Fundamentals of
High Strength High Performance
Concrete

Concrete Design and Construction Series

SERIES EDITORS

PROFESSOR F. K. KONG
Nanyang Technological University, Singapore

EMERITUS PROFESSOR R. H. EVANS CBE
University of Leeds

OTHER TITLES IN THE SERIES

Quality in Precast Concrete: Design—Production—Supervision
by John G. Richardson

Concrete Structures: Materials, Maintenance and Repair
by Denison Campbell-Allen and Harold Roper

Assessment and Renovation of Concrete Structures
by E. Kay

Concrete Bridges: Design and Construction
by A. C. Liebenberg

Fire Safety Design and Concrete
by T. Z. Harmathy

Concrete Structures: Eurocode EC2 and BS 8110 Compared
edited by R. S. Narayanan

Concrete at High Temperatures
by Z. P. Bažant and M. F. Kaplan

Concrete Structures in Earthquake Region: Design and Analysis
edited by E. Booth

Fracture Mechanics and Structural Concrete
by B. L. Karihaloo

Large Concrete Buildings
edited by B. V. Rangan and R. F. Warner

Fundamentals of High Strength High Performance Concrete

Dr. Edward G. Nawy, P. E., C. Eng.
Distinguished Professor

Department of Civil and Environmental Engineering
Rutgers University
The State University of New Jersey

Longman

Longman Group Limited
Longman House, Burnt Mill, Harlow
Essex CM20 2JE, England
and Associated Companies throughout the world

First published 1996

British Library Cataloguing in Publication Data
A catalogue entry for this title is available from the British Library.

ISBN 0-582-22699-6

Library of Congress Cataloging-in-Publication Data
A catalog entry for this title is available from the Library of Congress.

Printed and bound by Bookcraft (Bath) Ltd

Plate 1

Contents

Preface

Long-term performance of structures has become vital to the economics of all nations. Concrete has been the major instrument for providing stable and reliable infrastructures since the days of the Greek and Roman civilizations. While at the turn of the twentieth century concrete compressive strength was around 2000 psi (13.8 MPa), the 1960s have seen concrete strengths in the range of 4000–6000 psi (27.6–41.4 MPa), with the accepted ceiling of 6000 psi for normal-strength concrete. Deterioration, long-term poor performance and inadequate resistance to hostile environment, coupled with greater demands for more sophisticated architectural form, led to accelerated research into the micro-structure of cements and concretes and more elaborate codes and standards.

As a result, new materials and composites have been developed and improved cements produced. Today, concrete structures with a compressive strength exceeding 20 000 psi (138 MPa) are being built in the United States and Europe. In research laboratories, concrete strengths of 116 000 psi (800 MPa) are being produced. One major remarkable quality is the virtual elimination of voids in the concrete matrix which are mainly the cause of most of the ills that generate deterioration.

Engineering education in the science of concrete materials technology is poor if not lacking in most universities, particularly at the undergraduate level. As a result, practicing engineers and constructors, in many cases, lack the background for a workable understanding of the behavior and performance of concrete structural components both short-term and long-term. This problem is being compounded today by the emergence of high strength, high durability performance concretes. The reason is that high strength concretes and their components have characteristics that have to be well understood if such concretes and their mechanical properties are to be successfully produced and the end product enduring. It is for this reason that this book is written.

This book is aimed at the student and the designer who need to know how best to select and proportion a concrete system of high strength and high performance, and with optimum cost. It is equally aimed at the constructor and material specialist who needs to keep abreast of the state of the art in the emerging ultrahigh strength concrete technology and durability performance.

The text is the outgrowth of the author's experience over the past 36 years in research in materials and structures teaching at the undergraduate and MS and Ph.D. levels, as well structural design, consulting, and forensic engineering. He was the founding chairman of the ACI National Committee 224 on cracking which issued the first comprehensive report, *Control of Cracking in Concrete Structures*.

He has been the chairman of the ACI National Committee 435 on deflection which has just issued the voluminous report, *Control of Deflection in Concrete Structures*. The book is a coordinated treatment of the subject of high strength high performance concrete. It is not a collection of papers by various authors and it has the unique feature that it combines a treatment of the fundamentals of materials technology with the design expressions prescribed by the ACI code for both material proportioning and long-term structural member proportioning. It is also unique in that it summarizes in a single chapter the 1995 ACI 318-95 building code expressions for the flexural, shear, and torsional design of concrete members. It also contains numerous charts and tables for proportioning high strength blast furnace slag concretes, fly ash concretes, and silica fume concretes. The book is well suited for a one-semester specialized university course in concrete mechanics and materials combining theory with laboratory experimentation. It should also serve equally well the researcher, the design engineer, the material specialist, and the field constructor.

Chapter 1 deals with the general performance characteristics of cement including the most recently developed types in the production of high strength concrete, as well as the aggregates to be chosen and the performance comparisons of various cements. Chapter 2 covers the permeability effects on the performance of high strength concretes, freeze–thaw action and ACI recommendations on cold-weather concreting. Chapter 3 is a detailed discussion on the role of synthetic and mineral admixtures in achieving very high concrete strengths. It gives an extensive treatment to the use of polymers, superplasticizers (high range water reducing agents), latex modified concretes, fly ash, blast furnace slag, and silica fume.

Chapter 4 presents ACI procedures for the selection and proportioning of high strength concrete mixtures. It includes tables for recommended proportions and a step-by-step procedure for selecting these proportions. It also gives a detailed numerical example for the design of a concrete mix for a compressive strength of $\sim$12 000 psi (82.7 MPa) using mineral pozzolanic admixtures.

Chapter 5 deals with lightweight aggregate high strength concrete including the production and performance of lightweight aggregates and proportioning of lightweight structural concrete mixtures for normal as well as Arctic environmental conditions.

Chapter 6 covers in detail long-term creep and shrinkage and mechanisms for their prediction. It includes ACI charts, equations, and tables of values to assist the designer in evaluating the compressive strength f'_c, the modulus of rupture f_r, and the modulus of elasticity, E_c, of high strength concrete. It also presents expressions for evaluating the cracking moment and the cracked and effective moments of inertia for the computation of deflections. In addition, it presents the necessary expressions for the evaluation of flexural crack width in reinforced concrete beams and two-way slabs as well as prestressed concrete members and circular tanks. In effect, this chapter comprehensively covers all the performance and serviceability requirements needed for the design of durable high strength concrete structural systems. Chapter 7 stresses the material behavior aspects of the characteristics of high strength concretes. It details early age properties, mature concrete elastic strength expressions, workability and cohesiveness, volumetric stability, ductility and costructibility as well as fire resistance.

Chapter 8 treats in a compact manner the micro and macromechanics of high strength concrete. It presents a discussion of the classical failure theories, the fracture mechanics theory, shear friction transfer in two-layer systems such as bridge decks, and evaluation and proportioning of confining reinforcement in high strength concrete including design expressions and recommendations. Chapter 9 presents the state of the art on high strength concrete fiber composites and the mechanical properties of fibrous concrete structural elements. It includes numerous tables for mix proportioning including guidelines for producing ultrahigh strength slurry infiltrated fiber concretes (SIFCONs). It also discusses other types of cement composites including carbon fiber reinforced cement based composites.

Chapter 10 deals with the economics of high strength high performance concretes and the principal factors affecting cost. It also gives cost comparisons as affected by load and height of high-rise buildings as well as cost studies of using ultrahigh strength prestressed concrete girders in bridges. The chapter demonstrates that although the cost per unit cubic yard of high strength concrete is higher than lower strength concretes, the saving in member size, increase in rentable space, and reduced foundation costs more than offset the higher unit volume cost. Chapter 11 is devoted to the latest revisions in the ACI 318-95 building code. It presents a uniquely compact section dealing with all the most up-to-date code expressions so that the student, the researcher, the structural designer, and the material specialist can at a glance get access to both reinforced and prestressed concrete.

Chapter 12 considers high strength high performance concrete in the next millennium. It gives the author's expectations based on population and demographical considerations. In effect, it summarizes what has been achieved in the art and science of concrete technology in this century and the expected growth and development in the twenty-first century. It is expected and hoped that this text in its unique orientation towards the interaction of concrete material technology and the design of concrete elements, particularly high strength, would facilitate technology transfer from the materials technologist to the engineering student, the structural designer, and the constructor, with ease and efficiency.

Acknowledgements

Grateful acknowledgement is due to the American Concrete Institute for contribution to the author's accomplishments and for permitting use in this book of so many quotations and charts from its various Committee Codes and Reports, and to its Publications Director, Mr. Robert G. Wiedyke, for his generous cooperation over the years. Special mention is made of his original mentor, the late Professor A. L. L. Baker of London University's Imperial College of Science and Technology, who inspired him with the affection that he developed for systems constructed of concrete. Grateful acknowledgement is also made to the author's many students, both undergraduate and graduate, who have had much to do with generating the writing of this book; to the many who have assisted in his research activities in concrete over the past 35 years; to Dean Ellis H. Dill for his general encouragement; and to his many colleagues at other universities who have continuously used his Reinforced Concrete and Prestressed Concrete books and for their advice and suggestions.

Thanks are due to his friends and colleagues on the panel of authoritative reviewers: Professor R. N. Swamy of the University of Sheffield who reviewed the total manuscript on behalf of the publishers; to Professor Zdenek P. Bažant of Northwestern University, Professor Catherine W. French of the University of Minnesota, Dr. George C. Hoff, Senior Engineer, Mobil Research and Development Corporation and ACI Past President, Mr Thomas A. Holm, Vice President and Chief Engineer, Solite Corporation, Dr. V. Mohan Malhotra, Principal, Advanced Concrete Technology Program, Canada Center for Mineral and Energy Technology, Dr. Henry G. Russell, Consulting Engineer, and Professor Charles F. Scholer of Purdue University—who have all reviewed various individual chapters. Their meticulous and in-depth review and analysis of the manuscript and their valuable suggestions have immensely contributed to this book, for which the author is eternally grateful.

Thanks also to the Longman Group Ltd: Dr. Ian Francis, Publisher, and Dr. Chris Leeding, Senior Editor, Longman Higher Education, for continuous cooperation throughout the development of the manuscript; to Longman Consulting Editor, Professor F. K. Kong of Nanyang Technological University in Singapore and the University of Newcastle-upon-Tyne in the United Kingdom, for his advice and cooperation over the years, and to his son, Engineer Robert M. Nawy, Rutgers 1983 Class, for his general review of parts of the manuscript.

Last but not least, the author is deeply indebted to Ms. Kristi A. Latimer, MS candidate at Rutgers University, for her diligence, dedication and assistance in reviewing and processing the contents and to her overall work on the text.

1 General Performance Characteristics

1.1 INTRODUCTION

High strength concrete is a relative term. Normal strength in one practice can be considered as high strength concrete in another. At present, concrete having a cylinder compressive strength higher than 6000 psi (42 MPa) is considered in the United States as high strength. Up to the 1950s, concrete with 5000 psi strength was often difficult to produce. Concrete with cylinder compressive strength of 20 000 psi (140 MPa) is currently being used in high-rise structures in the United States and Europe. In certain laboratories, exotic concretes of 45 000 psi (315 MPa) have also been produced. Since concrete has to be reinforced for structural use, the level of ductility of the reinforcement becomes the limiting factor since higher strength concrete tends to exhibit lower ductility.

Savings in overall cost of concrete structural systems are achieved by the use of higher strength concretes. Components of a structure become smaller, thereby reducing the overall weight of the system on the foundations with the resulting reduction in the size and hence cost of all components. Additionally, reduction in member size increases available occupancy space, reducing rental costs. But strength is not the only criterion for the long-term performance of a system. Serviceability as determined by crack control as well as response to long-term environmental effects are as important. It is the intention of this book to discuss all these factors for a full utilization of the superior performance qualities of higher strength concretes.

1.2 CEMENT EFFECTS ON CONCRETE STRENGTH

In order to produce higher strength concretes, several parameters have to be optimized in addition to mix design, although the design of the concrete mixture is a major factor in achieving the desired strength. Several methods can be applied in order to achieve high strength. In general, high strength concrete contains strong aggregates, a higher portland cement content and a low water/cement or water/cementitious ratio. The addition of water-reducing admixtures, superplasticizers, polymers, blast furnace slag, or silica fume are common today. The following are the major factors that have to be taken into account:

Plate 2 Two Union Square, Seattle, Washington: composite steel and 20 000 psi concrete (Courtesy Portland Cement Association)

1. Cement characteristics and content
2. Water/cement, liquid/cement and water/cementitious ratios
3. Aggregate quality and interaction with cement paste
4. Chemical admixtures used
5. Mineral admixtures
6. Procedure and mixing time of constituents
7. Quality control and assurance

These factors control mortar strength, bond between the mortar and the aggregate, and the resulting interlock between the aggregate particles in the concrete. The strength of the coarse aggregate should at least be equivalent to the strength of the binding matrix in order to achieve the high compressive strength levels that are needed. If not, failure would result by fracture lines passing through the coarse aggregate while the higher strength binding matrix remained intact.

1.3   PORTLAND CEMENT CHARACTERISTICS AND CONTENT

1.3.1   Manufacture

Portland cement is a hydraulic cement which hardens by interacting with water and forms a water-resisting compound when it receives its final set. In comparison with nonhydraulic cements such as gypsum and lime which absorb water after hardening, it is highly durable and produces high compressive strengths in mortars and concretes. Portland cement is made of finely powdered crystalline minerals composed primarily of calcium and aluminium silicates. The addition of water to these minerals produces a paste which, when hardened, becomes of stone-like strength. Its specific gravity ranges between 3.12 and 3.16 and it weighs 94 lb/ft^3, which is the unit weight of a commercial sack or bag of cement. Its fineness measured by particle size can range between 10 and 50 microns. The size in portland cement used in concrete should not exceed 10 microns (μm). The raw materials that make cement are

1. Lime (CaO) from limestone
2. Silica (SiO$_2$) from clay
3. Alumina (Al$_2$O$_3$) from clay

Cement also contains very small percentages of magnesia (MgO) and sometimes some alkalis. Iron oxide is occasionally added to the mixture to aid in controlling its composition. The process of manufacture can be summarized as follows:

1. The raw mix of CaO, SiO$_2$, and Al$_2$O$_3$ is ground with the added other minor ingredients either in dry or wet form. The wet form is called slurry.
2. The mixture is fed into the upper end of a slightly inclined rotary kiln.
3. As the heated kiln operates, the material passes from its upper to its lower end at a predetermined, controlled rate.
4. The temperature of the mixture is raised to the point of incipient fusion, that is, the *clinkering temperature*. It is kept at that temperature until the ingredients combine to form at 2700°F (1500°C) the portland cement pellet product. The pellets, which range in size from 1/16 to 2 in. (1.6 to 50 mm), are called clinkers.
5. The clinkers are cooled and ground to a powdery form.
6. A small percentage of gypsum is added during grinding to control or retard the setting time of the cement in the field.
7. Most of the final portland cement goes into silos for bulk shipment; some is packed in 94 lb (42.6 kg) bags for retail marketing.

Figure 1.1 illustrates schematically the manufacturing process of portland cement. The form and properties of the manufactured compound are described in the following sections.

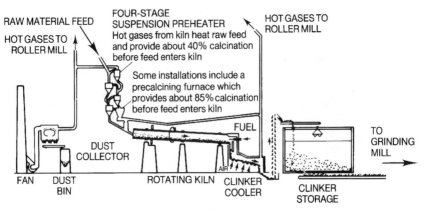

RAW MATERIAL FEED

FOUR-STAGE
SUSPENSION PREHEATER
Hot gases from kiln heat raw feed
and provide about 40% calcination
before feed enters kiln

HOT GASES TO
ROLLER MILL

HOT GASES TO
ROLLER MILL

Some installations include a
precalcining furnace which
provides about 85% calcination
before feed enters kiln

FUEL

TO
GRINDING
MILL

DUST
COLLECTOR

FAN   DUST
       BIN

ROTATING KILN   CLINKER
                 COOLER

AIR

CLINKER
STORAGE

Fig. 1.1 Portland cement manufacturing process[1.16]

1.3.2   Strength

The strength of cement paste is the result of a process of hydration. This chemical process results in recrystallization in the form of interlocking crystals producing the cement gel, which has high compressive strength when it hardens. Table 1.1 shows the relative contribution of each component of the cement toward the rate of gain in strength. The early strength of portland cement is higher with higher percentages of C_3S. If moist curing is continuous, later strength levels become greater with higher percentages of C_2S. The C_3S contributes to the strength developed during the first day after placing the concrete because it is the earliest to hydrate.

When Portland cement combines with water during setting and hardening, lime is liberated from some of the compounds. The amount of lime liberated is approximately 20 percent by weight of the cement. Under unfavorable conditions, this might cause disintegration of a structure owing to leaching of the lime from the cement. Such a situation should be prevented by addition to the cement of siliceous mineral such as pozzolan. The added mineral reacts with the lime in the presence of moisture to produce strong calcium silicate.

1.3.3   Average Percentage Composition

Since there are different types of cement for various needs, it is necessary to study the percentage variation in the chemical composition of each type in order to

Table 1.1 Properties of cements

Component	Rate of reaction	Heat liberated	Ultimate cementing value
Tricalcium silicate, C_3S	Medium	Medium	Good
Dicalcium silicate, C_2S	Slow	Small	Good
Tricalcium aluminate, C_3A	Fast	Large	Poor
Tetracalcium aluminoferrate, C_4AF	Slow	Small	Poor

Plate 3 A $4\frac{1}{2}$ in. slump mix (left) and a $1\frac{1}{2}$ in. slump mix (tests by Nawy *et al.*)

Table 1.2 Percentage composition of portland cements

Type of cement	Component (%)							General characteristics
	C_3S	C_2S	C_3A	C_4AF	$CaSO_4$	CaO	MgO	
Normal: I	49	25	12	8	2.9	0.8	2.4	All-purpose cement
Modified: II	45	29	6	12	2.8	0.6	3.0	Comparative low heat liberation: used in large structures
High early strength: III	56	15	12	8	3.9	1.4	2.6	High strength in 3 days
Low heat: IV	30	46	5	13	2.9	0.3	2.7	Used in mass concrete dams
Sulfate resisting: V	43	36	4	12	2.7	0.4	1.6	Used in sewers and structures exposed to sulfates

interpret the reasons for variation in behavior. Table 1.2, studied in conjunction with Table 1.1, gives concise reasons for the difference in reaction of each type of cement when in contact with water.

1.3.4   Influence of Fineness of Cement on Strength Development

The size of the cement particles has a strong influence on the rate of reaction of cement with water. For a given weight of finely ground cement, the surface area of the particles is greater than that of the coarsely ground cement. This results in a greater rate of reaction with water and a more rapid hardening process for larger surface areas. This is one of the reasons for the high early strength type III cement—it gives in 3 days the strength that type I gives in 7 days, and it gives in 7 days the strength that type I gives in 28 days—primarily because of the finer size of its particles.

1.3.5   Influence of Cement on the Durability of Concrete

Disintegration of concrete due to cycles of wetting, freezing, thawing, and drying and the propagation of resulting cracks is a matter of great importance. The presence of minute evenly distributed air bubbles throughout the cement paste increases the resistance of concrete to disintegration. This can be achieved by the addition of air-entraining admixtures to the concrete while mixing.

Disintegration due to chemicals in contact with the concrete surface, such as port structures and substructures in hostile environments, e.g., alkaline soils, can also be slowed down or prevented. Since the concrete in such cases is exposed to chlorides and sometimes sulfates of magnesium and sodium, it is sometimes necessary to specify sulfate-resisting cements. Usually, type II cement is adequate for use in seawater structures.

1.3.6   Heat Generation During Initial Set

Since the different types of cement generate different amounts of heat at different rates, the type of structure governs the type of cement to be used. The bulkier and heavier in cross-section the structure is, the less generation of heat of hydration is desired. In massive structures, such as dams, piers, and caissons, type IV cement is more advantageous to use. Frequently, this reduction in heat of hydration is accomplished in the presence of pozzolans and ASTM type II cements. From this discussion, it is seen that the type of structure, the weather and other conditions under which it is built and will exist during the life span of the structure are the governing factors in the choice of the type of cement that should be used.

1.4   OTHER HYDRAULIC CEMENTS

1.4.1   Blended Cements

Blended cements are composed of a portland cement uniformly blended with either fine granulated blast furnace slag where the slag content varies between 25 percent and 70 percent of the weight of portland blast furnace slag cement, or blended with fine pozzolan between 15 and 40 percent of the total weight. The former is labeled as type IS cement and the latter as type IP cement in ASTM C595 standard.

The Greeks and the Romans used pozzolanic materials to render the lime mortars hydraulic, hence nonwater-absorbing so that their structures were to endure the induced stresses. Pozzolans are siliceous or combined siliceous and aluminus compounds that in themselves do not possess any significant cementing power. However, when they are finely ground, they react chemically with the calcium hydroxide in the cement in the presence of moisture to form a cementitious compound.

1.4.2   Rapid Setting Cements

Rapid setting cements have their final set accomplished at a faster rate than type I or type III cements as well as hardening at a considerably faster rate. They are useful in underwater construction and in emergency repairs as well as emergency rapid construction. The time of set can be as little as 10 minutes as compared to 45–60 minutes for the normal type I and high early type III cements.

Rapid set is accomplished through ettringite formation by the addition of plaster of paris ($CaSO_4 \cdot \frac{1}{2}H_2O$) or calcium aluminate to the portland cement. These rapid setting cements generate high heat in mixing. After achieving the initial rapid hardening in 24 hours or less, they proceed to harden at the normal rate of other cements. Such cements can generate over 1000 psi (6.9 MPa) compressive strength in 1 hour and in excess of 4000 psi (28 MPa) in 3 days after initial hydration[1.9]. They set within 3–5 minutes if not retarded to a different setting time through the use of such additives as calcium hydroxide, citric acid, and others.

1.4.3   Expansive Cements (Type K)

Type K cements have the capacity to expand during and after the initial hydration period. If the concrete element is restrained from expanding, compressive prestressing forces are induced in the element preventing shrinkage cracking both short-term and long-term. The expansion characteristic is achieved through the formation of ettringite and the early hydration of calcium oxide in the mixture.

1.4.4   Very High Early Strength Cements

Very high early strength cements can produce in a concrete mix, within 10–24 hours, a compressive strength of 3000–7000 psi (20–48 MPa) and ultimate cylinder compressive strength, f'_c, of 10 000–15 000 psi (70–105 MPa). Their very rapid set and hardening seem to be achieved through the formation of large amounts of ettringite during the early hydration process and the addition of finer compounds to the cement during the production process.

1.4.5   Miscellaneous Cements

Other special use cements are also available such as colored and white cements, oil well cements, calcium aluminate cements, and dental cements. They are not intended for normal use in concrete structures and cost considerably more than the cements previously discussed.

1.4.6   Exotic Cements

As society moves towards the twenty-first century, new advances in cementitious materials technology will permit building structures in which concrete strength can be well in excess of 20 000 psi (140–150 MPa). Such strengths can be facilitated by newer cements, different proportioning and mixing procedures, and modified quality assurance and quality control actions.

Macrodefect free Cements
A new class of high strength, macrodefect free cements (MDF) developed at Oxford University is available[1.10]. They have relatively few large voids or defects that are normally extensively present in conventionally mixed cement pastes due to entrapped air and inadequate dispersion.

Densified Cement
Also new, the densified cement system (DSP) is composed of densely packed particles of portland cement and ultrafine particles of silica fume. The size of the particles is 0.5–100 μm with homogeneously arranged ultrafine particles ranging in size from about 5–500 nm placed in the spaces between the larger particles[1.11].

Table 1.3 Compressive strength comparison at early age for alkali-activated cements[1.11]

	f'_c, psi (MPa)	
Time	Commercial alkali-activated	Portland type III
(1)	(2)	(3)
5 hours	3 400 (23.4)	Not set
24 hours	6 820 (47.0)	12 100 (83.5)
3 days	8 570 (59.1)	13 200 (91.0)
7 days	10 100 (69.6)	15 940 (110)
14 days	11 400 (78.6)	17 750 (122)
21 days	11 970 (82.5)	17 160 (118)
28 days	12 270 (84.6)	15 530 (107)

Concrete cured at 25°C; water/cement ratio = 0.25.

Berlite Cement

Berlite cement (S_2S) and berlite–sulfoaluminate cement have the potential for reduced energy consumption during the production process by lowering the required clinkering temperature from the 2700°F (1500°C) in the production of normal cement to 2200–2400°F (1200–1300°C). They also have higher resistance to carbonation than normal portland cements. Their foreseen use at this time is for special applications such as hydraulic binder in the fixation of heavy metals and in soil stabilization[1.11].

Alkali-Activated Cement (CBC)

Alkali additions activate some pozzolanic materials so that almost 30 percent less water is needed than when using conventional cements, with the accompanying reduction in porosity. In these cements, the CaO/SiO_2 ratio is adjusted in order to eliminate the free calcium hydroxide remaining in the hydrated material. The alkaline activators could be caustic alkalis or silicate or nonsilicate salts. Table 1.3[1.11] compares the gain in the compressive strength of concrete with time at early age for this cement as compared to type III cement. A high strength of 12 270 psi (84.6 MPa) is achieved in 28 days.

1.5   PERFORMANCE COMPARISONS OF VARIOUS CEMENTS IN CONCRETE

The discussions in Sections 1.2 to 1.4 presented some of the differences of the various types of cement as they impact on the strength of concrete. An attempt is made here to present in graphical form the relative performances of these cements. The influence of the oxide C_3S ($3CaO$, SiO_2) on heat generation is shown in Fig. 1.2 for various C_3S contents. It is seen that the generated heat increases by more than 50 percent as the C_3S content is increased from 16 percent to 60 percent. The difference in heat generation for various cement types is shown in Fig. 1.3[1.12].

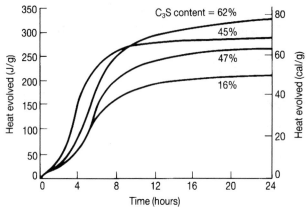

Fig. 1.2 Influence of C$_3$S content on heat evolution[1.12]

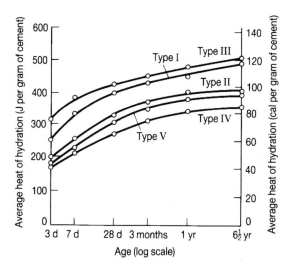

Fig. 1.3 Heat of hydration development for different cements cured at 70°F (21°C) having water/cement ratio 0.40[1.12]

For the same cement content in comparable mixes, the attained compressive strength with time for the various cements are shown in Fig. 1.4[1.12] and Fig. 1.5[1.13] for strengths up to 8000 psi (55 MPa). Figure 1.6 gives comparisons of compressive strengths with time in days for high strength concretes with f'_c in excess of 11 500 psi (80 MPa) while Fig. 1.7 shows the effect of low curing temperatures on the compressive strength of high alumina cement concretes[1.14].

Figure 1.8 gives another plot for the compressive strengths of concrete vs. age in days made from normal portland cement of types I to III achieving an f'_c of 12 000 psi (83 MPa) using 100 lb of fly ash with 846 lb of cement in the mix[1.15].

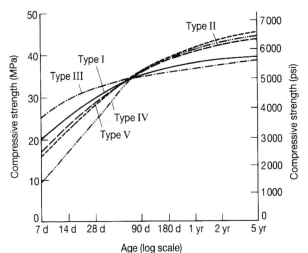

Fig. 1.4 Compressive strength of concretes vs. age up to 5 years made with different cement types[1.12] (cement content 565 lb/yd³, or 335 kg/m³)

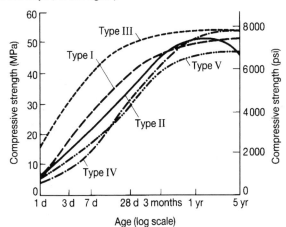

Fig. 1.5 Compressive strength of concretes vs. age up to 5 years made with different cement types[1.13] (water/cement ratio = 0.49)

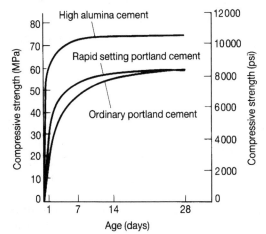

Fig. 1.6 Early age compressive strengths of high strength concrete at ambient temperatures[1.14]

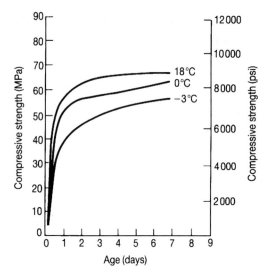

Fig. 1.7 Effect of low temperature curing on strength of high alumina cement concretes[1.14]

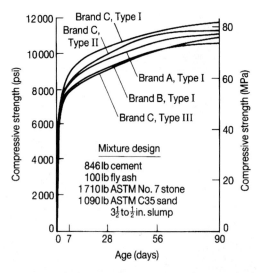

Fig. 1.8 Effect of cement type and mix proportions on compressive strength of concrete up to 90 days[1.15]

1.6   WATER/CEMENT, WATER CEMENTITIOUS MATERIALS, AND LIQUID CEMENT RATIO IN CONCRETES

1.6.1   Water and Air

Water is required in the production of concrete in order to precipitate chemical reaction with the cement, to wet the aggregate, and to lubricate the mixture for easy workability. Normally, drinking water is used in mixing. Water having harmful ingredients, contamination, silt, oil, sugar, or chemicals, is destructive to the strength and setting properties of cement. It can disrupt the affinity between the aggregate and the cement paste and can adversely affect the workability of a mix.

Since the character of the colloidal gel or cement paste is the result only of the chemical reaction between cement and water, it is not the proportion of water relative to the whole mixture of dry materials that is of concern, only the proportion of water relative to the cement. Excessive water leaves an uneven honeycombed skeleton in the finished product after hydration has taken place, while too little water prevents complete chemical reaction with the cement and leaves powder voids in the concrete. The product in both cases is a concrete that is weaker than and inferior to concrete without honeycombing.

Additionally, gradual evaporation of *excess* water from the concrete mix results in pores produced in the hardened concrete. If these pores are evenly distributed, they could give improved characteristics to the product. Very even distribution of pores by artificial introduction of finely divided uniformly distributed air bubbles

Plate 4 Cylinder compression test

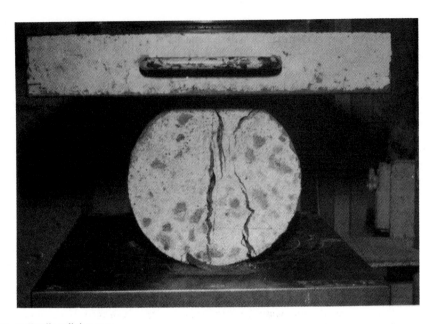

Plate 5 Tensile splitting test

Plate 6 Bennett Bay Ridge, Idaho: 1730 ft segmental girder with two center spans of 520 ft and end spans of 320 ft (Courtesy Portland Cement Association)

throughout the product is possible by adding air-entraining agents such as vinsol resin. Air-entrainment increases workability, decreases density, increases durability, reduces bleeding and segregation, and reduces the required sand content in the mix. For these reasons, the percentage of entrained air should be kept at the required optimum value for the desired performance quality of the concrete. The optimum air content is 6–9 percent of the mortar fraction of the concrete. Air entrainment in excess of 5–6 percent of the total mix proportionally reduces the concrete strength.

1.6.2   Water/Cement and Liquid/Cement Ratio

The discussion in Section 1.6.1 demonstrates that strict control has to be maintained of the water/cement ratio and the percentage of air in the mix. The water/cement ratio or the water/cementitious ratio is the real measure of strength of the concrete and consequently it should be the principal criterion governing the design strength of most structural concretes. It is usually given as the ratio of weight of water to the weight of cement or cement plus cementitious additives in the concrete mix.

Water content—the water/cement ratio in the fresh mix—determines the consistency of the concrete. Consistency is a measure of the viscosity or flow of the concrete as it is placed in the formwork. As the water/cement ratio is decreased, it proportionately decreases the slump in the concrete as a measure of its workability, making the concrete more difficult to place in the formwork. The resulting finished product will have honeycombing and large voids and gaps that reduce the strength of the structural element due to discontinuity and stress concentration. As mixtures are added, preferably in liquid form, such as latexes, polymers, or silica fume, they replace part of the water content while increasing, sometimes significantly, the slump of the mix. The introduction of these additives not only increases the workability of the mixture but enhances the compressive strength of the hardened concrete. Thus, the term liquid/cement ratio is parallel with the water/cement ratio. A discussion of the change in concrete properties due to decrease in slump and the contribution of the admixtures is given in Section 1.8.

1.7   AGGREGATES

Aggregates[1.16] are those parts of the concrete that constitute the bulk of the finished product. They comprise 60–80 percent of the volume of the concrete, and have to be so graded that the whole mass of concrete acts as a relatively solid, homogeneous, dense combination, with the smaller sizes acting as an inert filler of the voids that exist between the larger particles. Aggregates are of two types:

1.   *Coarse aggregate* such as gravel, crushed stone, or blast furnace slag
2.   *Fine aggregate* such as natural or manufactured slag

Since the aggregate constitutes the major portion of the mixture, the more aggregate in the mix, the cheaper is the concrete, provided that the mix is of reasonable workability for the specific job for which it is used.

1.7.1   Coarse Aggregate

Coarse aggregate is classified as such if the smallest size of the particle is greater than $\frac{1}{4}$ in. (6 mm). Properties of the coarse aggregate affect the final strength of the hardened concrete and its resistance to disintegration, weathering, and other destructive effects. The mineral coarse aggregate must be clean of organic impurities, and must bond well with the cement gel. The common types of coarse aggregate are:

1. *Natural crushed stone.* This is produced by crushing natural stone or rock from quarries. The rock could be of igneous, sedimentary, or metamorphic type. Although crushed rock gives higher concrete strength, it is less workable in mixing and placing than are the other types.
2. *Natural gravel.* This is produced by the weathering action of running water on the beds and banks of streams. It gives less strength than crushed rock but is more workable.
3. *Artificial coarse aggregates.* These are mainly slag and expanded shale, and are frequently used to produce lightweight concrete. They are the by-products of other manufacturing processes, such as blast furnace slag or expanded shale, or pumice for lightweight concrete.
4. *Heavyweight and nuclear-shielding aggregates.* With the specific demands of our atomic age and the hazards of nuclear radiation due to the increasing number of atomic reactors and nuclear power stations, special concretes have had to be produced to shield against x rays, gamma rays, and neutrons. In such concretes, economic and workability considerations are not of prime importance. The main heavy coarse aggregate types are steel punchings, barites, magnetites, and limonites. Whereas concrete with ordinary aggregate weighs about 144 lb/ft^3 (2300 kg/m^3), concrete made with these heavy aggregates weighs 225–330 lb/ft^3 (3600–5280 kg/m^3). The property of heavyweight radiation-shielding concrete depends on the density of the compact product rather than primarily on the water/cement ratio criterion. In certain cases, high density is the only consideration, whereas in others both density and strength govern.

1.7.2   Fine Aggregate

Fine aggregate is a smaller filler made of sand. It ranges in size from No. 4 to No. 100 U.S. standard sieve sizes. A good fine aggregate should always be free of organic impurities, clay or any deleterious material or excessive filler of size smaller than No. 100 sieve. It should preferably have a well-graded combination conforming to the American Society of Testing and Materials (ASTM) sieve analysis standards. For radiation-shielding concrete, fine steel shot and crushed iron ore are used as fine aggregate.

1.7.3 Grading of Normal Weight Concrete Mixes

The recommended grading of coarse and fine aggregates for normal weight concretes is presented in Table 1.4.

1.7.4 Grading of Lightweight Concrete Mixes

The grading requirements for lightweight aggregate for structural concrete are given in Table 1.5.

1.7.5 Grading of Heavyweight and Nuclear-Shielding Aggregates

The grading requirements to ensure heavyweight concrete are given in Tables 1.6 and 1.7.

1.7.6 Unit Weights of Aggregates

The unit weight of the concrete is dependent on the unit weight of the aggregate, which in turn depends on the type of aggregate, namely, whether it is normal weight, lightweight, or heavyweight (for radiation shielding). Table 1.7 gives the

Table 1.4 Grading requirements for aggregates in normal weight concrete (ASTM C-33)

	Percent passing				
	Coarse aggregate				
U.S. standard sieve size	No. 4 to 2 in.	No. 4 to $1\frac{1}{2}$ in.	No. 4 to 1 in.	No. 4 to $\frac{3}{4}$ in.	Fine aggregate
2 in.	95–100	100	—	—	—
$1\frac{1}{2}$ in.	—	95–100	100	—	—
1 in.	25–70	—	95–100	100	—
$\frac{3}{4}$ in.	—	35–70	—	90–100	—
$\frac{1}{2}$ in.	10–30	—	25–60	—	—
$\frac{3}{8}$ in.	—	10–30	—	20–55	100
No. 4	0–5	0–5	0–10	0–10	95–100
No. 8	0	0	0–5	0–5	80–100
No. 16	0	0	0	0	50–85
No. 30	0	0	0	0	25–60
No. 50	0	0	0	0	10–30
No. 100	0	0	0	0	2–10

Table 1.5 Grading requirements for aggregates in structural concrete (ASTM C-330)

Size designation	Percentages (by weight) passing sieves having square openings								
	1 in. (25.0 mm)	$\frac{3}{4}$ in. (19.0 mm)	$\frac{1}{2}$ in. (12.5 mm)	$\frac{3}{8}$ in. (9.5 mm)	No. 4 (4.75 mm)	No. 8 (2.36 mm)	No. 16 (1.18 mm)	No. 50 (300 μm)	No. 100 (150 μm)
Fine aggregate No. 4 to 0	—	—	—	100	85–100	—	40–80	10–35	5–25
Coarse aggregate 1 in. to No. 4	95–100	—	25–60	—	0–10	—	—	—	—
$\frac{3}{4}$ in. to No. 4	100	90–100	—	10–50	0–15	—	—	—	—
$\frac{1}{2}$ in. to No. 4	—	100	90–100	40–80	0–20	0–10	—	—	—
$\frac{3}{8}$ in. to No. 8	—	—	100	80–100	5–40	0–20	0–10	—	—
Combined fine and coarse aggregate $\frac{1}{2}$ in. to 0	—	100	95–100	—	50–80	—	—	5–20	2–15
$\frac{3}{8}$ in. to 0	—	—	100	90–100	65–90	35–65	—	10–25	5–15

Table 1.6 Grading requirements for coarse aggregate for aggregate concrete (ASTM C-637)

Sieve size	Percentage passing	
	Grading 1: for $1\frac{1}{2}$ in. (37.5 mm) max. size aggregate	Grading 2: for $\frac{3}{4}$ in. (19.0 mm) max. size aggregate
Coarse aggregate		
2 in. (50 mm)	100	—
$1\frac{1}{2}$ in. (37.5 mm)	95–100	100
1 in. (25.0 mm)	40–80	95–100
$\frac{3}{4}$ in. (19.0 mm)	20–45	40–80
$\frac{1}{2}$ in. (12.5 mm)	0–10	0–15
$\frac{3}{8}$ in. (9.5 mm)	0–2	0–2
Fine aggregate		
No. 8 (2.36 mm)	100	—
No. 16 (1.18 mm)	95–100	100
No. 30 (600 μm)	55–80	75–95
No. 50 (300 μm)	30–55	45–65
No. 100 (150 μm)	10–30	20–40
No. 200 (75 μm)	0–10	0–10
Fineness modulus	1.30–2.10	1.00–1.60

Source: Data in Tables 1.4 and 1.6 reprinted with permission from the American Society for Testing and Materials, Philadelphia, Pa.

Table 1.7 Unit weight of aggregates

Type	Unit weight of dry-rodded aggregate (lb/ft^3)^a	Unit weight of concrete (lb/ft^3)^a
Insulating concretes (perlite, vermiculite, etc.)	15–50	20–90
Structural lightweight	40–70	90–110
Normal-weight	70–110	130–160
Heavyweight	135	180–380

^{a}1 lb/ft^3 = 16.02 kg/m^3.

unit weights of the various aggregates and the corresponding unit weight of the concrete.

1.8   TYPES OF CHEMICAL ADMIXTURES

Admixtures[1.16] are materials other than water, aggregate, or hydraulic cement which are used as ingredients of concrete and which are added to the batch immediately before or during the mixing operation. Their function is to modify the properties of the concrete so as "to make it more suitable for the work at hand, or for economy, or for other purposes such as saving energy.[1.6]" The major types of admixtures can be summarized as follows:

1.   Accelerating admixtures
2.   Air-entraining admixtures

3. Chemical admixtures for reducing water demand: High Range Water Reducer, HRWR (called also superplasticizer) and set-controlling admixtures such as chlorides
4. Polymers and latexes
5. Finely divided mineral admixtures (such as items 6, 7, 8 in this list)
6. Granulated blast furnace slag
7. Fly ash
8. Silica fume
9. Admixtures for no-slump concrete

General characteristics are given in this section of the various common admixtures used today. Detailed discussion of their major properties, mixture proportions, quality control and assurance, and their performance are given in subsequent chapters.

1.8.1   Accelerating Admixtures

Accelerating admixtures are added to the concrete mix to reduce the time of setting and accelerate early strength development. The best known is calcium chloride. Other accelerating chemicals include a wide range of soluble salts, such as chlorides, bromides, carbonates, calcium acetates, silicates, and some other organic compounds such as triethanolamine. It must be stressed that calcium chlorides should not be used where progressive corrosion of steel reinforcement can occur. The maximum dosage should be less than 1 percent by weight of the portland cement.

1.8.2   Air-Entraining Admixtures

Air-entraining admixtures form minute bubbles 1 mm in diameter or smaller in the concrete or mortar during mixing. They are used to increase workability of the mix during placing and to increase the frost resistance of the finished product. Most of the air-entraining admixtures are in liquid form, although they may be obtained as powders, flakes, or semisolids. The amount of the admixture required to obtain a given air content depends on the shape and the grading of the aggregate used. The finer the size of the aggregate, the larger is the percentage of admixture needed. The amount is also governed by several other factors, such as type and condition of the mixer, use of fly ash or other pozzolans, and the degree of agitation of the mix. It can be expected that air entrainment reduces the strength of the concrete. Maintaining cement content and workability, however, offsets the partial reduction of strength because of the resulting reduction in the water/cement ratio.

1.8.3   Water-Reducing and Set-Controlling Admixtures

Water-reducing and set-controlling admixtures increase the strength of the concrete. They also allow the cement content to be reduced in proportion to the reduction in the water content. Most admixtures of the water-reducing type are water soluble. The water they contain becomes part of the mixing water in the concrete and is added to the total weight of water in the design of the mix. It has to be emphasized that the proportion of the mortar to the coarse aggregate should always remain the same. Changes in the water content, air content, or cement content are compensated by corresponding changes in the fine aggregate content so that the volume of the mortar remains the same.

1.8.4   Finely Divided Admixtures

Finely divided mineral admixtures are used to rectify deficiencies in the concrete mixture by providing missing fines from the fine aggregate, improving one or more qualities of the concrete, such as reducing permeability or expansion, and reducing the cost of concrete-making materials. Such admixtures include hydraulic lime, slag cement, fly ash, and raw or calcined natural pozzolan.

1.8.5   Admixtures for No-slump Concrete

No-slump concrete is defined as a concrete with a slump of 1 in. (25 mm) or less immediately after mixing[1.6]. The choice of the admixture depends on the desired properties of the finished product, such as its effect on the plasticity needed, setting time, strength development, freeze–thaw effects, compressive strength and cost.

1.8.6   Fly Ash

This admixture is fine particle ash that accumulates electrostatically from the exhaust fumes of coal-fired power stations. It is considered as artificial pozzolan and its particles have at least the same fineness as the cement particles (10 μm). The carbon content is at least 3 percent. Because of its pozzolanic property, its cementing effect as part of the cementitious percentage of the mixture can result in high strength concrete. Bottom ash which is also a by product in *liquid form* is not usable as cementing additive in concrete production.

1.8.7   Polymers

Polymer admixtures produce concretes of very high strength: compressive strength of 15 000 psi (103 MPa) or higher and tensile splitting strength of 1500 psi (10.3 MPa) or higher. Such concretes are generally produced using a polymerizing material through (1) modification of the concrete property through water reduction in the field, or (2) impregnation and irradiation under elevated temperature in a laboratory environment (rarely used today).

Polymer modified concrete (PMC), more often called polymer concrete (PC), is concrete made through the addition of resin and hardener as an "admixture." The principle is to replace part of the mixing water by the polymer so as to attain the high compressive strength and other high performance qualities to be subsequently discussed. The optimum polymer/cement ratio by weight seems to be 0.30–0.45 to achieve such high compressive strengths.

1.8.8   Superplasticizers

Superplasticizers are often referred to as high range water-reducing chemical admixtures (HRWRs). There are four types of plasticizers:

1. Sulfonated melamine formaldehyde condensates, with a chloride content to 0.005 percent (MSF)
2. Sulfonated naphthalene formaldehyde condensates, with negligible chloride content (NSF)
3. Modified lignosulfonates, which contain no chlorides
4. Carboxyl acrylic ester copolymer (CAF)

Most of these are made from organic sulfonates and are termed "superplasticizers" in view of their considerable ability to facilitate reducing the water content in a concrete mix while simultaneously increasing the slump in the range of 8 in. (206 mm) or more. Other superplasticizers are sulfonic acid esters and carbohydrate esters.

A dosage of $1-2\frac{1}{2}$ percent by weight of cement is advisable. Higher dosages can result in a reduction in compressive strength unless the cement content is increased to balance this reduction effect. It should be noted that the superplasticizers exert their action by decreasing the surface tension of water and by equidirectional charging of the cement particles. These properties, coupled with the addition of silica fume, help the concrete to achieve high strength and water reduction without loss of workability.

1.8.9   Silica Fume Admixture Use in High Strength Concrete

Silica fume is generally accepted as an efficient admixture for high strength concrete mixes. It is a relatively new pozzolanic material that has received considerable attention in both research and application. Silica fume is a by-product resulting from the use of high purity quartz with coal in the electric arc furnace in the production of silicon and ferrosilicon alloys. The size of silica fume particles as a measure of its fineness is 0.1 μm as compared to 10 μm on the average in portland cement and fly ash and 1.5 in metakaolin. Its main constituent, fine spherical particles of silicon dioxide, makes it an ideal cement replacement, simultaneously raising the concrete strength. Being a waste product with relative ease in collection as compared to fly ash or slag, silica fume is gaining rapid popularity. Norway first experimented with the product, followed by other Scandinavian countries in the 1970s. Canada and the United States embarked on extensive use of this product in the early 1980s.

Proportions of silica fume in concrete mixes vary from 5 to 30 percent by weight of the cement depending on the strength and workability requirements. However, water demand is greatly increased with increasing proportion of silica fume and high range water reducers. It is essential to keep the water/cementitious ratio low in order to produce higher strength, yet workable concrete. Silica fume seems to attain a high early strength in about 3–7 days with relatively less increase in strength at 28 days. The strength development pattern of flexural and tensile splitting strengths is similar to that of compressive strength gain for silica fume concrete. The addition of silica fume to the mixture can produce significantly increased strength, increased modulus of elasticity, and increased flexural strength.

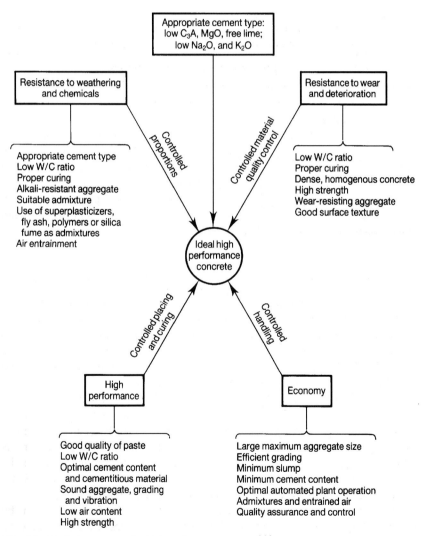

Fig. 1.9 Principal parameters for high performance concrete[1.16]

1.9   SUMMARY

In order to obtain high performance concrete, the major parameters to be considered can be summarized as follows:

1. Quality and type of cement
2. Proportion of cement in relation to water in the mixture
3. Strength, size, and cleanliness of aggregate
4. Interaction or adhesion between cement paste and aggregate
5. The type of admixture chosen
6. Adequate mixing of the ingredients
7. Proper placing, finishing, and compaction of the fresh concrete
8. Curing at a temperature not below 50°F (10°C) while the placed concrete gains strength
9. Chloride content not to exceed 0.15 percent in reinforced concrete exposed to chlorides in service and 0.5 percent for dry protected concrete

Figure 1.9[1.16] gives in graphical form a chart outlining the characteristics expected of high performance concretes.

REFERENCES

1.1   American Society for Testing and Materials, *Annual Book of ASTM Standards.* Part 4, *Concrete and Mineral Aggregates*, ASTM, Philadelphia, 1994

1.2   Popovices S 1979 *Concrete-Making Materials* McGraw-Hill, New York

1.3   ACI Committee 221 Selection and Use of Aggregate for Concrete. *Proceedings, ACI Journal* Vol. 58 No. 5, *American Concrete Institute, Detroit*, 1961, pp. 513–542

1.4   ACI Manual of Concrete Practice 1995 Part 1, *Materials*, American Concrete Institute, Detroit

1.5   Portland Cement Association 1979 *Design and Control of Concrete Mixtures* 12th ed., PCA, Skokie, Ill

1.6   ACI Committee 212 Chemical Admixtures for Concrete. *ACI Manual of Concrete Practice. ACI 212.3 R-91* American Concrete Institute, Detroit, 1994

1.7   Nawy E G, Ukadike M M, and Sauer J A 1977 High Strength Field Modified Concretes. *Proceedings, ASCE J. Structural Division* Vol. 103 No. ST12, pp. 2307–2322

1.8   *Super plasticizers in Concrete. ACI SP-62* American Concrete Institute, Detroit, 1979

1.9   Mehta P K, and Montiero P J M 1993 *Concrete-Structure Properties and Materials* 2nd ed., Prentice Hall, Englewood Cliffs, N.J

1.10   Young J F 1991 Microdefect-Free Cement: A Review. *Proceedings, Materials Research Society Symposium* Vol. 179, pp. 101–122

1.11   Roy D M, and Silsbec M R 1994 Novel Cements and Cement Products for Application in the 21st Century. *ACI SP-144* American Concrete Institute, Detroit, pp. 349–397

1.12   Verbeck G J, and Foster C W 1950 Long-Term Study of Cement Performance in Concrete. *Proceedings, ASTM* Vol. 50, pp. 1235–57

1.13   Gonderman H F, and Leach W 1951 Changes in Characteristics of Portland Cement as Exhibited by Laboratory Tests. *ASTM Special Publication 127*

1.14 Neville A M 1980 *Progress in Concrete Technology* ed. V M Malhotra, CANMET, Ottawa, pp. 293–231

1.15 ACI Committee 363 State of the Art Report on High Strength Concrete. *ACI Report 363-92* American Concrete Institute, Detroit, 1992

1.16 Nawy E G 1996 *Reinforced Concrete — A Fundamental Approach* 3rd ed. (1st ed. 1985), Prentice Hall, Englewood Cliffs, N.J.

1.17 Russell H G 1993 High Strength Concrete. *ACI Compilation 17* American Concrete Institute, Detroit, p. 3

1.18 Popovics S 1979 *Concrete-Making Materials* McGraw-Hill, New York

1.19 Jazrawi M 1995 High Strength Concrete — An Extension of Normal Strength Concrete *M.S. Thesis* under the direction of E G Nawy, Rutgers University, New Brunswick, N.J

2   Permeability Effects on Performance of Concrete

2.1   AIR VOIDS AND PERMEABILITY

Major air voids develop due to evaporation of the excess water in the chemical hydration process. The degree of compaction of the concrete, the extent of porosity due to the air voids, capillarity, and the pressure head of the retained liquid and its viscosity determine the degree of permeability of the concrete barrier. The degree of permeability is a measure of the ability of concrete to allow liquid or water to flow through the concrete barrier due to the difference in the hydraulic pressure gradient between the opposite faces of the concrete element. The voids can be essentially classified into the following categories:

1. *Small, closely spaced air voids.* Their size ranges from 0.003 to 0.004 in. (0.07 to 0.10 mm). These small voids or air bubbles, if evenly distributed, are advantageous in resisting freezing and thawing deterioration of concrete subjected to freezing temperatures. An average of 5–6 percent in concrete is recommended. They can be generated by adding air-entrainment to the concrete mix
2. *Large air voids.* They are the result of entrapped air and range from small size to $1/2$ in. in diameter (12.7 mm). They should not exceed an average of 1 percent by volume. They can be caused by poor consolidation or compaction
3. *Capillary voids.* They represent the space not occupied by the hydrated cement in the hydration process. Hence, the higher the water/cement ratio the higher is the capillary voids percentage. The size of capillary voids in low water/cement or water/cementitious ratio pastes ranges at early age from 3 to 5 μm
4. *Gel pores.* They are the solid-to-solid distance and they form in the concrete gel, namely, the solid part of the hardened concrete. Their size ranges from 5 to 20 Å (1 Å $= 10^{-8}$ cm $= 4 \times 10^{-9}$ in.)
5. *Aggregate pores.* The aggregate can contribute to increased permeability if it is porous. From one rock type to another, the total pore space varies between 0.5 and 20 percent. Table 2.1[2.1] gives the permeabilities of typical natural rocks and the water/cement ratios of cement pastes with similar permeability

Plate 7 Walt Disney World Monorail, Orlando, Florida: a series of hollow precast prestressed concrete box girders individually posttensioned to produce a six-span continuous structure (Designed by ABAM Engineers and reprinted courtesy of Walt Disney World Company)

Table 2.1 Permeabilities of typical natural rocks and cement pastes[2.1]

Rock type	Permeability of rocks (cm/ sec)	Water/cement ratio of mature cement paste for same permeability coefficient
(1)	(2)	(3)
Dense trap	0.003×10^{-10}	0.38
Quartz diorite	0.01×10^{-10}	0.42
Marble 1	0.03×10^{-10}	0.48
Marble 2	0.08×10^{-10}	0.66
Granite 1	7×10^{-10}	0.70
Sandstone	20×10^{-10}	0.71
Granite 2	20×10^{-10}	0.71

2.2   PERMEABILITY COEFFICIENTS

For a steady-state flow in a porous media, the permeability coefficient can be determined from the Darcy equation for the rate of fluid flow as

$$\frac{dQ}{dt} = K \frac{\Delta H A}{L \mu}$$

where K = permeability coefficient
dQ/dt = rate of flow
ΔH = pressure head
A = surface area
L = thickness of member in the flow direction
μ = fluid viscosity

Typical permeability coefficients for concrete vary: they may be 1×10^{-10} cm/sec for large aggregate concretes (1 in. size) and water/cement ratio (W/C) = 0.5; they may be 30×10^{-10} cm/sec. for low strength concrete in dams with W/C = 0.75.[2.4] For high strength normal weight concrete and small aggregate (3/8 in.), permeability can be as low as 5×10^{-11} cm/sec. This is because the W/C ratio can be as low as 0.26 for 15 000 psi (104 MPa) concrete with 3.5–4.9 in. slump (89–124 mm). Figure 2.1[2.8] shows that the permeability decreased by a ratio of 1/2.5 for concretes from W/C = 0.5 to 0.3. It should be expected that lightweight concrete has higher permeability than stone normal weight concrete. It should also be noted that concrete or mortar gives a lower permeability than neat cement paste of the same W/C ratio and degree of maturity. Also, concrete is considerably less permeable to vapor or air than to water or liquid. Table 2.2[2.9] lists water permeability for high strength lightweight concrete for concrete strengths ranging between 14 850 psi (109 MPa) and 12 820 psi (88.4 MPa).

It must be kept in mind that permeability decreases at a very fast rate with age. It is not unreasonable to expect a decrease by a factor of 10 between an age differential of 5 and 8 days from the start of the hydration process (from 4×10^{-8} to 4×10^{-9} respectively for cement paste with W/C ratio = 0.7).

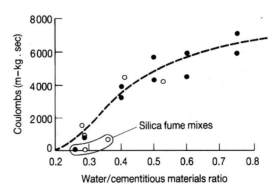

Fig. 2.1 Rapid chloride permeability vs. water/cementitious materials ratio[2.8]

Table 2.2 Water permeability for high strength lightweight concrete[2.9]

Mix. no.	Compressive strength, psi (MPa)	Density of fresh concrete, lb/ft³ (kg/m³)	Water permeability K (m/sec)	Relative pore volume (%)
(1)	(2)	(3)	(4)	(5)
1	14 850 (102.4)	116.5 (1865)	4.2×10^{-12}	16.6
			1.3×10^{-12}	15.5
			2.3×10^{-13}	14.8
2	13 300 (91.8)	114.5 (1835)	$< 10^{-14}$	16.0
			$< 10^{-14}$	17.1
			4.9×10^{-14}	16.6
3	13 550 (93.4)	109 (1750)	1.9×10^{-13}	17.6
			9.4×10^{-12}	17.1
			2.3×0^{-12}	17.3
4	12 260 (84.5)	113 (1815)	$< 10^{-14}$	16.8
			$< 10^{-14}$	17.3
			cracked	17.3
5	14 210 (98.0)	112.5 (1800)	$< 10^{-14}$	18.1
			$< 10^{-14}$	18.8
			2.8×10^{-13}	18.8
6	10 800 (74.4)	107 (1710)	cracked	19.6
			1.9×10^{-14}	20.4
			cracked	20.1
7	8 300 (57.3)	100 (1595)	9.2×10^{-15}	22.4
			$< 10^{-14}$	22.4
			1.7×10^{-13}	21.9
8	11 800 (81.5)	109 (1750)	1.8×10^{-13}	18.1
			1.9×10^{-14}	18.6
			1.9×10^{-14}	18.3
9	12 800 (88.4)	1175 (1880)	$< 10^{-14}$	22.7
			2.5×10^{-12}	22.2
			2.2×10^{-12}	22.4

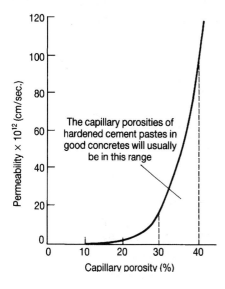

The capillary porosities of hardened cement pastes in good concretes will usually be in this range

Fig. 2.2 Permeability of portland cement paste with capillary porosity[2.9]

Plate 8 Afrikaans Language Monument, Stellenbosch, South Africa. Height of main dianamically designed hollow columns, 186 ft.

2.3   FREEZING AND THAWING ACTION

2.3.1   Frost Action in Hardened Concrete

Concrete deteriorates in freezing temperatures if exposed to the environment such as in the case of bridge decks and in pavements. This deterioration is caused when moisture fills the voids, freezes into ice, and expands within the pores. The high concentrated stresses on the walls of the pores induced by this expansion lead to cracking and spalling of the concrete surface in the mature concrete. Freezing and thawing cycles continue the propagation of the cracks and the serviceability of the structural element is gradually diminished. The dilation (expansion) pressure due to the expanding frost in the pores when exceeding the tensile strength of the surrounding concrete enclosure leads to localized fracture that propagates into surface scaling. Another cause of the dilation pressure is the water diffusion caused by osmotic pressure resulting from small bodies of ice which lead to frost damage.[2.14] With the spreading of salt for deicing bridge decks and road surfaces,

Plate 9 311 South Wacker Street, Chicago: 12 000 psi concrete (Courtesy Portland Cement Association)

an osmotic pressure is also produced resulting in the movement of water towards the coldest zones in the concrete element without freezing taking place. This process, combined with the scaling caused by the tensile forces due to the icicles, will cause additional scaling and surface damage to the concrete structure and the corrosion of the reinforcement that adds more expansive tensile stresses within the concrete.

2.3.2   Frost Action in Fresh Concrete

In the case of concreting in cold weather, frost action takes place by freezing the water in the mix resulting in the increase of the concrete volume, namely, the yield of the mixture. But the frozen portion of the design water content deprives

Plate 10 East Huntington Bridge, Ohio: 2000 ft segmental prestressed cable-stayed bridge over the Ohio River between West Huntington, West Virginia, and Proctorville, Ohio. Each segment was 45 ft long and weighed 250 tons; the two main spans were 900 and 680 ft long (Courtesy Portland Cement Association)

Plate 11 Skin concrete showing porous layer (Courtesy American Concrete Institute)

the cement from undergoing the full chemical hydration process for which the mixture is designed. The initial and final set are delayed or inhibited and a weak concrete with honeycombing results. Thereafter, freezing and thawing generates the cracking and spalling previously discussed and the concrete scales and deteriorates in a continuous process.

Figure 2.3[2.1] gives the relationship between the ambient temperature and relative setting time as a proportion of setting time at 59°F (15°C). Figure 2.4[2.10] gives the relationship for length of exposure to frost and increase in volume of concrete as a function of early age concrete, while Fig. 2.5 relates the increase in volume of the concrete as a function of the number of freezing cycles.

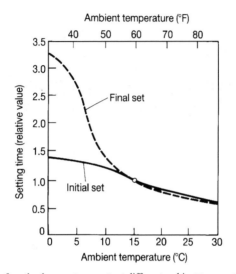

Fig. 2.3 Setting time of portland cement concrete at different ambient temperatures as a proportion of a base 15°C (59°F) setting time[2.1]

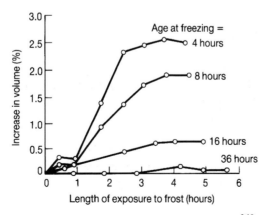

Fig. 2.4 Volume increase in early age concrete vs. exposure length to frost[2.10]

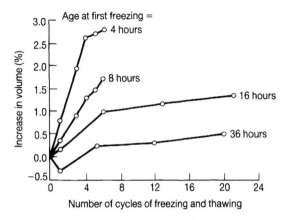

Fig. 2.5 Volume increase in early age concrete vs. freezing and thawing cycles[2.10]

2.4   CONCRETING IN COLD WEATHER

Special measures and precautions have to be taken when concreting in cold weather. When the temperature drops below 45°F (7°C) and particularly when freezing temperatures are encountered at 32°F (0°C). These measures can be summarized as follows:

1. Heating the aggregate to a maximum of 125°F (52°C), or heating the mixing water to 140–180°F (60–80°C)
2. Avoiding the use of cold cement in order to minimize the differential temperature gradient with the other mix components
3. Exercising rigorous controls on the temperature of the constituent materials.
4. Providing a steady supply of the mixture materials without dislocations
5. Using steam in the mix if the proper temperature levels cannot be maintained
6. Protecting the early age concrete for at least the first 3 days after placement such that its surface temperature does not drop below 50°F (10°C). A preferred temperature of 70°F (21°C) helps to develop the design concrete compressive strength in a timely manner
7. Using air-entraining agents in the mixture in order to prevent freeze–thaw effects as the concrete hardens (ACI Committee 306)
8. Using accelerators or calcium chloride but up to 0.5 percent in order to facilitate the hydration process
9. Preparing a well-defined curing procedure prior to placing the mix in the formwork
10. Using modest heat-generating cement in the mix
11. Using richer mixes by increasing the cement content, namely, lowering the water/cement ratio

Table 2.3[2.5] gives the age of concrete at which exposure to frost does not result in damage.

Table 2.3 Concrete age when frost exposure does not cause damage[2.5]

Type of cement	W/C ratio	5°C (41°F)	10°C (50°F)	15°C (59°F)	20°C (68°F)
		\multicolumn{4}{c}{Age (hours) at exposure when preceding curing temperature was}			
Ordinary portland	0.4	35	25	15	12
	0.5	50	35	25	17
	0.6	70	45	35	25
Rapid-hardening portland	0.4	20	15	10	7
	0.5	30	20	15	10
	0.6	40	30	20	15

2.5   AIR-ENTRAINING AGENTS

Air-entraining agents are vinsol resins that produce small air bubbles of 0.05–1 mm diameter evenly spaced in the concrete mix which can fill the voids that are expected to be at a spacing of approximately 0.10–0.25 mm. In this manner, the concrete can be protected against frost damage by the presence of these evenly distributed small voids that reduce the stresses resulting from the expanding frost. The percentage of the air-entraining agent should not exceed 6–7 percent as the concrete compressive strength decreases as a function of the percentage of air. Table 2.4 gives the total air content as a function of the aggregate size and exposure condition.

The advantages of adding air-entraining agents or admixtures to the concrete mix, whether in liquid or powder form, can be summarized as follows:

1. Reducing the W/C ratio if a liquid admixture is used. Part of the design mixture water is replaced by the liquid additive
2. Improving the durability of the concrete surface by reducing or eliminating the freezing and thawing effects
3. Increasing the concrete resistance to deicing chemicals

It should be emphasized that good quality control of the air content has to be maintained, particularly the mixing and vibrating process of the concrete. Overmixing and overvibration can drive out the entrapped air bubbles, thereby

Table 2.4 Total air content in structural frost-resisting concretes

Maximum aggregate size, in. (mm)	Moderate exposure	Severe exposure
	\multicolumn{2}{c}{Air content (%)}	
(1)	(2)	(3)
$\frac{3}{8}$ (9.5)	6	$7\frac{1}{2}$
$\frac{1}{2}$ (12.7)	$5\frac{1}{2}$	7
$\frac{3}{4}$ (19)	5	6
1 (25)	$4\frac{1}{2}$	6

losing the air-entraining component in the mix. Also, aggregate grading is important since ungraded larger aggregates cause larger unevenly distributed air voids that weaken the concrete and render it less resistant to frost cycles.

But variations in temperature, aggregate grading, fly ash, superplasticizers, and the mixing and placing methods are unavoidable. Their impact is to complicate the attainment of the air-entraining content designed for the mix. New air-entraining agents are available to produce possibly more stabilized air content and more evenly spaced air bubbles. They involve the use of hollow plastic microspheres with diameters in the range of 10–50 μm and a dosage of 1–2 percent by weight of cement.[2.17] This dosage corresponds to approximately one percent of extra air by volume of concrete. The appropriate percentage should be chosen on the basis of the W/C ratio and the maximum size of aggregate.

Alternatively, preformed bubble reservoirs can produce effective entraining systems. This can be accomplished by the addition of divided porous solid, such as brick or fly ash ground to smaller than 1 mm in size, which would act in the same manner as entrained air bubbles. This method is more expensive than the traditional air-entraining agents used for freeze and thaw resistance, but has the distinct advantage of independence from the effects previously discussed.

2.6   ACI RECOMMENDATIONS ON COLD WEATHER CONCRETING

ACI reports on cold weather concreting[2.15, 2.16] give guidelines for quality control in placing concrete in cold weather including guidelines on temperature loss during concrete delivery. Table 2.5 gives recommended concrete temperatures for placement in cold weather. Table 2.6 gives the length of the protection period required to prevent damage from early age freezing of

Table 2.5 Recommended concrete temperatures

Line	Air temperature	< 12 in. (300 mm)	12–36 in. (300–900 mm)	36–72 in. (900–1800 mm)	> 72 in (> 1800 mm)
		Section size, minimum dimension, in. (mm)			
		Minimum concrete temperature as placed and maintained			
1	—	55°F (13°C)	50°F (10°C)	45°F (7°C)	40°F (5°C)
		Minimum concrete temperature as mixed for indicated air temperature[a]			
2	Above 30°F (−1°C)	60°F (16°C)	55°F (13°C)	50°F (10°C)	45°F (7°C)
3	0 to 30°F (−18 to −1°C)	65°F (18°C)	60°F (16°C)	55°F (13°C)	50°F (10°C)
4	Below 0°F (−18°C)	70°F (21°C)	60°F (16°C)	60°F (16°C)	55°F (13°C)
		Maximum allowable gradual temperature drop in first 24 hr after end of protection			
5	—	50°F (28°C)	40°F (22°C)	30°F (17°C)	20°F (11°C)

[a]For colder weather a greater margin in temperature is provided between concrete as mixed and required minimum temperature of fresh concrete in place.

Table 2.6 Length of protection period required to prevent damage from early age freezing of air-entrained concrete

Line in Table 2.5	Exposure	Protection period at temperature indicated in line 1 of Table 2.5 (days)[a]	
		Type I or II cement	Type III cement, or accelerating admixture, or 100 lb/yd³ (60 kg/m³) of additional cement
1	Not exposed	2	1
2	Exposed	3	2

[a]A day is a 24 hr period.

Table 2.7 Length of protection period for concrete placed during cold weather

Line in Table 2.5	Service category	Protection period at temperature indicated in line 1 of Table 2.5 (days)[a]	
		Type I or II cement	Type III cement, or accelerating admixture, or 100 lb/yd³ (60 kg/m³) of additional cement
1	No load, not exposed	2	1
2	No load, exposed	3	2
3	Partial load, exposed	6	4
4	Full load	Extra days	Extra days

[a]A day is a 24 hr period.

Table 2.8 Maximum allowable temperature drop during first 24 hours after end of protection period

Maximum temperature for given section size, minimum dimensions, in. (mm)			
< 12 in.	12–36 in.	36–72 in.	> 72 in.
(< 300 mm)	(300–900 mm)	(900–1800 mm)	(> 1800 mm)
50°F (28°C)	40°F (22°C)	30°F (17°C)	20°F (11°C)

air-entrained concrete while Table 2.7 details the length of the protection period for concrete placed during cold weather. Table 2.8 gives the maximum allowable temperature drop during the first 24 hours after the end of the protection period.

2.7   FREEZING AND THAWING EFFECTS ON HARDENED HIGH STRENGTH CONCRETE

Dry concrete if properly air-entrained is not affected by freeze–thaw cycles. However, if the aggregate is nondurable with a large void percentage, the permeable water that fills the voids when the concrete is dry will cause the concrete to deteriorate in freezing and thawing cycles. Thus, in high strength

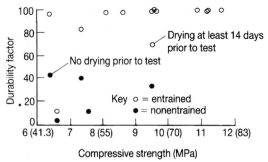

Fig. 2.6 Effect of air entrainment on the durability of high strength concrete[2.8] (Tests on 3 in. × 3 in. × 11¼ in. prisms, or 76 mm × 76 mm × 256 mm)

concrete, where the aggregate size is normally small (⅜ in. to ½ in.), durability quality is high while W/C ratio is very low and quality control is maximized. In this case, freezing and thawing effects can be considerably reduced, if not altogether eliminated. Air-entraining agents tend to reduce the compressive strength of the finished product, and the mix design has to take this strength reduction into account.

It has been found that larger doses of the air-entraining agent are needed in high strength concrete, particularly the rich low slump mixtures and those mixtures containing large quantities of fly ash, in order to provide the air void percentage and distribution needed to resist the freezing and thawing effects. Fiorato[2.8] found that high strength concretes can only perform well in resisting freezing and thawing if they are properly air-entrained. Figure 2.6 shows from test results that the durability factor for the nonair-entrained concretes is 5–40 percent of those that were air-entrained.[2.11, 2.12, 2.13]

2.8   HOT WEATHER CONCRETING

2.8.1   Introduction

Hot weather adversely affects the mixing, placing, and curing of concrete and its serviceability and long-term performance. Most of the problems arise because of the increased rate of cement hydration at higher temperatures and the increased evaporation rate of moisture from the freshly mixed concrete.[2.18] Hot weather is the combination of any of the following conditions:

1. High ambient temperature
2. High concrete temperature
3. Low relative humidity
4. Solar radiation
5. Wind velocity

The effects of the first four factors can be more pronounced with increases in wind velocity as shown in Fig. 2.7.[2.18] These potential problems arising from hot weather concreting can occur during the summer season in normal climates and at

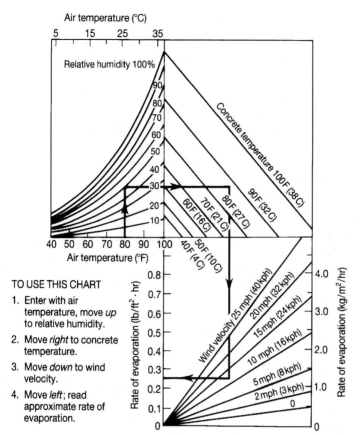

Fig. 2.7 Effect of concrete and air temperatures, relative humidity, and wind velocity on rate of evaporation of surface moisture in the concrete[2.18]

any time during the year in warm, tropical, or arid climates . As a result, cracking due to thermal shrinkage is more severe during hot seasons because the temperature differential, particularly during the late spring and early fall for each 24 hour period is greater during these times of the year. The major potential problems in hot weather concreting can be summarized as:

1. Increased water demand
2. Increased rate of slump loss and the need to add more water in the field
3. Increased difficulty in controlling the entrained air
4. Increased rate of setting with the accompanying increased difficulty with handling, compacting, and finishing and a greater risk of cold joints
5. Increased tendency for plastic shrinkage cracking in the freshly mixed concrete
6. Decreased compressive strength due to the added water
7. Increased drying shrinkage cracking resulting in increased permeability of harmful products, hence decreased durability and poor long-term performance

Plate 12 Skin concrete showing dense microstructure except for a few cracks (Courtesy American Concrete Institute)

8. Possible extensive scaling of concrete cover
9. Steel reinforcement corrosion
10. Increased cost of the finished concrete because of the need for special precautions with concreting in hot weather, such as handling and curing procedures and their duration

2.8.2   Hot Weather Concreting Practices

It is essential that detailed procedures be instituted prior to concreting for the mixing, placing, protection, curing, temperature monitoring, and testing of the concrete during hot weather. The primary factors that have to be considered are limits on concrete temperature, cement and cementitious additives content, heat of hydration of the particular cement needed for the specific job requirement, type and dosage rate of the chemical and mineral admixtures to be used, types of joints, and formwork stripping time.

The constructor should use concrete materials and mixture proportions based on prior successful performance in hot weather, and a cool concrete having a consistency that permits rapid placement and effective consolidation. Most important, the concrete surface has to be protected against moisture loss at all times during placement as well as during the entire curing period.

2.8.3   Plastic Shrinkage Cracking

Severe plastic shrinkage cracking is often the result of hot weather concreting. It develops in exposed concrete surfaces whenever the water evaporation rate is greater than the rate at which water rises by bleeding to the surface of recently

Table 2.9 Typical concrete temperatures[a] for various relative humidities potentially critical to plastic shrinkage cracking[2.18]

Concrete temperature, °F (°C)	Relative humidity (%)
105 (40.6)	90
100 (37.8)	80
95 (35.0)	70
90 (32.2)	60
85 (29.4)	50
80 (26.7)	40
75 (23.9)	30

[a]Based on 10 mph (16 km/hr) wind speed; 10°F (5.6°C) air–concrete temperature differential.

placed concrete. Table 2.9[2.18] gives the concrete temperatures for various relative humidities potentially critical to plastic shrinkage cracking. It should be noted that plastic shrinkage is rarely a problem in hot humid climates where the relative humidity is rarely less than 80 percent.

The effect of concrete temperature on slump and on the water quantity needed to modify the slump are shown in Fig. 2.8.[2.19] Figure 2.7 and Table 2.8 lead to the following observations:

1. If the humidity and wind remain the same and the air temperature changes from 60 to 90°F (16 to 32°C), evaporation rate increases by 300 percent
2. If air temperature and humidity remain the same and the wind speed increases from 5 to 20 mph (8 to 32 kph), evaporation rate increases by 300 percent

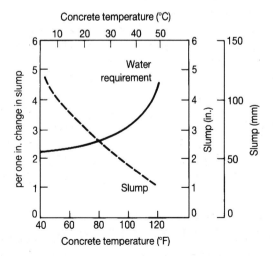

Fig. 2.8 Effect of concrete temperature on slump and water required to change slump for type I and II cements[2.19]

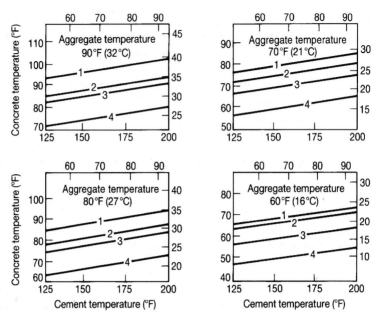

Curve (1): Mixing water at temperature of aggregate
Curve (2): Mixing water at 50°F (10°C)
Curve (3): Mixing water at temperature of aggregate; 25% of mixing water by weight replaced by ice
Curve (4): Mixing water at temperature of aggregate; 50% of mixing water by weight replaced by ice

Fig. 2.9 Influence of temperature of concrete ingredients on concrete temperature[2.18]

3. If air temperature and wind remain the same and the humidity decreases from 90 to 70 percent, evaporation rate increases by 300 percent
4. If the wind speed increases from 5 to 20 mph (8 to 32 kph), and if the temperature rises from 60 to 90°F (16 to 32°C) and the humidity decreases from 90 to 70 percent, the evaporation rate increases by 900 percent

Figure 2.9[2.18] shows the influence of temperature of the concrete ingredients on concrete temperature. Since the major portion of the produced concrete is the aggregate, reduction of aggregate temperature leads to the largest reduction in concrete temperature. Consequently, all practical measures have to be taken to keep the aggregate as cool as possible in the case of hot weather concreting. Also, chilling of batch water by water chillers, substituting crushed or flaked ice for part of the mixing water or cooling by liquid nitrogen might be undertaken depending on the size of the batch.

2.8.4   Curing and Protection of the Concrete

After placement, continuous protection of the concrete from high temperatures, direct sunlight, low humidity, and drying winds is essential. The concrete surface should be protected from rapid temperature drops, particularly during the first 24 hours after placement. This precaution is equally necessary in cold weather concreting. Cracking is often associated with a cooling rate of more than 5°F (3°C) per hour, or more than 50°F (28°C) in a 24 hour period for concrete with dimensions less than 12 in. (300 mm).[2.18] If these conditions occur, the concrete should be protected by placing several layers of waterproof paper or by using other insulating methods used in cold weather concreting.

Other means of protection in order to achieve a complete hydration process involve the application of membrane curing of flat work. This procedure involves the use of liquid membrane-forming compounds. These compounds are used when job site conditions do not permit continuous moisture curing through continuous water spraying or ponding, or covering with continuously wetted burlap. On surfaces exposed to the sun, white-colored heat-reflecting compounds need to be applied to the concrete surface. The capability of moisture retention considerably varies with the type of curing compound used. The material selected should provide as a minimum the requirements of ASTM C 309 specifications limiting the moisture loss to 0.55 kg/m^2 or less.

Formwork has also to be covered and kept continuously moist during the early curing period. But the forms should be loosened as soon as practicable, provided that no damage occurs to the enclosed concrete. The newly exposed surfaces should immediately receive a uniformly wet covering. The duration of the curing period should be at least seven and preferably 12 days. After the end of this period, the covering should be left in place for several days without wetting in order that the concrete surface can dry slowly and be subject to less shrinkage cracking.

REFERENCES

2.1   Powers T C 1958 The Physical Structure and Engineering Properties of Concrete. *Research Bulletin No. 90* Portland Cement Association, Skokie, Ill

2.2   Powers T C, Copeland L E, Hayes J C, and Mann H M 1958 Permeability of Portland Cement Paste. *Proceedings, ACI Journal* Vol. 51 American Concrete Institute, Detroit, pp. 285–298

2.3   Nawy E G 1996 *Reinforced Concrete—A Fundamental Approach* 3rd ed. (1st. Ed, 1985), Prentice Hall, Englewood Cliffs, NJ

2.4   Mehta P K, and Monteiro P J M 1993 *Concrete—Structure, Properties and Materials* 2nd ed., Prentice Hall, Englewood Cliffs, N.J

2.5   Neville A M 1981 *Properties of Concrete* 3rd ed., Pitman, London

2.6   Kong F K, Evans R H, Cohen E, Roll E (eds.) 1983 *Handbook of Structural Concrete* McGraw-Hill, New York

2.7   *Concrete Manual* 1975 8th ed., U.S. Bureau of Reclamation, Denver, p. 37

2.8   Fiorato A E 1994 PCA Research on High Strength Concrete. *ACI Compilation 17* American Concrete Institute, Detroit

2.9   Zhang M H and Gjorv O E 1991 Permeability of High Strength Lightweight Concrete. *Proceedings ACI Materials Journal* Vol. 88, No. 5, American Concrete Institute, Detroit, pp. 463–69

2.10   Moller G 1956 Test of Resistance of Concrete to Early Frost Action. *Proceedings RILEM Symposium on Winter Concreting, Copenhagen*

2.11   Klieger P 1960 Some Aspects of Durability and Volume Changes of Concrete for Prestressing. *Research Bulletin 118* Portland Cement Association, Skokie, Ill.

2.12   Perenchio W F, and Klieger P 1978 Some Physical Properties of High Strength Concrete. *Research and Development Bulletin* No. RD056-01T, Portland Cement Association, Skokie, Ill.

2.13   Whiting D 1987 Durability of High Strength Concrete. *Proceedings Katherine and Bryant Mather International Conference. ACI SP-100* American Concrete Institute, Detroit, pp. 169–86

2.14   Helmuth R A 1987 Capillary Size Restrictions in Hardened Portland Cement Pastes. *Proceedings 4th International Symposium on the Chemistry of Cement, Washington, D.C.* pp. 855–869

2.15   ACI Committee 306 Cold Weather Concreting. *ACI Report 306R-88* American Concrete Institute, Detroit, 1988, pp. 1–23

2.16   ACI Committee 306 Standard Specified for Cold Weather Concreting. *ACI Report 306-90* American Concrete Institute, Detroit, 1990, pp.1–5

2.17   Collepardi M 1994 Superplasticizers and Air Entraining Agents: State-of-the-Art and Future Needs. *ACI SP-144* ed. P Kumar Mehta, American Concrete Institute, Detroit, pp. 399–416

2.18   ACI Committee 305 Hot Weather Concreting. *ACI Report 305R-91* American Concrete Institute, Detroit, 1991, pp.1–20

2.19   Klieger P 1958 Effect of Mixing and Curing Temperatures on Concrete Strength. *Proceedings, ACI Journal,* Vol. 54 No. 12, American Concrete Institute, Detroit, pp. 1063–81

3 Mineral and Chemical Admixtures in High Strength Concrete

3.1 FLY ASH

Fly ash is a finely divided residue which is the by-product of the combustion of ground or powdered coal exhaust fumes of coal-fired power stations. It is known in the U.K. as pulverised fuel ash and possesses pozzolanic properties similar to natural pozzolans.[3.1] It is composed of siliceous and aluminous ingredients and possesses limited cementitious properties unless so finely divided that its fineness is at least equal or less than the fineness of the cement with which it is mixed. In the presence of the water in the mix, it reacts with the calcium hydroxide at ordinary temperatures, thereby forming compounds that have high cementitious qualities.[3.2]

The chemical and mineral composition of fly ashes is complex as they consist of heterogeneous combinations of glassy and crystalline phases. They are classified in two ASTM classes, C and F. The principal constituents are silica, SiO_2 (5–25 percent), alumina, As_2O_3 (10–30 percent), and ferric oxide, Fe_2O_3 (5–25 percent). In addition they contain calcium oxide, CaO, magnesium oxide, MgO, sulphur trioxide, SO_3, and alkali oxide, Na_2O.

ASTM Class F

In ASTM Class F the sum of SiO_2, Al_2O_3, and $Fe_2O_3 = 70$ percent or greater. This class normally has a *small* calcium oxide content (less than 10 percent), but a large proportion of high silica content of silicate glass, quartz, mullites and magnetites of low reactivity. High calcium fly ashes gain more early strength than low calcium fly ashes. The particle size ranges from 1 μm to 1 mm or greater and a specific gravity of solid fly ash particles ranging normally between 2.2 and 2.8.

ASTM Class C

In ASTM Class C the sum of SiO_2, Al_2O_3, and $Fe_2O_3 \geq 50\%$ but ≤ 70 percent. It has a *high* calcium oxide content (more than 10 percent and often 15–20 percent). It also has a high proportion of particles finer than 10 μm.

3.1.1 Fly Ash Effect on Fresh Concrete

ACI Committee 226[3.1] has published a comprehensive report on fly ash in concrete. Additionally, Malhotra, et al.[3.9–3.12] have contributed extensively to this area.

Plate 13   Ekofisk offshore oil drilling platform superstructure in the North Sea (Courtesy Portland Cement Association)

Workability
Whenever fly ash is used, the volume of cement and fly ash in the concrete mix would normally exceed that in no-fly ash concrete mix. The increased volume produces larger cementitious paste volume, hence better workability. As a result, a smaller water content is needed than in mixes where fly ash is not used.

Bleeding
Fly ash generally reduces bleeding as it provides greater fines volume and produces a lower water content in the mixture.

Time of Set
Class F fly ash retards the time of set of the concrete mix while ASTM Class C with the relatively higher content of CaO can either accelerate, retard, or have no effect on the time of set. The time of set in either of these types is greatly influenced by the ambient and concrete temperatures, the cement type, the water/ cementitious ratio, the percentage of fly ash that replaces the cement in the mix, the type of cement, and the use of other admixtures in addition to fly ash.

Need for Superplasticizers
Superplasticizers (HRWRs) are necessary in high volume fly ash concrete where the ratio $W/C + F$ is about 0.30. The dosage needed is a function of the required slump, generally about 1.5 percent of the total cementitious material, namely,

about $\frac{1}{2}$ lb/ft^3 ($\sim$5 kg/m^3). A superplasticizer that will not delay the setting time should be chosen for the mix.

3.1.2   Fly Ash Effect on Hardened Concrete

Compressive Strength

The use of ASTM Class F fly ash can result in a lower compressive strength at early ages (3–7 days). Thereafter, as the strength contribution rate of the portland cement decreases, the continued pozzolanic activity of the fly ash content in the hardening mix contributes to higher strength gain at later ages. This higher rate of strength gain continues with time, resulting in higher ultimate strengths than in concretes without fly ash content.[3.3] It was demonstrated[3.4–3.6] that fly ash is a very useful ingredient in the production of high strength concrete. On the other hand, ASTM Class C fly ashes sometimes exhibit at early ages a lower concrete strength, although they are more reactive than ASTM Class F at early age because of the presence of Ca(OH)$_2$.

High volume Class F fly ash in concrete can produce a strength varying from 1000 psi (8 MPa) to 5500 psi (38 MPa) at early age, i.e. 1–28 days, depending on the type of fly ash, moist- or air-cured, water/cementitious ratio, and combinations with other admixtures.[3.7] It is not unusual that the compressive strength can reach almost 12 000 psi (83 MPa).[3.10] Figure 3.1 gives the rate of strength gain for Class C fly ash concrete compared with no-fly ash concrete. Figure 3.2 using type III high early cement in the mix and Class F fly ash gives strength gain with age for a water/cementitious ratio (W/(C + F)) of 0.31. Test 3 in Fig. 3.2, shows that a compressive strength of almost 8700 psi (60 MPa) at one year age is achieved. Figure 3.3 shows a strength vs. age for W/(C + F) ratio

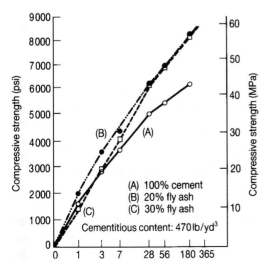

Fig. 3.1 Rates of strength gain of ASTM Class C fly ash and no-fly ash concretes[3.1]

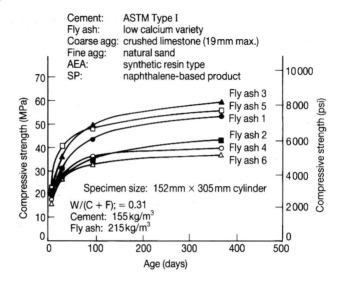

Fig. 3.2 Compressive strength vs. age of high volume fly ash concretes (W/C+F = 0.31)[3.10]

of 0.27, where a strength of 12 000 psi (83 MPa) is reached. In Table 3.1,[3.10] the different characteristics of high volume fly ash concretes are presented.

Modulus of Elasticity

From Figs. 3.1 and 3.4,[3.1] it can be deduced that the modulus of elasticity of fly ash concrete, particularly at early ages, is slightly higher than plain concrete as the slope of the tangent to the stress–strain and strength–age diagrams for the fly ash concrete is smaller. From Table 3.1, it is seen that the 90 day modulus of elasticity for Batch A ranged from 5.4×10^6 psi (37.3 GPa) to 6.7×10^6 psi

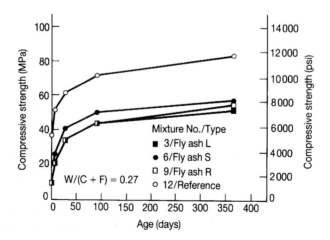

Fig. 3.3 Compressive strength vs. age in high volume fly ash concretes (W/C+F = 0.27)[3.10]

Table 3.1 Densities, compressive strength, and modulus of elasticity of fly ash concrete[3.10]

Mixture no.	W/(C + FA) ratio	Cement (kg/m³)	Fly ash (kg/m³)	Densities of cylinders at one day (kg/m³)			Compressive strength (MPa)[b]							91-day modulus of elasticity (GPa)
				A	B	C	1 d	7 d	28 d[a]			91 d	365 d	
							A	A	A	B	C	A	A	A
1	0.38	126	173	2435	2430	2410	3.9	11.2	21.1	21.2	18.6	30.1	39.4	37.3
2	0.31	156	215	2440	2445	2420	6.8	16.0	28.3	28.3	25.2	37.1	47.1	40.4
3	0.27	180	248	2440	2420	2425	8.6	20.5	33.7	33.8	32.0	44.1	51.9	43.7
4	0.39	124	172	2360	2375	2390	3.2	13.2	27.5	29.7	27.8	35.9	41.1	39.1
5	0.31	155	214	2365	2350	2380	6.5	22.0	36.9	36.8	41.6	46.0	51.4	40.8
6	0.27	182	251	2380	2385	2370	9.9	26.4	41.0	42.8	45.2	50.3	56.8	40.3
7	0.39	124	170	2410	2405	2395	3.9	11.2	20.2	20.1	19.3	30.9	42.7	38.2
8	0.31	155	213	2425	2425	2410	7.0	17.0	29.3	28.1	27.5	41.2	51.4	40.7
9	0.27	181	250	2425	2430	2430	9.2	20.9	34.8	37.6	36.8	44.2	55.0	40.7
10	0.39	292	0	2455	2445	2425	16.4	27.8	34.6	40.7	34.1	40.3	47.1	40.3
11	0.31	368	0	2475	2480	2465	27.8	43.3	55.1	56.4	52.7	66.4	78.9	45.1
12	0.27	428	0	2485	2490	2480	37.2	51.2	61.3	61.3	60.2	71.8	83.7	46.2

[a] Average between batches coefficient of variation = 3.9%.
[b] MPA = N/mm²; psi × 0.006895 = MPa; lb/ft³ = 16.02 kg/m³.

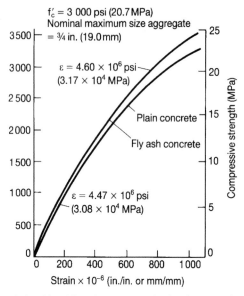

Fig. 3.4 Stress–strain relationship of fly ash concrete at 91 days in comparison to no-fly ash concrete[3.11]

Plate 14 Scotia Plaza, Toronto: a 68-storey office tower of 10 000 psi silica fume concrete (Courtesy Portland Cement Association)

(46.2 GPa). In comparing the plots of the two concretes, the differential is not too great and is probably caused by the larger percentage of aggregate content in the mix.

Long-Term Behavior

Long-term behavior is measured by creep and drying shrinkage deformations. Creep is the transverse flow of the material under external load or stress. But it is affected also by the duration of the load, the strength of the concrete, the aggregate content, temperature effects, and moisture conditions. Since creep is primarily load-induced, it was expected that fly ash would affect the creep behavior as a function of its contribution to the mechanical properties of the fly ash concrete versus the no-fly ash concrete. However, many investigations have demonstrated[3.1] that fly ash concretes generally exhibit lower long-term creep strains because of their higher rate of late age strength gain as discussed earlier.

Drying shrinkage is influenced by environmental conditions such as ambient temperatures, humidity, cement content and type, water/cementitious ratio, and aggregate type. The addition of fly ash does not seem to affect the shrinkage behavior of the concrete. Figures 3.5 and 3.6[3.11, 3.12] respectively give the creep and shrinkage strains relationship with age for high volume fly ash concrete.

Air Entrainment

Fly ash use in concrete necessitates a dosage rate of the air-entraining admixture which depends on the fly ash composition such as its carbon content, fineness, percentage of organic material in the fly ash, and loss of ignition. The carbon content is a major factor as it is similar to porous activated carbon; it

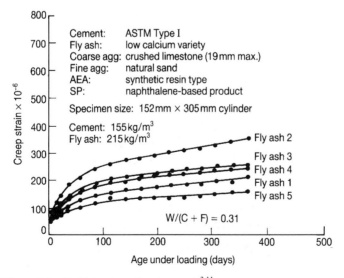

Fig. 3.5 Creep strains for high volume fly ash concrete[3.11]

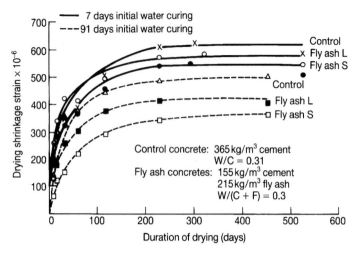

Fig. 3.6 Drying shrinkage of high volume fly ash and control concrete after 7 and 981 days of initial water-curing[3.12]

absorbs the air-entraining admixture and hence reduces its effectiveness.[3.1] There seems to be a relationship between the required dosage of air-entraining admixture and the loss of air in fly ash concrete such that fly ashes requiring higher admixture dosages lose more air.[3.13, 3.14] The air content in the hardened concrete, however, does not decrease to below 3.5 percent. It should be noted that it is difficult to entrain high percentages of air if the carbon content in the fly ash exceeds 6 percent.[3.11]

Freezing and Thaw Resistance

As discussed in Sections 1.8.2 and 2.5, the increased amount of cementitous content in a mix due to the use of fly ash would require a higher percentage of air-entraining admixture such as neutralized vinsol resin. The mixture proportions aim to achieve a concrete with a compressive strength of at least 3500 psi (24 MPa) prior to freezing and thawing regardless of whether it is fly ash concrete or no-fly ash concrete.

Alkali–Silica Reaction

Use of fly ash reduces the degree of aggregate–silica reaction and its harmful expansion effects on the concrete. The siliceous glass in the fly ash neutralizes the alkali hydroxides in the cement paste. In order to prevent the alkali–silica reaction in concretes containing reactive aggregates, use cements with an alkali content not exceeding 0.6 percent along with pozzolans or slag. In high volume fly ash concretes (50–60 percent by volume of the total binder), it is important that the alkali content in the fly ash is not so high that it affects the ability of the fly ash to reduce or control the expansive reaction of the reactive aggregate.

Sulfate Resistance

The sulfate resistance of fly ash concretes is controlled by the same factors which affect no-fly ash concretes. The major factors are exposure, W/(C + F) ratio, curing conditions, and permeability resistance. Generally, Class F fly ash can improve the sulphate resistance of the concrete provided, particularly because its permeability is very low in comparison to the no-fly ash concrete.

3.2   SUPERPLASTICIZERS

As discussed in Section 1.8.8, superplasticizers are high-range water-reducing chemical admixtures.[3.15] There are four types of superplasticizers:

1.   Sulfonated melamine formaldehyde condensates, with a chloride content of 0.005 percent (MSF)
2.   Sulfonated naphthalene formaldehyde condensates, with negligible chloride content (NSF)
3.   Modified lignosulfonates, which contain no chlorides
4.   Carboxyl acrylic ester copolymer (CAE)

Most of these admixtures are made from organic sulfonates and are termed "superplasticizers" in view of their considerable ability to facilitate reducing the water content in a concrete mix while simultaneously increasing the slump in the range of 8 in. (200 mm) or more. Other superplasticizers are sulfonic acid esters and carbohydrate esters. Depending on the solid content of the mixture, a dosage of 1–2 percent by weight of cement is advisable. Higher dosages can result in a reduction in compressive strength unless the cement content is increased to balance this reduction effect. It should be noted that the superplasticizers exert their action by decreasing the surface tension of water and by equidirectional charging of the cement particles. These properties, coupled with the addition of silica fume, help the concrete to achieve high strength and water reduction without loss of workability.

They are primarily used in concrete mixes in order to accomplish the following effects[3.16]:

1.   Increasing the workability without altering the mix composition
2.   Reducing both water and cement content in the mix for the purpose of reducing creep, shrinkage, and thermal strains caused by cement hydration
3.   Reducing the mixing water volume and the water/cement (W/C) or water/ cementitious materials ratio (such as $W/C + F$) in order to increase concrete strength and improved durability

The superplasticizers can change a zero-slump concrete to a concrete with a slump of almost 8 in. (200 mm). But the method of addition of the plasticizers can affect the increase in slump significantly. According to Collepardi,[3.16] it is advisable to treat the cement initially with a small amount of water (1–2 percent) about one minute prior to introducing the plasticizer MSF or NSF. He found that for a mix with 0.48 percent sulphonate naphthalene formaldehyde plasticizer (NSF), an increase in slump from 4 in. (100 mm) to 9 in. (230 mm) was achieved by delaying the addition of NSF one minute after a small percentage of water was

Plate 15 101 Park Avenue, New York City: 8000 psi concrete (Courtesy Portland Cement Association)

added to the cement. It is apparent that the addition of an initial part of the design mixing water to the cement causes

> . . . the incorporation of the superplasticizer into the C_3A–gypsum system, leaving only small amounts for dispersion of C_3A and C_2S. Consequently, the adsorption of MSF or NSF polymer molecules in the prehydrated cement surface is reduced and the subsequent dispersing action appears to be much more effective than that recorded in the absence of preliminary water treatment.

A new superplasticizer based on carboxylated acrylic ester (CAE) copolymer is available. It contains carboxylic instead of the sulfonic (SO_3) groups present in the MSF and NSF polymers. It acts as a dispersant in such a manner that no initial hydration of the cement particles is needed to achieve higher slump. In such a

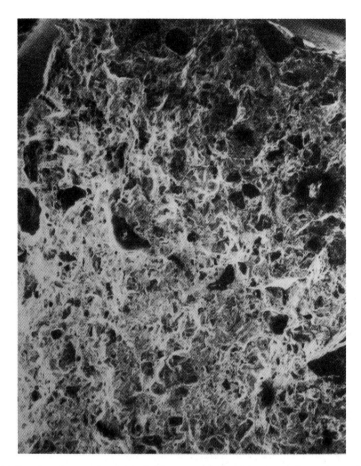

Plate 16 Scanning electron micrograph of polymer cement mortar fracture surface under tension (tests by Nawy *et al.*)

case, the addition of the superplasticizer and the water to the mix can be made simultaneously—a convenient field mixing. Table 3.2[3.16] shows the effect of the addition of the NSF or CAE plasticizer on the slump of the concrete mix.

Table 3.2 Effect of method of addition of NSF or CAE superplasticizer on the slump of concrete mix[3.16]

	Admixture			
Type	Dosage (%)[a]	Method of addition[b]	W/C ratio	Slump (mm)
NSF	0.48	Immediate	0.40	100
NSF	0.48	Delayed	0.40	230
CAE	0.30	Immediate	0.39	230
CAE	0.30	Delayed	0.39	235

[a]As dry polymer by weight of cement.
[b]Immediate: admixture with mixing water; delayed: admixture after 1 min of mixing.

3.2.1   Slump Loss

Transportation of a concrete mix over long distances reduces the slump made available at source particularly in hot weather. Addition of further water to increase the slump reduces the durability, strength, and other properties of the concrete. But slump loss is unavoidable and the mix designer has to strive to use the appropriate measures which can reduce slump loss to a minimum. In particular, concretes with MSF or NSF superplasticizers would suffer greater slump loss than nonplasticized concrete.

Current methods of reducing slump loss can be summarized as follows for the addition of the superplasticizer:

1. At source in the batching plant
2. Use of higher than normal dosage or with retarders
3. Redosing at several intervals before placement

All three alternatives have their drawbacks; an ideal condition would be to have a superplasticizer that could maintain slump for enough time, perhaps 1–2 hours, regardless of the temperature or cement type. Presently, some existing nonwater soluble plasticizers can reduce the slump loss. But the nonsolubility has serious drawbacks in actual source and field applications. CAE as a water soluble monocomponent copolymer seems to act both as an immediate disperser and slump loss reducing agent. Figure 3.7[3.16] shows both slump loss and strength gain with time. It is noted from the plots that the CAE with even a lower content than

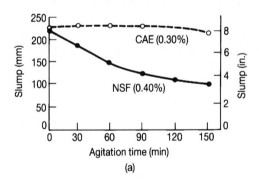

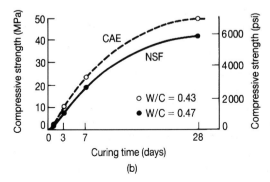

Fig. 3.7 Superplasticizer effect on slump and strength of concrete[3.16]: (a) agitation time vs. slump; (b) curing time vs. strength (cured at 41°F, or 5°C)

the NSF is able to maintain a relatively constant slump in $2\frac{1}{2}$ hours and can reach a higher compressive strength in 28 days for essentially the same W/C ratio (7250 psi vs. 5800 psi), although setting may be retarded.

3.3   POLYMERS

3.3.1   Types of Polymer Concretes

Polymer admixtures produce concretes with considerably high strength in the range of 15 000 psi (100 MPa) or higher and a tensile splitting strength of 1500 psi (10 MPa) or higher.[3.15] They modify the performance of concrete through one of the following mechanisms:

1.   Impregnation and irradiation under elevated temperatures in a laboratory environment to produce polymer impregnated concrete (PIC), rarely used today due to application complexity and cost
2.   Modification of concrete property by water reduction in the field through the use of polymer resins and monomers at site. The monomers include methyl methacrylate (MMA), styrene (STY), unsaturated polyester resins (PEs) and vinyl esters (VEs). They produce high strength, high performance concretes that are described as polymer concretes (PC) or polymer modified concretes (PMC)
3.   Latex modification by polymer dispersion through use of synthetic latexes made of vinyl acetates or butadiene and styrene under normal temperatures in the field. They are described as polymer portland cement concretes (PPCC) or as latex modified concretes (LMC). They are less amenable to producing very high strength concretes with higher performance than the types previously described, but are used on a large scale as overlays on bridge decks

3.3.2   Polymer Impregnated Concrete

Polymer impregnated concrete (PIC) is a hydrated portland cement concrete that is impregnated with a monomer which is subsequently polymerized. The impregnation process removes the free water from the pores in the concrete. The monomer is introduced into the concrete by pressure or atmospheric soaking until the element is fully impregnated—about 85 percent of the available voids are filled when the specimen is dry.[3.17]

After impregnation, the concrete element is subjected to a polymerization process where the monomer is converted to polymer. Polymerization is accomplished by a thermal catalytic process or by ionized radiation. The resulting composite material becomes essentially composed of two networks: (a) a hydrated concrete and (b) a polymer network which fills all the voids in the concrete. Figure 3.8[3.29] compares the stress–strain relationship for PIC and unimpregnated concrete. Note the increase in strength to 17 000 psi (117 MPa).

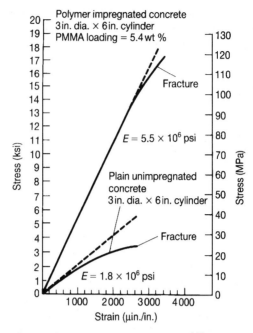

Fig. 3.8 Polymer impregnated concrete stress–strain relationship[3.29]

One of the drawbacks is the evaporation of the monomer. Another is the need for application under laboratory conditions. Also, the hazards involved in pressure impregnation and radiation make the use of PIC impractical; it is rarely used today.

3.3.3   Polymer Concrete

Polymer concrete (PC) or polymer modified concrete (PMC), the usage preferred in this book, is a composite material in which the aggregate is bound together by a polymer binder. The composites do not contain a hydraulic cement phase, and part of the cement acts as a filler in the same manner as the fine aggregate is a filler. In other words, PMC is a concrete composite in which the cement is replaced by the organic polymer as a cementing phase. This material is used in the construction industry either to fill potholes or as overlays over normal concrete, particularly in bridge decks, because it has good resistance to abrasion, negligible permeability, and good binding characteristic to existing concrete surfaces.

There are several different formulations of polymers for use in concrete. The most widely used include methyl methacrylate (MMA), styrene (STY), unsaturated polyester resins (PEs), and polyurethane. These monomers could be free-flowing powders or granules, pastes, or liquid dispersions. The promoters for the monomers are tertiary amines such as dimethylaniline and dimethyl-*p*-toluidine. They are straw-colored light liquids that quickly disperse in the monomer system.[3.17]

The total epoxy compound is generally formulated in two parts. Part A is usually the portion containing the resin while part B is the hardener (or promoter).

The principal characteristics of polymer modified concretes can be summarized as follows:

1. High slump (6–10 in.)
2. Rapid curing at ambient temperature from 0 to 104°F (− 18 to +4°C)
3. Good bond to the parent concrete surface
4. High compressive tensile and flexural strength
5. Low or negligible permeability to water and aggressive solutions
6. Good freezing and thawing cycles
7. Long-term durability.

Extensive research was undertaken at Rutgers University on the use of polymers in concrete mixtures and on the structural behavior of polymer concrete reinforced concrete elements. Figure 3.9[3.18] gives the wide range of slump values for different polymer/cement (P/C) and water/cement (W/C) ratios for PMC concretes using liquid epoxy resins. Figure 3.10 gives the tensile splitting strength for W/C ratios up to 0.6 and P/C ratios of 0.2, 0.4, and 0.6. Figure 3.11 gives the compressive strength for various percentages of mixing water replaced by polymer, giving a strength close to 15 000 psi (103 MPa). Table 3.3[3.30] gives a summary of the mechanical and durability properties of high molecular weight methacrylate polymer concretes with a maximum compressive strength at 75°F mix of 11 950 psi (82 MPa).

Use as Patching Material
Two good properties of this type of polymer concrete are fast cure and high strength, even at subfreezing temperatures. Reports[3.21] describe using three types of polymer: MMA, MPC, and PEs at temperatures of 15–20°F (− 7 to +9°C). A compressive strength of the methacrylate concrete of 9000 psi (62 MPa) in 3-day-old patching material and a slant shear strength of 4600 psi (32 MPa) in 1-day-old patching material were achieved. Figure 3.12(a), (b), and (c) show the levels of early age compressive and shear strength of polymer concrete patching material under subfreezing temperatures.

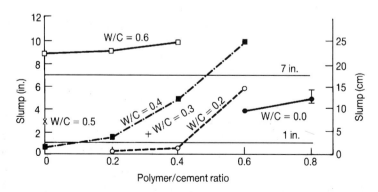

Fig. 3.9 Slump vs. polymer/cement ratio in polymer concrete specimens[3.18]

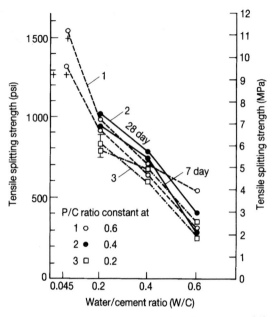

Fig. 3.10 Tensile splitting strength vs. water/cement ratio in polymer concrete[3.18]

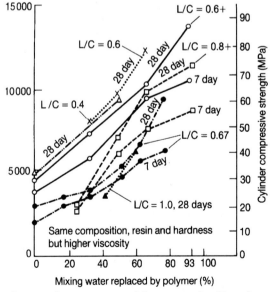

Fig. 3.11 Compressive strength vs. percentage mixing water replaced by polymer in polymer concrete[3.18]

Table 3.3 Mechanical and curability properties of high molecular weight methacrylate polymer concrete[3.30]

Property	High molecular weight methacrylate type		
(1)	(2)	(3)	(4)
	PC I	PC II	PC III
Compressive strength at 75°F (psi)	11 950	12 550	15 700
Flexural strength at 75°F (psi)	3 500	3 200	3 500
Flexural bond modulus of rupture (psi)[a]	602	501	1 031
Modulus of elasticity (psi)	3.05×10^6	2.86×10^6	1.5×10^6
Poisson's ratio	0.21	0.23	0.29
Coefficient of thermal expansion (in./in./°F)	12.65×10^{-6}	12.56×10^{-6}	2.48×10^{-6}
Shrinkage (in./in.)	0.00241	0.00328	0.00284
Freeze–thaw/freeze–thaw shear bond	Good resistance	Good resistance	Excellent resistance
Chemical resistance (% weight loss)	< 1	< 1	Not available
Water absorption (%)	~ 0	~ 0	~ 0

[a] 1000 psi = 6.895 MPa.

Use as Overlay

Polymer concrete can be used as a durable and wear-resisting surface for the parent portland cement concrete. It is particularly suitable for bridge decks as it has a negligible chloride permeability from deicing salts. Polymer concrete has a very high frictional bond interaction; after only 1–3 days it may still exceed 800 psi (5.5 MPa).[3.22] The surface of the parent concrete should be well prepared, tested for delaminations and subjected to dry or wet sandblasting. All laitance and any other surface contamination has to be removed by pressure hosing. The monomer and aggregate system used for the PMC overlay is similar to that used for patching. A coarse aggregate not exceeding ½ in. (12.7 mm) in size is recommended.

Safety Measures

It is important to recognize that the chemical reaction of the monomer and the activator and the odor of the completed mix can have injurious effects. Hence, care should be taken in the mixing and placing process.

3.3.4 Latex Modified Concrete

Polymer Portland Cement Concrete

Polymer portland cement concretes (PPCCs) are normal portland cement mixtures to which a water soluble or emulsified polymer is added during the mixing process. As the concrete hardens, the polymer simultaneously hardens forming a continuous matrix of polymer throughout the concrete specimen.

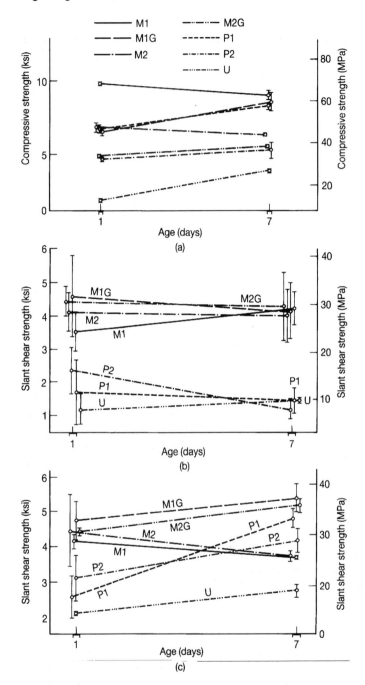

Fig. 3.12 Early age behavior of polymer concrete patching material at subfreezing temperatures (15–20°F)[3.21]: (a) compressive strength vs. age; (b) slant shear strength vs. age, dry-patched; (c) slant shear strength vs. age, moist-patched

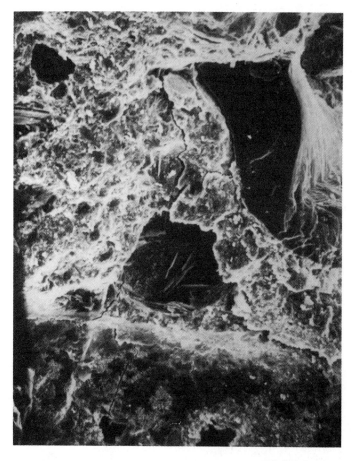

Plate 17 Scanning electron micrograph of polymer concrete fracture surface (tests by Nawy et al.)

Although a real polymer, the PPCC latex system can be considered as a polymer system consisting of very small (0.05–1.0 μm diameter) spherical particles of high molecular weight polymer held in suspension in water by the use of surface-active agents.[3.17] The latex is formed by emulsion polymerization of the monomer and typically contains approximately 50 percent solids by weight. Several types are available. The most commonly used types are styrene, butadiene, and acrylic polymers. An estimated 1.5 million square yards of bridge deck surfaces are annually overlaid with latex modified concrete (LMC) in addition to parking garage decks. The maximum compressive strength that can be achieved in reasonably and cost-effectively proportioned LMC is about 5000 psi (34.5 MPa), as discussed by Ramakrishuan.[3.31] The composite concrete is not intended for construction of structural components and does not fall in the category of high strength concrete. In summary, Table 3.4 compiled by Mehta[3.23] gives the relative strengths of the three categories discussed.

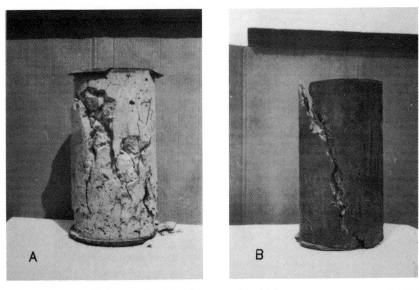

Plate 18 Concrete cylinders tested to failure in compression: (A) low epoxy cement content; (B) high epoxy cement content (tests by Nawy *et al.*)

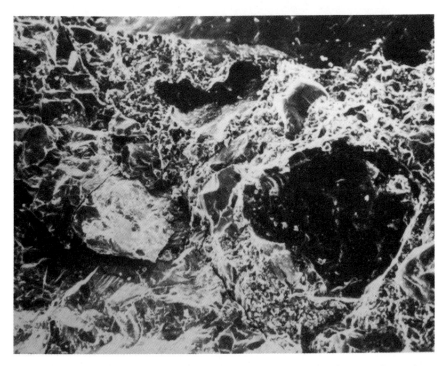

Plate 19 Electron micrograph of concrete from specimen in Plate 17A (tests by Nawy, Sun, and Sauer)

Table 3.4 Typical mechanical properties of concretes with polymer systems[3.23]

Strength (psi)[a]	PC		LMC			PIC	
	Polyester (1:10 polymer/aggregate ratio)	Polymerized MMA (1:15)	Control		LMC containing styrene–butadiene air-cured	Control unimpregnated	MMA impregnated, thermal-catalytical polymerization
			Moist-cured	Air-cured			
Compressive strength	18 000	20 000	5 800	4 500	4 800	5 300	18 000
Tensile strength	2 000	1 500	535	310	620	420	1 500
Flexural strength	5 000	3 000	1 070	610	1 430	740	2 300
Elastic modulus $\times 10^6$	5	5.5	3.4	—	1.56	3.5	6.2

[a]1000 psi = 6895 MPa.

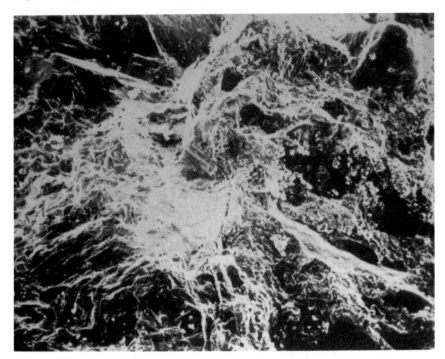

Plate 20 Electron micrograph of concrete from specimen in Plate 17B (tests by Nawy, Sun, and Sauer)

3.4   SILICA FUME

3.4.1   General Characteristics

Silica fume (SF) is a relatively new pozzolanic material that has received considerable attention in both research and application. It is a by-product resulting from the use of high purity quartz with coal in the electric ore furnace in the production of silicon and ferrosilicon alloys.[3.15] Reduction of the quartz to silicon is made at temperatures up to 2000°C producing silicon oxide vapors (SiO) which oxidize and condense into minute spherical particles as the temperature decreases. These particles of noncrystalline silica are removed by filtering the gases into bag filters. The diameter of the particles is 0.1–0.12 μm and their surface area is 15–25 m^2/g. In comparison, ASTM conforming portland cement or fly ash particle sizes are almost two orders of magnitude larger than silica fume particles (10–12 μm).

Being a waste product with relative ease in collection as compared to fly ash or slag, silica fume has gained rapid popularity. Still, its annual use in the United States today is limited to about 20 000 tons and worldwide to 150 000 tons as compared to fly ash (7 million and more than 60 million tons respectively).

Silica fume is available in loose bulk form, densified form, slurry form, and in the form of blended silica fume portland cement. It can also be delivered in truck

Plate 21 Compressive brittle failure of high strength concrete

loads or large containers. Proportions of silica fume in concrete mixes generally vary from 5 to 20 percent by weight of cement, depending on the strength and workability requirements, although in special situations up to 30 percent has been used. However, water demand is greatly increased with increasing proportion of silica fume. Thus, high range water reducers are essential to keep the water/cement ratio low, yet produce high strength and also workable concrete. SF seems to attain high early age strength in 3–7 days with relatively less increase in strength at 28 days.

3.4.2   Water Demand

The small size (0.1–0.12 μm) and spherical shape of the silica fume particles allows them to fill the voids between the larger cement particles (10–12 μm)

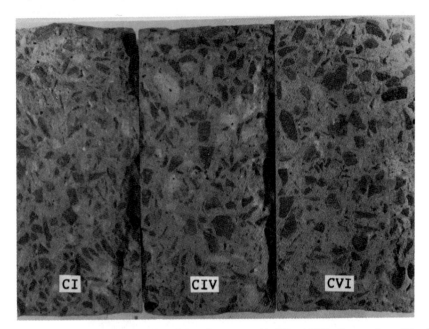

Plate 22 Fracture surfaces in tensile splitting of concretes with different W/C ratios: specimens CI and CIV have a higher W/C ratio hence more bond failure than CVI (tests by Nawy et al.)

which would have otherwise been filled with mix water. The entrapped water is consequently unable to contribute to the consistency, namely the degree of fluidity of the concrete mix.[3.33] In spite of the better particle distribution, the larger specific area of the silica fume particles increases their capacity to absorb water with the resulting need for more water in the mix.

Aitcin's compilation of the effect of using silica fume on water demand on the concrete mix is shown in Fig. 3.13. It can be seen that in cases where the silica content by weight of cement approaches 16 percent, the water demand can increase by almost 40 percent unless high range water reducers are adequately used in the mix; HRWRs eliminate the need for any additional water with the increase in the SF content. This behavior is due to the extensive dispersal of the cement particles and the silica fume with decreased contact between their particles. In addition, with high cementitious content, hence a low $W/(C + SF)$ ratio, the cohesiveness of the paste increases considerably due to the reduction of internal bleeding in the mixture. As a result, more water or water-reducing agents are needed.

3.4.3   Permeability and Curing Effect on Strength Development

Moist-curing greatly facilitates the gain in compressive strength. The 28 day compressive strength in air-dried SF concretes can be lower by almost 20 percent than moist-cured SF concretes, as continuous gain in strength is achieved with time.

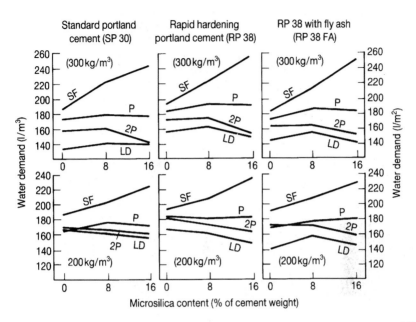

Fig. 3.13 Water demand in silica fume concrete (SF) vs. others for 5 in. slump (120–130 mm)[3.33]:
P and 2P = lignosulphonate, LD = superplasticizers, FA = fly ash, SP = standard portland,
RP = rapid hardening

Permeability is reduced in the concrete element through the addition of SF to the mix as the permeability of the cement paste decreases. This is due to the great dispersion of the finer SF particles as discussed earlier, filling most of the voids occupied by the mixing water. The addition of 10 percent by weight of SF replacement to concrete containing 6–7 lb/ft^3 (~ 100 kg/m^3) of cement reduces the water permeability coefficient from 1.6×10^{-5} to 4×10^{-8} cm/sec.

If the SF replacement percentage is increased to 20–25 percent, the permeability almost approaches zero. This great reduction in permeability improves the freeze–thaw resistance of the concrete since very little water can diffuse through the concrete surface. It should be emphasized that air-entraining agents have always to be used if protection against freezeing and thawing is required. Figure 3.14[3.34] shows the vast decrease of deicer scaling of SF concretes.

3.4.4   Silica Fume Effect on Hardened Concrete

Permeability and strength improvement are the two major reasons for the use of SF in concrete. If a large percentage of cement such as 20 percent is replaced by SF, the compressive strength of the concrete increases considerably. The improved qualities of hardened concrete[3.32] with the addition of SF replacement in the mix can be summarized as follows:

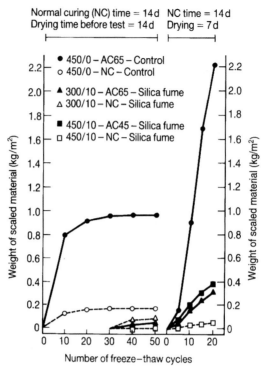

Fig. 3.14 Deicer Scaling of Air-Entrained Concrete in 3 percent NaCl solution (7 and 14 day curing)[3.34]

1. Considerably reduced permeability
2. High compressive, tensile, and flexural strengths
3. At similar water/cementitious materials ratio, drying shrinkage of silica fume is often lower than that of non-SF fume concrete
4. Creep deformations are 40–70 percent of nonsilica fume type III cement concrete
5. An ultimate shrinkage strain of $600–700 \times 10^{-6}$, similar to normal concrete
6. An increase of 50–100 percent in bond to the steel reinforcement
7. Reduced reinforcement corrosion
8. Better freeze–thaw resistance comparable to properly entrained non-SF concrete
9. Dry curing tends to result in a compressive strength about 10–20 percent less than moist curing

Table 3.5[3.36] gives the properties of mixes with a range of SF replacement percentages of 10–30 percent. An early age 2 day strength of 7800–18 550 psi (54–128 MPa) is achieved, and a maximum compressive strength of 26 000 psi (182 MPa) is achieved in one test at 28 days.

   Long-term strength development of SF concretes has been studied by Malhotra *et al.*[3.35] They used a W/(C + SF) ratio of 0.25 for nonair-entrained mixes and 0.30 and 0.4 for air-entrained mixes using a maximum aggregate size of $\frac{3}{4}$ in. (19.7 mm). A superplasticizer was used to maintain a slump of

Table 3.5 Silica fume concrete characteristics[3.36]

No.	W/C ratio	Silica fume (wt%)	Super-plasticizer (wt%)	Water-content (kg/m³)[a]	Matrix-content (%)	Density dry (kg/m³)[a]	Compressive strength (MPa)[b]			E (GPa) at 28 d		Ultimate shrinkage strain (10^{-6} m/m)
							2 d	7 d	28 d	Dynamic	Static	
1	0.30	20	3.0	159	0.37	2580	71	112	152	54	43	700
2	0.25	20	2.5	154	0.40	2580	90	129	162	55	44	590
3	0.20	20	3.0	167	0.52	2530	94	125	160	51	40	710
4	0.30	20	2.5	151	0.35	2590	95	127	158	55	44	510
5	0.30	—	1.5	186	0.37	2570	69	109	131	52	41	610
6	0.25	—	2.5	184	0.42	2560	70	98	117	50	41	160
7	0.25	10	2.5	153	0.38	2590	96	130	160	56	46	500
8	0.25	30	2.5	153	0.44	2550	94	141	163	54	44	510
9	0.30	20	2.0	168	0.40	2530	112	143	172	53	43	630
10	0.25	20	3.0	163	0.44	2540	128	148	182	53	42	640
11	0.25	20	2.5	151	0.41	2930	83	116	150	67	58	460
12	0.25	20	3.0	160	0.44	2890	115	135	163	63	53	430
13	0.25	20	0.75	159	0.42	5320	69	87	104	80	69	290
14	0.25	20	1.5	102	0.28	5230	87	118	148	90	78	160
15	0.30	20	0.5	161	0.39	5380	75	96	102	75	69	170
16	0.25	20	0.5	307	0.80	3320	94	109	125	41	33	820
17	0.25	20	1.0	230	0.60	4400	92	106	119	55	48	480
18	0.25	20	1.2	149	0.41	5330	88	102	120	79	70	270
19	0.20	20	3.0	134	0.43	5220	97	118	138	78	67	280
20	0.25	20	3.0	104	0.28	5530	102	127	146	93	85	200
21	0.30	20	1.0	433	1.00	2180	54	101	127	32	25	1640
22	0.20	20	1.5	286	1.00	2260	75	112	144	34	27	1620
23	0.25	—	0.7	452	1.00	2270	67	96	133	33	24	1890
24	0.30	20	1.0	428	1.00	2160	81	113	151	32	24	1460
25	0.20	20	1.5	284	1.00	2240	107	129	149	35	28	1370

[a] 1 lb/ft³ = 16.02 kg/m³,
[b] 1000 psi = 6.895 MPa.

Table 3.6 Compressive strength development with age in silica fume[a] concretes[3.35]

	Curing	\multicolumn{9}{c}{Compressive strength (MPa) at given age (days)[b]}
		7	28	56	91	180	365	540	910	1275
W/(C+SF) = 0.25										
Control										
G-1	Water	55.3	66.3	74.7	81.6	87.5	88.4	—	98.9	100.3
G-2	Air	55.5	65.8	72.2	74.8	75.4	73.3	—	73.9	75.0
Silica fume										
G-3	Water	69.7	81.7	84.4	93.4	95.4	95.0	100.9	104.6	107.4
G-4	Air	70.2	84.3	86.4	90.2	92.3	88.9	87.6	86.5	86.2
W/(C+SF) = 0.3										
Control										
G-5	Water	37.5	45.6	45.9	53.0	56.4	59.9	64.4	64.9	69.1
G-6	Air	39.5	47.9	48.6	51.1	53.5	52.1	53.9	50.5	52.0
Silica fume										
G-7	Water	42.2	53.2	55.7	57.3	58.7	60.2	60.6	63.6	65.2
G-8	Air	41.4	56.5	56.3	57.9	56	54.0	53.8	51.0	51.7
W/(C+SF) = 0.4										
Control										
G-9	Water	27.7	34.4	37.3	41.2	43.1	46.0	47.7	50.4	51.7
G-10	Air	27.4	34.8	37.5	40.4	40.6	38.8	39.2	39.7	40.4
Silica fume										
G-11	Water	33.9	42.8	47.6	46.1	48.2	49.8	50.0	51.9	52.7
G-12	Air	33.1	45.2	46.8	47	45.6	43.4	41.0	40.2	39.8

[a]SF content 10%.
[b]1000 psi = 6.895 MPa.

6–7 in. (150–175 mm). The following conclusions were made after $3\frac{1}{2}$ years:

1. Some retrogression in compressive strength between the ages of 91 days and $2\frac{1}{2}$ years. It becomes more pronounced as the W/(C + SF) ratio is increased from 0.25 to 0.45. However this decrease in strength should not be of significance in structures (see Table 3.6)
2. Flexural strength of SF concretes exhibit gain of strength with age.
3. Carbonation measured at the end of $3\frac{1}{2}$ years does not seem to be of any significance with W/(C + SF) ratio not exceeding 0.25. As this ratio increases, carbonation penetration becomes significant. At 0.40 ratio, a carbonation depth of 8 mm was observed

Table 3.6[3.35] gives a summary of concrete strength development over a $3\frac{1}{2}$ year period for W/(C + SF) ratio levels of 0.25, 0.30, and 0.40 for a mix of a constant silica fume content by weight of 10 percent.

3.5   GRANULATED BLAST FURNACE SLAG

3.5.1   General Characteristics

Blast furnace slag as defined by ASTM C 989-89 is a nonmetallic product, consisting essentially of silicates and aluminosilicates of calcium and other bases simultaneously developed in a molten condition with iron in a blast furnace in a process of iron production. The blast furnace is continuously charged with iron oxide sources such as iron ore, with fluxing stone such as limestone and dolomite, and with coke fuel. Two products are obtained from the furnace, molten iron which collects in the bottom of the furnace and a liquid iron blast furnace slag *floating* on the pool of iron.[3.37] Both products are tapped periodically from the furnace at a temperature of about 1500°C.

The slag (S) is rapidly quenched by immersion in water, producing granules which are then ground to cement fineness for use in concrete mixes as a cementing component that replaces part of the portland cement in the mix. The chemical composition of the finished slag product is as follows in percent (ASTM C 109)

SiO_2	32 –40
Al_2O_3	7 –17
CaO	29 –42
MgO	8 –19
S	0.7–2.2
Fe_2O_3	0.1–1.5
MnO	0.2–1.0

The optimum percentage in a concrete mix is a 50 percent replacement of the total cementitious material and 70 percent in marine construction. Due to the greater solid volume and the *higher fineness* of the ground granulated blast furnace slag (GGBF), more coarse aggregate can be used without a noticeable decrease in consistency of the wet concrete. Design of the concrete mix is based more on trial batching of the blast furnace slag and other solid contents of the mixture, taking into consideration that more entraining agent and more superplasticizer contents are generally needed.

3.5.2   Mechanical Properties

ASTM C 989 (1992) grades the slag into three strength categories depending on their mortar strengths: Grades 120, 100, and 80. Figure 3.15[3.37] gives the relative compressive mortar strengths with age of the mortar for the three grades. Figure 3.16(a)[3.37] shows the change in concrete compressive strength with the change in slag content from 40 to 65 percent for a water/cement ratio of 0.55, while Fig. 3.16(b) gives the change in modulus of rupture strength. Figure 3.17 gives the relative shrinkage percentages for the various slag contents used in the mix.

As fineness of the slag is increased, higher concrete compressive strengths are expected to be achieved. Swamy et al.[3.37] describe the effect of slag fineness on strength. Three degrees of slag fineness—surface area (weight)—were used in the slag that replaced the portland cement content in the concrete mix: 453, 786, and 1160 m^2/kg. The water/binder ratio was kept at a low level of 0.30 and 0.40 and a high range water-reducing admixture was used to give concrete slumps of 6.3–7.9 in. (160–200 mm). Increased fineness of the slag would require higher water

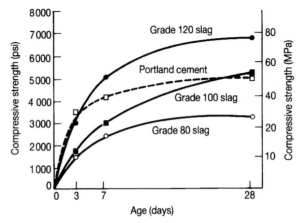

Fig. 3.15 Slag mortar compressive strength for the three slag strength grades[3.37, 3.38]

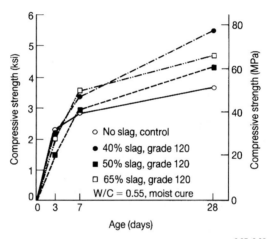

Fig. 3.16a Slag concrete compressive strength for various slag contents.[3.37, 3.38]

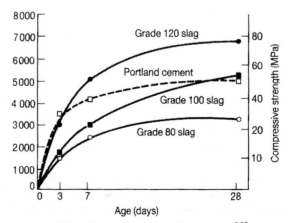

Fig. 3.16b Slag concrete modulus of rupture for various slag concretes[3.37]

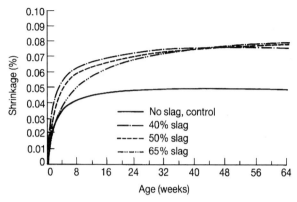

Fig. 3.17 Drying shrinkage of nonair-entrained concrete for various slag replacement percentages[3.37] (W/C ratio = 0.55)

demand. Table 3.7[3.39] lists the properties of the slag concrete for the three slag fineness levels. It is seen that a compressive strength of 15000 psi (104 MPa) is achieved by increasing the fineness from 453 to 1160 m^2/kg.

3.6   HIGH-REACTIVITY METAKAOLIN

High-reactivity metakaolin (HRM) mineral admixture is a reactive aluminosilicate pozzolan formed by calcining purified kaolinite at a specific temperature

Plate 23 Albemarle Sound Bridge, North Carolina: 3.5 mile long box girder bridge with typical 131 ft spans and a central 224 ft span (Courtesy Portland Cement Association)

Table 3.7 Slag concrete properties for different blast furnace slag fineness levels[3.39]

Mix no.	W/(C + S)	Fineness of ground slag (m²/kg)	Compressive Strength (MPa)[a]								Porosity				Water permeability	
			Wet curing				Air curing			Wet and air	Total pore volume (mm³/g)				Depth of penetration (mm)	Diffusion coefficient (10^{-2} mm²/sec)
			3 d	7 d	28 d	91 d	7 d	28 d	91 d	28 d	3 d	7 d	28 d	91 d		
1	0.40	None	38.6	48.9	59.5	69.3	39.7	46.5	47.4	63.1	64.9	57.4	46.7	33.5	12.3	2.27
2	0.40	453	15.2	27.7	58.7	69.5	23.5	28.5	34.7	52.3	60.4	55.9	30.7	13.0	8.1	0.99
3	0.40	786	17.9	36.4	67.8	90.6	28.0	36.8	40.0	66.3	68.5	47.6	22.8	12.0	7.1	0.76
4	0.40	1160	34.5	64.8	101.8	122.3	47.4	64.6	69.0	104.8	41.5	31.6	16.8	11.9	2.9	0.13
5	0.30	None	51.1	65.0	88.6	96.6	48.5	72.8	78.4	92.1	—	—	—	—	—	—
6	0.30	435	22.5	44.3	80.4	90.1	33.4	45.8	49.9	75.8	—	—	—	—	—	—
7	0.30	786	31.3	64.2	104.2	115.8	43.3	64.6	71.9	106.1	46.1	38.0	20.0	14.5	3.5	0.18
8	0.30	1160	49.4	76.9	110.0	121.5	55.8	71.5	73.5	104.2	—	—	—	—	—	—

[a]Based on 100 × 200 mm cylinders; 1000 psi = 6.895 MPa.

range. It combines with calcium hydroxide to form calcium silicate and calcium aluminate hydrates. The product conforms to ASTM C618 Class N pozzolan specifications and is processed to remove unreactive impurities, producing an essentially fully reactive pozzolan. The average particle size of HRM is 1.5 μm as compared to silica fume particle size (0.1–0.12 μm) and portland cement (10 μm). It is white in color as compared to the very dark silica fume color.

As a new cementitious admixture for producing high strength concrete, HRM as replacement for part of the cement in the mixture has produced compressive strengths in excess of 16000 psi (110 MPa) under well-controlled conditions. Tests have shown[3.42] that use of 5–10 percent by weight of metakaolin in the mixture produced high strength concretes with performance characteristics comparable to those of silica fume concretes with respect to strength development rate, chloride ion permeability, drying shrinkage, and resistance to freeze–thaw deterioration and scaling. Further tests are needed to confirm these findings.

REFERENCES

3.1   ACI Committee 226 Use of Fly Ash in Concrete. *ACI Report 226.3R-87* American Concrete Institute, Detroit, 1987, pp. 1–29

3.2   ACI Committee 116 Cement and Concrete Technology. *ACI Report 116R-90* American Concrete Institute, Detroit, 1990, pp. 1–67

3.3   Berry E E, and Malhotra V M 1986 Fly Ash for Use in Concrete—A Critical Review. *Proceedings, ACI Journal*, Vol. 77 No. 2, American Concrete Institute, Detroit, pp. 59–73

3.4   Mather B 1965 Compressive Strength Development of 193 Concrete Mixtures During Ten Years of Moist Curing. *Miscellaneous Paper No. 6-123* Report 12 (NTIS AD 756 324) U. S. Army Engineers Waterways Experiment Station, Vicksburg,.

3.5   Bliek R L, Peterson C F, and Winter M E 1974 Proportioning and Controlling High Strength Concrete. *ACI SP-46* American Concrete Institute, Detroit, pp. 141–163

3.6   Joshi R D 1979 Sources of Pozzolanic Activity—A Critical Review. *Proceedings, 5th International Ash Utilization Symposium. ACI SP-79* American Concrete Institute, Detroit, pp. 610–623

3.7   Read P, Carette G G, and Malhotra V M 1990 Strength Development Characteristics of High Strength Concrete Incorporating Supplementary Cementing Materials. *ACI SP-121* ed. W. Hester, American Concrete Institute, Detroit, pp. 527–547

3.8   Cook J E 1983 Fly Ash in Concrete—Technical Considerations. *Proceedings Concrete International, Design and Construction* Vol. 5 No. 9, American Concrete Institute, Detroit, pp. 51–59

3.9   Malhotra V M 1994 CANMET Investigation Dealing with High-Volume Fly Ash Concrete. *Advances in Concrete Technology* ed. V M Malhotra, 2nd ed., CANMET, Ottawa, Ontario, pp. 445–482

3.10   Bilodeau A, and Malhotra V M 1992 Concrete Incorporating High Volumes of ASTM Class F Fly Ashes: Mechanical Properties and Resistance to Deicing Salt Scaling and to Chloride—Ion Penetration. *Proceedings CANMET/ACI International Conference on Fly Ash, Silica Fume, Slag and Natural Pozzolans in Concrete, Istanbul ACI SP-132* Vol. 1, American Concrete Institute, Detroit, pp. 319–349

3.11   Sivasundaram V, Carette G G, and Malhotra V M 1989 Mechanical Properties,

Creep, and Resistance to Diffusion of Chloride Ions of Concretes Incorporating High Volumes of ASTM Class F Fly Ash From Different Sources. *MSL Division Report 89-126 (J)* Energy, Mines, Resources Canada, Ottawa

3.12   Sivasundaram V, Carette, G G, and Malhotra V M 1989 Properties of Concrete Incorporating Low Quantity of Cement and High Volumes of Low-Calcium Fly Ash. *ACI SP-114* Vol. 1, ed. V M Malhotra, American Concrete Institute, Detroit, pp. 45–71

3.13   Meininger R C 1981 Use of Fly Ash in Air-Entrained Concrete. *NSGA–NRMCA Report* National Ready Mixed Concrete Association, Silver Spring

3.14   Gebler S, and Klieger P 1983 Fly Ash, Silica Fume, Slag and Other Mineral By-Products in Concrete. *ACI SP-79* American Concrete Institute, Detroit, pp. 103–142

3.15   Nawy E G 1996 *Reinforced Concrete—A Fundamental Approach* 3rd ed. (1st ed., 1985). Prentice Hall, Englewood Cliffs, N.J., 838 pp.

3.16   Collepardi M 1994 Superplasticizer and Air-Entraining Agents: State of the Art and Future Needs. *Proceedings V Mohan Malhotra Symposium. ACI SP-144* ed. P K Mehta, American Concrete Institute, Detroit, pp. 399–416

3.17   ACI Committee 548 Guide of Use for Polymers in Concrete. *ACI Report 548.1R-92* American Concrete Institute, Detroit, 1992, pp. 1–33

3.18   Nawy E G, Ukadike M M, and Sauer J A 1977 High Strength Field Polymer Modified Concretes. *Proceedings, ASCE J. Structural Division* ST12, pp. 2307–2322

3.19   Nawy E G 1981 Shear Transfer Behavior in Concrete and Polymer Modified Concrete Two-Layered Systems with Application to Infrastructure Rehabilitation and New Designs. *ACI SP 89-4* American Concrete Institute, Detroit, pp. 51–90

3.20   Nawy E G, and Ukadike M M 1983 Shear Transfer in Concrete and Modified Concrete Members Subjected to Shearing Loads. *Proceedings, ASTM Journal* March, pp. 89–97

3.21   Kudlapur P, Hanoar A, Balguru P N, and Nawy E G 1989 Evaluation of Cold Weather Patching Materials. *Proceedings, ACI Materials Journal* Vol. 86 No. 1, American Concrete Institute, Detroit, pp. 36–44

3.22   Kudlapur P, and Nawy E G 1990 Shear Interaction of High Strength Two-Layered Concretes at Early Ages Placed in Subfreezing Temperatures. *Transactions No. 1284* Transportation Research Board, National Research Council, Washington, D.C., pp. 32–52

3.23   Mehta P K 1993 *Concrete—Structures, Properties and Materials* 2nd ed., Prentice Hall, Englewood Cliffs, N.J., pp. 548

3.24   Fowler D W, Houston J T, and Paul D R 1973 Polymer-Impregnated Concrete Surface Treatment for Highway Bridge Decks. *ACI SP-40* American Concrete Institute, Detroit, pp. 93–117

3.25   Fowler D W 1983 Polymers in Concrete. *Handbook of Structural Concrete.* McGraw Hill, New York, pp. 8.1–8.32

3.26   Popovics S 1985 Modification of Portland Cement Concrete with Epoxy as Admixture. *ACI SP 89-11* American Concrete Institute, Detroit, pp. 207–229

3.27   Dikeou J T 1980 Development and Use of Polymer Concrete and Polymer Impregnated Concrete. *Proceedings on Progress in Concrete Technology* ed. V M Malhotra, CANMET, Ottawa, Ontario, pp. 539–581

3.28   Dikeou J T, Kukacka L E, Backstrom J E, and Steinberg M 1969 Polymerization Makes Tougher Concrete. *Proceedings, ACI Journal* Vol. 66 No. 10, American Concrete Institute, Detroit pp. 829–839

3.29   Steinberg M 1973 Polymers in Concrete. *ACI SP-40* American Concrete Institute, Detroit, pp. 25

3.30   Kushner R G, Fowler D W, and Wheat D L 1985 Mechanical and Durable Properties of High Molecular Weight Methacrylate Polymer Concrete. *ACI SP 99-7 on Polymer Modified Concrete* American Concrete Institute, Detroit, pp. 113–135

3.31   Ramakrishman V 1992 Properties and Applications of Latex Modified Concrete. *Proceedings CANMET International Conference on Advances in Concrete Technology* ed. V M Malhotra, Ottawa, Ontario, pp. 839–890

3.32   Ayers M E, and Khan M S 1992 Overview of Fly Ash and Silica Fume Concretes: The Need for Rational Curing Standards. *Proceedings, Malhotra Symposium on Concrete Technology—Past, Present, and Future.* ACI SP-144 ed. P K Mehta, American Concrete Institute, Detroit, pp. 605–622

3.33   Khayat K H, and Aitcin P C 1992 Silica Fume in Concrete—An Overview. *Proceedings CANMET/ACI 4th International Conference on Fly Ash, Silica Fume, Slag and Natural Pozzolans in Concrete,* Istanbul. ACI SP-132 Vol. 2, ed. V M Malhotra, American Concrete Institute, Detroit, pp. 835–872

3.34   Johnston C D 1992 Durability of High Early Strength Silica Fume Concretes Subjected to Accelerated and Normal Curing. *Proceedings CANMET/ACI 4th International Conference on Fly Ash, Silica Fume, Slag and Natural Pozzolans in Concrete,* Istanbul. ACI SP-132 Vol. 2, ed. V M Malhotra, American Concrete Institute, Detroit, pp. 965–986

3.35   Carette G G, and Malhotra V M 1992 Long-Term Strength Development of Silica Fume Concrete. *Proceedings CANMET/ACI 4th International Conference on Fly Ash, Silica Fume, Slag and Natural Pozzolans in Concrete,* Istanbul. ACI SP-132 Vol. 2, ed. V M Malhotra, American Concrete Institute, Detroit, pp. 1017–1044

3.36   Alfes C 1992 Modulus of Elasticity and Drying Shrinkage of High Strength Concrete Containing Silica Fume, *Proceedings CANMET/ACI 4th International Conference on Fly Ash, Silica Fume, Slag and Natural Pozzolans in Concrete,* Istanbul. ACI SP-132 Vol. 2, ed. V M Malhotra, American Concrete Institute, Detroit, pp. 1651–1671

3.37   ACI Committee 226 1987 Ground Granulated Blast-Furnace Slag as a Cementitious Constituent in Concrete, *ACI Report 226.1R.87* American Concrete Institute, Detroit, pp. 1–16

3.38   Hogan F J, and Meusel J W 1981 Evaluation for Durability and Strength Development of a Ground Granulated Blast-Furnace Slag. *Proceedings, Cement and Concrete Aggregate* Vol. 3 No. 1, pp. 40–52

3.39   Nakamura N, Sakai M, and Swamy R N 1992 Effect of Slag Fineness on the Development of Concrete Strength and Microstructure. *Proceedings CANMET/ACI 4th International Conference on Fly Ash, Silica Fume, Slag and Natural Pozzolans in Concrete,* Istanbul. ACI SP-132 Vol. 2, ed. V M Malhotra, American Concrete Institute, Detroit, pp. 1343–1366

3.40   Sprinkel M M 1992 Twenty Year Performance of Latex Modified Concrete Overlays. *Transactions Record No. 1335* Transportation Research Board, National Research Council, Washington, D.C., pp. 27–35

3.41   Ramakrishman V 1992 Latex Modified Concretes and Mortars. *NCHRP Synthesis 179* Transportation Research Board, National Research Council, Washington, D.C., pp. 1–58

3.42   Caldarone M A, Gruber K A, and Burg R G 1994 High Reactivity Metakaolin: A New Generation Admixture. *Concrete International,* Nov. American Concrete Institute, Detroit, pp. 37–40

4   Design of Concrete Mixtures for High Strength High Performance Concretes

4.1   SCOPE

High strength concrete by present ACI definitions covers concretes whose cylinder compressive strength exceeds 6000 psi (41.4 MPa). Proportioning concrete mixtures is more critical for high strength concrete than for normal strength concrete. The procedure is similar to the proportioning process for normal strength concrete[4.1] except that adjustments have to be made for the admixtures that replace part of the cement content in the mixture and often for the need to use smaller aggregates in very high strength concretes.

As discussed in Chapter 3, there are several types of strength-modifying admixtures: high range water reducers (superplasticizers), fly ash, polymers, silica fume and blast furnace slag. However, in mix proportioning for very high strength concrete, isolating the water/cementitious materials ratio (W/C + P) from the paste/aggregate ratio due to the very low water content can be more effective in arriving at the optimum mixture with fewer trial mixtures and field trial batches. But few other methods are available today. The very low W/C + P ratio required for strengths in the range of 20 000 psi (138 MPa) or higher require major modifications to the present standard approach used in mix proportioning[4.2] that seems to work well for strengths up to 12 000 psi (83 MPa). The optimum mixture that can be chosen with minimum trials has to produce a satisfactory concrete product both in its plastic and its hardened states.

One approach[4.5] is based on mortar volume/stone volume ratio, proportioning the solids in the mortar on the basis of the ratio:

$$\frac{\text{solid sand volume} + \text{cementitious solid volume}}{\text{mortar volume}}$$

The ACI standard is well established for fly ash concretes (FAC).[4.2] Ample mixture proportioning results are available for polymers. The same is true for silica fume concretes (SFC) and slag concrete (SC or GGBFSC). They are, however, not established in the form of a standard such as the committee reports of the ACI Manual of Concrete Practice.[4.3] Additionally, several sections in this book list mixture proportions for all the types of strength-generating admixtures that have been discussed. The computational example in this chapter on fly ash concrete design (FAC) for strengths up to 12 000 psi (83 MPa) should serve as a

Plate 24 Two Prudential Plaza, Chicago: 12 000 psi concrete (Courtesy Portland Cement Association)

systematic step-by-step guide for proportioning mixtures using polymers, silica fume, and granulated blast furnace slag within its intended compressive strength range.

4.2   STRENGTH REQUIREMENTS

The age at test is a governing criteria for selecting mix proportions. The standard 28 day strength for normal strength concrete penalizes high strength concrete since the latter continues gaining strength after that age. One has also to consider that a structure is subjected to service load at 60–90 days at the earliest. Consequently, mixture proportioning has to be based in this case on these latter age levels and also on either *field experience* or *laboratory batch trials*. The average compressive field strength results should exceed the specified design

compressive strength by a sufficiently high margin so as to reduce the probability
of lower test results.

4.2.1   Mixture Proportions on the Basis of Field Experiences

If the concrete producer chooses the mixture on the basis of field experience, the
required average strength f'_{cr} should be the larger of

$$f'_{cr} = f'_c + 1.34s \qquad\qquad\qquad [4.1]$$

$$f'_{cr} = 0.90f'_c + 2.33s \qquad\qquad\qquad [4.2]$$

$$s = \left[\frac{(n_1 - 1)(s_1)^2 + (n_2 - 1)(s_2)^2}{(n_1 + n_2 - 2)} \right]^{\frac{1}{2}} \qquad\qquad [4.3]$$

where f'_c = specified design compressive strength, psi
      s = sample standard deviation, psi

4.2.2   Mix Proportions on the Basis of Laboratory Trial Batches

In this case, the laboratory trial batches should give

$$f'_{cr} = \frac{(f'_c + 1400)}{0.90} \text{ psi} \qquad\qquad\qquad [4.4a]$$

In SI units,

$$f'_{cr} = \frac{(f'_c + 27.6)}{0.90} \text{ MPa} \qquad\qquad\qquad [4.4b]$$

In addition to the attainment of the required compressive strength, other factors
have to be taken into account in the selection of the mix and its constituent
materials. These can be summarized as follows[4.2]:

1. Modulus of elasticity
2. Flexural and tensile strengths
3. Heat of hydration
4. Creep and drying shrinkage
5. Durability
6. Permeability
7. Time of set
8. Mixing procedure

9. Type of admixture
10. Workability
11. Method of placement

It is important to note that high strength, high performance concrete requires special attention to the selection and control of the ingredients in the mix in order to obtain optimum proportioning and maximum strength. To achieve this aim, care in the choice of the particular cement, admixture brand, dosage rate, mixing procedure, and quality and size of aggregate becomes paramount. Since all the cement does not hydrate, it is advisable that the cement content be kept minimum for optimum mixture proportioning.

4.3   SELECTION OF INGREDIENTS

4.3.1   Cement and Other Cementitious Ingredients

A proper selection of types and source of cement is extremely important. ASTM cement requirements are only minimum requirements, and certain brands are better than others due to the variations in the physical and chemical properties of the various cements. High strength concrete requires high cementitious materials content, namely a low water/cementitious materials ratio $W/(C+P)$ and the fineness of the cementitious materials has a major effect on the workability of the fresh mix and the strength of the hardened concrete. They contribute to the reduction in water demand and lower the temperature of hydration. Hence, a determination has to be made whether to choose fly ash Class F or G, silica fume, or granulated slag; Chapter 3 gives guidelines.

4.3.2   Coarse Aggregate

Aggregates greatly influence the strength of the hardened concrete as they comprise the largest segment of all the constituents. Consequently, only hard aggregate should be used for normal weight high strength concrete so that the aggregate would *at least* have the strength of the cement gel. As higher strength is sought, the aggregate size should be decreased. It is advisable to limit aggregate size to $\frac{3}{4}$ in. (19 mm) maximum size for strengths up to 9000 psi (62 MPa). For higher strengths, a $\frac{1}{2}$ in. or preferably $\frac{3}{8}$ in. size aggregate should be used (12.7–9.5 mm). For strengths in the range of 15 000–20 000 psi (103–138 MPa), higher strength trap rock from selected quarries should be used in order to achieve such very high strengths. Beyond 20 000–30 000 psi strength, the aggregate size should not exceed $\frac{3}{8}$ in. in structural components.

4.3.3   Fine Aggregate

A fineness modulus (FM) in the range of 2.5–3.2 is recommended for high strength concrete to facilitate workability. Lower values result in decreased workability and a higher water demand. The mixing water demand is dependent on the void ratio in the sand. The basic void ratio is 0.35 and should be adjusted for other void ratios such that the void content V in percent can be evaluated from

$$\left(1 - \frac{\text{oven-dry rodded unit weight } (\text{lb/ft}^3)}{\text{Bulk dry specific gravity} \times 62.4}\right) \times 100\% \qquad [4.5a]$$

in SI units,

$$\left(1 - \frac{\text{oven-dry rodded unit weight } (\text{kg/m}^3)}{\text{Bulk dry specific gravity} \times 10^3}\right) \times 100\% \qquad [4.5b]$$

The mixing water has to be accordingly adjusted to account for the change in the basic void ratio such that the mixing water adjustment would be as follows:

$$\text{Mixing water adjustment } (\text{lb/yd}^3) \ A = 8(V - 35) \qquad [4.6a]$$

in SI units,

$$\text{Mixing water adjustment } (\text{kg/m}^3) \ A = 4.7(V - 35) \qquad [4.6b]$$

4.3.4   Workability-enhancing Chemical Admixtures

High strength mixes have a rich cementitious content that requires a high water content, with the knowledge that excessive water reduces the compressive strength of the concrete and affects its long-term performance. Thus, water-reducing admixtures become mandatory. High range water-reducing admixtures (HRWR) discussed in Chapter 3 are used. These are sometimes called superplasticizers. The dosage rate is usually based on fluid oz per 100 lb (45 kg) of total cementitious materials if they are in liquid form. If the water-reducing agent is in powdered form, the dosage rate would be on a weight ratio basis. The optimum admixture percentage should be determined on a trial and adjustment basis as it can reduce the water demand by almost 30–35 percent with a corresponding increase in compressive strength. A slump of 1–2 in. (25–50 mm) is considered adequate. If, however, no HRWR admixtures are used, the slump should be increased to 2–4 in. (50–100 mm). In addition, air-entraining admixtures are used if the concrete is exposed to freezing and thawing cycles in severe environmental conditions. For structural components in building systems, air entrainment is unnecessary as these are usually not subjected to the type of frost action that exposed bridge decks or sea oil platforms endure.

4.4   RECOMMENDED PROPORTIONS

Tables 4.1 to 4.9 adapted from several sources[4.1–4.4] recommend the necessary ingredient contents for proportioning mixes for high strength concrete.

4.5   STEP-BY-STEP PROCEDURE FOR SELECTING PROPORTIONS

The following are the steps necessary in the selection process. Select

1. Slump and required strength f'_{cr}, Table 4.1 and
    (a) Based on field experience: f'_{cr} the larger of $f'_c + 1.34s$ or $0.9f'_c + 2.33s$
    (b) Based on laboratory batching: $(f'_c + 1400)/0.9$
2. Maximum size of aggregate (Table 4.2)
3. Optimum coarse aggregate content (Table 4.3)
4. Estimate mixing water and air content (Table 4.5)
5. Select the water to cementitious ratio $W/(C+P)$ where C is the cement content and P is the pozzolanic content by weight (Tables 4.6 and 4.7)
6. Compute the necessary content of the cementitious material P. This can be obtained by dividing the amount of mixing water per yd^3 or m^3 of concrete (step 4) by $W/(C+P)$ ratio
7. Proportion a basic mixture without the cementitious material P
8. Proportion a companion mixture using the cementitious pozzolanic material P such as fly ash
9. Produce a trial mix for each of the trial mix proportions designed in steps 1 to 8.
10. Adjust the mixture proportions to achieve the required slump by changing the contents, adjusting the HRWR agent rate for several trial mixes
11. Select the optimum mixture

Figure 4.1 is a flowchart for proportioning high strength, high performance concrete trial mixes giving in graphical form the steps 1 to 11 previously outlined. Figure 4.2 is a flowchart for the selection and documentation of concrete proportions[4.4] for the two methods for the choice of a trial mix: (a) prior field batch data, and (b) laboratory trial mixes. The optimum mix proportion chosen should satisfy most economically the field workability and placement requirements and the specified design strength f'_c from the f'_{cr} level chosen for the mix design.

4.6   MIX PROPORTIONING DESIGN EXAMPLE

Design a high strength concrete mix for the columns in a multistory structure for a specified 28 day compressive strength of 10 000 psi (69 MPa). A slump of 9 in. (229 mm) is required for workability needed in congested reinforcement in the columns. Do not use an aggregate size exceeding $\frac{1}{2}$ in. (12.7 mm). Use a high range water reducer (HRWR) to obtain the 9 in. slump and a set-retarding admixture. Assume that the ready-mix producer has no prior history with high strength concrete.

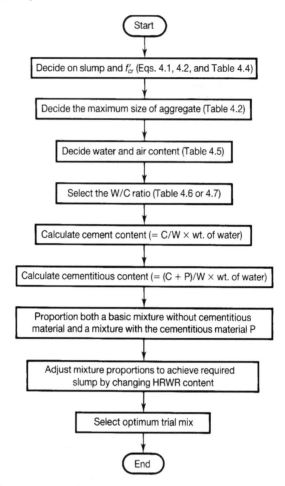

Fineness modulus of sand = 2.6
Dry-rodded weight of coarse aggregate = 100 lb/ft³
Moisture absorption = 3% for coarse aggregate and 2% for fine aggreg

Fig. 4.1 Flowchart for mix proportioning of high strength, high performance concrete[4.1]

Given the Following Sand Properties

Fineness modulus (FM)	$= 2.90$
Bulk specific gravity, over dry, (BSG_{dry})	$= 2.59$
Absorption based on dry weight (Abs)	$= 1.1\%$
Dry rodded unit weight (DRUW)	$= 103$ lb/ft³
	$(1620$ kg/m³$)$
Moisture content in sand	$= 6.4\%$

Solution

1.   Select Slump and Required Concrete Strength

Because an HRWR agent is used, choose strength on the basis of 1–2 in. slump prior to the addition of HRWR. Also, since the ready mix producer has no prior

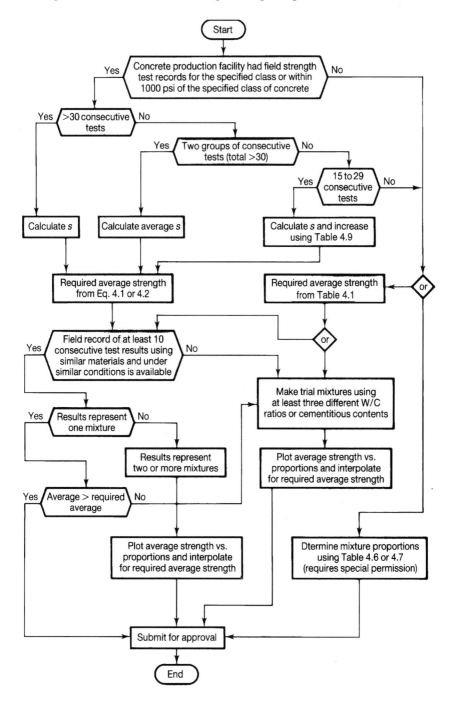

Fig. 4.2 Flowchart for selection and documentation of concrete proportions[4.4]

Table 4.1 Required average compressive strength when data are not available to establish a standard deviation

Specified strength f'_{cr}, psi (MPa)	Required strength f'_{cr}, psi (MPa)
> 5000 (34.5)	$f'_c + 1400$ $(f'_c + 9.7)$

history with high strength concrete, laboratory trial mixtures have to be designed for the selection of the optimum proportions. From Eq. 4.4(a),

$$f'_{cr} = (f'_c + 1400)/0.90$$
$$= (10\,000 + 1400)/0.90$$
$$= 12\,670 \text{ psi } (87 \text{ MPa})$$

2. Select Maximum Aggregate Size

A crushed limestone graded $\frac{1}{2}$ in. (12.7 mm) maximum size is selected with $BSG_{dry} = 2.76$, $Abs = 0.70$ and $DRUW = 101 \text{ lb/ft}^3$, stone moisture content $= 0.5\%$.

3. Select Optimum Coarse Aggregate Content

From Table 4.3, fractional ratio $= 0.68$
Dry weight of coarse aggregate/yd^3 of concrete is

$$W_{dry} = (\% \text{ DRUW}) \times (\text{DRUW} \times 27)$$
$$= 0.68 \times 101 \times 27 = 1854 \text{ lb}(841 \text{ kg})$$

4. Estimate Mixing Water and Air Content

From Table 4.5, the first estimate of the required mixing water is 295 lb/yd^3 (174 kg/m^3) of concrete and the entrapped air content when HRWR is used $= 2.0\%$

Table 4.2 Maximum size for coarse aggregate

Required concrete strength f'_c, psi (MPa)	Maximum aggregate size, in. (mm)
< 9000 (62)	$\frac{3}{4}-1$ (19–25)
≥ 9000 (62)	$\frac{3}{8}-\frac{1}{2}$ (9.5–12.7)

Table 4.3 Coarse aggregate to concrete fractional volume ratio (sand fineness modulus 2.5–3.2)

Nominal max. size, in. (mm)	$\frac{3}{8}$ (9.5)	$\frac{1}{2}$ (12.7)	$\frac{3}{4}$ (19)	1 (25)
Fractional volume of oven-dry rodded coarse aggregate	0.65	0.68	0.72	0.75

Table 4.4 Recommended slump

With HRWR,[a] in. (mm)	No HRWR, in. (mm)
1–2	20–4
$(25–50)^b$	(50–100)

[a]Adjust slump to that desired in the field by adding
high range water reducer (HRWR).

Table 4.5 Mixing water requirement and air content of fresh concrete using sand with 35%
void ratio—first trial water content[4.2]

	Mixing water, lb/yd³ (kg/m³)[a] for given max. size coarse aggregate, in. (mm)			
	$\frac{3}{8}$ (9.5)	$\frac{1}{2}$ (12.7)	$\frac{3}{4}$ (19)	1 (25)
Slump, in. (mm)				
1–2 (25–50)	310 (183)	295 (174)	285 (168)	280 (165)
2–3 (50–75)	320 (189)	310 (183)	295 (174)	290 (171)
3–4 (75–100)	330 (195)	320 (189)	305 (180)	300 (177)
Entrapped air (%)[b]	3 (2.5)[c]	2.5 (2.0)	2 (1.5)	1.5 (1.0)

[a]1 lb/yd³ $= 0.59$ kg/m³.
[b]Adjust mixing water values for sand void ratio other than 35%, where void content V is
given by

$$V(\%) = \left(1 - \frac{\text{Oven-dry rodded unit wt.}}{\text{Bulk specific gravity (dry)} \times 62.4}\right) \times 100$$

and mixing water adjustment is

$$\text{lb/yd}^3 = (V - 35) \times 8$$
$$\text{kg/m}^3 = (V - 35) \times 4.7$$

From Eq. 4.5(a), the void content of the sand to be used is

$$V = \left[1 - \frac{103}{2.59 \times 62.4}\right] \times 100 = 36\%$$

From Eq. 4.6(a), the mixing water adjustment

$$A = 8(V - 35) = (36 - 35) = +8 \text{ lb/yd}^3 (4.7 \text{ kg/m}^3) \text{ of concrete}$$

Hence, total mixing water $W = 295 + 8 = 303$ lb (138 kg)

   5.   *Select Water/Cementitious Materials Ratio*, W/(C + P)
The values in Table 4.6 and 4.7 are average field strengths values. Hence, strength
f'_{cr} for which the W/(C + P) ratio is to be found is

$$f'_{cr} = 0.90 \times 12\,670 = 11\,400 \text{ psi} \,(77 \text{ MPa})$$

Table 4.6 W/(C + P) ratio for concrete without high range water reducer (without HRWR)

Field strength f'_{cr},[a] psi (MPa)		W/(C+P) ratio for given max. size coarse aggregate, in. (mm)			
		$\frac{3}{8}$ (9.5)	$\frac{1}{2}$ (12.7)	$\frac{3}{4}$ (19)	1 (25)
7 000 (48)	28 day	0.42	0.41	0.40	0.39
	56 day	0.46	0.45	0.44	0.43
8 000 (55)	28 day	0.35	0.34	0.33	0.33
	56 day	0.38	0.37	0.36	0.35
9 000 (62)	28 day	0.30	0.29	0.29	0.28
	56 day	0.33	0.32	0.31	0.30
10 000 (69)	28 day	0.26	0.26	0.25	0.25
	56 day	0.29	0.28	0.27	0.26

[a]For psi: $f'_{cr} = f'_c + 1400$. For MPa: $f'_{cr} = f'_c + 9.7$. These are average field values; enter into the table 0.9 (required f'_{cr}).

Table 4.7 W/(C + P) ratio for concrete with high range water reducer (with HRWR)

Field strength f'_{cr},[a] psi (MPa)		W/(C+P) ratio for given max. size coarse aggregate, in. (mm)			
		$\frac{3}{8}$ (9.5)	$\frac{1}{2}$ (12.7)	$\frac{3}{4}$ (19)	1 (25)
7 000 (48)	28 day	0.50	0.48	0.45	0.43
	56 day	0.55	0.52	0.48	0.46
8 000 (55)	28 day	0.44	0.42	0.40	0.38
	56 day	0.48	0.45	0.42	0.40
9 000 (62)	28 day	0.38	0.36	0.35	0.34
	56 day	0.42	0.39	0.37	0.36
10 000 (69)	28 day	0.33	0.32	0.31	0.30
	56 day	0.37	0.35	0.33	0.32
11 000 (76)	28 day	0.30	0.29	0.27	0.27
	56 day	0.37	0.31	0.29	0.29
12 000 (83)	28 day	0.27	0.26	0.25	0.25
	56 day	0.30	0.28	0.27	0.26

[a]For psi: $f'_{cr} = f'_c + 1400$. For MPa: $f'_{cr} = f'_c + 9.7$. These are average field values; enter into the table 0.9 (required f'_{cr}).

A comparison of the values contained in Tables 4.6 and 4.7 permits, in particular, the following conclusions: (1) for a given water cementitious material ratio, the field strength of concrete is greater with the use of HRWR than without it, and this greater strength is reached within a shorter period of time; and (2) with the use of HRWR, a given concrete field strength can be achieved in a given a period of time using less cementitious material than would be required when not using HRWR.

From Table 4.7 for $\frac{1}{2}$ in. size aggregate, the desirable

W/(C + P) ratio = 0.272 by interpolation

6. *Compute Content of Cementitious Material*

From before, mixing water W = 303 lb, hence, C + P = 303/0.272 = 1114 lb (505 kg).

7.   Proportion the Basic Mixture With Cement Only
Volumes of all materials except sand per yd^3 are as follows:

Cement	$= 114 \div (3.15 \times 62.4)$	$= 5.67 \text{ ft}^3$
Stone	$= 1884 \div (2.76 \times 62.4)$	$= 10.77$
Water	$= 303 \div 62.4$	$= 4.86$
Air	$= 0.02 \times 27$	$= 0.54$
		$\overline{}$
Total		$= 21.77 \text{ ft}^3 \ (0.62 \text{ m}^3)$

$(1 \text{ m}^3 = 35.31 \text{ ft}^3)$

Hence the required volume of sand per yd^3 of concrete $= 27 - 21.77 = 5.23 \text{ ft}^3$
Converting the sand volume to weight,

$$\text{Sand} = 5.23 \times 62.4 \times 2.59 = 845 \text{ lb}(384 \text{ kg})$$

The mix proportions by weight for the no-fly ash concrete would be:

	$lb/yd^3 \ (kg/m^3)$
Cement	$= 1114 \ (661)$
Sand, dry	$= \ 845 \ (501)$
Stone, dry	$= 1854 \ (1100)$
Water, incl. 3 oz/cwt retarding admixture	$= \ \ 303 \ (180)$
(cwt $=$ hundred weight of cement)	$\overline{}$
Total	$= 4116 \text{ lb/yd}^3 \ (2442 \text{ kg/yd}^3)$

8. Proportion Companion Mixtures Using Cement and Fly Ash
Use in this case ASTM Class C fly ash (FA) which has bulk specific gravity
s.g. $= 2.64$

From Table 4.8, the FA replacement $= 20$–35%
Use four trial mixtures: 20, 25, 30, 35% levels
For trial mixture No.1, SF $= 0.20 \ (1114) = 223$ lb
Hence, cement $= 1114 - 223 = 891$ lb

In a similar manner, the weights of the cementitious materials would be

Mixture no.	Cement lb (kg)	Fly ash lb (kg)
1	891 (404)	223 (101)
2	835 (379)	279 (126)
3	780 (354)	334 (151)
4	724 (328)	390 (177)

Table 4.8 Fly ash values to replace part of the cement[4.2]

Type	Replacement (wt%)
ASTM Class F	15–25
ASTM Class C	20–35

Table 4.9 Modification factor for standard deviation when fewer than 30 tests are available

Number of tests[a]	Modification factor for standard deviation[b]
< 15	Use Table 4.1
15	1.16
20	1.08
25	1.03
> 30	1.00

[a]Interpolate for intermediate number of tests.
[b]Modified standard deviation to be used to determine required average strength f'_{cr} in Eqs. 4.1 and 4.2.

Taking mixture No. 1, the volumes of components except sand per yd^3 of concrete are

$$\text{Cement} = 891 \div (3.15 \times 62.4) = 4.53 \text{ ft}^3$$
$$\text{FA} \quad = 223 \div (2.64 \times 62.4) = 1.35$$

From before,

Stone	$= 10.77 \text{ ft}^3$
Water, incl. 2.5 oz/cwt retarder	$= 4.86$
Air	$= 0.54$
Total	$= 22.05 \text{ ft}^3$

$$\text{Cement Volume} = 27 - 22.05 = 4.95 \text{ ft}^3$$
$$= 4.95 \times 62.4 \times 2.59 = 800 \text{ lb}$$

The mix proportions by weight for the fly ash concrete would be

	lb/yd^3 (kg/m^3)
Cement	$= 891$ (526)
Fly Ash	$= 223$ (132)
Sand, dry	$= 800$ (472)
Stone, dry	$= 1854$ (1094)
Water, incl. retarder	$= 303$ (179)
Total	$= 4071 \text{ lb/yd}^3$ (2402 kg/m^3)

(1 lb/yd^3 = 0.59 kg/m^3)

In a similar manner, the mix proportions for 25, 30, and 35% fly ash content are computed to give the following companion mixtures.

9. Trial Mixtures Adjustment for Absorbed Water Content in Aggregate
From before,

$$\text{moisture content in sand} = 6\%$$
$$\text{moisture content in stone} = 0.5\%$$

From Table 4.10, corrections in the basic mixture for the wetness of the aggregates,

$$\text{wet sand} = 845(1 + 0.064) = 899 \text{ lb}$$
$$\text{wet stone} = 1854(1 + 0.005) = 1863 \text{ lb}$$

From input data, sand absorption based on dry weight $= 1.1\%$ and stone absorption $= 0.7\%$ hence water correction

$$= 303 - 845(0.064 - 0.011) - 1854(0.005 - 0.007)$$
$$= 303 - 45 + 4 = 262 \text{ lb}(119 \text{ kg})$$

Accordingly, the batch weight of water has to be corrected to account for the excess moisture contributed by the aggregates = total moisture − aggregate absorbed moisture.

Hence, Table 4.10 is modified to Table 4.11.

10.   Size of Laboratory Trial Mixture
The usual size of the trial mixture is 3.0 ft^3 (0.085 m^3). The reduced batch weights to yield 3.0 ft^3 of concrete would be 1/9 the values tabulated in Table 4.11 to give the value in Table 4.11a.

Table 4.10 Mixture proportion in the design example without moisture trial batch adjustment

		C + CF mixes			
Ingredient	Basic mix: C only	#1	#2	#3	#4
(1)	(2)	(3)	(4)	(5)	(6)
Cement (lb/yd^3)	1 114	891	835	780	724
Fly ash (lb/yd^3)	0	223	279	334	390
Sand, dry (lb/yd^3)	845	800	790	781	773
Stone, dry (lb/yd^3)	1 854	1 854	1 854	1 854	1 854
Water + retarder (lb/yd^3)	303	303	303	303	303
Total, lb/yd^3 (kg/m^3) concrete^a	4 116 (2 428)	4 071 (2 402)	4 061 (2 396)	4 052 (2 391)	4 044 (2 386)

^{a} lb/yd^3 = 0.59 kg/m^3.

Table 4.11 Moisture adjusted mixture proportions in the design example

Ingredient	Basic mix: C only	C + CF mixes			
		#1	#2	#3	#4
(1)	(2)	(3)	(4)	(5)	(6)
Cement (lb/yd^3)	1 114	891	835	780	724
Fly ash (lb/yd^3)	0	223	279	334	390
Sand, dry (lb/yd^3)	899	851	841	831	823
Stone, dry (lb/yd^3)	1 863	1 863	1 863	1 863	1 863
Water, + retarder (lb/yd^3)	262	262	262	262	262
Total, lb/yd^3 (kg/m^3) concrete^a	4 138 (2 441)	4 090 (2 413)	4 080 (2 407)	4 070 (2 401)	4 062 (2 397)

^{a}1 lb/yd^3 = 0.59 kg/m^3.

Table 4.11a Reduced batch weight yielding 3 ft^3 of concrete

Ingredient	Basic mix: C only	C+CF mixes			
		#1	#2	#3	#4
(1)	(2)	(3)	(4)	(5)	(6)
Cement	123.78	99.00	92.78	86.67	80.44
Fly ash	0	24.78	31.0	37.11	43.33
Sand, dry	99.89	94.56	93.44	92.33	91.44
Stone, dry	207.00	207.00	207.00	207.00	207.00
Water + retarder	29.11	29.11	29.11	29.11	29.11
Total, lb/3 ft (kg/0.1 m^3) concrete^a	460 (245.3)	455 (242.7)	453 (241.6)	452 (241.1)	451 (240.5)

^{a}1 lb/yd^3 = 0.59 kg/m^3.

11. Adjustment of Trial Mixture Due to Slump Observation

Basic Mix

Assume that the water calculated to produce the 1–2 in. slump, namely, 29.11 lb was found not to be adequate and has to be increased to 30 lb/3 ft^3 including the 2.5 oz/cwt retarding admixture.

The actual batch weights have therefore to be adjusted so that the actual batch weight for the basic mix (no fly ash) becomes

    Cement = 123.78 lb
    Sand   = 99.89
    Stone = 207.00
    Water = 30.00

These values have to be adjusted for moisture correction to dry weight.
The basic total added water = 30 × 9 = 270 lb/yd^3.
From before, the absorbed water in the aggregates = 45 − 4 = 41 lb.

Actual total water content $= 270 + 41 = 311$ lb/yd^3 $= 34.56$ lb 3 ft^3.

Cement $= 123.78$ lb
Sand $= 99.89 \div 1.064 = 93.88$
Stone $= 207 \div 1.005 = 205.97$
Batch water $= 30.00 + 45/9 - 4/9 = 34.56$

Yield of Trial Batch
Consequently the actual yield of the trial mixture becomes

Cement $= 123.78 \div (3.15 \times 62.4) = 0.63$
Sand $= 93.88 \div (2.59 \times 62.4) = 0.50$
Stone $= 205.97 \div (2.76 \times 62.4) = 1.20$
Water $= 34.56 \div 62.4$ $= 0.55$
Air $= 0.02 \times 3$ ft^3 $= 0.06$

Total yield volume of trial batch $= \overline{2.94 \text{ ft}^3}$

The yield in lb/yd^3 of concrete is obtained by multiplying all the previous values by 9 and converting the volumes to weights, giving

Cement $= 1114$ lb
Sand, dry $= 845$
Stone $= 1854$
Water, incl. retarder $= 311$

The new mixture proportions result in a water/cementitious materials

ratio $W/(C + P) = 311/1114 = 0.28$

versus the desirable ratio of 0.272 previously obtained from Table 4.7. In order to maintain the 0.272 ratio, the weight of cement should be increased to $309/0.272 = 1136$ lb/yd^3 of concrete. The increase in volume due to the adjustment of the weight of cement

$$= (1136 - 1114) \div (3.15 \times 62.4) = 0.11 \text{ ft}^3.$$

This increase in volume should be adjusted for by the removal of an equal volume of sand. Hence, weight of sand to be removed $= 0.11 \times 2.59 \times 62.4 = 17.79$ lb/yd^3, say 18 lb/yd^3.
    The resulting adjusted mixture proportions become

Cement $= 1136$ lb
Sand, dry $= 845 - 18 = 827$
Stone, dry $= 1854$
Water $+ 2.5$ oz/cwt retarder $= 311$

Increasing Slump to 9 in. (229 mm)

The required slump in this example is 9 in. (229 mm). To achieve this value without the addition of water that will reduce the strength, a high range water reducer, namely, a plasticizer is used.

The dosage recommended by the manufacturer of the HRWR ranged between 8 and 16 oz per 100 lb of cementitious material. Laboratory tests in a laboratory with ambient temperature of 74°F, indicated the following:

> 8 oz dosage produced 5 in. slump
> 11 oz dosage produced 10 in. slump
> 16 oz dosage produced segregation of the fresh concrete.

In all these cases, a constant dosage rate of retarding admixture of 2.5 oz/cwt was also added to the mixture with the mixing water.

The HRWR was added to the mix about 15 minutes after initial mixing. It was determined that

1. The mixture with 10 in. (255 mm) slump had adequate workability, hence no correction needed to the coarse aggregate content
2. Air content of the HRWR concrete mix was found to be 1.9%; hence no correction needed
3. 28 day compressive strength of the basic mix was found to be 12 700 psi, satisfying the required $f'_{cr} = 12\,670$ psi.

Note: It is important to have recognized whether additional water at this stage was needed to produce the required slump and workability, then an additional cycle of corrections to actual batches of aggregate have to be executed in the same manner as in the previous steps.

Table 4.12 Laboratory final trial mixtures

		C + CF mixes			
	Basic mix: C only	#1 20% CF	#2 25% CF	#3 30% CF	#4 35% CF
(1)	(2)	(3)	(4)	(5)	(6)
Ingredient					
Cement (lb/yd³)	1136	891	835	780	724
Fly ash (lb/yd³)	—	223	279	334	390
Sand, dry (lb/yd³)	827	782	772	763	755
Stone, dry (lb/yd³)	1854	1863	1863	1863	1863
Water, + retarder (lb/yd³)	311	304	300	298	297
Slump, in. (mm)	1.00	1.20	1.15	1.50	1.90
	(25)	(31)	(29)	(38)	(48)
Retarder (oz/cwt)	3.5	2.5	2.0	2.5	2.0
HRWR (oz/cwt)	10.00	10.50	11.00	10.25	9.00
Slump, in. (mm)	10.00	10.75	8.75	10.50	9.25
	(250)	(270)	(220)	(270)	(235)
Strength at 28 days, psi (MPa)	12 600	12 400	12 550	12 750	12 250
	(87)	(85)	(87)	(88)	(84)

12.   Summary of Trial Mixtures Laboratory Performance

The following is a summary table of the performance of the five mixtures, namely the basic no-FA concrete and the four concretes with FA at 20, 25, 30, and 35% content of the total cementitious material. Slump values for no-HRWR mixtures and those with HRWR were measured in the laboratory slump tests.

In addition, field trials have to be made to verify the chosen laboratory trial mix. In this case, No. 3 from Table 4.12 gives the highest 28 day compressive strength of 12 750 psi (88 MPa) and is the closest to the required $f'_{cr} = 12\,670$ psi that can give an average compressive strength $f'_c = 10\,000$ psi required in this example.

REFERENCES

4.1   Nawy E G 1996 *Reinforced Concrete—A Fundamental Approach* 3rd ed. (1st ed., 1985). Prentice Hall, Englewood Cliffs, N.J.

4.2   ACI Committee 211 Guide For Selecting Proportions for High Strength Concrete with Portland Cement and Fly Ash. *ACI Report 211.4R-93* American Concrete Institute, Detroit, 1993

4.3   *ACI Manual of Concrete Practice* 1995 Vols. 1, 2, 3, 4, 5, American Concrete Institute, Detroit

4.4   ACI Committee 318 Building Code Requirements For Reinforced Concrete, *ACI Standard 318-95* and Commentary *ACI 318R-95*, *ACI 318M-95*, and *ACI RM-95*, American Concrete Institute, Detroit, 1995

4.5   Addis B J, and Alexander M G 1990 A Method of Proportioning Trial Mixes for High Strength Concrete. *Proceedings 2nd International Symposium on High Strength Concrete, Berkeley. ACI SP-121* American Concrete Institute, Detroit, pp. 287–308

5 Lightweight Aggregate High Strength Concrete

5.1 AGGREGATE PRODUCTION

Structural lightweight concrete is made with artificial lightweight aggregates instead of crushed stone or riverbed gravel used in normal weight concrete. The raw materials used in the commercial production of structural lightweight aggregates are from natural deposits of shales, clays, or slates. The aggregate is produced by one of several methods presented in this section.

5.1.1 Rotary Kiln Processes

Unscreened Material

Raw material is introduced in its natural size or form to the top of a slightly tilted horizontal cylinder with a refractory lining and rotating at a slow speed. The lower end of the cylinder is the burning end. As the raw material moves slowly to the lower end of the cylinder, the high heat level in excess of 2000°F (1100°C) causes simultaneous formation of gases and onset of a pyroplastic condition in the material.[5.1] The level of viscosity of the softened mass of the raw material is regulated so as to be able to entrap the gases and form an internal cellular structure which becomes vitrified hard material upon cooling. The hardened material is thereafter removed for crushing and screening.

Intermediately Removed Material

The hot material is removed from the rotary kiln, cooled externally, and then crushed and screened to the specified aggregate size. The resulting particles have angular shapes with some smooth shell.

Presized Material

The raw material is presized by crushing and screening before being introduced to the rotary kiln.

5.1.2 Sintering Processes

The raw material is blended with a carbonaceous fuel source. The carbon content serves as fuel and sometimes is mixed with fuel such as finely ground coke or coal.

Plate 25 Transamerica Pyramid Tower, San Francisco, California

Crushed Material

A premoistened layer of this mixture of carbonaceous particles and coal is carried by a traveling grate under drying and ignition hoods and subsequent burners. The burning process starts at the surface then projects through the entire depth of the mixture layer, producing gases that simultaneously cause expansive action with the onset of pyroplasticity. The material becomes sufficiently viscous, as in the case of the rotary kiln process, in entrapping the gases and creating the cellular structure. The clinker formed can then be crushed and screened to the proper size after cooling.

Pelletized Material

Clay, pulverized shale, or both are mixed with moisture and finely ground coal as fuel and then extruded before burning. The resulting product tends to be round pellets. These pellets may receive a surface treatment before burning in order to improve the outer shell or after burning to reduce the absorption ability of the aggregate.

5.2   AGGREGATE PROPERTIES

5.2.1   Particle Shape and Surface Texture

The shape of the particles can be rounded, angular, or irregular depending on the source and the production process. The surface texture may be relatively smooth with small exposed pores or irregular having small or large exposed pores. Thus, the surface texture and the degree of water absorption controls the mixture design process and the workability of the plastic concrete, as is the case of natural stone aggregate but in a more magnified manner. Plate 26 shows the relative shapes of the three major sizes of lightweight aggregate.

5.2.2   Bulk Density

The specific gravity (density) of lightweight aggregate is lower than that of the normal weight natural aggregate. It also varies with particle size, being highest in the case of fine lightweight aggregate and lowest in the case of coarse aggregate. Hence, it is more difficult to determine a standard bulk density in this case. It can be assumed, however, that the bulk density of lightweight aggregate can range between one-third and two-thirds of that for normal weight natural coarse aggregate such as crushed stone. The bulk density is 45–50 lb/ft^3 (720–800 kg/m^3).

5.2.3   Unit Weight and Maximum Size

Because of its cellular structure and large void content, the unit weight of lightweight aggregate is significantly lower than that of the natural normal weight aggregate. It also differs within its varieties by as much as 10 lb/ft^3 (160 kg/m^3) depending on the grading and size distribution. The maximum size grading designation is nominally $\frac{3}{4}$ in. (19 mm), $\frac{1}{2}$ in. (13 mm) and $\frac{3}{8}$ in. (10 mm). Table 5.1 lists the comparative physical gradation properties of natural stone and Solite lightweight. Plate 26 shows the relative shapes of the three major sizes of lightweight aggregate.

Here is an example of how to analyze the void ratio of a typical sample of expanded coarse aggregates:

$$\text{Bulk density, } \gamma_{blk} = 45 \text{ lb/ft}^3 \ (720 \text{ kg/m}^3)$$
$$\text{Specific density, } \gamma_{sp} = 150 \text{ lb/ft}^3 \ (2400\text{SF24kg/m}^3)$$
$$\text{Particle density, } \gamma_p = 90 \text{ lb/ft}^3 \ (1440 \text{ kg/m}^3)$$

Table 5.1 Physical property comparisons of natural stone and lightweight aggregate[5.3]

Physical properties of aggregate	Lightweight aggregate			Natural aggregate		
	Solite coarse 20–5 mm ($\frac{3}{4}$ in. to No. 4)	Solite medium 10–2 mm ($\frac{3}{8}$ in. to No. 8)	Solite fine 5–0 mm (No. 4 to 0)	Natural sand 5–0 mm (No. 4 to 0)	Natural stone 15–5 mm ($\frac{1}{2}$ in. to No. 4)	Natural stone 15–5 mm ($\frac{1}{2}$ in. to No. 4)
(1)	(2)	(3)	(4)	(5)	(6)	(7)
Gradation (percent passing by weight)						
25 mm (1 in.)	100					100
20 mm ($\frac{3}{4}$ in.)	95				100	98
15 mm ($\frac{1}{2}$ in.)	50	100			95	70
10 mm ($\frac{3}{8}$ in.)	25	95			55	40
5 mm (No. 4)	5	40	100	100	10	8
2.4 mm (No. 8)		5	85	95	2	4
1.2 mm (No. 16)			55	75		
0.6 mm (No. 30)			40	50		
0.3 mm (No. 50)			25	10		
0.15 mm (No. 100)			12	2		
Bulk dry loose density, lb/ft³ (kg/m³)	45 (720)	50 (800)	55 (880)	90 (1440)	95 (1520)	95 (1520)
Dry particle density, lb/ft³ (kg/m³)	90 (1420)	94 (1500)	103 (1650)	164 (2620)	165 (2650)	174 (2790)
Moisture content (wt%) for 1 day soak[a]	9	10	12	2	1	1

[a]Other experiences have shown that finer sizes have lesser absorption than coarser sizes.

This data gives the pore content of an individual particle as

$$\frac{(2400 - 1440)}{2400} \times 100\% = 40\%$$

And the bulk voids as

$$\frac{(1400 - 720)}{1440} \times 100\% = 50\%$$

5.3 PROPORTIONING, MIXING, AND PLACEMENT

5.3.1 Proportioning Methods

While normal weight concrete mixes are designed by the absolute $W/(C + P)$ method, lightweight concrete mix design is often principally based on the cementitious material content of the mix, namely, the cement plus supplementary pozzolanic cementing materials replacing part of the cement (e.g., fly ash, blast furnace slag or silica fume) that can fill all the voids in the matrix and produce the recommended slump of 3–4 in. (76–100 mm). In *the absolute volume method*, as with normal weight concrete, the trial mix is based on estimating the volumes of cement, cementitious materials such as fly ash, lightweight coarse aggregate, and preferably natural sand, for high strength concretes, with *sufficient* added water or chemical admixtures or both to produce the required slump. The resulting mix is tried for workability and finishability properties, modifying the chemical admixtures and air content as needed. Typically, water-reducing admixtures and superplasticizers are used either by themselves or in combination. Small amounts of air may be used to improve workability.

Calculations are thereafter made for the yield, which is the total batch weight divided by the plastic unit weight, as well as the actual weights of materials per unit volume in lb/yd^3 or kg/m^3. Adjustments are made and additional trial mixes developed until optimum proportions are achieved.

During trial and adjustment batching, it is important to have a full knowledge of the properties of the lightweight aggregate and the compatibility of the other constituent materials of the mix prior to embarking on the proportioning computations.

5.3.2 Compressive Strength

As with normal weight concrete, the water content has a significant effect on the compressive strength of the concrete. As today's lightweight high strength concrete should have a strength of 6000–9000 psi (41.4–62.1 MPa), special care is needed in controlling the water/cementitious ratio, selecting the appropriate lightweight aggregate, and ensuring the workability of the fresh mix. It is advisable for achieving higher compressive strength to use normal weight sand in

Plate 26 Coronado Bridge, San Diego, California: 11 719 ft (3527 m) length and 50–200 ft height; girders of precast prestressed sand lightweight concrete (Copyright Steven Simpson Inc., San Diego, 1992)

the mix, although this increases the unit weight of the hardened concrete to 100 lb/ft^3 (1600 kg/m^3) or more. The strength ceiling of the lightweight aggregate can also be increased for the same W/(C + P) ratio by using smaller aggregate, limiting it to $\frac{3}{8}$ in. (9.5 mm) for high strength concrete. Some trials have indicated that it is possible as a result of limiting the size to $\frac{3}{8}$ in. (9.5 mm) to increase the strength from 6500 psi (44.8 MPa) to in excess of 8000 psi (55 MPa).[5.1] If the strength ceiling is not reached, it has been found that the long-term strength gain of structural lightweight concrete is greater in many cases than for normal concrete of similar proportions.[5.2] This behavior is due to the continuous hydration of the binder due to the availability of the absorbed moisture within the particle pores of the aggregate. Such an *internal curing process* can proceed if the water content present in the aggregate is in excess of the content achieved after *soaking the aggregate at least 24 hours* prior to use.

This *soaking* can be achieved by continuous spraying at the production plant for this period while the aggregate is spread on conveyor belts. In laboratory trial mixes, a continuous soaking in a container bath is most effective.

One parameter that affects the strength levels is the Young's modulus E_c of the concrete. The E_c value is affected by the moduli of the constituent materials of the hardened concrete, particularly the modulus of the lightweight aggregate. Being less rigid than the surrounding mortar, such incompatibility makes it more difficult to fully transmit the interactive internal forces in the hardened product. For this reason, it is important to select the highest density, highest modulus, and highest particle strength lightweight aggregate to achieve high strength, in addition to limiting the maximum size of the graded aggregate to $\frac{3}{8}$ in. (9.5 mm).

The addition of other cementitious materials, such as fly ash or silica fume, tends to increase the total cement plus cementitious materials content $(C+P)$, so the internal curing process is further enhanced through the presoaking of the aggregate. In a manner similar to that of normal weight concrete, these added pozzolans, which have a fineness modulus often one-tenth that of the cement, contribute to filling all the matrix voids, leading to an increase in the density of the concrete and higher compressive strength. The addition of high range water reducers discussed in Chapter 3 further contributes to enhancing the strength, both short-term and long-term. The increased compact density of the gel results in considerable increase in the compressive strength as Fig. 5.1[5.5] demonstrates, and an increase in strength from 4350 psi (30 MPa) to more than 10 000 psi (69 MPa) by increasing the density from 85 lb/ft³ (1360 kg/m³) to 120 lb/ft³ (1900 kg/m³).

Table 5.2[5.3] gives the mix proportions and resulting compressive strengths and modulus of elasticity of six mixes, giving a range of compressive strength of 6800 psi (46.8 MPa) and 9800 psi (67.4 MPa).

Table 5.3[5.1] gives an approximate relationship between the average compressive strength and cement content for all-lightweight and sand lightweight concrete, *without* the inclusion of other cementitious materials to the cement. A general guideline, it is subject to variations and is based on 3–4 in. slump (76–

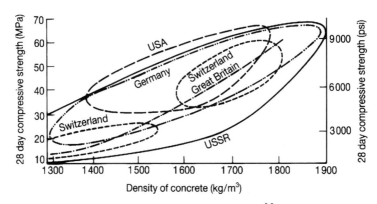

Fig. 5.1 Compressive strength vs. density of lightweight aggregate[5.5]

Table 5.2 Physical properties of high strength concretes (superplasticizers plus commercial retarder)[5.3]

Properties	Type I cement			Type IP cement (fly ash interground)		
	1	2	3	4	5	6
Mix proportions						
Cement, lb/yd³ (kg/m³)	950 (560)	560 (950)	560 (950)	850 (500)	850 (500)	850 (500)
Fly ash (interground), lb/yd³ (kg/m³)				100 (60)	100 (60)	100 (60)
Water, lb/yd³ (litre)	360 (210)	200 (335)	180 (295)	300 (180)	325 (190)	320 (190)
Natural sand, lb/yd³ (kg/m³)	1110 (660)	760 (1290)	720 (1220)	1110 (660)	1290 (760)	1220 (720)
Coarse aggregate Type Size, in. (mm)	LWA $\frac{3}{8}$ in. to No. 8 (10-2)	LWA $2\frac{3}{4}$ in. to No. 4 (20-5)	Nat. stone 1/2 in. to No. 4 (15-5)	LWA $1\frac{3}{8}$ in. to No. 8 (10-2)	LWA $\frac{3}{4}$ in. to No. 4 (20-5)	Nat. stone $\frac{1}{2}$ in. to No. 4 (15-5)
Quantity, lb/yd³ (kg/m³)	1100 (650)	530 (900)	990 (1670)	1100 (650)	900 (530)	900 (1670)
Concrete						
Air content (%)	2.25	2.25	2.0	2.0	2.0	2.0
Slump, in. (mm)	4 (100)	6 (150)	4 (100)	4 (100)	5.5 (140)	5.0 (130)
Density—Fresh, lb/ft³ (kg/m³)	126 (2020)	123 (1960)	151 (2410)	127 (2040)	125 (1990)	148 (2370)
Equilibrium, lb/ft³ (kg/m³)	122 (1950)	120 (1930)	148 (2380)	124 (1990)	120 (1920)	147 (2360)
Oven dry, lb/ft³ (kg/m³)	120 (1920)	118 (1900)	147 (2360)	122 (1960)	117 (1880)	145 (2330)
Strength properties						
Compressive strength at 28 days, ksi (MPa)	9.78 (67.4)	7.61 (52.5)	7.73 (53.3)	8.96 (61.8)	6.70 (46.8)	7.91 (54.5)
Compressive mod. of elast. at 210 days, psi$\times 10^6$ (MPa)	3.48 (24.0)	3.18 (21.9)	6.36 (43.8)		3.93 (27.1)	7.20 (43.9)
E_{test}/E_{calc}	0.76	0.82	1.21		0.99	0.90

100 mm). Through utilizing these additional pozzolans, such as fly ash or silica fume, appreciably higher levels can by achieved.

In general it is the cementitious content vs. slump in the lightweight aggregate concrete rather than the W/(C + P) ratio that controls the mix proportioning for the reasons previously discussed. As an example, Table 5.4, courtesy Solite Corp., gives alternate mixes for fly ash and lightweight aggregate concrete adding 40 lb of fly ash and achieving strengths of 6810 psi in 7 days for concrete pumped 830 ft (268 m).

Figure 5.2 gives the stress–strain relationships of high strength lightweight concretes having different size aggregates in the mix[5.7] in the range of $\frac{3}{8}$ to $\frac{3}{4}$ in. (9.5–19.5 mm). It is seen that the $\frac{3}{8}$ in. aggregate attained a strength close to 11 300 psi (78 MPa) at 200 days age. Figure 5.3 shows the stress–strain relationship of high strength lightweight aggregate concrete in Fig. 5.2 compared with that of normal weight concrete. The diagram also shows the stress–strain

Table 5.3 Approximate relationship between average compressive strength and cement content[5.1]

	Cement content, lb/yd^3 (kg/m^3)	
Compressive strength, psi (MPa)	All-lightweight	Sand lightweight
2500 (17.2)	400–510 (237–303)	400–510 (237–303)
3000 (20.7)	440–560 (261–332)	420–560 (249–332)
4000 (27.6)	530–660 (314–392)	490–660 (291–392)
5000 (34.5)	630–750 (374–445)	600–750 (356–445)
6000 (41.4)	740–840 (439–498)	700–840 (415–498)

Table 5.4 Mix proportions for fly ash lightweight aggregate pumped concrete[a]

	Mix 1	Mix 2[b]	Mix 3
Mix proportions			
Cement type III (lb)	550	650	750
Fly ash (lb)	140	140	140
Solite $\frac{3}{4}$ in to No. 4 (lb)	900	900	900
Sand (lb)	1370	1287	1203
Water (gal.)	35.5	36.5	37.2
WRA (oz)	27.6	31.6	35.6
Superplasticizer	55.2	81.4	80.1
Fresh concrete properties			
Initial slump (in.)	$2\frac{1}{2}$	2	$2\frac{1}{4}$
Slump after superplasticizer	$5\frac{1}{2}$	$7\frac{1}{2}$	$6\frac{3}{4}$
Percent air	2.5	2.5	2.3
Unit weight (pcf.)	117.8	118.0	118.0
Compressive strength (psi)			
4 days	4290	5110	5710
7 days	4870	5790	6440
28 days (avg.)	6270	6810	7450
Splitting tensile strength (psi)	520	540	565

[a]Nations Bank Building, Charlotte, N.C., 1991, pumped 830 ft (268 m).

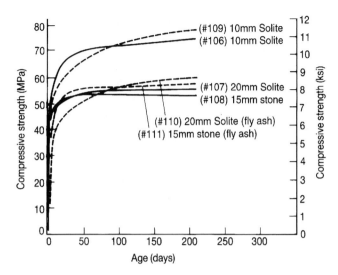

Fig. 5.2 Compressive strength vs. age of lightweight and normal weight concretes[5.7]

relationship of concrete cored from the 60-year-old USS *Selma*. Note that the rate of increase in strength with age for the lightweight concrete is higher in comparison to normal weight concrete due to the internal curing process discussed earlier. It is also seen in Figs. 5.2 and 5.3 that the addition of the fly ash pozzolan to the mix is further enhanced by the internal curing process.

5.3.3   Modulus of Elasticity E_c and Poisson's Ratio μ

Concrete modulus of elasticity E_c as a function of the rigidity of the concrete is controlled by the relative proportions of the aggregate and the cementitious paste. Sand and crushed stone or gravel concrete are expected to have a higher E_c value than the modulus of structural lightweight concrete. For high strength concretes, E_c for lightweight aggregate concrete is *one-half* to *two-thirds* that of stone concrete of the same strength, depending on the modulus of the aggregate and the relative volume of the cementitious paste and the aggregate.

For concretes of density 90–155 lb/ft^3 (1440–2480 kg/m^3) and strengths up to 5000 psi (34.5 MPa), the ACI 318 code recommends a secant modulus

$$E_c = w^{1.5}\,33\sqrt{f_c'}\ \text{psi}\ (w^{1.5}0.0043\sqrt{f_c'}\ \text{MPa}) \qquad [5.1]$$

For concretes with strengths of 6000–12 000 psi (41.4–52.7 MPa), the following secant modulus expression can be used[5.6]:

$$E_c = (40\,000\sqrt{f_c'} + 1 \times 10^6)\left(\frac{w_c}{145}\right)^{1.5}\text{psi} \qquad [5.2]$$

1975–1979 HIGH STRENGTH PROGRAM					
Mix	Size and Type of Coarse Aggregate	Compressive Strength		Comp. Modulus of Elasticity	
		MPa	ksi	MPA×10³	ksi×10³
106	10mm LWA	77.1	11.2	24.0	3.48
107	20mm LWA	53.2	7.72	21.9	3.18
108	15mm Nat. Stone	56.0	8.12	49.6	7.20
110	20mm LWA	60.6	8.79	27.1	3.93
111	15mm Nat. Stone	51.6	7.48	43.9	6.36
1919 "SELMA"		70.0	10.15	24.7	3.59

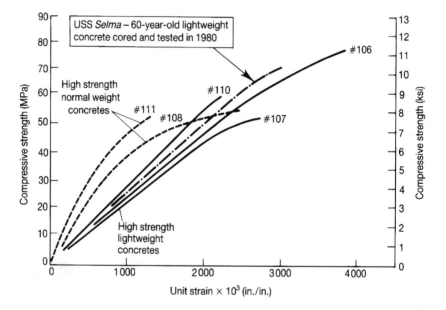

Fig. 5.3 Stress–strain relationship for high strength lightweight and normal weight concretes, including 60-year-old USS *Selma* concrete[5.7]

or

$$E_c = (3.32\sqrt{f_c'} + 6895)\left(\frac{w_c}{2320}\right)^{1.5} \text{MPa} \qquad [5.3]$$

Hence, for high strength lightweight aggregate concrete, Eqs. 5.2 and 5.3 are more applicable. However, a more accurate value of E_c should be obtained from laboratory tests of the chosen trial batch mix through the establishment of the stress–strain relationship of the hardened concrete. At the same time, one can obtain from these tests the Poisson's ratio μ. While the value of this ratio can vary between 0.15 and 0.25, it is sufficiently accurate to use an average value of $\mu = 0.20$.

Figure 5.4 adapted from an ACI report[5.1] gives the modulus E_c as a function of the 28 day compressive strength f_c', for both normal weight and lightweight

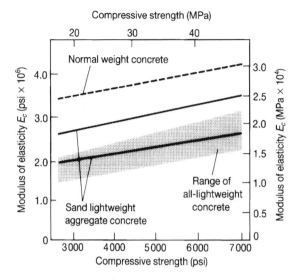

Fig. 5.4 Modulus of elasticity vs. compressive strength of lightweight and normal weight concretes

Plate 27 Gradation sizes of Solite lightweight aggregate (Courtesy Solite Corporation, Richmond, Virginia)

Plate 28   Micrograph of lightweight aggregate concrete (Courtesy Solite Corp., Richmond, Virginia)

concretes. Note that the rate of increase in the modulus with strength is essentially the same for both types of concrete.

5.3.4   Water Absorption and Moisture Content

Lightweight coarse aggregate has a high degree of absorption because of its large cellular structure. It generally absorbs 5–20 percent by weight of the dry aggregates depending on the size, percentage, and distribution of the pores. The rate of absorption is also substantially higher than that of the normal weight aggregate which absorbs less than 2 percent moisture. For this reason, it is important in the design of the mixtures and the evaluation of the workability of the plastic mix to take this factor into account as a major parameter.

As stated earlier, the compressive strength of lightweight aggregate concrete is more related to the cementitious materials content rather than the $W/(C + P)$ ratio. This is due to the uncertainty in determining the water portion in the mix that is utilized in the hydration process. Since placement of the finished product is affected by the viscosity of the fresh mix, its workability is controlled to a major extent by the water content in the mix.

A measure of the workability is the slump value. The slump should typically be 3–4 in. (76–100 mm) in order to allow for good workability. A slump of 3 in. maintains cohesiveness, thereby preventing the lighter coarse particles from migrating to the surface segregation. This behavior is contrary to that in normal weight concrete, where segregation causes the excess mortar rather than the aggregate to migrate to the surface. If the slump is more than 4 in. (100 mm) finishing delays and difficulties could ensue. However, mixtures using large doses of superplasticizers can have much higher slumps without segregation, provided there is sufficient binder in the mixture.

5.3.5   Permeability

The water permeabilities of ordinary and lightweight aggregate concrete are essentially similar in magnitude. This is because the resistance of the concrete surface to water penetration is determined by the capillary porosity of the mortar fraction, not by the degree of water absorption. Hence, the high absorption of lightweight aggregate concrete does not adversely affect its permeability performance.

5.3.6   Placement, Finishability, and Curing

A properly proportioned mix with a slump not exceeding 4 in. can be placed in the forms without difficulty. The surface has to be prepared before troweling through the use of aluminum or magnesium screens and floats so as to prevent or minimize surface tearing or pullout. The finishing activities should only commence after free surface bleeding water has disappeared.

When the finishing process is completed, protection of the concrete should commence as soon as possible as the strength and long-term behavior will be greatly affected by the manner and duration of the curing process. Curing is accomplished by one of two methods

1. *Water curing* by wet covering, or soaking through ponding or sprinkling
2. *Moisture retention curing* by using waterproof paper, polyethylene film, or a spray-applied compound membrane.

In general, 7 days of curing is adequate with temperatures exceeding 50°F (10°C).[5.1]

5.4   CREEP AND SHRINKAGE OF LIGHTWEIGHT CONCRETE

5.4.1   Creep

Creep is the lateral flow of the material under sustained loading. In other words, it is the increase of strain caused by sustained imposed stress. It is affected by the aggregate properties and its gradation, type of cement and cementitious material, water content in the mix and the moisture content in the aggregate at mixing time, amount of entrained air, age of initial loading, and the magnitude and duration of load application.

The magnitude of creep is affected also by the duration and type of curing, namely, whether normal wet curing or steam curing is applied. Creep strain is reduced in low pressure steam-cured specimens by 25–40 percent of the creep strain in moist-cured similarly constructed and loaded specimens. In the case of high pressure steam curing, this reduction can be as high as 60–80 percent.[5.1] Figure 5.5 demonstrates the specific creep strain, assuming that shrinkage strains can be separated from creep strains. Note that as the concrete strength is increased, the creep strain is reduced so that higher strength lightweight aggregate concretes can have considerably reduced creep, with the creep magnitude comparable to that in normal density concrete.

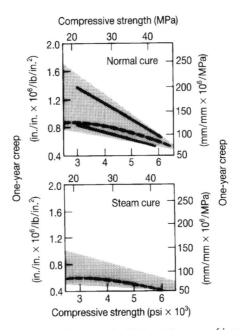

Fig. 5.5 Specific creep vs. compressive strength of lightweight concrete[5.1] (dotted line represents normal weight concrete)

5.4.2   Drying Shrinkage

The factors affecting drying shrinkage are the same as those listed in Section 5.4.1 affecting creep, but not the sustained load. It is also a function of the curing type and process, relative humidity of surrounding air and the temperature of the environment. As shrinkage results in cracking, leading to reduced stiffness, it is important to apply an effective curing regime to reduce the initial drying shrinkage considerably. Figure 5.6 gives the relative effect of reducing shrinkage through steam curing. The shaded area is the range of lightweight concretes of varying densities and performance.

5.5   DURABILITY

Freeze and thaw cycles and deicing salts significantly affect the durability of all concretes. Deterioration can take place in walls and columns exposed to moisture and in flat surfaces exposed to freezing of the absorbed water such as concrete highways and bridge decks. Durability is measured by the durability factor, which is the percentage of the dynamic modulus of elasticity *retained* after 300 freeze and thaw cycles. The higher the W/(C + P) or W/C ratio the less is the durability.

Hence, higher strength lightweight aggregate concretes have a higher durability factor than lower strength concretes as their water content is considerably reduced by the addition of plasticizer, air-entraining agents, and pozzolans. As with normal weight concrete it is essential to provide curing and protection for saturated aggregates at mixing time because of the vulnerability of frost damage

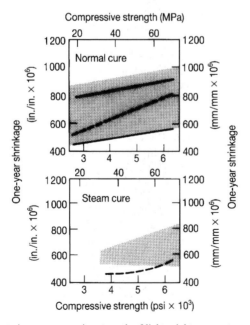

Fig. 5.6 Shrinkage strain vs. compressive strength of lightweight aggregate concrete[5.1] (dotted line represents normal weight concrete)

to concrete in the initial life of the hardened concrete. With protection in accordance with ACI 318 and 301, freeze–thaw resistance is gained as the drying process continues.

5.6   THERMAL EXPANSION AND THERMAL CONDUCTIVITY

5.6.1   Thermal Expansion

As with normal weight concrete, the thermal expansion of lightweight aggregate concrete affects the cracking performance of continuous members that form part of a structural system. The stresses develop due to the restraint on expansion caused by continuity. The coefficient of thermal expansion of lightweight aggregate concrete is less than that of normal weight concrete and is primarily a function of the coefficient of expansion of the constituent materials and the degree of compactness of the hardened concrete. The range of values of the coefficient of thermal expansion for lightweight concretes is

$$\alpha = 4 - 6 \times 10^{-6} \text{ in./in./}^\circ\text{F}$$

or

$$\alpha = 8 - 12 \times 10^{-6} \text{ mm/mm/}^\circ\text{C}$$

For normal weight concretes the coefficient of thermal expansion is

$$\alpha = 5 - 7 \times 10^{-6} \text{ in./in./}^\circ\text{F}$$

or

$$\alpha = 9 - 13 \times 10^{-6} \text{ mm/mm/}^\circ\text{C}$$

It is not anticipated that for high strength concretes these values would be appreciably changed. Table 5.5 gives the thermal properties of concrete constituents for concretes in general.[5.8]

Thermal expansion coefficients, the results of extensive tests on lightweight aggregate concrete, are given in Table 5.6 and appear to depend on the mix proportions.[5.11]

5.6.2   Thermal Conductivity

Thermal conductivity is a measure of the rate at which heat energy perpendicularly passes through a unit area of homogeneous material of unit thickness per one degree temperature gradient. This measure is defined by a thermal conductivity coefficient k where in U.S. units (Btu/ft^2 hr $^\circ$F)

$$k = 0.5e^{0.02w} \qquad \qquad [5.4]$$

Table 5.5 Thermal properties of concrete constituents[5.7]

	Thermal conductivity, W/m·K (Btu/ft·hr·°F)		Specific heat, J/kg·°C (Btu/lb·°F)	Coefficient of linear expansion, 10^{-6}/°C (10^{-6}/°F)	
Aggregate					
Granite	3.1	(1.8)	800 (0.19)	7–9	(4–5)
Basalt	1.4	(0.8)	840 (0.20)	6–8	(3.3–4.4)
Limestone	3.1	(1.8)	—	6	(3.3)
Dolomite	3.6	(2.1)	—	7–10	(4–5.5)
Sandstone	3.9	(2.3)	—	11–12	(6.1–6.7)
Quartzite	4.3	(2.5)	—	11–13	(6.1–7.2)
Marble	2.7	(1.6)	—	4–7	(2.2–4)
Cement paste[a]					
W/C = 0.4	1.3	(0.75)	—	18–20	(10–11)
W/C = 0.5	1.2	(0.7)	—	18–20	(10–11)
W/C = 0.6	1.0	(0.6)	1600 (0.38)	18–20	(10–11)
Concrete	1.5–3.5	(0.9–2.0)	840–1170 (0.2–0.28)	7.4–11	(4.1–7.3)
Water	0.5	(0.3)	4200 (1.0)	—	—
Air	0.03	(0.02)	1050 (0.25)	—	—
Steel	120	(70)	460 (0.11)	11–12	(6.1–6.7)

Table 5.6 Coefficient of thermal expansion

Mixture	Moisture condition, relative humidity (%)	Specimen size, in. × in. (mm × mm)	Coefficient of thermal expansion between 70°F (21.1°C) and −22°F (−30°C), microstrain/°F (°C)
LWC1	100	0.5×3 (13×75)	3.4 (6.1)
LWC1	50	0.5×3 (13×75)	4.3 (7.7)
LWC1	0	0.5×3 (13×75)	3.5 (6.3)
LWC1	50	6 × 12 (150 × 300)	4.1 (7.4)
LCW3	100	6 × 12 (150 × 300)	7.1 (12.8)
LCW3	50	6 × 12 (150 × 300)	6.1 (11.0)
LCW3	0	6 × 12 (150 × 300)	3.2 (5.8)
LCW4	100	6 × 12 (150 × 300)	5.0 (9.0)
LCW4	50	6 × 12 (150 × 300)	4.5 (8.1)
LCW4	0	6 × 12 (150 × 300)	3.9 (7.0)
HSLWC	100	6 × 12 (150 × 300)	7.1 (12.8)
HSLWC	50	6 × 12 (150 × 300)	3.9 (7.0)
HSLWC	0	6 × 12 (150 × 300)	3.9 (7.0)

and in SI units (Calorie W/min °C)

$$k = 0.072e^{0.00125w}$$ [5.5]

where
e = 2.71828
w = unit weight of the concrete
W = calories/cc volume

As in thermal expansion, the thermal conductivity of concrete is primarily dependent on the density and moisture content of the concrete, the size and distribution of the pores, the microstructure of the constituents, and the temperature level. Figure 5.7 gives the average k values versus the concrete dry density[5.1] for a complete range of concrete dry densities up to 140 lb/ft³ (2240 kg/m³). The thermal conductivity of concretes is independent of temperature within the normal climatic range. But it starts to decrease linearly above 212°F (100°C) temperatures due to the resulting decrease in moisture caused by the drying of the concrete element.

The standard test method for steady-state thermal transmission properties by means of the guarded hot plate generally involves placing two slabs of test material between "hot" and "cold" plates regulated to provide nominally constant one-dimensional heat flow through the test slab thickness. Once constant flow is established, thermal conductivity is calculated by the following equation:

$$k = \frac{Qt}{A(T_1 - T_2)}$$

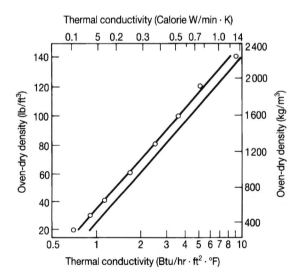

Fig. 5.7 Thermal conductivity vs. oven-dry density in concretes[5.1]

Table 5.7 Thermal conductivity of lightweight aggregate concrete[5.11]

Mixture	Specimen thickness, in. (mm)		Oven-dry density, lb/ft³ (kgs/m³)		Tempera-ture, °F (°C)		Apparent thermal conductivity, Btu/ft²·hr·°F (W/m²·K)		Thermal resistance hr. sq ft.°F per Btu (sq m.°K per W)	
LWC1	2.01	(51.0)	107.7	1727	−50	−46	5.64	0.814	0.36	0.063
					0	−18	5.89	0.850	0.34	0.060
					32	0	6.06	0.874	0.33	0.058
					70	21	6.24	0.900	0.32	0.057
HSLWC	2.01	(51.0)	119.5	1915	−50	−46	7.66	1.10	0.26	0.046
					0	−18	7.56	1.09	0.27	0.047
					32	0	7.51	1.08	0.27	0.047
					70	21	7.45	1.07	0.27	0.048

where k = thermal conductivity, Btu · in./hr · ft² · °F

Q = time rate of heat flow, Btu/hr

t = specimen thickness, in.

A = effective area, ft²

T_1 = temperature of warm surface of specimen, °F

T_2 = temperature of cold surface of specimen, °F

Extensive work by Hoff[5.11] involved prisms 5.7 in. × 5.7 in. (145 mm × 145 mm) in plan and 2 in. (51 mm) thick. The properties of the fresh concrete used to cast these specimens are shown in Table 5.9. The specimens were removed from the mold after 1 day and cured in a moist room at 73°F ± 3°F (22.8°C ± 1.7°C) until reaching an age of 14 days. They were then kept at 50 percent ± 5 percent relative humidity and 73°F ± 3°F (22.8°C ± 1.7°C) until they were approximately 6 weeks old, then oven dried at 230°F (110°C) until a constant weight was obtained. The tests were conducted on the oven-dried specimens at mean temperatures of − 50°F, 0°F, 32°F, and 70°F (− 46°C, − 18°C, 0°C, and 21°C). The results are given in Table 5.7.

5.7   CARBONATION IN LIGHTWEIGHT CONCRETE

Carbonation in concrete is the reaction of carbon dioxide from the air with calcium hydroxide from the hydration process. This continuous process transforms the calcium hydroxide to calcium carbonate, thereby lowering the pH of the concrete from 12 to about 8 or 9. As a result, the effectiveness of the concrete cover in protecting the steel reinforcement from corrosion is considerably reduced, with the ensuing scaling and deterioration of a concrete structural element. The results of core tests reported in Holm et al.[5.9] on the depth of carbonation penetration are given in Table 5.5. The carbonation coefficient K_c as a function of depth penetration and time in years[5.10] can be defined as

$$K_c = \frac{d}{\sqrt{t}} \qquad [5.6]$$

Table 5.8 Carbonation progression in 20-year-old structural concretes of varying mixes[5.10]

	Mix 1	Mix 2	Mix 3
Coarse aggregate type, kg/m³ (pcy)	Gravel 1068 (1800)	SLWA[a] 445 (750)	SLWA[a] 549 (925)
Fine aggregate type, kg/m³ (pcy)	Nat. sand 712 (1200)	Nat. sand 718 (1210)	SLWA[a] 771 (1300)
Cement, kg/m³ (pcy)	335 (564)	377 (635)	335 (564)
Water, kg/m³ (pcy)	182 (307)	178 (300)	178 (300)
W/C	0.54	0.47	0.53
Fresh density, kg/m³ (pcf)	2290 (143)	1730 (108)	1870 (117)
Density at 28 days, kg/m³ (pcf)	2240 (140)	1610 (100)	1820 (114)
Air content (%)	5.0	7.0	5.0
Slump, mm (in.)	125 (5)	125 (5)	125 (5)
Strength at 28 days MPa (psi)	25.2 (3650)	25.4 (3680)	23.8 (3450)
Average carbonation depth mm (in.)	23 (0.91)	23 (0.91)	24 (0.94)
Carbonation coefficient K_c	5.1	5.1	5.4

where d = carbonation depth in mm determined by spraying a freshly exposed surface with phenolphthalein

t = time in years

As seen from Table 5.8, the average carbonation penetration depth for structural lightweight concrete was essentially similar after 20 years to that of normal weight concrete $\simeq 0.9$ in. (23 mm). Hence, if the concrete clear cover is more than $1\frac{1}{2}$ in., and the concrete is dense and impermeable, adequate corrosion protection to the reinforcement is possible.

5.8   HIGH STRENGTH LIGHTWEIGHT AGGREGATE CONCRETE IN OFFSHORE ARCTIC ENVIRONMENTS

Concrete can be a durable construction material not only at normal or subfreezing temperatures, but also at subarctic and arctic temperatures. Lightweight aggregate high strength concrete having a design compressive strength range of 7000–9000 psi (48.3–62.1 MPa) at 28 days was developed for offshore oil platforms.[5.11] Coarse lightweight aggregate having a maximum loose weight of 55 lb/ft³ (850 kg/m³) was used in the mix together with natural sand of 1.6 percent absorption and a fineness modulus of 2.89. Two types of aggregate were used, crushed and pelletized. Type I/II portland cement together with cement replacement cementitious materials. Table 5.9 gives a summary of the mix proportions for the six types of mixes used where silica fume, fly ash, or blast furnace slag were used where indicated. Two densities of concrete were used, 120 and 133 lb/ft³ (1920 and 2082 kg/m³).

Figure 5.8 shows the gain in strength with age for the different types of concretes used, 28 day moist-cured then air-cured. The mix using silica fume as replacement for part of the cement attained a cylinder compressive strength of

Table 5.9 Mix proportioning of high strength lightweight aggregate concrete in arctic environments[5.11]

	Tested by United States						Tested by Japan		
	LWC1	LWC2	HSLWC	LWC3	LWC4	NWC	LWC1	LWC2	NWC
Type I/II cement, lb/yd³ (kg/m³)	799 (474)	799 (474)	846 (502)	700 (415)	600 (356)	658 (390)	799 (474)	799 (747)	657 (390)
Fine aggregate, lb/yd³ (kg/m³)	1004 (596)	965 (573)	1575 (934)	896 (532)	1004 (596)	1140 (676)	979 (581)	947 (562)	1123 (666)
Coarse aggregate, lb/yd³ (kg/m³)									
Crushed type	1012 (600)	—	—	—	—	—	1075 (638)	—	—
Pelletized type	—	1022 (606)	613 (364)	924 (548)	920 (546)	—	—	979 (581)	—
Normal weight	—	—	—	—	—	1990 (1180)	—	—	1986 (1178)
Silica fume, lb/yd³ (kg/m³)	80 (47)	80 (47)	110 (65)	—	—	— (47)	79 (47)	79	—
Fly ash, lb/yd³ (kg/m³)	—	—	—	200 (119)	—	—	—	—	—
Slag, lb/yd³ (kg/m³)	—	—	—	—	200 (119)	—	—	—	—
High range water reducer, oz (l)	160 (4.7)	160 (6.2)	169 (6.5)	132 (5.0)	104 (4.0)	95.4 (3.7)	116.2 (6.2)	116.2 (6.2)	78.8 (2.9)
Air-entraining admixture, oz (l)	32.0 (1.25)	32.0 (1.25)	16.9 (0.66)	19.6 (0.73)	17.4 (0.63)	55.9 (2.15)	33.2 (1.25)	25.6 (0.94)	10.5 (0.43)
Mix water[a] lb/yd³ (kg/m³)	237 (141)	234 (139)	256 (152)	236 (140)	247 (147)	215 (128)	238 (141)	234 (139)	212 (126)
Water/cement ratio	0.30	0.30	0.31	0.34	0.41	0.33	0.31	0.30	0.33
Water/cementitious ratio	0.28	0.27	0.28	0.26	0.31	—	0.28	0.28	—

[a]Water added in addition to that contained in chemical admixtures.

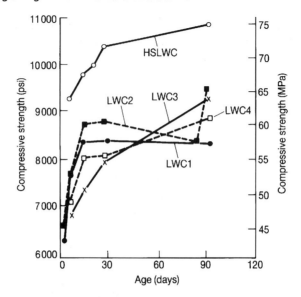

Fig. 5.8 Compressive strength vs. age of high strength lightweight aggregate concrete in Arctic environment[5.11] (28 day moist cure followed by air cure)

10 540 psi (73 MPa) at 90 days, moist-cured. Figure 5.9 gives the freeze–thaw behavior of this concrete in percent of the relative dynamic modulus, using the rapid freezing and thawing procedure. It was found from these tests that the low water/cementitious materials ratio of 0.26–0.31 detailed in Table 5.6 using the finely divided replacement pozzolans (W/(C + P)) left little excess moisture to promote further hydration at later ages. It was also found that the curing regimes

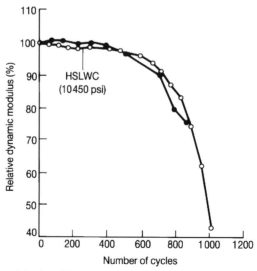

Fig. 5.9 Freeze–thaw behavior of high strength lightweight aggregate concrete in Arctic environment[5.11]

for these concretes have a significant effect on the strength development of these concretes similar to what happens in normal weight concrete. All mixtures attained 86–92 percent of the 28 day strength at 7 days.[5.11]

REFERENCES

5.1   ACI Committee 213 Guide for Structural Lightweight Aggregate Concrete. *ACI Report 213R-87* American Concrete Institute, Detroit, 1987, pp. 1–27.

5.2   Holm T A 1983 Structural Lightweight Concrete. *Handbook of Structural Concrete* McGraw Hill, New York, Ch. 7, pp. 1–34.

5.3   Holm T A 1980 Physical Properties of Lightweight Aggregate Concretes. *Proceedings 2nd International Congress on Lightweight Concrete, London* Solite Corporation, Richmond, Va.

5.4   Haynes H H 1980 Permeability of Concrete in Sea Water. *ACI SP-65* American Concrete Institute, Detroit, pp. 21–38.

5.5   CEB-FIP 1977 Lightweight Aggregate Concrete. *Manual of Design and Technology* Paris.

5.6   Nilson A H 1985 Design Implications of Current Research on High Strength Concrete. *ACI SP-87* American Concrete Institute, Detroit, pp. 85–118.

5.7   Holm T A 1980 Performance of Structural Lightweight Concrete in a Marine Environment. *ACI SP-65* American Concrete Institute, Detroit.

5.8   Mindess S, and Young J F 1981 *Concrete* Prentice Hall, Englewood Cliffs, N. J., pp. 1–671.

5.9   Holm T A, Bremner T W, and Vaysburd A 1986 Carbonation of Marine Structural Lightweight Concretes. *Solite Corp. Report* Richmond, Va., pp. 1–7.

5.10 Meyer A 1968 Investigation of the Carbonation of Concrete. *Proceedings 5th International Symposium of Chemistry of Cement, Tokyo* Supplementary Paper III-52, pp. 394–401.

5.11 Hoff G C 1992 High Strength Lightweight Aggregate Concrete For Arctic Applications. *Structural Lightweight Aggregate Concrete. ACI SP-136* eds. T A Holm and A M Vaysburd, American Concrete Institute, Detroit, pp. 1–245.

5.12 Bremner T A, and Holm T A 1986 Elastic Compatibility and the Behavior of Concrete. *Proceedings, ACI Journal* American Concrete Institute, Detroit.

6 Long-Term Effects

6.1 CREEP IN CONCRETE

Creep or lateral material flow is the increase in strain with time due to sustained load.[6.1] Initial deformation due to load is the *elastic strain*, while the additional strain due to the same sustained load is the *creep strain*. This practical assumption is quite acceptable since the initial recorded deformation includes few time-dependent effects. Figure 6.1 illustrates the increase in creep strain with time, and as in the case of shrinkage, it can be seen that the rate of creep decreases with time. Creep cannot be measured directly but determined only by deducting elastic strain and shrinkage strain from the total deformation. Although shrinkage and creep are not independent phenomena, it can be assumed that superposition of strains is valid; hence

$$\text{total strain}(\epsilon_t) = \text{elastic strain}(\epsilon_e) + \text{creep}(\epsilon_c) + \text{shrinkage}(\epsilon_{sh})$$

An example[6.2] of the relative numerical values of strain due to the foregoing three factors is presented for a normal concrete specimen subjected to 900 psi in compression:

Immediate elastic strain,	$\epsilon_e = 250 \times 10^{-6}$ in./in.
Shrinkage strain after 1 year,	$\epsilon_{sh} = 500 \times 10^{-6}$ in./in.
Creep strain after 1 year,	$\epsilon_c = 750 \times 10^{-6}$ in./in.
	$\epsilon_t = 1500 \times 10^{-6}$ in./in.

These relative values illustrate that stress–strain relationships for short-term loading in normally reinforced or plain concrete elements lose their significance and long-term loadings become dominant in their effect on the behavior of a structure. For large heavily reinforced columns in buildings, elastic strain can be a more significant component of the total strain.

Figure 6.2 is a qualitative three-dimensional model of these three types of strain resulting from sustained compressive stress and shrinkage. Since creep is time-dependent, this model has to be such that its orthogonal axes are deformation, stress, and time.

Numerous tests have indicated that creep deformation is proportional to the applied stress, but the proportionality is valid only for low stress levels. The upper limit of the relationship cannot be determined accurately but can vary between 0.2

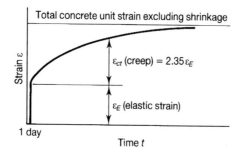

Fig. 6.1 Long-term creep stress–time curve[6.1]

and 0.5 of the ultimate strength f_c'. This range in the limit of the proportionality is expected due to the large extent of microcracks that exist at about 40 percent of the ultimate load.

Figure 6.3(a) shows a section of the three-dimensional model in Fig. 6.2 parallel to the plane containing the stress and deformation axes at time t_1. It indicates that both elastic and creep strains are linearly proportional to the applied stress. In a similar manner, Fig. 6.3(b) illustrates a section parallel to the plane containing the time and strain axes at a stress f_1; hence it shows the familiar creep time and shrinkage time relationships.

As in the case of shrinkage, creep is not completely reversible. If a specimen is unloaded after a period under a sustained load, an immediate elastic recovery is obtained which is less than the strain precipitated on loading. The instantaneous recovery is followed by a gradual decrease in strain, called *creep recovery*. The extent of the recovery depends on the age of the concrete when loaded, with older concretes presenting higher creep recoveries, while residual strains or deformations become frozen in the structural element as in Fig. 6.4.

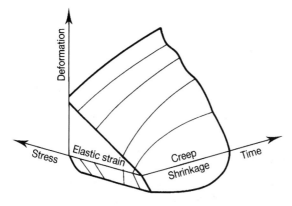

Fig. 6.2 Three-dimensional model of time-dependent structural behavior[6.1]

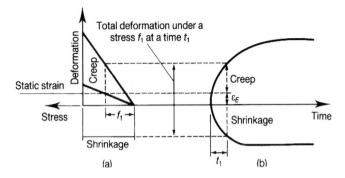

Fig. 6.3 Two-dimensional section of deformations in Fig. 6.2[6.1]: (a) section parallel to stress–deformation plane; (b) section parallel to deformation–time plane

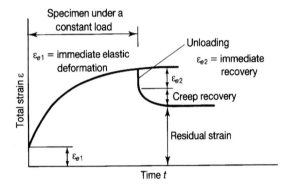

Fig. 6.4 Creep recovery vs. time[6.1]

6.1.1   Creep Effects

As in shrinkage, creep increases the deflection of beams and slabs, and causes loss of prestress in prestressed elements. In addition, the initial eccentricity of a reinforced concrete column increases with time due to creep, resulting in the transfer of the compressive load from the concrete to the steel in the concrete section.

Once the steel yields, additional load has to be carried by the concrete. Consequently, the resisting capacity of the column is reduced and the curvature of the column increases further, resulting in overstress in the concrete, leading to failure. Similar behavior occurs in axially loaded columns.

6.1.2   Rheological Models

Rheological models are mechanical devices that portray the general deformation behavior and flow of materials under stress. A model is basically composed of elastic springs and ideal dashpots denoting stress, elastic strain, delayed elastic strain, irrecoverable strain, and time. The springs represent the proportionality between stress and strain, and the dashpots represent the proportionality of stress to the rate of strain. A spring and a dashpot in parallel form a Kelvin unit; and in series they form a Maxwell unit.

Two rheological models will be discussed: the Burgers model and the Ross model. The Burgers model in Fig. 6.5 is shown since it can approximately simulate the stress–strain–time behavior of concrete at the limit of proportionality, with some limitations. This model simulates the instantaneous recoverable strain (a), the delayed recoverable elastic strain in the spring (b), and the irrecoverable time-dependent strain in dashpots (c and d). The weakness in this model is that it continues to deform at a uniform rate as long as the load is sustained by the Maxwell dashpot—a behavior not similar to concrete, where creep reaches a limiting value with time, as shown in Fig. 6.1.

A modification in the form of the Ross rheological model[6.3] in Figure 6.6 can eliminate this deficiency. A in this model represents the Hookian direct proportionality of stress-to-strain element, D represents the Newtonian element, and B and C are the elastic springs that can transmit the applied load $P(t)$ to the enclosing cylinder walls by direct friction. Since each coil has a defined frictional resistance, only those coils whose resistance equals the applied load $P(t)$ are displaced; the others remain unstressed, symbolizing the irrecoverable deformation in concrete. As the load continues to increase, it overcomes the spring resistance of unit B, pulling out the spring from the dashpot and signifying failure in a concrete element. More rigorous models have been used, such as Roll's model to assist in predicting the creep strains. Mathematical expressions for such predictions can be very rigorous. One convenient expression due to Ross defines creep C under load after a time interval t as follows:

$$C = \frac{t}{a + bt} \qquad\qquad [6.1]$$

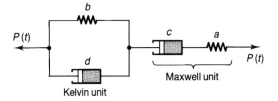

Fig. 6.5 Burgers rheological model[6.1]

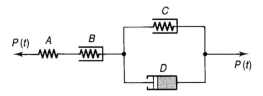

Fig. 6.6 Ross rheological model[6.1]

where a and b are constants determinable from tests. As will be discussed in Sections 6.2.3 and 6.2.4, this model seems to represent the creep deformation of concrete and is the background for the ACI equations for creep.

6.2 CREEP PREDICTION

6.2.1 Creep Prediction for Standard Conditions

Creep and shrinkage are interrelated phenomena because of the similarity of the variables affecting both including the forms of their strain–time curves seen from Fig. 6.3. The ACI[6.4] proposes similar format for expressing both creep and shrinkage behavior.

The expression for creep is as follows:

$$C_t = \frac{t^\alpha}{a + t^\alpha} C_u \qquad [6.2]$$

where a and α are experimental constants and t in days is the duration time of loading.

Work by Branson[6.6,6.7] formed the basis of Eqs. 6.2 and 6.3 in a simplified creep evaluation. The additional strain ϵ_{cu} due to creep can be defined as

$$\epsilon_{cu} = \rho_u f_{ci} \qquad [6.3]$$

Plate 29 Sydney Opera House, Sydney, Australia (Courtesy Australian Information Service)

where $\rho_u =$ unit creep coefficient, generally called *specific creep*

$\quad\quad f_{ci} =$ stress intensity in the structural member corresponding to initial unit strain ϵ_{ci}

$$C_u = \frac{\epsilon_{cu}}{\epsilon_{ci}} = \rho_u E_c \quad\quad\quad\quad [6.4]$$

If C_u is the ultimate creep coefficient, an average value of $C_u \simeq 2.35$.

Branson's model, verified by extensive tests, relates the creep coefficient C_t at any time to the ultimate creep coefficient *for standard conditions* as follows:

$$C_t = \frac{t^{0.6}}{10 + t^{0.6}} C_u \quad\quad\quad\quad [6.5]$$

or alternatively,

$$\rho_t = \frac{t^{0.6}}{10 + t^{0.6}} \quad\quad\quad\quad [6.6]$$

where t is the time in days during which the load is applied. Standard conditions are summarized in Table 6.1 for both creep and shrinkage.[6.4]

6.2.2   Factors Affecting Creep

Creep is greatly affected by the concrete constituents. The coarse aggregate modulus affects the creep strain level. But the cementitious paste and its shear-friction interaction with the aggregate are the constituents that influence significantly the time-dependent load induced strain. Other factors are the environmental effects; here is a summary.

1. *Sustained load.* Creep is proportional to the sustained stress and is recoverable up to 30–50 percent of the ultimate strain.
2. *Water/cementitious materials ratio* $(W/C+P)$. The higher this ratio, the larger is the creep, as seen in Fig. 6.7 relating specific creep to the $W/(C+P)$ ratio.[6.8]
3. *Aggregate modulus and aggregate/paste ratio.* For a constant paste volume content, an increase in the aggregate volume decreases creep. As an example, an increase from 65 to 75 percent lowered creep by 10 percent.[6.9] This behavior is the same whether the coarse aggregate is natural stone or lightweight artificial aggregate.
4. *Age at time of loading.* The older the concrete is at the time of loading, the smaller is the induced creep strain for the same load level.
5. *Relative humidity.* Reconditioning the concrete at a lower relative humidity before applying the sustained external load reduces the resulting creep strain. If creep is considered in two categories—drying creep and wetting creep—

Table 6.1 Standard conditions for creep and shrinkage factors[6.4]

Factors		Variable considered	Standard conditions
		Concrete composition and curing	
Concrete composition	Cement paste content	Type of cement	Type I and III
	W/C ratio	Slump	2.7 in. (70 mm)
	Mix proportions	Air content	$\leq 6\%$
	Aggregate characteristics	Fine aggregate percentage	50%
	Degree of compaction	Cement content	470–752 lb/yd^3 (279–446 kg/m^3)
Initial curing	Curing length	Moist cured	7 days
		Steam cured	1–3 days
	Curing temperature	Moist cured	73.4 ± 4°F (23 ± 2°C)
		Steam cured	≤ 212°F (100°C)
	Curing humidity	Relative humidity	≥ 95
		Member geometry and environment	
Environment	Concrete temperature	Concrete temperature	7.34 ± 4°F (23 ± 2°C)
	Concrete water content	Ambient relative humidity	40%
Geometry	Size and shape	Volume/surface ratio, (V/S)	V/S = 1.5 in. (38 mm)
		Minimum thickness	6 in. (150 mm)
		Creep effects of loading	
Loading history	Concrete age at load	Moist cured	7 days
	Application	Steam cured	1–3 days
	Duration	Sustained load	Sustained load
	Duration of unloading period	—	—
	Number of unloading cycles		
Stress conditions	Type of stress and distribution across the section	Compressive stress	Axial compression
	Stress/strength ratio	Stress/strength ratio	≤ 0.50

the creep strain develops irrespective of the direction of change,[6.8] provided that the exposure is above 40 percent.

6. *Temperature.* Creep increases with the increase in temperature if the concrete is maintained at elevated temperatures while under sustained load. It increases in a linear manner up to a temperature of 175°F (80°C). Its value at this temperature level is almost three times the creep value at ambient temperatures.

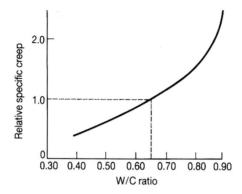

Fig. 6.7 Water/cement ratio effect on the relative specific creep[6.8]

7. *Concrete member size.* Creep strain decreases with the increase in the thickness of the concrete member.
8. *Reinforcement.* Creep effects are reduced by use of reinforcement in the compressive zones of concrete members.

6.2.3 Creep Prediction for Nonstandard Conditions

As the standard conditions for creep described in Table 6.1 change, corrective modifying multipliers have to be applied to the ultimate creep coefficient C_u in Eq. 6.5.

If the average ultimate creep $C_u = 2.35$ for standard conditions, it has to be adjusted by a multiplier γ_{CR} so that

$$C_u = 2.35\gamma_{CR} \tag{6.7}$$

γ_{CR} has component coefficients that account for the change in conditions enumerated in Section 6.2.2. ACI Committee 209 recommends in detailed tabular form the various component coefficients for the γ_{CR} multiplier.[6.4] These are generally based on the studies by Branson[6.6] The tabulated values are given in graphical form[6.6,6.10,6.11] in Fig. 6.8 for the multiplier as follows,

$$\gamma_{CR} = K_h^c \, K_d^c \, K_s^c \, K_f^c \, K_{ac}^c \, K_{to}^c \tag{6.8}$$

where $\gamma_{CR} = 1$ for standard conditions
  K_h^c = relative humidity factor
  K_d^c = minimum member thickness factor
  K_s^c = concrete consistency factor
  K_f^c = fine aggregate content factor
  K_{ac}^c = air content factor
  K_{to}^c = age of concrete at load application factor.

Values of these factors are given in Fig. 6.8.

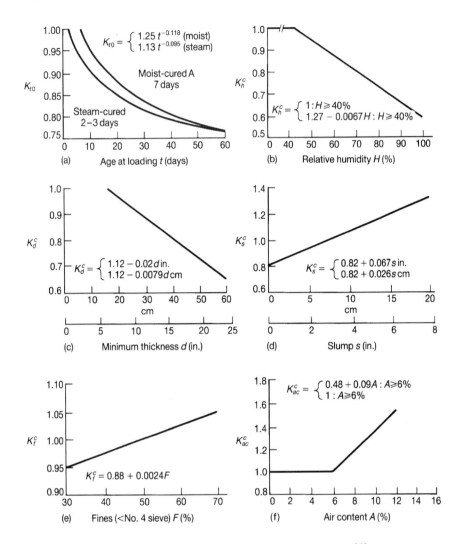

Fig. 6.8 Creep correction factors for nonstandard conditions, ACI 209 method[6.10]

6.3   SHRINKAGE IN CONCRETE

6.3.1   General Shrinkage Behavior

There are two basic types of shrinkage: plastic shrinkage and drying shrinkage; carbonation shrinkage is a third form of shrinkage.

Plastic shrinkage occurs during the first few hours after placing fresh concrete in the forms. Exposed surfaces such as floor slabs are more easily affected by exposure to dry air because of their large contact surface. In such cases, moisture evaporates faster from the concrete surface than it is replaced by the bleed water from the lower layers of the concrete elements. *Drying shrinkage*, on the other hand, occurs after the concrete has already attained its final set and a good portion of the chemical hydration process in the cement gel has been accomplished.

Drying shrinkage is the decrease in the volume of a concrete element when it loses moisture by evaporation. The opposite phenomenon, that is, volume increase through water absorption, is termed swelling. In other words, shrinkage and swelling represent water movement out of or into the gel structure of a concrete specimen due to the difference in humidity or saturation levels between the specimen and the surroundings irrespective of the external load.

Shrinkage is not a completely reversible process. If a concrete unit is saturated with water after having fully shrunk, it will not expand to its original volume. Figure 6.9 relates the increase in shrinkage strain ϵ_{sh} with time. The rate decreases with time since older concretes are more resistant to environmental effects and consequently undergo less shrinkage, such that the shrinkage strain becomes almost asymptotic with time.

Several factors affect the magnitude of drying shrinkage:

1. *Aggregate.* The aggregate acts to restrain the shrinkage of the cement paste; hence concretes with high aggregate content are less vulnerable to shrinkage. In addition, the degree of restraint of a given concrete is determined by the properties of aggregates; those with high modulus of elasticity or with rough surfaces are more resistant to the shrinkage process. See Figures 6.10 and 6.11.[6.8]
2. *Water/cementitious ratio.* The higher the water/cementitious ratio, the higher the shrinkage effects. Figure 6.12 is a typical plot relating shrinkage to aggregate content and significantly to the water/cement ratio.
3. *Size of the concrete element.* Both the rate and total magnitude of shrinkage decrease with an increase in the volume of the concrete element. However, the duration of shrinkage is longer for larger members since more time is needed for drying to reach the internal regions. It is possible that 1 year may be needed for the drying process to begin at a depth of 10 in. from the

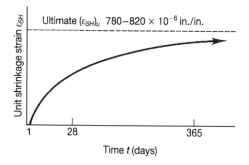

Fig. 6.9 Concrete shrinkage vs. time curve[6.1]

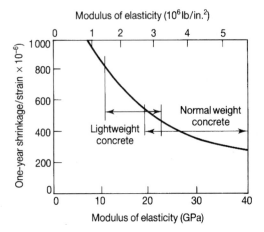

Fig. 6.10 Aggregate modulus effect on shrinkage strain[6.8]

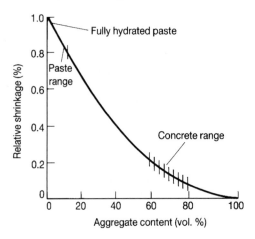

Fig. 6.11 Aggregate content effect on drying shrinkage[6.8]

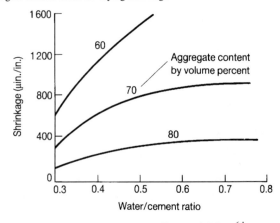

Fig. 6.12 Water/cement ratio and aggregate content effect on shrinkage[6.1]

exposed surface, and 10 years to begin at 24 in. below the external surface, with large members never drying out completely.

4. *Medium ambient conditions.* The relative humidity of the medium affects greatly the magnitude of shrinkage; the rate of shrinkage is lower at high states of relative humidity. The environment temperature is another factor in that shrinkage becomes stabilized at low temperatures.

5. *Amount of reinforcement.* Reinforced concrete shrinks less than plain concrete; the relative difference is a function of the reinforcement percentage.

6. *Admixtures.* This effect varies depending on the type of admixture. An accelerator such as calcium chloride, used to accelerate the hardening and setting of the concrete, increases the shrinkage. Pozzolans can also increase the drying shrinkage, whereas air-entraining agents have little effect.

Plate 30 Society Center, Cleveland, Ohio: composite steel concrete frame (Courtesy Portland Cement Association)

7. *Type of cement.* Rapid-hardening cement shrinks somewhat more than other types, while shrinkage-compensating cements minimize or eliminate shrinkage cracking if used with restraining reinforcement.

8. *Carbonation.* Carbonation shrinkage is caused by the reaction between carbon dioxide (CO_2) present in the atmosphere and that present in the cement paste. The amount of combined shrinkage from carbonation and drying varies according to the sequence of occurrence of carbonation and drying processes. If both phenomena take place simultaneously, less shrinkage develops. The process of carbonation, however, is dramatically reduced at relative humidities below 50 percent.

6.3.2   Shrinkage Prediction for Standard Conditions

The mathematical model for shrinkage prediction in Eq. 6.3 is

$$(\epsilon_{SH})_t = \frac{t^\beta}{b + t^\beta}(\epsilon_{SH})_u$$

where β is a constant and t in days is the time after curing when the concrete has hardened. The value of the ultimate shrinkage strain at *standard conditions* defined in Table 6.1 has the following range;

$$(\epsilon_{SH})_u = 415 \times 10^{-6} \text{ to } 1070 \times 10^{-6} \text{ in./in. (mm/mm)}$$

An average value of $(\epsilon_{SH})_u$ as recommended by ACI Committee 209[6.4] is

Moist-cured for 7 days	$(\epsilon_{SH})_u = 800 \times 10^{-6}$ in./in.(mm/mm)
Steam-cured for 1–3 days	$(\epsilon_{SH})_u = 730 \times 10^{-6}$ in./in.(mm/mm)

A common average shrinkage strain in standard conditions for both moist-cured and steam-cured concretes can be used[6.4] with sufficient accuracy having a value

$$(\epsilon_{SH})_u = 780 \times 10^{-6} \text{ in./in.(mm/mm)}$$

The constant b in the mathematical model of Eq. 6.2 is $b = 35$ for 7 days moist-cured specimens and $b = 55$ for 1–3 days steam-cured specimens. Hence, the shrinkage strain prediction expressions for standard conditions become

After 7 days of moist curing $\qquad (\epsilon_{SH})_t = \dfrac{t}{35 + t}(\epsilon_{SH})_u \qquad$ [6.9a]

where t is the age of concrete in days after curing.

After 1–3 days of steam curing $\qquad (\epsilon_{SH})_t = \dfrac{t}{55 + t}(\epsilon_{SH})_u \qquad$ [6.9b]

6.3.3 Shrinkage Prediction for Nonstandard Conditions

As the standard conditions for shrinkage described in Table 6.1 change, corrective multipliers have to be applied to the ultimate value of the shrinkage strain $(\epsilon_{SH})_u$ in Eqs. 6.8 and 6.9.

If γ_{SH} is the shrinkage-adjusting multiplier, the average ultimate shrinkage strain for nonstandard conditions becomes

$$(\epsilon_{SH})_u = 780 \times 10^{-6} \gamma_{SH} \qquad [6.10]$$

or

$$(\epsilon_{SH})_{u,n} = \gamma_{SH}(\epsilon_{SH})_u \qquad [6.11]$$

where $(\epsilon_{SH})_{u,n}$ = average ultimate strain for nonstandard conditions. Hence, for *nonstandard* conditions, Eqs. 6.9a and 6.9b respectively become

$$(\epsilon_{SH})_t = \frac{t}{35 + t} \gamma_{SH}(\epsilon_{SH})_u \qquad [6.12a]$$

and

$$(\epsilon_{SH})_t = \frac{t}{55 + t} \gamma_{SH}(\epsilon_{SH})_u \qquad [6.12b]$$

The multiplier γ_{SH} has component coefficients that account for the change in conditions enumerated in Section 6.3.1. ACI Committee 209 recommends in detailed tabular form the various component coefficients for the γ_{SH} multiplier.[6.11]

They are generally based on the studies by Branson.[6.6] The tabulated values are given in graphical form[6.6,6.10,6.11] in Fig. 6.13 for

$$\gamma_{SH} = K_H^s K_d^s K_s^s K_F^s K_B^s K_{AC}^s \qquad [6.13]$$

where $\gamma_{SH} = 1$ for standard conditions
K_H^s = relative humidity factor
K_d^s = minimum member thickness factor
K_s^s = slump factor
K_F^s = fine aggregate content factor
K_B^s = cement content factor
K_{AC}^s = air content factor

Values of these factors are given in Fig. 6.13.

6.3.4 Alternate Method for Shrinkage Prediction in Prestressed Concrete Elements

The Prestressed Concrete Institute stipulates for standard conditions an average value of nominal ultimate shrinkage strain $(\epsilon_{SH})_u = 820 \times 10^{-6}$ in./in. (mm/mm).

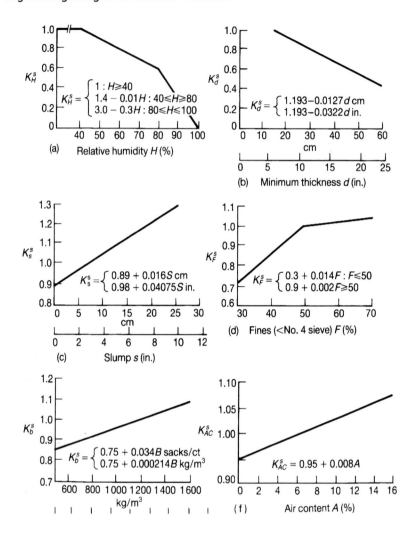

Fig. 6.13 Shrinkage correction factors for nonstandard conditions, ACI method[6.10]

If ϵ_{SH} is the shrinkage strain after adjusting for relative humidity at volume-to-surface ratio V/S, the shrinkage strain is

$$\epsilon_{SH} = 8.2 \times 10^{-6} K_{SH}\left(1 - 0.06\,\frac{V}{S}\right)(100 - \text{RH}) \qquad [6.14]$$

where $K_{SH} = 1.0$ for pretensioned members.

RH = relative humidity in percent

V/S = volume to surface ratio, in.

Table 6.2 Values of K_{SH} for posttensioned members

Time from end of moist curing to application of prestress (days)	1	3	5	7	10	20	30	60
K_{SH}	0.92	0.85	0.80	0.70	0.73	0.64	0.58	0.45

Source: Precast/Prestress Concrete Institute (PCI)

Table 6.2 gives the values of K_{SH} for posttensioned members. Adjustment of shrinkage losses for standard conditions as a function of time t in days is made using Eqs. 6.9a and 6.9b for standard conditions and Eqs. 6.12a and 6.12b for nonstandard conditions.

RH = Relative humidity in percent

V/S = Volume to surface ratio, in.

6.4   STRENGTH AND ELASTIC PROPERTIES OF CONCRETE VERSUS TIME

6.4.1   Compressive Strength f_c'

The cylinder compressive strength increases with time as the cement hydration reaction progresses in the presence of water. As a function of time, the developing strength[6.8] is

$$(f_c')_t = \frac{t}{\alpha/\beta + t} (f_c')_u \qquad [6.15]$$

where α/β = age of concrete in days at which *one-half* of the ultimate (*in time*) compressive strength of concrete $(f_c')_u$, is reached.

t = age of concrete in days.

The range of α and β for normal weight, sand lightweight, and all-lightweight concrete is

$$\alpha = 0.05\text{--}9.25 \qquad \beta = 0.67 - 0.98$$

These constants are a function of the type of cement and the type of curing applied. Typical values for α/β and time ratio are given in Table 6.3 adapted from ACI 209.[6.4]

6.4.2   Modulus of Rupture f_r and Tensile Strength f_t'

The modulus of rupture f_r can be expressed as

$$f_r = g_r \sqrt{w(f_c')_t} \qquad [6.16]$$

g_r has a range of 0.6–1.00 with an average value of 0.65 (In SI units, this range is 0.012–0.021 with an average of 0.0135 for f_r in MPa). And w = unit weight of the

Table 6.3 Values of constant α/β and the time ratio

	Constant (α/β)	Time ratio $(f'_c)_t/(f'_c)_u$ at a given age									
		Days							Years		Ultimate (in time)
		3 d	7 d	14 d	21 d	28 d	56 d	91 d	1 yr	10 yr	
Moist-cured cement											
Type I	4.71	0.39	0.60	0.75	0.82	0.86	0.92	0.95	0.99	1.0	1.0
Type III	2.5	0.54	0.74	0.85	0.89	0.92	0.96	0.97	0.99	1.0	1.0
Steam-cured cement											
Type I	1.50	0.74	0.87	0.93	0.95	0.96	0.98	0.99	1.0	1.0	1.0
Type III	0.71	0.81	0.91	0.95	0.97	0.97	0.99	0.99	1.0	1.0	1.0

concrete in lb/ft^3 for f_r in psi or kg/m^3 for f_r in MPa. Hence, Eq. 6.16 becomes

$$f_r(\text{psi}) = 0.65\sqrt{wf_c'} \tag{6.17a}$$

and

$$f_r = (\text{MPa}) = 0.013\sqrt{wf_c'} \tag{6.17b}$$

Equation 6.17 is applicable for concrete strengths up to 12 000 psi (83 MPa). For normal weight concrete, $w = 145$ lb/ft^3 (2320 kg/m^3); Eq. 6.17 becomes

$$f_r(\text{psi}) = 7.5\sqrt{f_c'} \tag{6.18a}$$

$$f_r(\text{MPa}) = 0.60\sqrt{f_c'} \tag{6.18b}$$

ACI Committee 363 on high strength concrete[6.1] recommends higher values for the modulus of rupture as follows for normal weight concrete:

$$f_r(\text{psi}) = 11.7\sqrt{f_c'} \tag{6.19a}$$

$$f_r(\text{MPa}) = 0.94\sqrt{f_c'} \tag{6.19b}$$

The tensile splitting strength f_t' as recommended by ACI[6.12,6.13] for normal weight concrete of compressive strength range up to 12 000 psi (83 MPa) is

$$f_t'(\text{psi}) = 7.4\sqrt{f_c'} \tag{6.20a}$$

$$f_t'(\text{MPa}) = 0.59\sqrt{f_c'} \tag{6.20b}$$

6.4.3 Modulus of Elasticity E_c

The modulus of elasticity of concrete is strongly influenced by the concrete materials and mix proportions used. The increase in compressive strength is accompanied by an increase in the modulus since the slope of the ascending branch of the stress–strain diagram becomes steeper. For concretes with densities of 90–155 lb/ft^3 (1440–2320 kg/m^3), based on the secant modulus at 0.45 f_c' intercept and compressive strength up to 6000 psi (42 MPa)

$$E_c(\text{psi}) = 33w^{1.5}\sqrt{f_c'} \tag{6.21a}$$

$$E_c(\text{MPa}) = 0.0143w_c^{1.5}\sqrt{f_c'} \tag{6.21b}$$

As the strength of the concrete increases beyond 6000 psi, the measured value of E_c increases at a slower rate such that the value expressed in Eq. 6.21 underestimates the actual value of the modulus. The value of the modulus for compressive strength range 6000–12 000 psi (42–83 MPa)[6.14] can be predicted by

$$E_c(\text{psi}) = (40\,000\sqrt{f_c'} + 1.0 \times 10^6)\left(\frac{w_c}{145}\right)^{1.5}$$ [6.22a]

$$E_c(\text{MPa}) = (3.32\sqrt{f_c'} + 6895)\left(\frac{w_c}{2320}\right)^{1.5}$$ [6.22b]

Figure 6.14[6.14] gives the best fit for E_c vs. f_c' for high strength concretes. Deviations from the predicted values are highly sensitive to the properties of the coarse aggregate such as size, porosity, and hardness. When very high strength concretes—20 000 psi (140 MPa) or higher—are used in major structures or when deformation is critical, E_c should be determined from actual field cylinder test values and the $0.45f_c'$ intercept in the resulting stress–strain diagram.

Long-term effects on the modulus can be viewed in terms of the gain in the compressive strength $(f_c')_t$ such that

$$E_{ct} = E_c\sqrt{(f_c')_t/f_c'}$$ [6.23]

where $(f_c')_t$ = compressive strength at later ages and f_c' = 28 days' compressive strength.

6.5   SERVICEABILITY: LONG-TERM CONSIDERATIONS

Serviceability is evaluated in concrete structural members by their cracking and deflection behavior. Creep and shrinkage effects on cracking and deflection are well established. Both deflections and crack widths increase with time. As a section cracks, its gross moment of inertia is reduced, resulting in reduced stiffness hence larger deformations and deflections. The crack width w and the cracking moment M_{cr} are the principal parameters together with the contribution of the reinforcement (compressive reinforcement in the case of deflection) that determine the long-term behavior of structural elements and systems.

6.5.1   Cracking Moment M_{cr} and Effective Moment of Inertia I_e

Reinforced Concrete Beams

Tension cracks develop when the externally imposed loads cause bending moments in excess of the cracking moment M_{cr}. As a result, the tensile stresses in the concrete at the tensile extreme fibers exceed the modulus f_r of the concrete. The cracking moment for a noncracked section can be computed from the basic

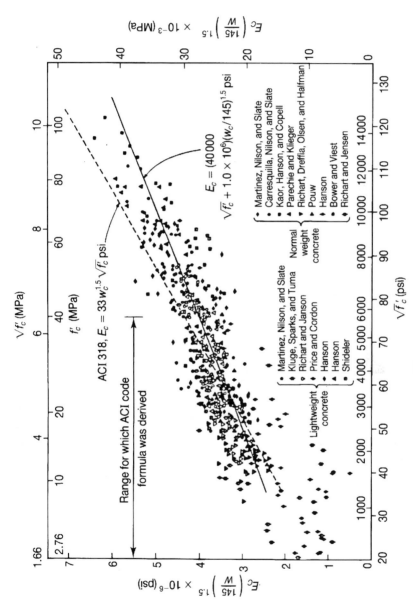

Fig. 6.14 Modulus of elasticity vs. concrete strength[6.14]

flexural formula,

$$M_{cr} = \frac{f_r I_g}{y_t}$$
[6.24a]

$$M_{cr} = \frac{f_r}{S_t}$$
[6.24b]

where f_r = modulus of rupture
  I_g = gross moment of inertia
  y_t = distance form the neutral axis to the extreme *tension* fibers
  S_t = section modulus at the extreme tension fibers

Cracks develop at several sections along a member length. At those sections where the modulus of rupture f_r is exceeded, cracks develop and the moment of inertia is reduced to a cracked moment I_{cr}. At other sections along a span where cracks did not develop, I_g is used for evaluating the stiffness of those sections.

Branson's work[6.6] as the basis of the ACI 318 code, proposes using the effective moment of inertia I_e for cracked section as follows:

$$I_e = \left(\frac{M_{cr}}{M_a}\right)^3 I_g + \left[1 - \left(\frac{M_{cr}}{M_u}\right)^3\right] I_{cr} \leq I_g$$
[6.25]

where M_{cr} = cracking moment
  M_a = maximum moment at the stage at which deflections are being considered
  I_g = gross moment of inertia of the section
  I_{cr} = moment of inertia of the cracked transformed section

The two moments I_g and I_{cr} are based on the assumption of bilinear load–deflection behavior as seen in Fig. 6.15.[6.1] The cracked moment

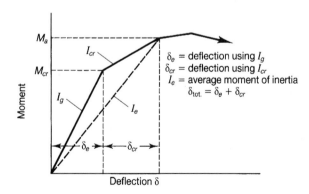

Fig. 6.15 Bilinear moment of inertia diagram[6.11]

of inertia I_{cr} is

$$I_{cr} = nA_s d(1 - 1.6\sqrt{n\rho}) \qquad [6.26]$$

where n = modular ratio = E_s/E_c
$\rho = A_s/bd$
d = effective depth

Equation 6.25 can be rewritten as

$$I_e = I_{cr} + \left(\frac{M_{cr}}{M_a}\right)^3 (I_g - I_{cr}) \leq I_g \qquad [6.27]$$

Continuous Members
For continuous beams, ACI 318-95 stipulates that I_e may be taken as the average value obtained from Eqs. 6.25 or 6.26 for the critical positive and negative moment sections. For prismatic sections, I_e may be taken as the value obtained at midspan for continuous spans. If the designer chooses to average the effective moments of inertia I_e, the following expression can be used

$$I_e = 0.5I_{e(m)} + 0.25(I_{e1} + I_{e2}) \qquad [6.28]$$

where m, 1, and 2 refer to midspan and the two beam ends, respectively.

Improved results for continuous prismatic members can, however, be obtained using a weighted average as follows[6.11] for beams *continuous on both ends*

$$I_e = 0.70I_{e(m)} + 0.15(I_{e1} + I_{e2}) \qquad [6.29a]$$

For beams continuous on one end:

$$I_e = 0.85I_{e(m)} + 0.15(I_{e1}) \qquad [6.29b]$$

Prestressed Concrete Beams
The effective moment of inertia I_e in Eqs. 6.25 or 6.27 is based on different moment levels for M_{cr} and M_a in the case of prestressed concrete beams because of the initial compressive stress imposed by the prestressing force. The M_{cr}/M_a value is defined by

$$\left(\frac{M_{cr}}{M_u}\right) = \left(1 - \frac{f_{TL} - f_r}{f_L}\right) \qquad [6.30]$$

where $f_r = 7.5\lambda\sqrt{f_c'}$
f_{TL} = *total* calculated stress in the member

f_L = calculated stress due to *live load*

M_{cr} = moment due to that portion of the unfactored *live load* moment that causes cracking

M_a = maximum unfactored live load moment

y_t = distance from the neutral axis to the tensile face

($\lambda = 1.0$, normal concrete; $\lambda = 0.85$, sand lightweight concrete; $\lambda = 0.75$, all-lightweight concrete)

In prestressed beams that are partially prestressed by the addition of mild steel reinforcement,

$$I_{cr} = (n_p A_{ps} d_p^2 + n_s A_s d^2) \times \left[(1 - 1.6\sqrt{n_p \rho_p + n_s \rho}\,\right] \qquad [6.31]$$

Plate 31 NCNB Tower, Charlotte, North Carolina: 9000 psi concrete (Courtesy Portland Cement Association)

Effect of Compression Reinforcement

Compression reinforcement in reinforced flexural members and nontensioned reinforcement in prestressed flexural members tend to offset the movement of the neutral axis caused by creep.[6.4] A reverse movement towards the tensile fibers can thus result.

A multiplier λ has to be used to account for increases in deflection as required in the ACI 318 Building Code,

$$\lambda = \frac{\xi}{1 + 50\rho'} \qquad [6.32]$$

where ξ = time-dependent factor for long-term increase in deflection obtained from Fig. 6.16[6.11].

$\rho' = A_s'/bd$

A_s' = area of compression reinforcement (in.^{2})

Nilson[6.14] suggested that two modifying factors should be applied to Eq. 6.32: material modifier μ_m to be applied to ξ and section modifier μ_s to be applied to ρ'. Both μ_m and μ_s have a value of one or less. Combining the two multipliers without significant loss in accuracy, Eq. 6.32 becomes

$$\lambda = \frac{\mu\epsilon}{1 + 50\mu\rho'} \qquad [6.33]$$

For 6000–9500 psi (42–66 MPa) compressive strength tests were conducted with the following range of μ values:

$$\mu \geq 0.7$$
$$\mu \leq (1.3 - 0.00005f_c') \leq 1.0 \qquad [6.34a]$$

Equation 6.34 in SI units for f_c' in MPa:

$$\mu \leq (1.3 - 0.0072f_c') \leq 1.0 \qquad [6.34b]$$

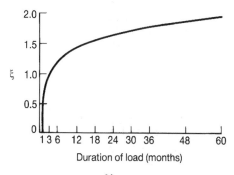

Fig. 6.16 Multipliers for long-term deflection[6.1]

Further evaluations are needed for cases where the concrete strength is higher than 12 000 psi (83 MPa).

6.5.2 Flexural Crack Width Development

External load results in direct and bending stresses causing flexural, bond, and diagonal tension cracks. Immediately after the tensile stress in the concrete exceeds its tensile strength at a particular location, internal microcracks that might have formed start to propagate into macrocracks. These cracks generate into macrocracks propagating to the external fiber zones of the element.

Immediately after the full development of the first crack in a reinforced concrete element, the stress in the concrete at the cracking zone is reduced to zero and is assumed by the reinforcement.[6.1] The distribution of ultimate bond stress, longitudinal stress in the concrete, and longitudinal tensile stress in the reinforcement can be schematically represented as shown in Fig. 6.17.

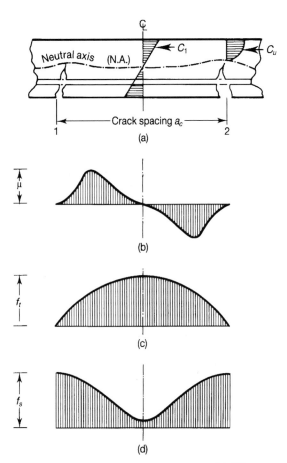

Fig. 6.17 Schematic stress distribution between two flexural cracks[6.1, 6.19]

Crack width is a primary function of the deformation of reinforcement between the two adjacent cracks 1 and 2 in Fig. 6.17 if the small concrete tensile strain along the crack interval a_c is neglected. The crack width would hence be a function of the crack spacing up to the load level at which no more cracks develop, leading to the stabilization of the crack spacing as in Fig. 6.18.

The major parameters affecting the development and characteristics of the cracks are percentage of reinforcement, bond characteristics and size of bar, concrete cover, and the concrete area in tension. On this basis, one can propose the following mathematical model:

$$w = \alpha a_c^\beta \epsilon_s^\gamma \qquad\qquad [6.35]$$

where w = maximum crack width, and α, β, and γ are nonlinearity constants. Crack spacing a_c is a function of the factors enumerated previously, being inversely proportional to bond strength and active steel ratio (steel percentage in terms of the concrete area in tension). ϵ_s is the strain in the reinforcement induced by external load.

The basic mathematical model in Eq. 6.35 with the appropriate experimental values of the constants α, β, and γ can be derived for the particular type of structural member. Such a member can be a one-dimensional element such as a beam, a two-dimensional structure such as a two-way slab, or a three-dimensional member such as a shell or circular tank wall. Hence, it is expected that different forms or expressions apply for the evaluation of the macrocracking behavior of different structural elements consistent with their fundamental structural behavior.[6.15-6.22]

6.5.2.1 Reinforced Concrete Beams and One-Way Slabs

Requirements for crack control in beams and thick one-way slabs, 10 in. (250 mm) or thicker, in the ACI building code[6.16] are based on the statistical analysis of maximum crack width data from a number of sources. Based on the analysis, the following general conclusions were reached[6.15-6.18]

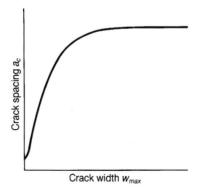

Fig. 6.18 Schematic variation of crack width with crack spacing[6.1, 6.19]

1. The steel stress is the most important variable.
2. The thickness of the concrete cover is an important variable.
3. The area of concrete surrounding each reinforcing bar is also an important geometric variable.
4. The bar diameter is not a major variable.
5. The size of the bottom crack width is influenced by the amount of strain gradient from the level of the steel to the tension face of the beam.

The simplified expression relating crack width to steel stress is given as follows.[6.18]

$$w_{max}(\text{in.}) = 0.076\beta f_s \sqrt[3]{d_c A} \times 10^{-3} \qquad [6.36]$$

where f_s = reinforcing steel stress, ksi

A = area of concrete symmetric with reinforcing steel divided by number of bars, in.^{2} divided by number of bars, in.^{2}

d_c = thickness of concrete cover measured from extreme tension fiber to center of bar or wire closest thereto, in.

$\beta = h_2/h_1$ where h_1 = distance from neutral axis to the reinforcing steel, in.

h_2 = distance from neutral axis to extreme concrete tensile surface

In the ACI code,[6.16] when the design yield strength f_y for tension reinforcement exceeds 40 ksi (276 MPa) cross sections of maximum positive and negative moment have to be so proportioned that the quantity z given by Eq. 6.37

$$z = f_s \sqrt[3]{d_c A} \qquad [6.37]$$

does not exceed 175 kips per in. (30 MN/m) for interior exposure and 145 kips per in. (25 MN/m) for exterior exposure. Calculated stress in the reinforcement at service load f_s (ksi) is computed as the moment divided by the product of steel area and internal moment arm. In lieu of such computations, it is permitted to take f_s as 60 percent of specified yield strength f_y.

When the strain, ϵ_s, in the steel reinforcement is used instead of stress, f_s, Eq. 6.37 becomes

$$w = 2.2\beta \epsilon_s \sqrt[3]{d_c A} \qquad [6.38]$$

Eq. 6.38 is valid in any system of measurement.

The cracking behavior in thick one-way slabs is similar to that in shallow beams. For one-way slabs having a clear concrete cover at around 1 in. (25.4 mm), Eq. 6.38 can be adequately applied if $\beta = 1.25$–1.3 is used.

6.5.2.2 Prestressed Concrete Beams

Crack Spacing Primary cracks form in the region of maximum bending moment when the external load reaches the cracking load. Sometimes, in posttensioned parking garage elements, cracks form in the draped region before forming at the maximum moment region. They can also form at debonded tendon locations. As loading is increased, additional cracks will form and the number of cracks will be stabilized when the stress in the concrete no longer exceeds its tensile strength at further locations regardless of load increase. This condition is important as it essentially produces the absolute minimum crack spacing which can occur at high steel stresses, to be termed the stabilized minimum crack spacing. The maximum possible crack spacing under this stabilized condition is twice the minimum, to be termed the *stabilized maximum crack spacing*. Hence, the stabilized mean crack spacing a_{cs} is deduced as the mean value of the two extremes.

The total tensile force T transferred from the steel to the concrete over the stabilized mean crack spacing[6.17, 6.23, 6.24] can be defined as

$$T = \gamma a_{cs} \mu \sum 0 \qquad\qquad [6.39a]$$

where γ = a factor reflecting the distribution of bond stress
μ = maximum bond stress which is a function of $\sqrt{f_c'}$
$\sum 0$ = sum of reinforcing elements' circumferences

Figure 6.19 illustrates the forces that cause the formulation of the stabilized crack. The resistance R of the concrete area in tension A_t can be defined as

$$R = A_t f_t' \qquad\qquad [6.39b]$$

where f_t' = tensile splitting strength of the concrete. By equating Eqs. 6.39a and 6.39b, the following expression for a_{cs} is obtained, where c is a constant to be developed from the tests:

$$a_{cs} = c \frac{A_t f_t'}{\sum 0 \sqrt{f_c'}} \qquad\qquad [6.40a]$$

The concrete stretched area, namely the concrete area A_t in tension for both the evenly distributed and nonevenly distributed reinforcing elements, is illustrated in Fig. 6.20. With a mean value of $f_t' \sqrt{f_c'} = 7.95$ the mean stabilized crack spacing becomes

$$a_{cs} = 1.20 \frac{A_t}{\sum 0} \qquad\qquad [6.40b]$$

Crack Width   If Δf_s is the net stress in the prestressed tendon or the magnitude of the tensile stress in the normal steel at any crack width load level in which the decompression load (decompression here means $f_c' = 0$ at the level of the reinforcing steel) is taken as the reference point,[6.23,6.24] then for the prestressed tendon

$$\Delta f_s = f_{nt} - f_d \qquad\qquad [6.41]$$

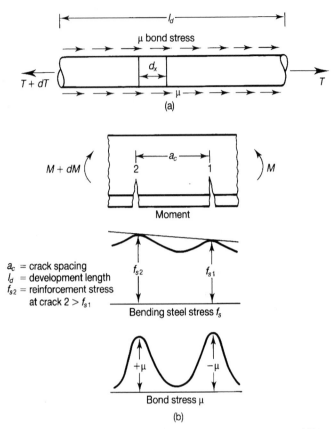

a_c = crack spacing
l_d = development length
f_{s2} = reinforcement stress
at crack 2 > f_{s1}

Fig. 6.19 Force and stress distribution in a stabilized crack in a prestressed beam[6.23]

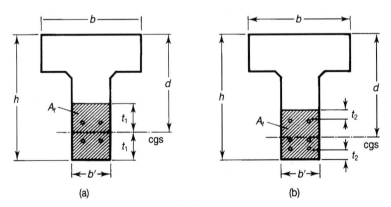

Fig. 6.20 Effective concrete area in tension[6.1, 6.23] (a) even reinforcement distribution; (b) noneven reinforcement distribution

where f_{nt} = stress in the prestressing steel at any load beyond the decompression load

f_d = stress in the prestressing steel corresponding to the decompression load

The unit strain $\epsilon_s = \Delta f_s / E_s$. It is logical to disregard as insignificant the unit strains in the concrete caused by temperature, shrinkage, and elastic shortening effects. The maximum crack width as defined in Eq. 6.35 can be taken as

$$w_{max} = k a_{cs} \epsilon_s^{\alpha} \qquad [6.42a]$$

or

$$w_{max} = k' a_{cs} (\Delta f_s)^{\alpha} \qquad [6.42b]$$

where k' is a constant in terms of constant k.

Expression for Pretensioned Beams   Eq. 6.42a is rewritten in terms of Δf_s to give the maximum crack width at the reinforcement level as follows:

$$w_{max}(\text{in.}) = 5.85 \times 10^{-5} \frac{A_t}{\sum 0} (\Delta f_s) \qquad [6.43a]$$

where A_t units are in.^{2}, $\sum 0$ units are in. and Δf_s units are ksi.

$$w_{max}(\text{mm}) = 8.48 \times 10^{-5} \frac{A_t}{\sum 0} (\Delta f_s) \qquad [6.43b]$$

(where A_t units are cm^2, $\sum 0$ units are cm and Δf_s units are MPa). The maximum crack width (in.) at the tensile face of the concrete is

$$w'_{max} = 5.85 \times 10^{-5} R_i \frac{A_t}{\sum 0} (\Delta f_s) \qquad [6.43c]$$

where R_i is the distance ratio $= h_2/h_1$ with h_2 being the distance from the neutral axis to the extreme tension fibers and h_1 the distance from the neutral axis to the reinforcement centroid.

A plot of the pretensioned beams tests data and the best-fit expression for Eq. 6.43a is given in Fig. 6.21 with a 40 percent spread, which is reasonable in view of the randomness of crack development.

Expressions for Posttensioned Beams   The expression developed for the crack width in posttensioned *bonded* beams which contain mild steel reinforcement is

$$w_{max}(\text{in}) = 6.51 \times 10^{-5} \frac{A_t}{\sum 0} (\Delta f_s) \qquad [6.44a]$$

$$w_{max}(\text{mm}) = 9.44 \times 10^{-5} \frac{A_t}{\sum 0} (\Delta f_s) \qquad [6.44b]$$

for the width at the reinforcement level closest to the tensile face. At the tensile face, the crack width for the posttensioned beams becomes

$$w_{\max}(\text{in.}) = 6.51 \times 10^{-5} R_i \frac{A_t}{\sum 0}(\Delta f_s) \qquad [6.44c]$$

For nonbonded beams, the factor of 6.51 in Eqs. 6.44a and 6.44c becomes 6.83. A plot of the data and the best-fit expression for Eq. 6.44a is given in Fig. 6.22.

Plate 32 101 Park Avenue, New York City: 8000 psi concrete (Courtesy Portland Cement Association)

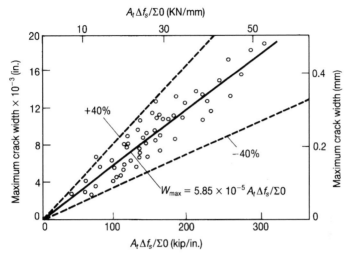

Fig. 6.21 Linearized maximum crack width vs. $(A_t/\sum 0)\Delta f_s$ for pretensioned beams[6.1, 6.17, 6.23]

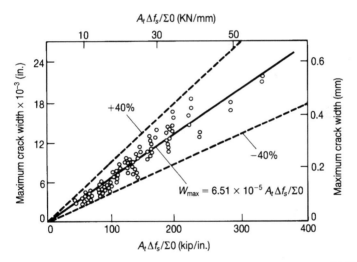

Fig. 6.22 Linearized maximum crack width vs. $(A_t/\sum 0)\Delta f_s$ for posttensioned beams[6.1, 6.17, 6.23]

A typical plot of the effect of the various steel percentages on the crack spacing at the various stress levels Δf_s is given in Fig. 6.23. It is seen from this plot that crack spacing stabilizes at a net stress level range of 30–36 ksi (207–248 MPa).

Cracking of High Strength Prestressed Beams   Analysis of recent work at Rutgers University on the cracking behavior of pretensioned and nonbonded posttensioned beams having cylinder compressive strengths in 10 200–14 200 psi (70.3–97.9 MPa) have resulted in the following expression for the crack width at

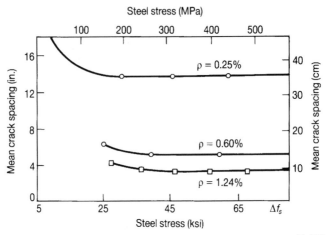

Fig. 6.23 Effect of steel percentage on mean crack spacing in prestressed beams[6.1, 6.17, 6.23]

the reinforcement level of pretensioned members:

$$w_{max}(\text{in.}) = 2.75 \times 10^{-5} \frac{A_t}{\sum 0} (\Delta f_s) \qquad [6.45a]$$

or

$$w_{max}(\text{mm}) = 4.0 \times 10^{-5} \frac{A_t}{\sum 0} (\Delta f_s) \qquad [6.45b]$$

The factor of 2.75 is an average of values from the following statistical expression[6.17] for a reduction multiplier λ_r of w_{max} in Eq. 6.43 such that

$$\lambda_r = \frac{2}{(0.75 + 0.06\sqrt{f'_c})\sqrt{f'_c}} \qquad [6.45c]$$

This reduced crack width due to use of high strength concrete is expected in view of the increased bond interaction between the concrete and the reinforcement.

Other Work on Cracking in Prestressed Concrete Based on the analysis of results of various investigators,[6.25,6.26] Naaman produced the following modified expression for partially prestressed pretensioned members:

$$w_{max}(\text{in.}) = \left(42 + 5.58 \frac{A_t}{\sum 0} (\Delta f_s)\right) \times 10^{-5} \qquad [6.46]$$

This regression expression is very close to Eq. 6.43 by the author. If plotted against the experimental results of the various researchers it gives a best fit as shown in Fig. 6.24.

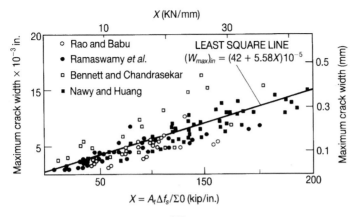

Fig. 6.24 Reinforcement stress vs. crack width[6.17] (best-fit data of several investigators)

6.5.2.3 Two-Way Supported Slabs and Plates

Flexural crack control is essential in structural floors, most of which are under two-way action. Cracks at service load and overload conditions can be serious in such floors as in office buildings, schools, parking garages, industrial building, and other floors where the design service load and overload levels exceed those in normal size apartment building panels. Such cracks can only lead to detrimental effects on the integrity of the total structure, particularly in adverse environmental conditions.

Flexural Cracking Mechanism and Fracture Hypothesis Flexural cracking behavior in concrete structural floors under two-way action is *significantly different* from that in one-way members. Crack control equations for beams underestimate the crack widths developed in two-way slabs and plates, and do not tell the designer how to space the reinforcement. Cracking in two-way slabs and plates is controlled primarily by the steel stress level and the spacing of the reinforcement in the two perpendicular directions. In addition, the clear concrete cover in two-way slabs and plates is nearly constant, $\frac{3}{4}$ in. (20 mm) for interior exposure, whereas it is a major variable in the crack control equations for beams.

The results from extensive tests on slabs and plates by Nawy et al.[6.15–6.20] demonstrate this difference in behavior in a fracture hypothesis on crack development and propagation in two-way plate action. Referring to Fig. 6.25, stress concentrations develop initially at the points of intersection of the reinforcement in reinforcing bars and at the welded joints of wire mesh, that is, at the grid nodal points, thereby dynamically generating fracture lines along the paths of least resistance, namely, along A_1B_1, A_1A_2, A_2B_2, B_2B_1. The resulting fracture pattern is a total repetitive cracking grid, provided that the spacing of the nodal points A_1, A_2, B_1 and B_2 is close enough to generate this preferred initial fracture grid of orthogonal cracks, narrow in width, as a preferred fracture mechanism.

If the spacing of the reinforcing grid intersections is too large, the magnitude of stress concentration and the energy absorbed per unit grid is too low to generate

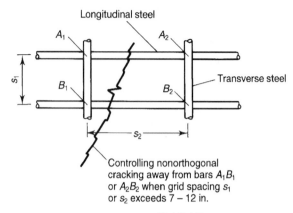

Fig. 6.25 Grid unit in two-way action reinforcement[6.1, 6.17, 6.19]

cracks along the reinforcing wires or bars. As a result, the principal cracks follow diagonal yield-line cracking in the plain concrete field away from the reinforcing bars early in the loading history. These cracks are wide and few.

The hypothesis also leads to the conclusion that surface deformations of the individual reinforcing elements have little effect in arresting the generation of the cracks or controlling their type or width in a two-way-action slab or plate. In a similar manner, one may conclude that the scale effect on two-way-action cracking behavior is insignificant, since the cracking grid would be a reflection of the reinforcement grid if the preferred orthogonal narrow cracking widths develop. Therefore, to control cracking in two-way-action floors, the major parameter to be considered is the reinforcement spacing in the two perpendicular directions. Concrete cover has only a minor effect, since it is usually small, constant, and equal to 0.75 in. (20 mm).

For a constant area of reinforcement determined for bending in one direction, that is, for energy absorption per unit slab area, the smaller the spacing of the transverse bars or wires, the smaller should be the diameter of the longitudinal bars. If one considers that the magnitude of fracture is determined by the energy imposed per specific volume of reinforcement acting on a finite element of the slab, a proper choice of the reinforcement grid size and bar size can control cracking into preferred orthogonal grids.

It must be emphasized that this hypothesis is important for serviceability and reasonable overload conditions both for short-term and long-term behavior. In relating orthogonal cracks to yield-line cracks, the failure of a slab ultimately follows the generally accepted rigid-plastic yield-line criteria.

Crack Control Equation   The basic Eq. 6.35 for relating crack width to strain in the reinforcement is

$$w = \alpha a_c^\beta \epsilon_s^\gamma$$

[6.47]

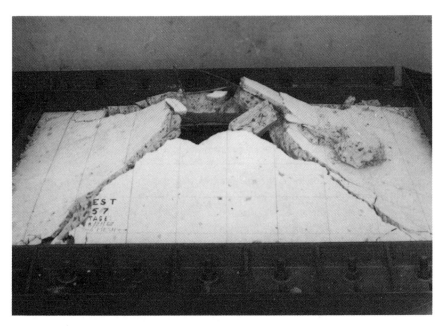

Plate 33 Yield line failure of two-way slab (Tests by Nawy et al.)

The effect of the tensile strain in the concrete between the cracks is neglected as insignificant. The parameter a_c is the crack spacing, ϵ_s the unit strain in the reinforcement, and α, β, and γ are constants to be evaluated by tests. As a result of the fracture hypothesis presented, the mathematical model in Eq. 6.47 and the statistical analysis of the data of 90 slabs tested to failure, the following crack-control equation emerges[6.15, 6.19]:

$$w(\text{in.}) = K\beta f_s \sqrt{G_I} \qquad [6.48]$$

Using SI units, the expression becomes

$$w_{\max}(\text{mm}) = 0.145 k\beta f_s \sqrt{G_I} \qquad [6.49]$$

where f_s is in MPa and all the terms for the grid index G_I in Eq. 6.50 are in mm. $G_I = d_{b1}s_2/\rho_{t1}$, is termed the grid index defining the reinforcement distribution in two-way action slabs and plates. It can be transformed in Eq. 6.48 to

$$G_I = \frac{s_1 s_2 d_c}{d_{b1}} \frac{8}{\pi} \qquad [6.50]$$

where K = fracture coefficient, having a value of $K = 2.8 \times 10^{-5}$ for uniformly loaded restrained two-way-action square slabs and plates. For concentrated loads or reactions, or when the ratio of short to long span is less than 0.75 but larger than 0.5, a value of $K = 2.1 \times 10^{-5}$ is applicable. For a span aspect ratio of 0.5, $K = 1.6 \times 10^{-5}$. Units of coefficient K are in.^{2}/lb.

β = ratio of the distance from the neutral axis to the tensile face of the slab to the distance from the neutral axis to the centroid of the reinforcement grid (to simplify the calculations use $\beta = 1.25$, although it varies between 1.20 and 1.35).

f_s = actual average service load reinforcement stress level, or 40 percent of the design yield strength f_s, ksi.

d_{b1} = diameter of the reinforcement in direction 1 closest to the concrete outer fibers, in.

s_1 = spacing of the reinforcement in perpendicular direction 1, in., closest to the tensile face.

s_2 = spacing of the reinforcement in perpendicular direction 2, in.

1 = direction of the reinforcement closest to the outer concrete fibers; this is the direction for which crack control check is to be made.

ρ_{t1} = active steel ratio in direction 1.

$$= \frac{\text{area of steel } A_s \text{ per foot width}}{12(d_{b1} + 2c_1)}$$

where c_1 is clear concrete cover measured from the tensile face of the concrete to the nearest edge of the reinforcing bar in direction 1.

w = crack width at face of concrete caused by flexural load, in.

Subscripts 1 and 2 pertain to the directions of reinforcement. Detailed values of the fracture coefficients for various boundary conditions are given in Table 6.4. A graphical solution of Eq. 6.48 is given in Fig. 6.26 for $f_y = 60$ ksi (414 MPa) and $f_s = 40$ percent of $f_y = 24$ ksi (165.5 MPa) for rapid determination of the reinforcement size and spacing needed for crack control.

Table 6.4 Fracture coefficients for slabs and plates[6.19,6.22]

Loading type[a]	Slab shape	Boundary condition[b]	Span ratio,[c] S/L	Fracture coefficient (10^{-5} K)
A	Square	4 edges r	1.0	2.1
A	Square	4 edges s	1.0	2.1
B	Rectangular	4 edges r	0.5	1.6
B	Rectangular	4 edges r	0.7	2.2
B	Rectangular	3 edges r and 1 edge h	0.7	2.3
B	Rectangular	2 edges r and 2 edges r	0.7	2.7
B	Square	4 edges r	1.0	2.8
B	Square	3 edges r and 1 edge h	1.0	2.9
B	Square	2 edges r and 2 edges h	1.0	4.2

[a]Loading type: A, concentrated; B, uniformly distributed.
[b]Boundary condition: r, restrained; s, simply supported; h, hinged.
[c]Span ratio S/L: S, clear short span; L, clear long span.

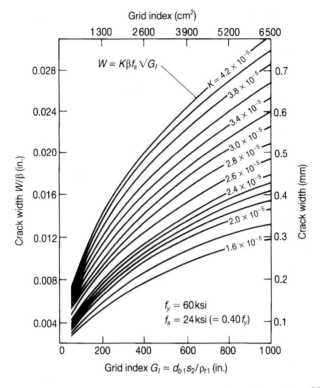

Fig. 6.26 Crack control reinforcement distribution in two-way action slabs and plates[6.1, 6.17, 6.19]

Since cracking in two-way slabs and plates is primarily controlled by the grid intersections of the reinforcement, concrete strength would not be of major consequence. Hence, the value of crack width in two-way action predicted by Eq. 6.48 should not be significantly affected if higher strength concretes are used in excess of 6000 psi (41.4 MPa). It has to be pointed out that in two-way normal slab floors, the use of much higher strengths is not justified in economic terms.

Tolerable Crack Widths in Concrete Structures   The maximum crack width that a structural element should be permitted to develop depends on the particular function of the element and the environmental conditions to which the structure is liable to be subjected to. Table 6.5 is a reasonable guide on the tolerable crack

Table 6.5 Maximum tolerable flexural crack widths[6.1,6.15]

Exposure condition	Crack width, in. (mm.)
Dry air or protective membrane	0.016 (0.40)
Humidity, moist air, soil	0.012 (0.30)
Deicing chemicals	0.007 (0.18)
Seawater and seawater spray: wetting and drying	0.006 (0.15)
Water-retaining structures (excluding nonpressure pipes)	0.004 (0.10)

widths in concrete structures under the various environmental conditions that are normally encountered. Its values are in close agreement with the CEB recommendations[6.22] for most conditions of exposure.

The crack control equation and guidelines presented are important not only for the control of corrosion in the reinforcement but also for deflection control. The reduction of the stiffness EI of the two-way slabs or plates, due to orthogonal cracking when the limits of permissible crack widths in Table 6.5 are exceeded, can lead to excessive deflection both short-term and long-term. Deflection values several times those anticipated in the design, including deflection due to construction loading, can be reasonably controlled through camber and control of the flexural crack width in the slab or plate. Proper selection of the reinforcement spacing s_1 and s_2 in the perpendicular directions as discussed in this section, and *not exceeding* 12 in. (30 cm) center to center, can maintain good serviceability performance of a slab system under normal and reasonable overload conditions.

Long-term Effects on Cracking   In most cases, the magnitude of crack widths increases in long-term exposure and long-term loading. The increase in crack width can vary considerably in cases of cyclic loading, such as in bridges. But the width increases at a decreasing rate with time. In most cases, a doubling of crack width after several years under sustained loading is not unusual.

6.5.2.4   Cracking in Prestressed Concrete Circular Tanks

Circular prestressed tanks are cylindrical shell elements of very large diameter in relation to their height. Hence, it is possible to treat the wall with respect to flexural cracking in a manner similar to the behavior of two-way-action plates. Vessey and Preston[6.27] modified the Nawy expressions developed for two-way-action slabs and plates[6.19] so that the maximum crack width can be defined as

$$w_{max}(\text{in.}) = 4.1 \times 10^{-6} \epsilon_{ct} E_{ps} \sqrt{G_I} \qquad [6.51]$$

Using SI units, the expression becomes

$$w_{max}(\text{mm}) = 0.6 \times 10^{-6} \epsilon_{ct} E_{ps} \sqrt{G_I} \qquad [6.52]$$

where E_{ps} is in MPa and the dimensions of all the parameters of the grid index G_I are in mm. And

where ϵ_{ct} = tensile surface strain in the concrete = $\lambda_t f_p / E_{ps}$
  f_p = actual stress in the reinforcement
  f_{pi} = initial prestress before losses
  λ_t = f_p / f_{pi}
  G_I = grid index = $\dfrac{s_1 s_2 d_c}{d_{b1}} \dfrac{8}{\pi}$
  d_{b1} = diameter of steel in direction 1
  s_1 = spacing of the reinforcement in direction 1 closest to the tensile face

s_2 = spacing of the reinforcement in direction 2

d_c = concrete cover to center of reinforcement, in.

Note that $w_{max} = 0.004$ in. (0.1 mm) should be the limit crack width for liquid-retaining tanks.

REFERENCES

6.1   Nawy E G 1996 *Reinforced Concrete—A Fundamental Approach* 3rd ed. (1st ed. 1985), Prentice Hall, Englewood Cliffs, N.J.

6.2   Ross A D 1937 Creep Concrete Data. *Proceedings Institution of Structural Engineers, London* Vol. 15, pp. 314–326.

6.3   Ross A D 1958 The Elasticity, Creep and Shrinkage of Concrete. *Proceedings of the Conference on Non-Metallic Brittle Materials* Interscience Publishers, London, pp. 157–174.

6.4   ACI Committee 209 Prediction of Creep, Shrinkage and Temperature Effects in Concrete Structures. *ACI Report 209R-92* American Concrete Institute, Detroit, pp. 1–47.

6.5   Shah S P, and McGarry F J 1971 Griffith Fracture Criteria and Concrete. *Proceedings, ASCE J. Engineering Mechanics Division* Vol. 47 No. EM6, pp. 1663–1676.

6.6   Branson D E 1977 *Deformation of Concrete Structures* McGraw-Hill, New York.

6.7   Branson D E 1971 Compression Steel Effects on Long-Term Deflections. *Proceedings, ACI Journal* Vol. 68, American Concrete Institute, Detroit, pp. 555–559.

6.8   Mindess S, and Young J F 1981 *Concrete* Prentice Hall, Englewood Cliffs, N.J.

6.9   Neville A M 1981 *Properties of Concrete* 3rd ed., Pitman Books, London, 1981, 779 p.

6.10   Meyers B L, and Thomas E W 1983 Elasticity, Shrinkage, Creep and Thermal Movement of Concrete. *Handbook of Structural Concrete* ed. F K Kong, R H Evans, E Cohen, and E Roll, McGraw-Hill, Ch. 11, pp. 1–33.

6.11   ACI Committee 435 1995 Control of Deflection in Concrete Structures. *ACI 435 Report* chairman, E G Nawy, American Concrete Institute, Detroit.

6.12   ACI Committee 363 State-of-the-Art Report on High Strength Concrete. *ACI Report 363R-92* American Concrete Institute, Detroit, 1992, pp. 1–55.

6.13   ACI 1995 *Manual of Concrete Practice* Vols. 1–5, American Concrete Institute, Detroit 77 p.

6.14   Nilson A H 1985 Design Implications of Current Research on High Strength Concrete *ACI SP 87-7* American Concrete Institute, Detroit, pp. 85–118.

6.15   ACI Committee 224 Control of Cracking in Concrete Structures. *Proceedings, ACI Journal* Vol. 20 No. 10, American Concrete Institute, Detroit, Oct. 1980, pp. 35–76, Updated version (1995) to be published.

6.16   ACI Committee 318 Building Code Requirements for Reinforced Concrete. *ACI 318-95* and Commentary *ACI 318R-95* American Concrete Institute, Detroit, 1996.

6.17   Nawy E G 1992 Cracking of Concrete: ACI and CEB Approaches. *Proceedings CANMET International Symposium on Advances in Concrete Technology,* Athens 2nd ed., Canada Center for Mineral and Energy Technology (CANMET), ed. V M Malhotra, Ottawa, pp. 203–242.

6.18   Gergely P, and Lutz L A 1968 Maximum Crack Width in Reinforced Concrete Flexural Members. *Causes, Mechanism, and Control of Cracking in Concrete. ACI SP-20* ed. E G Nawy, American Concrete Institute, Detroit, pp. 87–117.

6.19 Nawy E G, and Blair K W 1971 Further Studies on Flexural Crack Control in Structural Slab Systems. *Cracking, Deflection, and Ultimate Load of Concrete Slab Systems. ACI SP-30* ed. E G Nawy, American Concrete Institute, Detroit, pp. 1–41.

6.20 Nawy E G 1972 Crack Control Through Reinforcement Distribution in Two-Way Acting Slabs and Plates. *Proceedings, ACI Journal* Vol. 69 No. 4, American Concrete Institute, Detroit, pp. 217–219.

6.21 Nawy E G 1972 Crack Control in Beams Reinforcement with Bundled Bars. *Proceedings, ACI Journal* October, American Concrete Institute, Detroit, pp. 637–639.

6.22 CEB-FIP 1990 Model Code for Concrete Structures. *CEB-FIP* Vols. 1, 2, 3, 1990.

6.23 Nawy E G 1990 Flexural Cracking Behavior of Partially Prestressed Pretensioned and Post-Tensioned Beams—State-of-the-Art. *Cracking in Prestressed Concrete Structures. ACI SP-113* American Concrete Institute, Detroit, pp. 1–42.

6.24 Nawy E G 1996 *Prestressed Concrete—A Fundamental Approach* 2nd ed., Prentice Hall, Englewood Cliffs, N.J.

6.25 Harajli M H, and Naaman A E 1989 Cracking in Partially Prestressed Beams Under Static and Fatigue Loading. *ACI SP-113* American Concrete Institute, Detroit, pp. 29–56.

6.26 Naaman A E, and Siriaksorn A 1979 Serviceability Based Design of Partially Prestressed Beams, Part I—Analysis. *Proceedings, PCI Journal*, Vol. 24 No. 2, pp. 64–89.

6.27 Vessey J V, and Preston R L 1978 A Critical Review of Code Requirements for Circular Prestressed Concrete Reservoirs. *FIP Bulletin* Federation International Precontrainte, Paris.

7 High Performance Characteristics of High Strength Concrete

7.1 INTRODUCTION

High performance concrete is characterized by special performance both short-term and long-term and uniformity in behavior. Such requirements cannot always be achieved by using only conventional materials or applying conventional practices. The U.S. construction industry is responsible for in excess of $425 billion in new construction (1992), which amounts to approximately 7.3 percent of the GDP and in excess of 6 million relatively skilled and highly paid jobs.[7.1] Concrete is involved as a major component of the total cost of construction. More than 500 million tons of concrete are produced in the United States annually and several times this volume worldwide. It is used in buildings, bridges, roads, airports, seaports, mass transportation systems, waterways, wastewater treatment plants, solid waste facilities, offshore platforms, missile defence silos, and space launching pads. The estimated cost of *replacement* of these concrete-based structures in the United States is estimated to be in excess of $6 trillion.[7.2] Hence, the deteriorating infrastructure is extremely costly to replace. An estimate of more than 400 billion dollars is needed by the turn of the century to replace just the existing highway and bridge system in the United States.

New concrete construction, in recognition of all these statistics, has to utilize the currently available new technology of high strength concrete that has high performance qualities which can eliminate costly future rehabilitation. Consequently, performance characteristics of high strength concrete and allied composites are essential to consider prior to the selection of the type, composition, and compressive strength of the concrete to be used in a structural system.

The main parameters to be considered in determining high performance are

1. Early age strength f'_{ci}
2. Compressive strength f'_c
3. Elastic modulus E_c
4. Modulus of rupture f_r
5. Tensile strength f'_t
6. Strength/density ratio λ
7. Workability and cohesiveness
8. Low permeability to resist:

Plate 34 In 1975 Beryl A became the first drilling and production platform for the North Sea; 118 m water depth and 52 000 m^3 of 50 MPa concrete (Courtesy Dr. George C. Hoff)

       freeze–thaw attack
       chemical attack
       salt penetration
       reinforcement corrosion

9.   Volumetric stability
10.   Ductility and energy absorption as defined by toughness (fatigue resistance)
11.   Constructibility
12.   Bond to parent concrete
13.   Abrasion resistance
14.   Fire resistance

In general, the primary characteristics of high performance concretes can be summarized as easy placement, high early age strength, toughness, superior long-term mechanical properties, and prolonged life in severe environments. The classification of high strength and high performance is given in Table 7.1.

7.2   EARLY AGE PROPERTIES

Early age properties of concrete are important because of the significant construction loads that a structure can be subjected to in the first few days after placement. They are also significant as they impact on its long-term performance. The properties of concrete develop as a result of hydration, namely, the exothermic reactions between water and cement and the interaction with the other pozzolanic cementitious components in the mix. The two principal factors to be considered are described in Sections 7.2.1 and 7.2.2.[7.3]

Table 7.1 High strength, high performance concrete classification[7.16]

Parameter	High strength	Very high strength	Ultrahigh strength
(1)	(2)	(3)	(4)
Strength, psi (MPa)	6 000–14 500 (42–100)	14 500–21 750 (100–150)	> 21 750 (150)
W/(C+P) ratio	0.45–0.30	0.30–0.24	< 0.24
Chemical admixture[a]	WRA/HRWR	HRWR	HRWR
Mineral admixture	Fly ash or combined with SF	Silica fume[b]	Silica fume[b]
Permeability coefficient (cm/sec)	[c]10^{-11}	10^{-12}	< 10^{-14}
Freeze–thaw protection	Air entrainment	Air entrainment	No freezable water

[a]HRWR = high range water reducer (superplasticizer)
[b]Also may contain fly ash.
[c]Coefficient for normal strength concrete $\approx 10^{-10}$.
WRA = water reducing agent.

7.2.1   Influence of Cement Paste Microstructure on the Long-term Performance of Concrete and the Effects of Early Age History on the Microstructure

Cement/cementitious paste is the binding matrix in concrete and is primarily responsible for properties such as strength, impermeability, and volume stability. The rate of the chemical reaction is highest at early age but proceeds at a continuously reducing pace for many years. Factors that control the early age structure of the hardening paste include mix proportions, the temperature and humidity conditions that control the curing process, water/cementitious ratio (W/C + P), other chemical and mineral admixtures, amount of shear during mixing, and degree of compaction or segregation in case of overvibrating. Use of cementitious additives replacing part of the cement in high strength concrete sometimes reduces the impact of some of these factors on long-term performance.

7.2.2   Controlling Temperature Rise at Early Ages

Because of the heat of hydration, the early age temperature of concrete can rise above the ambient temperature. The magnitude of temperature increase determines the extent of its harmful effect on long-term strength, cracking due to high thermal gradients and subsequent cooling, internal cracking of the cementitious paste due to the restraining effects of the aggregate particles, even if they are limited to $\frac{3}{8}$ in. (9.5 mm) size, and the increase in permeability resulting in reduced durability. The use of high strength concretes, which normally achieve high strengths at early age, and less heat generation because of the replacement of part of the cement content in the mix alleviates the effects of temperature rise at early age.

7.2.3   Monitoring High Performance Concretes at Early Age

A *maturing approach* relating the effect of curing temperatures on the rate of concrete strength development is available to monitor the gain in strength.[7.4, 7.5] It is based on the apparent activation energy in kJ/mol. Carino proposes the following expression for computing the equivalent age t_e as follows:

$$t_e = \sum_0^t \exp B(T - T_r) \Delta t \qquad\qquad [7.1]$$

where B = temperature sensitivity factor, $°C^{-1}$
$\quad\quad T$ = average concrete temperature during time internal Δt, $°C$
$\quad\quad T_r$ = reference temperature, $°C$

Work by Carino at the U.S. National Institute of Standards and Technology (NIST) has demonstrated the suitability of this method to high performance concrete mixtures as they are characterized by low ratios of W/C + P and the use of silica fume. Table 7.2 lists the activation energies in kJ/mol for different cementitious combinations.

Another approach is to relate the chemical process to the mechanical consequences in the cementitious matrix.[7.6] The following parameters are continuously recorded:

1. *Electrical conductivity* gives the variations in composition of the aqueous phase in the capillary pores.
2. *Thermal flow* measured by isothermal calorimetry obtains the heat of hydration. This is particularly important as the heat of hydration causes volumetric expansion as a result of the increase in porosity due to crystalline growth and chemical contraction.
3. *Ultrasonic-wave dissipation* measurements monitor the progressive change from the viscoplastic to the solid state.
4. *Speed of sound* values determine the dynamic modulus.

Figure 7.1 shows a typical plot of temperature rise with time in hours after batching.[7.7] Five thermocouples were placed in each 4 ft (122 cm) cube

Table 7.2 Apparent activation energies in kJ/mol obtained from isothermal strength development of concrete and mortar specimens[7.5]

Cementitious materials	W/C = 0.45		W/C = 0.60	
	Concrete	Mortar	Concrete	Mortar
Type I	63.6	61.1	48.0	43.6
Type II	51.1	55.4	42.7	41.1
Type III	43.6	40.1	44.0	42.6
Type I + fly ash	30.0	33.1	31.2	36.6
Type I + slag	44.7	42.7	56.0	51.3
Type I + accelerator	44.6	54.1	50.2	52.1
Type I + retarder	38.7	41.9	38.7	34.1

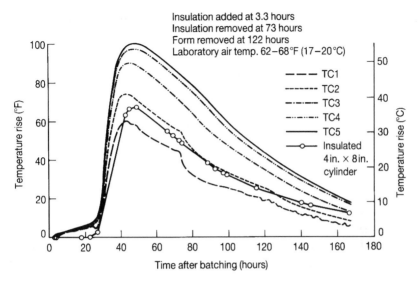

Fig. 7.1 Temperature rise in concrete mix[7.7]

specimen. The maximum temperature differential occurred between 28 and 60 hours after casting and ranged from 28 to 45°F (15.5 to 25°C) between the thermocouple at the center of the cube and the thermocouple at the surface.

7.2.4 Prediction of Strength Gain With Age of Silica Fume High Performance Concrete

Silica fume has an accelerating effect on the early hydration of portland cement as it reduces the retarding effect of lignosulfonate retarders. At standard curing conditions, its contribution as a pozzolan to compressive strength occurs in the first 4–7 days. Consequently, modifications have to be made to the standard equations for the strength f'_{ci} in terms of f'_c. Sadvik and Gjorv[7.8] proposed the following expression:

$$f'_{c,28} = \alpha f'_{ci,n} + \beta (\text{MPa}) \qquad [7.2]$$

where α, β = constants, functions of the silica fume percentage
     n = early age (days)
     $f'_{ci,n}$ = early age compressive strength at age n
     $f'_{c,28}$ = 28 day compressive strength

Table 7.3 gives the values of the constants in Eq. 7.2 so that for 5 percent silica fume content, f'_c at 28 days $= 1.14 f'_{c,4 \text{ day}} + 6.7$ MPa.

Figure 7.2 gives the early age strength development for a 9430 psi (65 MPa) silica fume concrete and the relative strength of the concrete to the 28 day compressive strength f'_c.

Table 7.3 Coefficients for predicting 28
day strength from early age strength

Silica fume (%)	α	n	β
5	1.14	4	6.7
10	1.15	7	10.2
20	1.15	7	15.6

1000 psi = 6.895 MPa.

In summary it is important to monitor the concrete characteristics and mechanical behavior of high strength concrete during the first few days of its placement. Its long-term performance is dependent on its initial development including microcracking and macrocracking, porosity, and deformation due to construction loading at early age. The structural member would have to be designed with an adequate knowledge of the changes in the microstructure of the matrix, the nature of the additives, the composition of the binders, the production process and the rate of strength development through techniques such as those previously described.

7.3 MATURE ELASTIC STRENGTH EXPRESSIONS

Mature elastic strength characteristics denote compressive strength f'_c at 7, 28, 56, or 90 day design levels, elastic modulus E_c, modulus of rupture f'_r, tensile strength f'_t, and the strength/density ratio λ. They define the performance of the material and the structure at initial loading prior to the formation of stiffness-reducing cracks. The values of f'_c, E_c, f_r, and f'_t have already been discussed in detail in Chapter 6 as well as the modification factors that have to be applied due to long-term effects such as shrinkage, creep, and temperature effects. Only a summary of these parameters is given here for completeness.

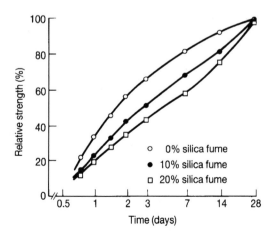

Fig. 7.2 Strength gain in high performance silica fume concrete, $f'_c = 9430$ psi (65 MPa) at 28 days[7.7]

Elastic Modulus E_c

$$E_c \text{ (psi)} = \left(40\,000\sqrt{f_c'} + 1.0 \times 10^6\right)\left(\frac{w_c}{145}\right)^{1.5} \qquad [7.3]$$

where w_c = unit weight of concrete, lb/ft^3
$\qquad f_c'$ = compressive strength, psi

$$E_c \text{ (MPa)} = \left(3.32\sqrt{f_c'} + 6895\right)\left(\frac{w_c}{2320}\right)^{1.5} \qquad [7.4]$$

where w_c = unit weight of concrete, kg/m^3
$\qquad f_c'$ = compressive strength, MPa

This expression is adequate for f_c' up to 12 000 psi (83 MPa). For strengths of around 20 000 psi (140 MPa), a stress–strain diagram based on field tests should be used to determine E_c at this time. Long-term effects on E_c give

$$E_{ct} = E_c\sqrt{(f_c')_t/f_c'} \qquad [7.5]$$

where E_c, f_c' are 28 day values, $(f_c')_t$ = compressive strength at later ages.

Modulus of Rupture f_r

$$f_r \text{ (psi)} = 11.7\sqrt{f_c'} \qquad [7.6]$$

$$f_r \text{ (MPa)} = 0.94\sqrt{f_c'} \qquad [7.7]$$

f_c' in Eq. 7.7 is in MPa.

Tensile Splitting Strength f_t'

$$f_t' \text{ (psi)} = 7.4\sqrt{f_c'} \qquad [7.8]$$

$$f_t' \text{ (MPa)} = 0.59\sqrt{f_c'} \qquad [7.9]$$

Strength/Density Ratio λ

The strength/density ratio is an important parameter because of recent development of several types of concretes and cement-based composites. It serves also as an indicator in cost/strength analysis and optimization of costs.

7.4   WORKABILITY AND COHESIVENESS

High strength concrete performance requires a dense, void-free mass with full contact with the steel reinforcement.[7.9] Slumps have to be compatible with these fundamental needs to achieve high performance. To do so, mix proportioning should provide a workable mixture, easy to vibrate and fluid enough to be able to pass through closely placed reinforcing bars. A slump of 4 in. (102 mm) should provide adequate workability although many high strength concretes with 8–10 in. (200–250 mm) slump have been used. A lower slump would require use of consolidation equipment such as external vibrators with appropriate compaction procedures.

Flow property of a mix depends on its cohesiveness. Aggregates larger than 3/8 in. (9.5 mm) should be avoided in using high strength concretes. They make it easier to achieve high strength, although 1/2 in. (12.7 mm) maximum size aggregate has been successfully used in some locations. Aggregate selection and proper grading is essential to reduce the need for higher water content if stone aggregates are used. High strength concretes have an inherent cohesiveness because of the high volume of fine particles in the matrix.

As discussed in other sections of this book, use of silica fume is fundamental for obtaining very high strength concretes; it produces a fineness almost *one-hundredth* the fineness of portland cement particles (0.1–0.12 μm vs. 10–12 μm) and results in elimination of most of the voids. To achieve the goal of workable high strength and high performance concrete, an increase in the superplasticizer content is necessary.

As stated by Aitcin,[7.10] no high performance concrete can be developed without the use of high range water reducers (superplasticizers). The efficiency of their dispensing action in a high performance quality is well established since such quality essentially depends on the behavior of the binder in the presence of the superplasticizer. It is not difficult to produce commercially a high performance concrete with a W/(C + P) ratio of 0.25–0.30 and obtain a concrete strength of 10 000–14 500 psi (70–100 MPa) with the addition of 17–18 lb/yd^3 (10 kg/m^3) of superplasticizer (see Table 9.4).

As workability is measured by the slump, a loss of slump in the first 20 minutes of mixing can be compensated by the addition of more superplasticizer (high-range water (reducer). Table 7.4[7.7] gives a five-mix range of HRWR plasticizer for different mixes of high performance, high strength concretes. A maximum strength f_c' of 17 250 psi (119 MPa) was achieved in mix No. 4. Compare strengths with Table 9.4 for high strength reactive powder concrete where a strength of 24 000–33 000 (170–230 MPa) is achieved for type RPC200 concrete used in certain bridge structures.

A desirable superplasticizer is not susceptible to slump loss and at the same time improves durability and resistance to sulphate attack. A new superplasticizer in the form of carboxylated acrylic ester (CAE) seems to have these qualities.[7.11] Figure 7.3 shows the loss in slump as a function of agitation time for CAE and for naphthalene sulfonate formaldehyde (NSF) at 70°F (21°C). The slump dropped from 9–7 in. (230–179 mm) using the CAE as compared to a drop from 9 in. to 1.2 in. (230 mm to 30 mm). At 41°F (5°C), the slump drop in the CAE concrete was similar to its drop at 70°F as seen from Fig. 7.4.

The NSF concrete, on the other hand, had a lower slump loss at the reduced temperature of 41°F. It dropped from 9 in. to 4 in. instead (230 mm to 102 mm). Figure 7.5 shows a higher gain in the 28 day compressive strength by using the CAE plasticizer instead of the NSF type (7100 psi vs. 6100 psi respectively). The plasticizer fraction was also lower (0.30 percent by weight of cement for the CAE vs. 0.40 percent for the NSF). The concrete mix did not contain pozzolanic admixtures. Hence, for high performance concretes, a slump-loss-resisting superplasticizer should be used where possible.

Table 7.4 Proportions of commercially available high strength concrete mixtures, US (SI metric) units[7.71]

Ingredient, units per yd³ (m³) concrete	Mix 1	Mix 2	Mix 3	Mix 4	Mix 5	Mix 6
Cement, type I, lb (kg)	950 (564)	800 (475)	820 (487)	950 (564)	800 (475)	551 (327)
Silica fume, lb (kg)	—	40 (24)	80 (47)	150 (89)	125 (74)	45 (27)
Fly ash, lb (kg)	—	100 (59)	—	—	175 (104)	147 (87)
Coarse agg., SSD, lb (kg)[a]	1 800 (1 068)	1 800 (1 068)	1 800 (1 068)	1 800 (1 068)	1 800 (1 068)	1 890 (1 121)
Fine agg., SSD, lb (kg)	1 090 (647)	1 110 (659)	1 140 (676)	1 000 (593)	1 000 (593)	1 251 (742)
HRWR, type F, fl oz (liter)	300 (11.60)	300 (11.60)	290 (11.22)	520 (20.11)	425 (16.44)	163 (6.30)
HRWR, type G, fl oz (liter)	—	—	—	—	—	84 (3.24)
Retarder, type D, fl oz (liter)	29 (1.12)	27 (1.05)	25 (0.97)	38 (1.46)	39 (1.50)	—
Total water, lb (kg)[b]	267 (158)	270 (160)	262 (155)	242 (144)	254 (151)	238 (141)
Water/cement ratio	0.281	0.338	0.320	0.255	0.318	0.432
Water/cementitious materials ratio	0.281	0.287	0.291	0.220	0.231	0.320
28 day compressive strength, psi (MPa)[c]	11 400 (79)	12 840 (89)	13 3300 (92)	17 250 (119)	15 520 (107)	10 600 (73)

[a]Maximum aggregate size: mixes 1–5, ½ in. (12.7 mm); mix 6, 1 in. (25 mm).
[b]Weight of total water in mix including water in admixture.
[c]Tests on 6 × 12 in. cylinders.

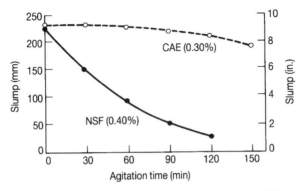

Fig. 7.3 Slump loss vs. time at 70°F using CAE and NSF superplasticizers[7.11]

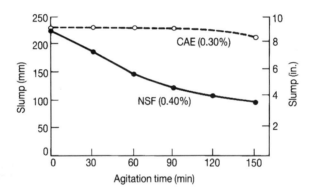

Fig. 7.4 Slump loss vs. time at 41°F using CAE and NSF superplasticizers[7.11]

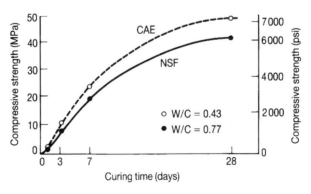

Fig. 7.5 Compressive strength comparison vs. time for CAE and NSF concretes at 41°F curing[7.11]

7.5   PERMEABILITY

7.5.1   General

While concrete deterioration is rarely caused by one single factor, it is somewhat difficult to isolate one single factor from the other interacting causes. Because concrete is subject to external effects that can be chemical, physical, or mechanical, it can be damaged by these adverse factors. Any penetration of the concrete by materials in solution reduces its long-term durability. Hence, permeability which is the degree of penetration of solutions through the concrete, is often the major cause of internal degradation. It is a function of the pore or void structure of the concrete matrix. As the permeability of concrete is lowered, its resistance to chemical attack increases.

The long-term high performance of high strength concrete is due to its compact, extremely low void structure because of the occupation of most of the pore content through the incorporation of supplementary low fineness cementing materials such as slag, natural pozzolan, fly ash, and silica fume. The decrease in permeability is highest when silica fume is incorporated because of its pozzolanic activity and the virtual elimination of bleeding.[7.12] Figure 7.6 gives the relationship between permeability and capillary porosity of cement pastes.[7.13]

Plate 35 Sunshine Skyway Bridge across Tampa Bay, Florida: 4.2 mile long segmental prestressed cable-stayed bridge, one of the longest in the world (Courtesy Portland Cement Association)

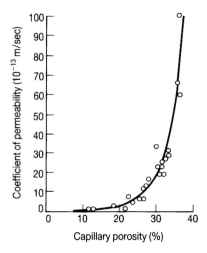

Fig. 7.6 Permeability vs. capillary porosity percentage of cement paste[7.13]

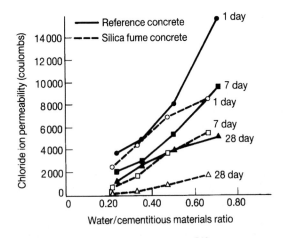

Fig. 7.7 Water/cementitious ratio vs. chloride ion permeability[7.15]

It is important to note that the permeability of the aggregate in the matrix affects the behavior of concrete. If the aggregate has a very low permeability, its presence reduces the effective area through which the flow of liquid can penetrate.[7.14] Hence, the choice of quality coarse aggregate in conjunction with the use of the fine particulate pozzolans such as silica fume reduce permeability to a level below capillary attraction or make the concrete impermeable, as shown in Table 7.1. It is seen that permeability was reduced from 10^{-11} to less than 10^{-13} cm/sec as the strength of the concrete was increased from 6000 psi (42 MPa) to $> 21\,750$ psi (150 MPa). Figure 7.7 shows the chloride ion permeability in Coulombs vs. water/cementitious ratio and the influence of silica fume on the reduction of concrete permeability.[7.15]

7.5.2   Permeability Measurement and Depth of Penetration

In steady flow, the permeability of liquid can be exposed by Darcy's coefficient K (m/sec) in the following expression:

$$\frac{dQ}{dt} = AK \frac{\Delta h}{t} \qquad [7.10]$$

where dQ/dt = rate of water flow, m³/sec
A = cross-sectional area of sample, m²
Δh = drop in the hydraulic head through the concrete thickness, m
L = sample thickness, m
t = flow time, sec.

The depth of penetration d_p can be expressed[7.14] as follows:

$$d_p = \sqrt{2Kht} \qquad [7.11]$$

where h = water head.

7.5.3   Freezing and Thawing Resistance in High Performance Concretes

The freezable water content in a concrete matrix determines the freeze–thaw damage level in a concrete element. Long-term performance as affected by freeze–thaw and wetting–drying principally depends on the degree of water penetration as determined by the coefficient of permeability of the concrete matrix. High strength concretes with high cementitious pozzolan content replacing part of the portland cement, particularly silica fume, possess the lowest permeability, as discussed earlier. Consequently, their long-term performance in their resistance to freeze–thaw and scaling is expected and established.

However, as the silica fume content is increased to 20–30 percent of the cementitious content, freeze–thaw resistance becomes marginal. This is probably due to the high volume content of the condensed silica fume in the matrix making it very dense and adversely affecting water movement.[7.12] This is seen in Fig. 7.8 relating the freeze–thaw cycles to the relative dynamic modulus in percent. Air entrainment seems to perform well regardless of the water/cementitious ratio with up to 15 percent condensed silica fume, and partial cement replacement. On the other hand, nonair entrainment reduces significantly the durability of concrete.

It has also been found that air-entrained lower strength concretes performed somewhat better in long-term resistance to deicing salts and freeze–thaw than higher strength air-entrained concretes.[7.16] Surprisingly, lightweight concrete can be less permeable than normal weight concrete of the same strength. This can be attributed to lightweight concrete mixes with the lightweight aggregate containing very low moisture content, less than 5 percent. The hardened concrete seems to have a water penetration resistance as high as normal weight concrete.

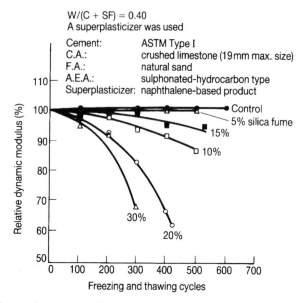

W/(C + SF) = 0.40
A superplasticizer was used

Cement: ASTM Type I
C.A.:   crushed limestone (19 mm max. size)
F.A.:   natural sand
A.E.A.:   sulphonated-hydrocarbon type
Superplasticizer: naphthalene-based product

Fig. 7.8 High strength concrete performance in freeze–thaw resistance for different silica fume contents[7.12]

7.5.4   Chemical Resistance

Chemical attack on concrete results in destructive expansion and decomposition of the cement paste leading to severe deterioration. As discussed by Malhotra et al.,[7.12]

> A permeating solvent as innocuous as water can result in the leaching of calcium hydroxide liberated from the hydration of cement. The ingress of chemicals and acids into concrete react with the calcium hydroxide to form water soluble salts which leach out of concrete, increasing the permeability of concrete, and allowing further ingress of the chemicals. Sulphate reacts with the calcium hydroxide forming ettringite which causes expansion and cracking of the concrete. Silica fume concretes have better chemical resistance than comparable portland cement concretes due to the depletion of calcium hydroxide liberated during the hydration of portland cement by means of pozzolanic reaction with silica fume, thus reducing the amount of lime available for leaching, and due to decrease in permeability resulting from the refined pore structure of the mortar phase of the concrete.

Popovics[7.17] found that silica fume, essential for high strength concretes, inhibited ammonium sulphate corrosion. In those tests, mortar specimens were made with portland cement, blended cement with 20 percent slag, blended cements with 15 percent natural pozzolan, and portland cement with 15 percent silica fume. The specimens were exposed to 10 percent ammonium sulphate solution after 28 days of water curing.

7.5.5 Carbonation

Carbonation is the chemical reaction caused by the diffusion of carbon dioxide (CO_2) in the air into the permeable concrete and its reaction with $Ca(OH)_2$ compound of the hydrated cement such that it carbonates to $CaCO_3$. This decomposition of the calcium compounds in the hydrated matrix combined with alternating wetting and drying in air containing CO_2 leads to an increase in the magnitude of irreversible shrinkage, contributing to crazing of the exposed surface and increase in the weight of the concretes, with progressive scaling of the concrete protective cover to the reinforcement.

Corrosion of the steel reinforcement accelerates with accelerating oxidation because surface scaling leads to progressive deterioration of the concrete. This reaction takes place in spite of the fact that carbonation decreases the size of the pores in the concrete matrix and neutralizes the alkalinity of the cement paste, reducing the pH from 12 to 8 or less. Section 5.7 discusses carbonation in lightweight high strength concrete and gives the penetration depth as a function of time. If K_c is the carbonation coefficient, then, as in the case of lightweight concrete,

$$K_c = \frac{d}{\sqrt{t}} \qquad\qquad [7.12]$$

where d = carbonation depth, mm
  t = time, years

Use of pozzolanic cementitious replacements in concrete such as silica fume or fly ash does not seem to have any significant effect on the carbonation development or rate. However, if scaling is prevented because of the higher tensile strength of the high strength concrete, its dense composition and extremely low pore volume and permeability inhibit the oxidation process that causes corrosion of the reinforcement.

7.6 VOLUMETRIC STABILITY

7.6.1 General

Volumetric changes in concrete affect its long-term durability performance. They are caused by shrinkage, both plastic and dry types, and by creep, which is the lateral flow of the material under external load. Chapter 6 on long-term effects covered in detail the factors, mechanisms, and design expressions which define these volumetric changes. The discussion presented here addresses the high volumetric stability of high strength concretes as it relates to its long-term performance. It also includes the alkali–aggregate reaction and performance, which is a form of volumetric change. It has resemblance to drying shrinkage cracking although it is chemically induced, resulting in excessive expansion of the concrete element, subsequent serious deterioration, and progressive serviceability loss.

7.6.2   Shrinkage

Plastic Shrinkage

Plastic shrinkage occurs during the first few hours after placing fresh concrete in the forms. It is caused by loss of water through evaporation, resulting in *map* cracking in the concrete. It can also result from the downward suction of the water by a subbase or by the formwork material. As a result, negative capillary pressure causes contraction of the paste. Capillary pressures continue to rise within the paste until a critical stage is reached when water is no longer dispersed in the paste.[7.19]

Thereafter, plastic shrinkage stops. If the rate of surface water evaporation exceeds 0.1 $lb/ft^2 \cdot hr$ (0.5 $kg/m^2 \cdot hr$), loss of moisture could exceed the rate at which bleed water reaches the surface, creating negative capillary pressure that leads to the plastic shrinkage cracks. Consequently, it is necessary for high performance of the concrete to protect the fresh concrete from losing moisture through evaporation when it is in its plastic state as well as preventing water loss through negative capillarity towards a subbase such as in highway construction or absorbent formwork.

Drying Shrinkage

Drying shrinkage occurs in the hardened concrete, as discussed in detail in Chapter 6. Relatively limited information is available on the drying shrinkage of high strength concrete.[7.9] A relatively high initial rate of shrinkage has been reported, but after 180 days of drying, little difference has been noted between the *rate* of shrinkage development of normal strength and high strength concretes. Figure 7.9 shows the shrinkage values as a function of age based on tests of high strength prisms after 28 day moist curing.[7.7] The prism sizes are the standard ASTM sizes.

It is important to recognize that the initial curing period and the conditioning of the test specimens before exposure to any drying environment plays a significant role in the performance of concrete, particularly if it is high strength. High strength concrete in general develops less drying shrinkage than normal strength concrete and hence less shrinkage cracking. A one-year drying shrinkage strain in high strength concretes with different mineral pozzolanic cementitious replacements was shown to be $540–610 \times 10^{-6}$ in./in. at 1200 days as compared to normal strength concrete which recorded a value of 930×10^{-6} in./in.[7.19] Normal strength concrete in these tests had W/C = 0.57; the high strength concrete had W/C + S = 0.22, 0.25, and 0.28.

Figure 7.10[7.20] corroborates the findings of Tachibana *et al.*[7.19] in that the incorporation of additional cementitious materials in the mix, such as fly ash and slag, significantly reduces the drying shrinkage, with the silica fume being relatively more effective than the other cementitious materials. This can also be seen in Fig. 7.9.

It is evident that as silica fume or fly ash is incorporated in high strength concrete, the pores in the hardened concrete are reduced in size and in number, thereby increasing the surface tension in the concrete and producing increased

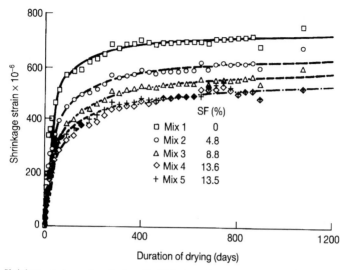

Fig. 7.9 Shrinkage strain vs. time in days for high strength concretes with different cementitious admixtures[7.20]

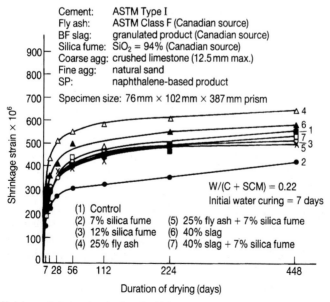

Fig. 7.10 Shrinkage strain vs. time in days for high strength concrete with max. SF/C = 4.8–13.5 percent (28 days f'_c = 11 400–17 250 psi)[7.7]

autogenous shrinkage.[7.12] The permeability of the water vapor through the hardened concrete is also lowered, thereby reducing the drying shrinkage depth in the concrete.

Autogenous Shrinkage

Autogenous shrinkage develops in concretes with low W/C ratios due to internal consumption of water during hydration and when no additional water is provided beyond that added during mixing.[7.18] Drying shrinkage is the difference between the total shrinkage of a drying specimen and the autogenous shrinkage of an identical specimen which has undergone no desiccation. The magnitude of the autogenous part of the total shrinkage is limited in a specimen subjected to normal drying conditions and placed with the appropriate mixing water content to effect a reasonable slump for constructibility. Other conditions which reduce the

Plate 36 One Peachtree Center, Atlanta, Georgia: 12 000 psi concrete 55-floor building 1020 ft high (Courtesy Portland Cement Association)

7.5μm

Plate 37 Portland cement paste with silica fume at 14 days (Courtesy American Concrete Institute)

free water content would promote autogenous shrinkage. But in any case, autogenous shrinkage stabilizes a few weeks after placement, then drying shrinkage becomes controlling.

As indicated by Larrard,[7.21] silica fume, for a given W/C ratio, reduces the mean size of the pores in the hardened concrete as previously discussed. At the same time, it refines the distribution of the pores in the hardened matrix leading to the lowering of the vapor permeability with the accompanying reduction in depth of drying at a given age. His test results also showed that drying shrinkage is lower in high strength than in normal strength concretes. A shrinkage strain of 300×10^{-6} in./in. after demolding (~ 3 days average after casting) was registered for silica fume concrete, and $400-500 \times 10^{-6}$ in./in. in 196 days, as seen from Fig. 7.11. The mix had a cementitious ratio $S/(C + S) = 7.4$ percent, using the mix proportions shown in Table 7.5. Sample size was 3.28 ft (1.0 m) in length.

From the plots of Fig. 7.11 for both portland cement and silica fume high strength concretes, the shrinkage strain ϵ_{SH} is within a range of 400–

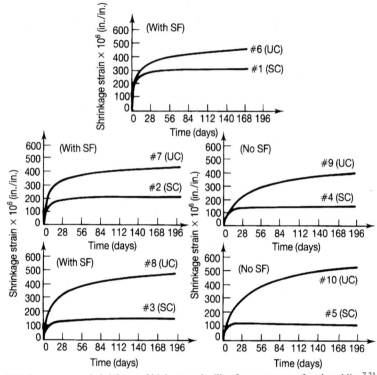

Fig. 7.11 Long-term total shrinkage of high strength silica fume concrete after demolding[7.21]:
SC = sealed curing, UC = unsealed curing, SF = silica fume used in mixes 1, 2, and 3 (unsealed) and
6, 7, 8 (sealed)

550×10^{-6} in./in. (mm/mm) at 196 days, with the silica fume concrete exhibiting
less shrinkage. This is consistent with the values in Figs. 7.9 and 7.10 for a
comparable age obtained by PCA and Malhotra, respectively. The 28 day
compressive strength attained for a similar mix in the Larrard investigation but
with the addition of silica fume raised the strength to 13 700 psi (94.5 MPa) as
compared with the portland cement concrete that achieved only 10 500 psi
(72.5 MPa). See Table 7.5.

From this discussion, it is clear that higher performance resistance to shrinkage
is provided by high strength concretes, with lower shrinkage strain accompanying
higher strengths. Silica fume seems to be comparatively more effective than the
other cementitious supplements in high performance. Shrinkage multipliers for
long-term deflection are presented in Section 6.3 and in an ACI report.[7.22]

7.6.3   Creep

Creep, the flow of material under sustained load, is a very important factor in the
long-term deformational performance of structures. It has been found that the
specific creep and hence the creep coefficient value are less in high strength
concrete (HSC) than in normal strength concrete (NSC) as shown in Fig. 7.12[7.9]

Table 7.5 Mix proportions for shrinkage and creep studies-adapted[7.21]

Ingredient, lb/yd³ (kg/m³)	Portland cement concrete		Silica fume concrete		
	Mix 4	Mix 5	Mix 1	Mix 2	Mix 3
Aggregate	1 715 (1 018)	1 722 (1 022)	1 734 (1 029)	1 710 (1 015)	1 710 (1 015)
Sand	1 163 (690)	1 168 (693)	1 176 (698)	1 166 (692)	1 166 (693)
Cement	763 (453)	767 (455)	768 (456)	763 (453)	763 (453)
Silica fume	—	—	60.7 (36)	60.7 (36)	60.7 (36)
Superplasticizer	33.7 (20)	20.2 (12)	59.0 (35)	55.6 (33)	30.3 (18)
Retarder	3.82 (2.27)	3.82 (2.27)	3.82 (2.57)	3.82 (2.27)	3.82 (2.27)
Added water	263 (156)	295 (175)	204 (121)	248 (147)	290 (172)
Compressive strength f'_c (28 hr), psi (MPa)					
$f'_{c,1}$	3 800 (26.3)	—	—	—	4 000 (27.6)
$f'_{c,14}$	9 200 (63.3)	8 600 (59.3)	12 840 (88.5)	11 170 (77.0)	9 820 (67.7)
$f'_{c,28}$	10 500 (72.5)	9 300 (64.0)	13 700 (94.5)	12 080 (83.3)	10 700 (73.8)
Tensile splitting f'_t psi (MPa)					
$f'_{t,14}$	650 (4.5)	580 (4.0)	—	740 (5.1)	680 (4.7)
$f'_{t,28}$	730 (5.0)	610 (4.2)	840 (5.8)	860 (5.9)	710 (4.9)

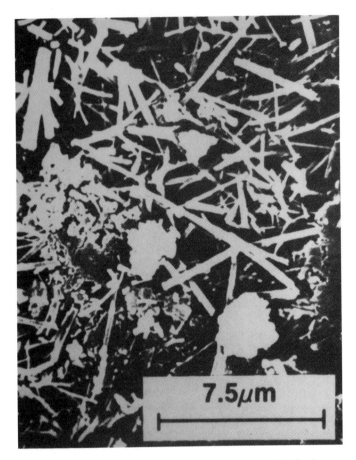

Plate 38 Portland cement paste at 14 days (Courtesy American Concrete Institute)

and Table 7.6.[7.23] It is seen from the data that the ratio of creep strain under sustained axial compression to initial elastic strain in high strength concrete may be as low as one-half the value for low strength concrete. Swamy[7.24] has also demonstrated that both the specific creep and the creep coefficients for high strength concretes are sufficiently lower than those of normal strength concretes to give distinctive performance benefit to HSC. Table 7.7[7.24] gives the creep coefficients and specific creep for portland cement concretes of strength 9140–15 950 psi (63–110 MPa).

Malhotra and coworkers,[7.20] using cementitious replacement additives, gave creep strains lower than values obtained for portland cement concretes, as seen in Table 7.8. The creep strain in concrete with mixes containing silica fumes was in the order of 713–846×10^{-6} unit strain compared to 1005–1505×10^{-6} unit strain in portland cement concrete. Tests by Burg and Ost[7.7] resulted in specific creep values for mixes containing silica fume (mixes 3, 4, and 5) compared with the control non-SF mix 1 shown in Fig. 7.13. It is seen that the specific creep C_c (in./in. $\times 10^{-6}$ per psi) in silica fume high strength concrete (SFHSC) is *one-*

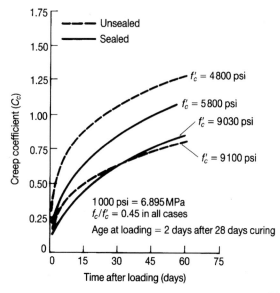

Fig. 7.12 Creep coefficient vs. time for sealed and unsealed concrete specimens[7.9, 7.23]

Table 7.6 Creep coefficient comparisons for normal strength and high strength portland cement concretes[7.23]

Type of concrete	$f'_{c,28}$ psi (MPa)	C_u	$C_{u,HSC}/C_{u,NSC}$
(1)	(2)	(3)	(4)
Low strength	3 000 (20.7)	3.1	1.0
Medium strength	4 000 (27.6)	2.9	0.94
Medium strength	6 000 (41.4)	2.4	0.77
High strength	8 000 (55.2)	2.0	0.65
High strength	10 000 (69.0)	1.6	0.52

third to one-half that of the control concrete (HSC). The values are comparable to those in Table 7.7. Creep multipliers for long-term deflection are presented in Section 6.3 and in an ACI report.[7.22]

Because of the significantly lower creep coefficients for high strength concrete, the volumetric change is kept drastically lower in the SFHSF than the NSC throughout the loading history of the concrete element. This volumetric stability contributes significantly to the high performance characteristics of high strength concretes.

7.6.4   Alkali-Aggregate Reaction

General

Alkali–aggregate reaction is essentially a chemical reaction between the cement matrix and the aggregates in the concrete caused by the interaction between the

Table 7.7 Creep coefficients and specific creep in high strength portland cement concretes[7.24]

Type of concrete	28 day strength f'_c, psi (MPa)	Stress strength[a]	Creep strain × 10^{-6}, in./in. (mm/mm)	Creep coeff.	Specific creep[b]
(1)	(2)	(3)	(4)	(5)	(6)
Granite, 3 day curing (mix 1:2:3:0.43)					
Warm moist	14 790 (102)	33–47	1 475–3 090	2.2–3.0	0.30–0.41 (43–60)
Normal moist	15 950 (110)				
Granite (mix 1:0.625:1.875:0.34)	11 600 (80)	40–58	1 670–2 280	2.1–2.9	0.34–0.55 (50–80)
Expanded slate, lightweight (mix 1:0.88:1.12:0.44)	9 140 (63)	38–56	1 600–2 600	2.3–2.5	0.48–0.86 (70–125)

[a] Age at loading 1–28 days.
[b] Sp. creep × 10^{-6} in./in. per psi (sp. creep × 10^{-6} m/m per MPa) at 650 days for granite aggregates and 500 days for expanded slate.

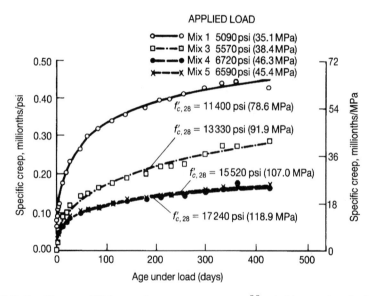

Fig. 7.13 Specific creep of high strength concretes vs. age at test[7.7]: mix 1 is control portland cement concrete; mixes 3 and 4 are with silica fume; and mix 5 is with silica fume + fly ash

hydroxyl ions in the pore water and certain types of rocks. As a result, water-absorbing gel is formed, exerting internal pressure in excess of the tensile strength of the concrete and leading to severe cracking and ultimate loss of serviceability. The factors that cause alkali–aggregate reaction (AAR) are (a) significant amounts of reactive silica in the aggregate, (b) sufficient alkali in the concrete, and (c) presence of substantive moisture.[7.25] AAR is a time-dependent reaction

Table 7.8 Specific creep characteristics of high strength concrete containing cementitious pozzolans: silica fume, fly ash[7.20]

Mix no.	W/(C + SCM)	Silica fume (%)	Fly ash (%)	Slag (%)	Age at loading (days)	Applied stress (MPa)	Duration of loading (days)	Initial elastic strain, $\times 10^{-6}$	Creep strain,[a] $\times 10^{-6}$
1	0.22	0	0	0	35	28.0	385	717	1505
2	0.22	7	0	0	35	28.0	380	677	713
3	0.22	12	0	0	35	28.0	378	694	836
4	0.22	0	25	0	36	28.0	372	750	1069
5	0.22	7	25	0	35	28.0	371	645	749
6	0.22	0	0	40	35	28.0	366	690	1005
7	0.22	7	0	40	35	28.0	364	632	641

that can occur at any time in the service life of the structure if a combination of the three factors is present.

It is important to remember that alkalinity is always present in the concrete to varying degrees (pH 12–8 on average) due to the inherent alkalinity of the cement. If the aggregate also possesses a high degree of alkalinity, the total level of alkalinity of the hardened concrete can result in a very high reactivity that can disintegrate the concrete and a collapse of total structures such as a retaining wall.

If external alkalinity is also present, such as a marine environment or deicing salts, the problem can become very serious. Many cases of failures of retaining walls, piers, and bridge abutments have occurred where the aggregate used in the concrete was unknowingly alkali-reactive. Low alkali portland cements with sodium oxide (Na_2O) content not exceeding 0.6 percent should be used in the concrete mix whenever the aggregate is considered to have even a low alkali content.

Reactive Aggregates

The presence of silica in aggregates, and almost all aggregates contain some silica, is the most serious in alkali–aggregate reactions, depending on the magnitude present. The silica content determines the extent of chemical reaction between the alkalis contained in the cement paste and the reactive forms of silica within the aggregate. Table 7.9[7.18] gives the types of reactive silica in rocks which can precipitate alkali–aggregate reaction, resulting in expansion of the concrete and the accompanying internal tensile stresses. Figure 7.14 gives the percentage expansion relative to the percentage of reactive silica in the aggregate,[7.26] while Fig. 7.15 relates the size of the reactive material to the expansion percentage. The

Table 7.9 Reactive components in rocks causing alkali–aggregate reaction[7.18]

Reactive component	Physical form	Rock types in which it is found	Occurrence
Opal	Amorphous	Siliceous (opaline) limestones, cherts, shales, flints	Widespread
Silica glass	Amorphous	Volcanic glasses (rhyolite, andesite dacite) and tuffs; synthetic glasses	Regions of volcanic origin; river gravels originating in volcanic areas; container glass
Chalcedony	Poorly crystallized quartz	Siliceous limestones and sandstones, cherts and flints	Widespread
Tridymite, cristobalite	Crystalline	Opaline rocks, fired ceramics	Uncommon
Quartz	Crystalline	Quartzite, sands, sandstones, many igneous and metamorphic rocks (e.g., granite and schists)	Common, but reactive only if microcrystalline or highly strained

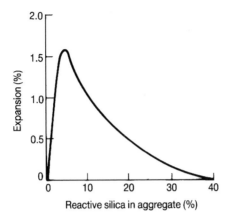

Fig. 7.14 Reactive silica in aggregate vs. concrete expansion[7.26]

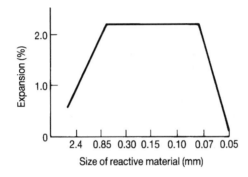

Fig. 7.15 Size of reactive material vs. expansion percentage of concrete[7.26]

alkali content in the cement generating the reaction is schematically described in Fig. 7.15, with maximum expansion occurring at about 0.9 percent alkali content.

The rate of expansion and the total expansion depend, therefore, on the type of reactive aggregate, the alkalinity of the concrete, and the moisture content in the behavior described in Figs. 7.14, 7.15, and 7.16.

Procedures to Neutralize Alkali–Aggregate Reaction

Alkali concentrations in a matrix can be reduced by using cements with sodium oxide content (Na_2O) less than 0.6 percent by weight (see Fig. 7.16). But this is not always possible particularly due to continuing changes in manufacturing processes that make it difficult to achieve such reduction. Another alternative is to use aggregates with the lowest reactive silica content based on petrographic examination and analysis. This is not always economically feasible taking into consideration the increase in cost if the aggregate has to be transported over long distances.

Since the presence of moisture is a prerequisite to alkali–aggregate reaction (AAR), it is important to reduce the W/C or W/C + P ratios to the absolute

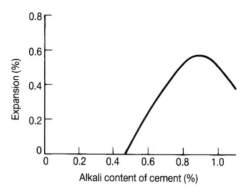

Fig. 7.16 Expansion percentage vs. cement alkali content[7.26]

practical minimum. In this manner, permeability would be drastically reduced as discussed in Section 7.5 and no absorbed water would be available for the long-term alkali–aggregate reaction. In such a case, no adverse expansion can occur when external moisture is not available, as elaborated by Mindess and Young.[7.18]

In addition, cementing pozzolanic mixtures replacing part of the portland cement are found to be effective in controlling expansions associated with alkali–aggregate reaction. They react with the calcium hydroxide in the matrix thereby lowering the pH content of the pore solution. Also, their significant contribution to porosity reduction and the drastic lowering of the permeability of the concrete, as discussed in several other sections of the book, isolate the silica reactive aggregate content from chemically interacting with the alkali in the cement due to the water-tightness available.

Fly ash, blast furnace slag, and silica fume supplementary cementitious pozzolanic additions to the concrete mix (SCM) have shown to be effective ingredients in resisting alkali–aggregate reaction. Table 7.10 gives a good comparison of the effect of the added pozzolanic fly ash (PFA), blast furnace slag (BFS), and condensed silica fume (CSF) in reducing the expansion in concrete,

Table 7.10 Mineral admixtures effect on alkali-aggregate reaction-affected concretes[7.25]

Test series		Expansion (%)	Concrete strength (MPa)	
			Compression	Flexure
Control	Series A1	nil	52.5	4.6
AAR	Series B1	0.732	41.2	1.7
AAR+PFA	Series C1	0.136	51.3	4.5
AAR+BFS	Series D1	0.311	53.8	3.0
AAR − CSF	Series E1	0.256	63.9	5.9

AAR = alkali–aggregate reactive.
PFA = pozzolanic fly ash.
BFS = blast furnace slag.
CSF = condensed silica fume.

Table 7.11 Loss in engineering properties due to alkali–aggregate reaction[7.25]

Reactive aggregate	Expansion (%)	Loss (%)		
		Compressive strength	Flexural strength	Elastic modulus
Beltane opal	0.316	26.0	—	51.1
	0.883	35.5	—	55.8
	1.644	62.6	—	79.3
Fused Silica	0.260	18.4	65.9	45.7
	0.623	39.5	76.7	58.5

provided they are correctly used and of the appropriate quality and amount.[7.25] Coating the aggregates with acrylic or epoxy might be a solution, but its effectiveness and cost does not match the other solution.

Table 7.11 from Swamy's extensive work in this area shows the percentage losses in engineering properties of concrete structures due to the deleterious effect of alkali–aggregate reaction which lead to overstress in the concrete and the reinforcement, resulting in map cracking, splitting and scaling, discoloring of the concrete surface used, and in some cases, ultimate collapse. It is seen from this table that compressive strength can be reduced by as high as 62.6 percent and the elastic modulus by 79.3 percent in some cases with dire consequences.

In summary, high performance can be achieved through ensuring volumetric stability in shrinkage and creep, and in resisting alkali–aggregate reaction expansion by the addition of mineral supplementary cementitious replacements to a portion of the cement in the mixture. At the same time, concrete strengths are considerably increased through this process.

7.7   DUCTILITY AND ENERGY ABSORPTION

7.7.1   Ductility

An increase in concrete strength increases its brittleness. Very high strength concretes are considerably more brittle, as shown in the stress–strain relationship depicted in Fig. 7.17.[7.27] The falling branch of the stress–strain diagram is much steeper and develops at a faster rate as the compressive strength is increased. Confining the concrete not only can arrest the increase in brittleness but increases the ductility of concrete to very high levels such that the strain at failure can be as high as 13 percent or more as compared to 0.3–0.38 percent in nonconfined concrete.[7.28, 7.29]

As discussed in Section 8.8, this increase in ductility is the result of the triaxial state of stress which can raise the axial compressive stress σ_1, to one or more orders of magnitude depending on the magnitude of the lateral stress σ_2, σ_3. With the continuous advancement in concrete technology, it is now easily possible to produce concretes having an unconfined uniaxial compressive strength, f_c', at 28 days of 14 500–22 000 psi (100–150 MPa) in long-span bridges and high-rise buildings in particular. Ductility, as a measure of ability to undergo large

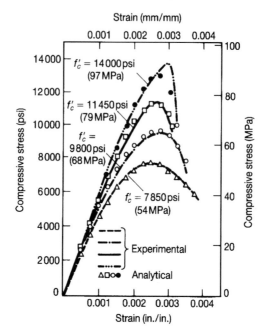

Fig. 7.17 Stress–strain relationships of various strength concretes[7.27]

deformations without failure, becomes important especially in seismic zones. Seismic codes are continually being modified, so designers are required to provide the energy absorbing and dissipating capabilities necessary for a structural system to survive strong earthquake motions; they do this through ductility increase.

Confinement is achieved through the use of spirals or rectangular ties to enclose the longitudinal reinforcement so as to form within the enclosed core a confined concrete area subjected to triaxial stress. The strength of the confined concrete, $\bar{f}_c$, becomes a multiple of the 28 day cylinder strength, f'_c, as shown in Eq. 8.58 of the next chapter so that

$$\bar{f}_c = K f'_c \qquad\qquad [7.13]$$

where K is a function of the confining reinforcement ρ'' in the structural member whether it is a column-beam or a column.

Ductility is measured by the displacement ductility index μ such that

$$\mu = \frac{\Delta u}{\Delta y}$$

where Δu = maximum deflection
  Δy = deflection at yield of reinforcement

A schematic example of the importance of ductility can be illustrated in Fig. 7.18 for a multistorey building subjected to earthquake motion. If one assumes that the ductility ratio for this system is $\mu = 3$, the lateral load acting on the elastic–plastic

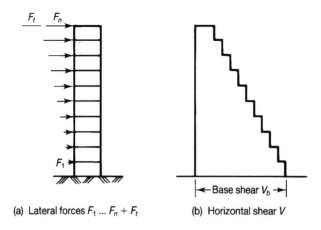

(a) Lateral forces $F_1 \ldots F_n + F_t$ (b) Horizontal shear V

Fig. 7.18 High-rise building ductility to resist earthquake forces

structure would be $1/\mu = 1/3$ of that on an elastic structure. The energy recovered in each loading cycle would be $1/(3)^2 = 1/9$ as great. Hence, a structure which is ductile can be designed for lower magnitudes of seismic forces. Tests[7.31] on both normal weight and lightweight high strength concretes at compressive stresses of 8700–16 680 psi (60–115 MPa) in axially loaded prisms have led to three conclusions.

1. Creep is significantly smaller for high strength concrete than for low strength concrete at the same load level. This confirms the discussions presented in Section 7.6.
2. Increased strength of concrete results in a higher creep–stress proportionality limit.
3. Ductile behavior was achieved only when the confining reinforcement ratio by volume reached 3.1 percent, on the basis of the geometry and size of the specimens tested.

Figure 7.19 demonstrates the significant increase in strain from no confinement in plain concrete to 3.1 percent confinement as the relative strain was increased sixfold.

Ghosh and coworkers[7.32] have studied the behavior of high strength confined concrete subjected to reversible loading. Concrete strengths up to 15 000 psi (103.4 MPa) were investigated. The load was applied to one-half the calculated yield deflection and repeated in both directions for sets of three cycles of reversible load. They found that with the repetition of load cycles at the same deflection level, there was a noticeable deterioration in the load-carrying capacity of beams with higher strength concretes and with smaller amount of confining reinforcement. Decreasing the spacing of the confining ties from 6 to 3 in. (54 to 76 mm) prevented the deterioration of the load-carrying capacity with the repetition of load cycles.

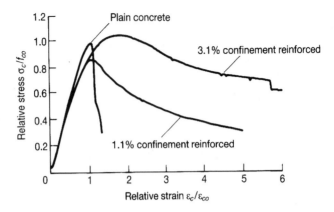

Fig. 7.19 Ductility increase in high strength concrete by confinement[7.31]

A typical confining reinforcement in a shear wall for a high-rise building designed to resist earthquake forces is shown in Fig. 7.20 from Chapter 15 of Nawy[7.27] on the seismic design of concrete structures.

In summary, confinement is a technique to achieve high performance in high strength concrete structural elements through the design of the required steel confining ties or spirals. Confinement can also inhibit long-term cracking and scaling of concrete cover due to other environmental causes.

7.7.2   Energy Absorption and Fatigue

Energy Absorption
Energy absorption is a measure of the toughness of the concrete elements. It is the energy absorbed in breaking a specimen in flexure due to fatigue or dynamic loading. The fatigue resistance of concrete is directly related to the total energy absorbed at failure. Tests in axial compression of high strength concretes at around 11 155 psi compressive strength (76.9 MPa) showed that after one million cycles the strength of specimens subjected to repeated loading varied between 66

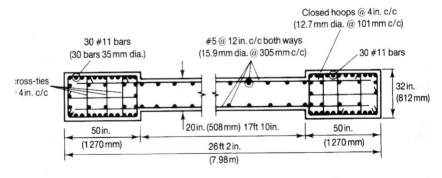

Fig. 7.20 Confining details of shear wall extremities for high-rise building[7.27]

and 71 percent of the static strength for a minimum stress level of 1250 psi (8.6 MPa).[7.9]

But the energy absorption strength can be considerably improved in high strength concrete through the use of steel fibers in the concrete mix, as will be discussed in more detail in Section 9.5. Ramakrishnan in his extensive work on flexural fatigue performance of high strength concretes, particularly lightweight concrete, has found that the endurance limit of lightweight concrete containing silica fume is 14–29 percent greater than that of normal density concrete which has an endurance limit of 0.55. This seems to be because cracks in normal density concrete initially start at the interface of the mortar and aggregate then propagate through the mortar. In lightweight concrete, the stiffness of the aggregate and mortar are mostly the same, producing a higher elastic compatibility and leading to reduced stress concentrations in the mortar/aggregate interface.[7.33] Table 7.12 gives a summary of flexural fatigue strength, endurance limit, and flexural strength after fatigue in the tested specimens.

Fatigue

A substantial increase in flexural fatigue strength results from the addition of fibers. It was found[7.34] that a fatigue limit of 76.3–77.2 percent can be reached in fibrous concrete as compared to 65.0 percent for plain concrete at 100 000 cycles, with the highest performance achieved when using hooked steel fibers. This is seen in Fig. 7.21 for concretes containing 0.5 percent fiber by volume. The fatigue endurance limit using 1.0 percent fiber fraction did not materially change. It was found that (a) fatigue strength is dependent on the anchorage and bond of the fiber reinforcement, and (b) fiber reinforced concrete reaches an endurance limit around 2 million cycles.

Chapter 9 on high strength fiber concrete composites discusses in more detail the toughness and contribution of fibers to the energy absorption of concretes and their high performance characteristics. Also, the dynamic strengths for various types of loading are 5–10 times greater for fiber reinforced concretes than for plain concretes giving them a higher long-term performance.

7.8   CONSTRUCTIBILITY

7.8.1   Definition

Constructibility is the art of placing the proportioned concrete efficiently and economically into a prescribed form such that it meets the short- and long-term requirements for which it is intended. This definition encompasses batching, mixing, transporting, placing or pumping, curing, and control procedures. The first control quality after mix batching is slump control to ensure the appropriate flow properties and cohesiveness. Thereafter all other steps are a logical extension for placement of the concrete.

Table 7.12 Summary of flexural strength, endurance limit, and flexural strength after fatigue[7.33]

Mix	Average compressive strength (MPa)		No. of specimens exceeding 2 million cycles	Average flexural fatigue strength f_{max} (MPa/day)	Average static flexural strength f_r (MPa/day)	Average endurance limit f_{max}/f_r	Average static flexural strength after fatigue (MPa/day)
	28 day	56 day					
				Tested in air			
1	45.0	45.3	6	2.96/63	4.50/60	0.66	4.66/63
2	46.4	48.0	3	3.09/68	4.35/67	0.71	4.48/68
3	52.8	55.2	4	3.03/71	4.74/69	0.64	5.09/71
4	62.4	62.7	2	3.88/74	5.71/74	0.68	5.09/74
5	65.2	66.7	5	3.46/78	5.19/75	0.66	5.19/78
6	56.1	64.3	5	3.12/84	4.73/75	0.66	5.21/84
				Tested in water			
7	50.8	51.9	7	4.05/98	6.12/93	0.66	7.14/102
8	51.6	51.9	6	3.82/106	6.09/96	0.63	6.90/111
9	51.9	52.4	9	4.17/115	6.16/96	0.68	6.85/123
10	61.7	53.1	9	4.03/124	5.98/94	0.67	6.87/132
11	60.8	53.6	6	4.02/134	5.81/94	0.69	6.78/142
12	54.2	53.3	5	3.95/143	5.97/93	0.66	7.12/147

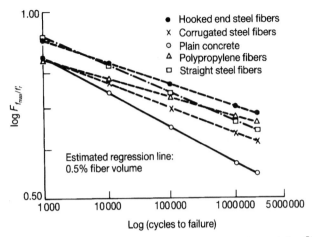

Fig. 7.21 Flexural fatigue strength of concrete with 0.5 percent by volume of fibers[7.34]

7.8.2   Slump

High strength concrete performance requires a dense, void-free mass with full contact with the reinforcement, be it steel or other composite reinforcing elements. Slump is an indirect measure of these qualities in providing a workable mixture, easy to vibrate, and mobile enough to pass through any closely spaced reinforcement.[7.9] As discussed in Chapters 1 to 4, a minimum slump of 3.5–4 in. (102 mm) is needed to provide the necessary workability. This applies to normal density and lightweight density high strength concretes. Additionally, high strength concrete tends to lose slump faster than lower strength concretes. Thus, it is important to prescribe a strict timing schedule for slump measurement and for concrete placement. Also, full attention has to be given for aggregate selection and proportioning, with aggregate size not to exceed 3/8 in. (9.5 mm) in concretes for normal structural elements and concrete strengths in the range of 12 000 psi (82.7 MPa) and higher.

In addition, mock-up forms and slump tests are recommended prior to the final approval of the mix proportions. These will help deciding on the placement procedures, vibration techniques, scheduling, and quality control during the construction period. In the case of pumping, particularly in lightweight concrete, presoaking the aggregate at the concrete plant is advisable. Aggregate suppliers should be consulted for mixture proportioning recommendations necessary to ensure pumpability.

Cohesiveness or stickiness is expected in high fineness mixtures required of high strength concretes, particularly those containing pozzolanic cementitious additions. The cementitious content should normally be the minimum needed for the chosen design strength together with the maximum coarse aggregate content within the workability requirement. Properly designed mixtures should not become too sticky in the field. Stickiness is an indication of possible false cement set, undesirable air entrainment, errors in batching or other changes.[7.9] A review of these factors becomes necessary.

7.8.3   Trial Batching

In high strength and ultrahigh strength concretes, a larger number of trial batches is always needed both in the laboratory and subsequently in field production-sized batching. Strength characteristics at various test ages need to be evaluated as well as the water demand, rate of slump loss, amount of bleeding, segregation, and setting time.

7.9   BOND TO PARENT CONCRETE

The bond between the interacting surfaces of a two-layer system is similar to sandwich construction. The bond between the new concrete and the parent concrete is primarily determined by the shear-friction bond interaction at the interface between the two layers. In order to develop full bond, the surface of the parent concrete has to be well prepared by scarifying the surface through sandblasting, removal of all laitance, *full* wetting of the old surface, and in certain cases applying a cement or other cementitious slurry layer, prior to the placement of the new concrete, or in the preparation of highway potholes for repair.

Research on shear-friction bond interaction has shown that high strength concrete develops a shear-friction bond strength even at early ages of 1–3 days in

Plate 39 Concrete base of Gulfaks C: constructed in 46 ft (14 m) deep dry dock (Courtesy American Concrete Institute)

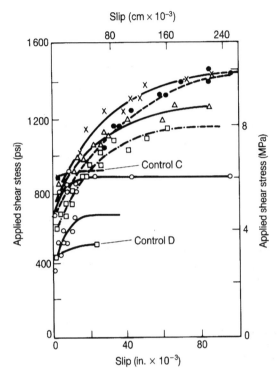

Fig. 7.22 Shear-friction bond strength in two-layer systems of high strength concrete[7.36]

subfreezing temperatures that are considerably higher than allowed by the ACI 318 building code.[7.35, 7.36] Sections 8.7.1 to 8.7.3 give in detail the theory and results of extensive testing. The ACI code limits the maximum frictional bond strength to 800 psi (5.5 MPa), using transverse reinforcement across the interface while these tests and others have shown that with high strength concrete, a strength of 1300 psi (9.0 MPa) is easily obtainable. Figure 7.22 shows that an interface friction-shear strength of 1350 psi can the obtained when using transverse bars through the interface.

In summary, high strength concrete placed against adequately prepared parent (old) concrete develops high frictional bond strength at the interface of a two-layer system and high performance against slip and delamination. Also, bonding of concrete to the reinforcement increases with the increase in compressive strength as the bond is a function of $\sqrt{f'_c}$. And better bond performance is achieved with an appropriate choice of the development length.

7.10   ABRASION RESISTANCE

Abrasion resistance of concrete is of major importance in highway pavements and concrete bridge decks. Service life is of major significance in terms of cost impact on the national economy. It is estimated that in excess of $400 billion will be spent on the replacement or rehabilitation of highway pavements before the end of this century. The largest share will have to be allocated to the deteriorating bridge decks that have been damaged by freeze–thaw, deicing salts and other adverse environmental effects.

Most concretes used thus far in highway pavements and bridge decks have had a lower compressive strength and a resulting lower performance. Strengths of 4000–5000 psi (27.6–34.5 MPa) have been the standard in bridge decks and sometimes lower in highway pavements. With the present availability of high strength, high performance concretes, it is economically sound to use these concretes particularly in bridge decks.

Work available on the abrasion resistance of high strength concretes has shown that an increase in strength results in substantially increased service life, as documented by Gjorv et al.[7.38] In this work, an increase in concrete strength from 7250 to 14 500 psi (50 to 100 MPa) can reduce the abrasion deterioration by almost 50 percent. While the type of aggregate and its abrasion resistance affects the performance of the concrete, its effect becomes less significant at the highest compressive strength levels. Figure 7.23 relates the compressive strength to abrasion. Service life of pavements ranged from 7 years in 5800 psi (40 MPa) to 31 years in 22 200 psi (153 MPa) ultrahigh strength concrete.

7.11   FIRE RESISTANCE

Limited information exists on fire performance of high strength concretes. Tests were reported by the Portland Cement Association[7.39] on 3 ft × 3 ft × 0.33 ft (914 mm × 914 mm × 101 mm) slab specimens with 56 day compressive strengths of 7000–17 500 psi (50–120 MPa). The slabs were fired for 4 hours in accordance with ASTM E199 fire testing procedure. The fire endurance of all the tested specimens was essentially similar, with no spalling of the exposed surfaces.

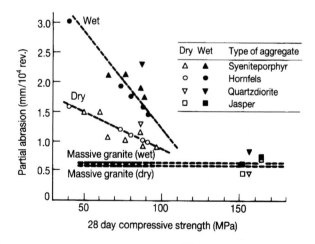

Fig. 7.23 Abrasion resistance of high strength concrete[7.38]

Other investigations, particularly in Norway, showed contradictory fire test results.[7.40] Different types of concretes were exposed to hydrocarbon fire where the temperature reached almost 2000°F (1100°C) in 30 minutes. The strength of the elements ranged between 5800 and 11 600 psi (40 and 80 MPa). Test results showed that spalling and damage occurred earlier than expected and that increasing the moisture content of the hardened concrete increased the severity of the effects. Tests by Williamson and Rashad[7.41] used two reference mixes of 4350 and 11 600 psi (30 and 80 MPa) and two mixes with silica fume having concrete strengths of 7250 and 14 500 psi (50 and 100 MPa). The relative humidity in the concrete was monitored during a storage period of 6 months, being 71–74 percent at testing. There was no internal spalling or internal damage to any of the specimens after being subjected to ASTM E119 fire testing procedures. While no conclusive recommendations can be made at present, it seems that the fire endurance performance of high strength concrete is not too different from that of lower strength concrete.

REFERENCES

7.1   U.S. Department of Commerce 1992 *U.S. Industrial Output* U.S. Dept. of Commerce, Washington, D.C., 1992

7.2   Office of Technology Assessment 1990 Rebuilding the Foundations. *Special Report on State and Local Public Works Financing and Management* Office of Technology Assessment, Washington, D.C., 1990.

7.3   Carino N J, Nawy E G, Jennings H M, and Snell L M 1989 Properties of Concrete at Early Ages. *Engineering Foundation Conference* Santa Barbara, cochair E G Nawy, N J Carino, *Concrete International-Design and Construction* Vol. 11 No. 4, American Concrete Institute, Detroit, pp. 51–54.

7.4   Carino N J, and Tank R C 1992 Maturity Functions for Concrete Made with Various Cements and Admixtures. *Proceedings, ACI Materials Journal* Vol. 89 No. 2, American Concrete Institute, Detroit, pp. 188–196.

7.5   Carino N J 1994 Nondestructive Testing of Concrete: History and Challenges. (*Proceedings, Malhotra Symposium on Concrete Technology: Past, Present and Future. ACI SP 144–30* ed. P K Mehta, American Concrete Institute, Detroit, pp. 623–678.

7.6   Vernet C, and Cadoret G 1992 Monitoring the Chemical and Mechanical Changes in High Performance Concretes During the First Days. *High Performance Concrete: From Material to Structure* Chapman and Hall, New York, pp. 145–159.

7.7   Burg R G, and Ost B W 1994 Engineering of Commercially Available High Strength Concrete. *PCAVR&D Publication No. 1914,* Portland Cement Association, Skokie, Ill., pp. 1–58.

7.8   Sandvik M, and Gjorv 1992 Prediction of Strength Development for Silica Fume Concretes. *Proceedings 4th CANMET/ACI International Conference on Fly Ash, Silica Fume, Slag and Natural Pozzolans, Istanbul ACI SP–132.* ed. V M Malhotra, American Concrete Institute, Detroit, pp. 987–996.

7.9   ACI Committee 363 State-of-the-Art Report on High Strength Concrete. *ACI Report 363R-92* American Concrete Institute, Detroit, 1992, pp. 1–55.

7.10 Aitcin P C 1992 The Use of Superplasticizers. *High Performance Concrete : From Material to Structure* Chapman and Hall, New York, pp. 14–33.

7.11 Collepardi M 1994 Superplasticizers and Air Entraining Agents: State of the Art and Future Needs. *Proceedings V M Malhotra Symposium on Concrete Technology–Past, Present and Future. ACI SP 144* American Concrete Institute, Detroit, pp. 399–418.

7.12   Malhotra V M, Carette G G, and Sivasundaram V 1992 Role of Silica Fume in Concrete: (A Review. *Proceedings International Symposium on Advances in Concrete Technology Athens* 2nd ed., ed. V M Malhotra, Canada Center for Mineral and Energy Technology (CANMET), Ottawa, 1994 pp. 915–990.

7.13   Powers T C, Copeland L E, Hayes J C, and Mann H M 1954 Permeability of Portland Cement Paste. *Proceedings, ACI Journal* Vol. 51, American Concrete Institute, Detroit, 285–298.

7.14   Neville A M 1981 *Properties of Concrete* 3rd ed., (Pitman Books, London, 1981.

7.15   Plante P, and Bilodeau A 1989 Rapid Chloride Ion Permeability Test: Data on Concretes Incorporating Supplementary Cementing Materials. *ACI SP-114* Vol. 1, ed. V M Malhotra, American Concrete Institute, Detroit, pp. 625–644.

7.16   Farny J A, and Panarese W C 1994 High Strength Concrete. *PCA Engineering Bulletin* Portland Cement Association, Skokie, Ill, pp. 1–48.

7.17   Popovics K, Ukrainick V, and Djurekovic A 1984 Improvement of Mortar and Concrete Durability by the Use of Condensed Silica Fume. *Durability of Building Material* Vol. 2, Elsevier Science Publishers, Amsterdam, pp. 171–186.

7.18   Mindess S, and Young J F 1981 *Concrete* Prentice Hall, Englewood Cliffs, N.J.

7.19   Tachibana D, Imai Y, Kawai T, and Inada Y 1990 High Strength Concrete Incorporating Several Admixtures. *ACI SP–121* ed. W T Hester, American Concrete Institute, Detroit, pp. 309–330.

7.20   Bilodeau A, Carette G G, and Malhotra V M 1989 Mechanical Properties of Non Air-Entrained High Strength Concrete Incorporating Supplementary Cementing Materials. *CANMET Division Report* MSL 89–129, CANMET, Energy Mines and Resources Canada, Ottawa.

7.21   Larrard F 1990 Creep and Shrinkage of High Strength Field Concrete. *Proceedings 2nd International Symposium on High Strength Concrete, Berkeley ACI SP 121–28* ed. W T Hester, American Concrete Institute, Detroit, pp. 577–598.

7.22   ACI Committee 435 Control of Deflection in Concrete Structures. *ACI Report 435–96* chairman, E G Nawy, American Concrete Institute, Detroit, 1996.

7.23   Nilson A H 1985 Design Implications of Current Research on High Strength Concrete. *ACI SP 87-7* American Concrete Institute, Detroit, pp. 85–118.

7.24   Swamy R N 1985 High Strength Concrete-Material Properties and Structural Behavior. *ACI SP 87-8* American Concrete Institute, Detroit, pp. 119–146.

7.25   Swamy R N 1994 Alkali–Aggregate Reaction–The Bogeyman of Concrete. *Proceedings V M Malhotra Symposium on Concrete Technology: Past, Present, and Future. ACI SP 144-6* ed. P K Mehta, American Concrete Institute, Detroit, pp. 105–139.

7.26   Woods H 1968 Durability in Concrete Construction. *ACI Monograph No. 4* American Concrete Institute, Detroit.

7.27   Nawy E G 1996 *Reinforced Concrete—A Fundamental Approach* 3rd ed. (1st ed., 1985), Prentice Hall, Englewood Cliffs, N.J.

7.28   Nawy E G, Danesi R F, and Grosko J J 1968 Rectangular Spiral Binder Effect on the Plastic Hinge Rotation Capacity in Reinforced Concrete Beams. *Proceedings, ACI Journal* Vol. 65 No.12, American Concrete Institute, Detroit, pp. 1001–1010.

7.29   Yong Y K, Nour M G, and Nawy E G 1988 Behavior of Laterally Confined High Strength Concrete Under Axial Load. *Proceedings, ASCE J. Structural Division* Vol. 114 No. 2, pp. 332–351.

7.30 Muguruma H, and Watanabe F 1990 Ductility Improvement of High Strength Concrete Columns with Lateral Confinement *Proceedings 2nd International Symposium on High Strength Concrete, Berkeley. ACI SP 121–4* American Concrete Institute, Detroit, pp. 47–60.

7.31 Bjerkeli L, Tomaszewicz A, and Jensen J J 1990 Deformation Properties and Ductility of High Strength Concrete. *Proceedings 2nd International Symposium on High Strength, Berkeley. ACI SP 121–12* ed. W T Hester, American Concrete Institute, Detroit, pp. 215–238.

7.32 Shin S W, Kamara M, and Ghosh S K 1990 Flexural Ductility, Strength Prediction, and Hysteretic Behavior of Ultra-High-Strength Concrete Members. *Proceedings 2nd International Symposium on High Strength Concrete, Berkeley. ACI SP 121–13* ed. W T Hester, American Concrete Institute, Detroit, pp. 223–264.

7.33 Ramakrishnan V, Hoff G C, and Shankar Y U 1994 Flexural Fatigue Strength of Structural Lightweight Concrete Under Water. *Proceedings V M Malhotra Symposium on Concrete Technology: Past, Present, and Future. ACI SP 144–13* Ed. P K Mehta, American Concrete Institute, Detroit, pp. 251–268.

7.34 Ramakrishnan V, and Lokvik B J 1992 Flexural Fatigue Strength of Fiber Reinforced Concrete. *Proceedings International RILEM/ACI Workshop, Stuttgart* Chapman and Hall, pp. 271–287.

7.35 Nawy E G 1985 Shear Transfer Behavior in Concrete and Polymer Concrete Two-Layered Systems with Application to Infrastructure Rehabilitation and New Design. *ACI SP 89–4* American Concrete Institute, Detroit, pp. 51–90.

7.36 Kudlapur S T, and Nawy E G 1992 Early Age Shear Friction Behavior of High Strength Concrete Layered Systems at Subfreezing Temperatures. *Proceedings Symposium on Designing Concrete Structures For Serviceability and Safety. ACI SP 133–9* ed. E G Nawy and A Scanlon, American Concrete Institute, Detroit, Ch. 133, pp. 159–185.

7.37 Transportation Research Board 1986 Strategic Highway Research Program. *TRB Report* National Research Council, Washington, D.C.

7.38 Gjorv O E, Baerland T, and Ronning H R 1993 Abrasion Resistance of High Strength Concrete Pavements. *ACI Compilation 17* American Concrete Institute, Detroit, pp. 81–84.

7.39 Shirley S T, Burg R G, and Fiorato A E 1988 Fire Endurance of High Strength Concrete Slabs. *Proceedings, ACI Materials Journal* Vol. 85 No. 2, American Concrete Institute, Detroit, pp. 102–108.

7.40 Gjorv O E 1992 High Strength Concrete. *Proceedings International CANMET Conference on Advances in Concrete Technology, Athens* ed. V M Malhotra, CANMET–Natural Resources Canada, Ottawa, 1992, pp. 19–82.

7.41 Williamson R B, and Rashad A I 1987 A Comparison of ASTM E119 Fire Endurance Exposure of Two EMSAC Concretes with Similar Conventional Concretes. *University of California Report* Fire Research Laboratory, University of California, Berkeley.

7.42 Mather B 1993 Concrete in Transportation: Desired Performance and Specifications. *Transactions No. 1382,* Transportation Research Board, National Research Council, Washington, D.C., pp. 5–10.

8 Micro and Macromechanics of High Strength Concrete

8.1 HISTORICAL REVIEW

Early studies of cracking in concrete led to the realization that the behavior of concrete whether under compressive or tensile loading is closely related to crack formation in concrete elements. With increased stress, microscopic cracks—called microcracks—form at the aggregate–mortar interface and propagate through the surrounding mortar. A microcrack is defined as a crack not discernible to the naked eye. The limit of ability for the naked eye is one-fifth of a millimeter (200 μm). The magnification capability of present electron microscopes is on the order of $10^5 \times$ the human eye capability, while a macrocrack is easily discernible to the naked eye. The importance of studying microcracking behavior lies in the fact that load–deformation behavior seems to be directly related to the microcracks. The initiation of major mortar cracking corresponds to an observed increase in the Poisson's ratio of the concrete and the term *discontinuity stress* is accepted as corresponding to the stress in which this change in material behavior occurs.[8.1]

At about the same time in the early 1960s, researchers started applying the principles of fracture mechanics to the studies of cracking of concrete under external stress. Griffith's fracture theory[8.2] served as an entry tool in studying the brittle failure of concrete. Kaplan[8.3] was the first to apply the Griffith theory to concrete, applying the stress intensity factor K_c approach. Additional extensive work since then was done by many, including Kaplan, Meyers, Slate, Bažant, Gerstle, Cohen, and others.[8.5] The accumulated research moved this area into a developed level of application. Yet, considerable progress is needed in order that the concept can be readily used for the evaluation and design of actual concrete elements and systems.

8.2 MICROSCOPIC AND MACROSCOPIC BEHAVIOR

The behavior of concrete under compressive and tensile loads is dependent on the level of developing cracks. Volume changes in the cement paste prior to loading generate interfacial *microscopic* bond cracks between the aggregate and mortar interface.[8.6] As additional short-term loading is applied to a specimen, additional significant cracks start to initiate through the matrix when the compressive stress

Plate 40 Dain-Bosworth/Neiman Marcus Plaza, Minneapolis, Minnesota: 14 000 psi concrete (Courtesy Portland Cement Association)

in the concrete achieves 30 percent of its strength. With further increase in loading, fracture lines and fracture surfaces develop with a rapid propagation of *macrocracks* through the medium.

Micromechanics studies of the cracking mechanisms in concrete and mortar are intended to predict the fundamental behavior of concrete by means of analyzing the microscopic cracking behavior of the constituent materials in the mix, particularly those of the cement paste matrix. Macromechanics studies, on the other hand, cover the planar and global behavior of the concrete element and interpret and analyze the development of fracture planes and curvilinear surfaces through such elements, including crack propagation and fracture.

Cracks are initiated when the stress conditions exceed the strength of the matrix, the bond frictional strength between the matrix and the aggregate, or the shear strength of the medium. At any point in a loaded continuum, it is always possible to find three mutually orthogonal planes subjected to zero shear. From basic mechanics, these planes are the planes of principal stresses σ_{p1}, σ_{p2}, and σ_{p3}. But concrete, being nonhomogeneous and not perfectly elastic, is found under a certain set of combined stresses to be able to support considerably higher stresses than the cylinder uniaxial strength. Under another set of combined stresses, the same concrete could crack or fail even though none of the acting sets of stresses are as high as the uniaxial cylinder strength of the medium.[8.7] This is because the deformation is high enough for the generation of cracks and fracture lines as the deformational behavior is totally dependent on the relative values and sense of the multiaxial stresses.

8.3   MICRO AND MACROMECHANICS THEORIES

To study the deformational characteristics resulting from the stress conditions described in Section 8.2, the failure mechanism can be interpreted by several means:

1. *Classical failure criteria* involving the maximum tensile strain criterion, the maximum octahedral shear stress criterion, and the empirical stress criterion.
2. *Crack propagation mechanics*
3. *Fracture mechanics* involving a stochastic crack theory and a blunt crack theory. The blunt crack theory will be emphasized within the scope of this chapter.

8.4   CLASSICAL FAILURE THEORIES

8.4.1   Maximum Tensile Strain Criterion

The maximum tensile strain criterion assumes that the concrete is a linear elastic material up to a limiting value of principal tensile strain ϵ_{tf} at which failure is assumed to precipitate. Hence, in uniaxial compression, failure occurs when

$$f'_c = \frac{E_c \epsilon_{tf}}{\mu} \qquad [8.1]$$

where μ =Poisson's ratio.

From classical mechanics, a specimen subjected to a triaxial state of stress undergoes a strain ϵ_3 in the direction of the minimum principal stress,

$$\epsilon_3 = \frac{[\sigma_3 - \mu(\sigma_1 + \sigma_2)]}{E_c} \qquad [8.2]$$

From Eqs. 8.1 and 8.2,

$$\sigma_{1f} = \frac{\sigma_{3f}}{\mu} - \sigma_2 + f'_c \qquad [8.3]$$

or

$$f'_c = \frac{\sigma_{3f}}{\mu} - \sigma_2 - \sigma_{1f} \qquad [8.4]$$

From Eq. 8.3b, this criterion seems to incorrectly predict that the strength goes down when the intermediate compressive stress σ_2 is increased,[8.7] hence cannot be used reliably.

8.4.2   Maximum Octahedral Shear Stress Criterion

The maximum octahedral shear stress criterion assumes that failure occurs when the octahedral shear stress, τ_0, reaches a value c characteristic of the material when subjected to triaxial state of stress:

$$c = \frac{1}{3} \left[(\sigma_{1f} - \sigma_{2f})^2 + (\sigma_{2f} - \sigma_{3f})^2 + (\sigma_{3f} - \sigma_{1f})^2 \right]^{1/2} \qquad [8.5]$$

For a biaxial stress condition where $\sigma_3 = 0$, one can reduce Eq. 8.4 to the following[8.7]:

$$\sigma_{1f}^2 + \sigma_{2f}^2 - \sigma_{1f}\sigma_{2f} = 9\frac{c^2}{2} \qquad [8.6]$$

From Eq. 8.5, $\sigma_{1f} = f'_c$ when $\sigma_{2f} = \sigma_{1f}$ and $= 1.15f'_c$ when $\sigma_{2f} = \frac{1}{2}\sigma_{1f}$.

While this criterion is in reasonable agreement with test results from biaxial compression it incorrectly predicts the strength in concrete when one of the principal stresses is in tension.

8.4.3   Other Classical Failure Criteria

Other classical criteria are mentioned for their historical significance. These include the Mohr–Coulomb criterion and the Prager–Drucker criterion. Additionally, Hobbs developed an empirical stress criterion[8.7] assuming that $\sigma_{1f} = f'_c(\sigma_{3f}/\mu)^k$ where $k = 0.4 + 7.7f'_c$. The latter, however, does not apply if σ_{3f} is in tension. This is because uniaxial tensile strength is more affected by the shear friction aggregate–paste interlock and the aggregate properties than by the compressive strength of concrete.

8.5   CRACK PROPAGATION THEORY

In the crack propagation theory the cement paste is initially considered at the microscopic level as the pores are at least ten times larger than the gel pores. Concrete which develops cracks because of bleeding, capillary shrinkage, and plastic shrinkage is analyzed at the macroscopic level. The crack length and propagation is modeled using a combination of linear elastic fracture mechanics and Monte Carlo computer simulation techniques to simulate the randomness of the pores and the cracks.[8.8]

A single crack is considered developing and stabilizing along the compressive axis, with the crack length increasing with the increase in load. If an arbitrary inclined crack in a homogeneous plate is subjected to uniaxial compression, it will extend at both ends along the compressive axis with the increasing load. Propagation of the crack becomes unstable when the crack length exceeds the critical length, thereby resulting in failure. The relation between the load and the crack length, as in Fig. 8.1, can be expressed[8.3] as

$$q = \frac{\sqrt{l_2}}{l_1} \frac{K_{1c}}{2A(\alpha_1 \rho)} \frac{\sqrt{\pi}}{l_1} \qquad [8.7]$$

where q = external compressive load intensity
l_1 = half the initial length of the inclined crack
l_2 = length of the branching crack
$A(\alpha_1 \rho) = \sin^2 \alpha \cos \alpha - \rho \sin^3 \alpha$
K_{1c} = strength factor

As the coarse aggregate is introduced into the matrix, a partial linear bond crack, which exists or initiates along the aggregate–mortar interface, continues to grow in an unstable manner until its length exceeds the projected length of the aggregate. This crack propagates parallel to the load axis and combines with the mortar cracks until failure precipitates.

A complete model of randomly oriented aggregates in a mortar matrix has to be considered, as the crack propagating from an aggregate piece meets the next aggregate piece. Depending on the angle of inclination of the second crack interface with the compressive axis, the crack may stop, go around the second aggregate piece, or penetrate through the aggregate without deviation from its linear path. Figure 8.2 shows the propagating path of the cracks[8.6] for both

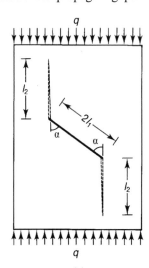

Fig. 8.1 Crack propagation from a random crack[8.6]

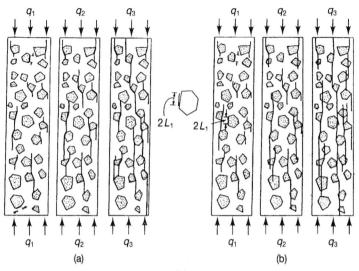

Fig. 8.2 Crack propagation in concrete medium[8.6]: (a) normal strength concrete; (b) high strength concrete

normal strength and high strength concretes. The crack, which grows parallel to the load and meets the next aggregate piece in its path, either propagates around the aggregate–gel interface or within the mortar medium depending on the strength factor K_{IC} of the mortar and K_{IIC} of the interface. The corresponding expressions for the compressive load intensity would be[8.8]

$$q_I = \frac{2K_{IC}\sqrt{\pi l_2}/L_1}{A(\alpha,\rho)[3\cos\frac{1}{2}\beta + \cos\frac{3}{2}\beta] - 3C(\alpha,\rho)[\sin\frac{1}{2}\beta + \sin\frac{3}{2}\beta]} \qquad [8.8]$$

and

$$q_{II} = \frac{2K_{IIC}\sqrt{\pi l_2}/L_1}{A(\alpha,\rho)[\sin\frac{1}{2}\beta + \sin\frac{3}{2}\beta] + C(\alpha,\rho)[\cos\frac{1}{2}\beta + 3\cos\frac{3}{2}\beta]} \qquad [8.9]$$

where L_1 = half the length of the bond crack
 β = angle of crack inclination similar to α of the first aggregate piece
 $C(\alpha,\rho) = (\sin\alpha\cos\alpha - \rho\sin^2\alpha)\cos\alpha.$

Further crack growth depends on both angles α and β. The crack which meets the next aggregate piece will pass through the aggregate if the strength of the aggregate is low compared to the resistance of the matrix and the interface. For the aggregate, the normal compressive stress intensity can be defined by

$$q_1^A = \frac{K_{IC}^A}{A(\alpha,\rho)} \frac{1}{2L_1}\sqrt{\pi l_2} \qquad [8.10]$$

where K_{IC}^A = stress intensity factor for the aggregate.

(a)

(b)

Fig. 8.3 Fracture surfaces in tensile splitting test[8.6]: (a) mortar failure, $f'_t = 450$ psi (3.1 MPa); (b) aggregate failure, $f'_t = 1550$ psi (10.7 MPa)

If K_{IC} of the matrix is less than K_{IC}^A of the aggregate, then the crack propagates *around the aggregate* piece and failure results from the inclined shear cracks. If the two factors have the same value, the crack propagates directly *through the aggregate* without deviating from the compressive axis path. In this case, split tension failure occurs as the crack runs parallel to the loading axis as seen in Fig. 8.2(b) in some of the aggregate pieces. Figures 8.3(a) and (b),[8.6] respectively, show mortar failure and aggregate failure.

8.6 FRACTURE MECHANICS THEORY

8.6.1 General Overview

The field of fracture mechanics was first applied to concrete by Kaplan[8.3] on the basis of the classical elastic theory of fracture originated by Griffith.[8.2] The theory serves to predict the rapid propagation of cracks through a homogeneous and isotropic elastic material using the stress intensity factor K_I under plane strain.

This factor is a function of the crack geometry and the stress condition such that failure is precipitated when it reaches the critical stress intensity factor K_{IC}. Hence, K_{IC} is considered a measure of the toughness of the material.

Naus[8.4] found that fracture toughness was not independent of the specimen geometry and that it is a function of the crack length. Several subsequent studies emphasized the importance of interfacial strength on the cracking behavior of concrete as discussed in Section 8.5 on the cracking propagation theory. Jenq and Shah,[8.9] in their two-parameter fracture model (TPFM), proposed an effective crack equivalent in compliance to the elastic component of the actual crack and an associated critical stress intensity factor. From all studies to date, specimen size seems to be a major controlling factor in the fracture mechanics approach as a failure theory for concrete.

8.6.2   Fracture Mechanics Concepts

As in the other methods previously presented, fracture mechanics is a hypo-thesis to predict cracking impact and propagation in a brittle medium such as concrete and also to allow the engineer to determine how the size of a struc-tural member affects its ultimate load capacity. In order to study the initiation and propagation of cracks, a notch is formed into a planar model and tested to failure.

The reasons for adopting the fracture mechanics approach are[8.5, 8.10]:

1. *Energy required for crack formation.* Crack initiation and propagation require energy to be supplied by the structure in resisting imposed external work.

2. *Smeared cracking concept.* In this concept, a finite element analysis of cracking is made. The stress in the finite element is limited to its tensile strength f_t'. The stress in a finite element must decrease if this is used as a limit. Initially it was assumed that the stress suddenly decreased to zero in a vertical drop. Thereafter it was determined that more realistic results can be obtained if the stress is gradually reduced, namely, that the material is assumed to exhibit strain-softening. The energy dissipated due to cracking decreases with the refinement of the finite element mesh. This is physically unjustified and corrective measures based on fracture mechanics have to be taken so that the energy dissipated per unit length of the crack is forced to be independent of the element subdivision. See Fig. 8.4(e) and 8.4(f).[8.5]

3. *Stress–strain relationship.* Two basic types of structural failure can develop, plastic and brittle. In plastic or ductile failure, various parts of a structure simultaneously proceed to fail, with a long yield plateau in the load–deflection diagram. In brittle failure, the plateau is absent as softening of the material occurs in the falling branch of the load–deflection diagram (Fig. 8.5). If the material is plastic, the cross section gradually plasticizes until all its points reach the yield limit. If the material exhibits softening, the stress peak leaves a reduced "softening" stress[8.5] as seen in Fig. 8.5.

4. *Energy absorption capability and ductility.* The area under the entire load–

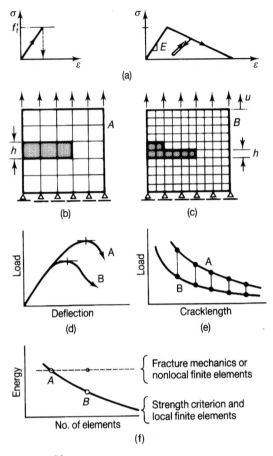

Fig. 8.4 Mesh size sensitivity[8.5]

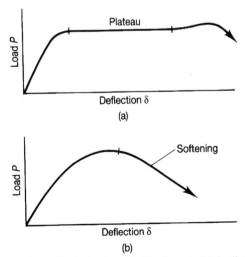

Fig. 8.5 Load–deflection relationship for ductile and brittle elements: (a) ductile (plastic) behavior; (b) brittle behavior

deflection diagram represents the energy absorbed by the structure at failure due to the applied load.

5. *Size Effect.* As stated earlier, the size effect in the fracture mechanics approach is the major parameter to be considered in evaluating the ultimate load of a structure. It is determined by comparing geometrically similar structures of different sizes, and is defined in terms of the nominal stress σ_N at ultimate load P_u. Zero size effect defines similar structures of different sizes but with the same σ_N value. If one assumes that

$b =$ thickness of a two-dimensional structure
$d =$ characteristic dimension of the structure

then, $\sigma_N = P_u/bd$ for two-dimensional similarity and $\sigma_N = P_u/d^2$ for three-dimensional similarity. All current theories used in design codes, elastic or plastic, assume that σ_N is constant for all structures. Failures governed by linear elastic fracture mechanics (LEFM) exhibited a strong size effect as seen in Fig. 8.6(a)[8.5] where the inclined dashed line represents the LEFM failure mode. In real structural systems, the solid transitional line is more reasonable.[8.11,8.12] It approaches the horizontal dashed line if the structure is small and the inclined dashed line if the structure is large.

6. *Effect of size on ductility.* Ductility is a measure of the degree of deformation of a structure at failure under a given type and magnitude of load. Depending on the size of the constituent members of the structure, it is found that *load-controlled* structures fail at the maximum load while *displacement-controlled*

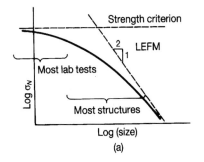

(a)

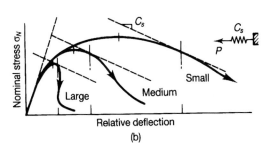

(b)

Fig. 8.6 Fracture mechanics size effect for geometrically similar structures of different sizes[8.5, 8.10]: (a) size effect; (b) load vs. deflection of geometrically similar structures of different sizes

structures (such as where stability controls) fail in the strain-softening range. Figure 8.6(b) gives the yield plots of geometrically similar structures of different sizes showing that failure occurs closer to the peak as the size is increased, because more strain energy is present for driving faster the propagation of failure region. A decrease in ductility represents an increase in brittleness, hence a more restricted failure region in the load–deformation relationship.

8.6.3　Linear Elastic Fracture Mechanics

Stress Components

The assumption is made in linear elastic fracture mechanics (LEFM) that the fracture occurs at the tip of the crack and that the entire body remains elastic. The crack produces stress concentrations near the crack tip. The stress field is singular at the crack tip, with all the nonzero stress components reaching infinity when the radial distance r from the crack tip tends to zero as seen in Fig. 8.7.[8.5] Considering that three elementary fracture modes can develop, as shown in Fig. 8.8, the stress components can be expressed[8.5] as

$$\sigma_{ij}^{\mathrm{I}} = K_{\mathrm{I}} f_{ij}(\theta)(2\pi r)^{-1/2} \qquad [8.11a]$$

$$\sigma_{ij}^{\mathrm{II}} = K_{\mathrm{II}} f_{ij}^{\mathrm{II}}(\theta)(2\pi r)^{-1/2} \qquad [8.11b]$$

$$\sigma_{ij}^{\mathrm{III}} = K_{\mathrm{III}} f_{ij}^{\mathrm{III}}(\theta)(2\pi r)^{-1/2} \qquad [8.11c]$$

where superscripts I, II, and III refer to the elementary modes in Fig. 8.8

θ = polar angle
$K_{\mathrm{I}}, K_{\mathrm{II}}, K_{\mathrm{III}}$ = stress intensity factors
$f_{ij}(\theta)$ = directional function, being the same irrespective of the body geometry and the manner of loading
$f_{11}^{\mathrm{I}}(\theta)$ = $\cos\alpha(1 - \sin\alpha\sin 3\alpha)$
$f_{22}^{\mathrm{I}}(\theta)$ = $\cos\alpha(1 + \sin\alpha\sin 3\alpha)$
$f_{12}^{\mathrm{I}}(\theta)$ = $\cos\alpha\sin 2\alpha\sin 3\alpha$ and so on with $\alpha = \frac{1}{2}\theta$.

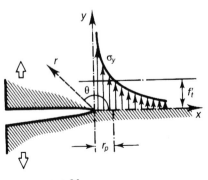

Fig. 8.7 Stress distribution near crack tip[8.5]

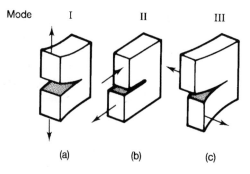

(a)   (b)   (c)

Fig. 8.8 Fracture modes: (a) direct opening; (b) plane shear; (c) anti-plane shear

Fracture Energy

As the crack tip propagates, energy flows into the crack where it is dissipated by the fracture process.[8.5,8.11] The energy flow is characterized by the energy release rate expressed as

$$G_b = \frac{\partial \Pi(a)}{\partial a} \qquad\qquad [8.12a]$$

giving

$$G_b \cong -\frac{1}{\Delta a}\left[\Pi\left(a + \frac{\Delta a}{2}\right) - \Pi\left(a - \frac{\Delta a}{2}\right)\right] \qquad\qquad [8.12b]$$

where $\Pi = U - W =$ potential energy of the structure

$U =$ strain energy of the structure as a function of the crack length a

$W =$ work done by the acting loads.

Griffith[8.2] stipulated that crack propagation at the *critical state* expressed as fracture energy G is

$$G = G_f \qquad\qquad [8.13]$$

where G has the dimension N/m or J/m^2 representing the basic material property. Three conditions for G are considered:

1. $G < G_f$: no crack propagation
2. $G > G_f$: disequilibrium
3. $G = G_f$: structural failure when $\partial G/\partial a = 0$

If $(\partial G/\partial a < 0)$ the crack can grow in a stable manner under limiting stress.[8.12]

Energy Release Rate

The energy release rate can be expressed in terms of the stress intensity factors K and the elastic constants of the materials so that

$$G_I = \frac{K_I^2}{E'} \qquad\qquad [8.14a]$$

$$G_{II} = \frac{K_{II}^2}{E'} \qquad\qquad [8.14b]$$

Plate 41 "Reflections" by R. H. Karol and the Rutgers civil engineering class of 1992: slices of 12 750 psi (88 Mpa) concrete reinforced with steel fabric mesh and epoxied together on site; height $8\frac{1}{2}$ ft (2.6 m)

$$G_{\mathrm{III}} = \frac{K_{\mathrm{III}}^2}{G}$$ [8.14c]

where G = elastic shear modulus

$E' = E$ = Young's elastic modulus in the case of plane stress

$E' = E/(1 - \mu^2)$ in the case of plane strain.

The total energy release becomes

$$G = G_{\mathrm{I}} + G_{\mathrm{II}} + G_{\mathrm{III}}$$ [8.15]

Stress Intensity Factors

These factors have to be proportional to the applied load. They can be expressed as

$$K_I = \frac{P}{bd} \sqrt{\pi a} f(\alpha) \tag{8.16a}$$

or

$$K_I = \frac{P}{bd} \sqrt{d} \Phi(\alpha) \qquad \text{where } \alpha = \frac{a}{d} \tag{8.16b}$$

where α = crack length

  $f(\alpha)$ = non-dimensional function of the relative crack length

  $f(\alpha)$ = 1 for the special condition of a single crack of length a in an infinite solid subjected at infinity to nominal stress σ_N in the direction normal to the crack plane

Equation 8.16a or 8.16b shows that for geometrically similar structures of different sizes; (a) the stress intensity factor is proportional to the square root of the size and (b) the energy release rate defined by Eqs. 8.14a, 8.14b and 8.14c is proportional to the size of the structure.

Since the stress intensity factor K is a measure of the fracture energy G, Eq. 8.13 can be represented by

$$K_I = K_{IC} \tag{8.17}$$

where K_{IC} = critical value of $K_I = G_f E'$.

K_{IC} is termed the fracture toughness of the material as it represents the material property. Substituting K_{IC} in Eq. 8.16 gives

$$\sigma_N = \frac{K_{IC}}{\sqrt{\pi a} f(\alpha)} \tag{8.18a}$$

or

$$\sigma_N = \frac{K_{IC}}{\sqrt{d} \Phi(\alpha)} \tag{8.18b}$$

According to Bažant, if the maximum aggregate size is assumed as d_a, the approximate effective length and width of the fracture zone in a third-point loaded specimen are respectively $12 d_a$ and $3 d_a$.

Brittleness Number

To characterize the nature of collapse, a dimensionless *brittleness number* β can be used in lieu of the stress intensity factor K_{IC} such that

$$\beta = \left[\frac{f_t' B}{K_{IC}}\right]^2 g(\alpha_0) h \tag{8.19}$$

where f_t' = average tensile stress in the plane that contains the crack
　　B = an empirical parameter
　　$g(\alpha_0)$ = nondimensional energy release rate corresponding to the initial crack length
　　h = cracking band length.

The lower the brittleness number the more brittle is the behavior of the structure. The brittleness number can also be expressed as a function of the elastic properties of the material so that if $b = h/2$,

$$B = \frac{\sqrt{EG_f}}{f_t'\sqrt{b}} = \frac{\sqrt{2EG_f}}{f_t'\sqrt{h}} \qquad\qquad [8.20]$$

The parameter B in Eq. 8.20 can thus explain why in a high strength concrete matrix, the tensile strength can be 2–5 times greater than the normal strength matrix[8.13] as the cement paste would have more fine microcracks than normal strength concrete. Silica fume, a very fine mineral admixture (0.10 μm particle size) often used as the dominant cementitious component replacing part of the portland cement, is an example where only minute voids result in the concrete. The silica fume fineness in terms of particle size is almost one-hundredth that of portland cement, reducing the void content in the matrix to a very low level and resulting in considerably more fine microcracks in the concrete gel of the hardened concrete and higher strength and durability properties, but appreciably increased brittleness.

The brittleness factor β has the following values depending on the stress condition:

　　plastic limit analysis:　　　　　　$\beta < 0.1$

　　nonlinear fracture mechanics:　　$0.1 \le \beta \le 10$

　　linear elastic fracture mechanics:　$\beta > 10$.

8.6.4　Nonlinear Fracture Mechanics with Softening Zone

General Behavior

Concrete develops a relatively *large* fracture zone which undergoes progressive softening damage due to microcracking. The large magnitude of the microcracking tends to reduce the energy that can be released into the crack tip and to increase the combined cracking surface area.[8.5] As a result, the energy absorption ability of the fracture zone is increased. It is for this reason that nonlinear fracture mechanics (NLFM) would be more representative of the actual fracture behavior and ultimate capacity of a concrete structure. Consequently, a relationship that can describe the softening damage has to be accounted for in the fracture model. As seen from Fig. 8.9, the fracture zone is large in both the ductile metal and the brittle concrete. In the case of concrete, the fracture zone is seen to occupy almost the entire nonlinear zone.

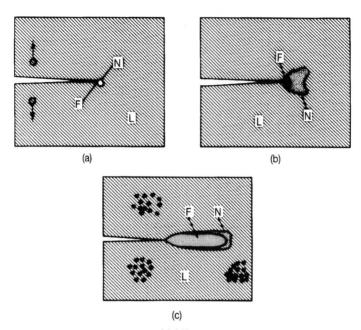

Fig. 8.9 Linear vs. nonlinear fracture pattern[8.5, 8.10]: (a) linear fracture; (b) fracture in metals; (c) fracture in concrete (L = linear zone, N = nonlinear zone, F = fracture)

Softening Stress–Displacement Relationship

Cracks in concrete do not follow straight paths and microcracking develops ahead of the crack tip, resulting in a *fracture process zone*. This zone was simplified by Bažant into a *smeared crack band model* through a strain-softening constitutive relationship. It also imposes a fixed width w_c of the front of the strain-softening zone, namely the *crack band*, representing the material property. This model had to be developed because of the difficulty of introducing additional strains over the length of the fracture zone due to its elongation.[8.10] The imposition of a constant width w_c assures that the energy dissipation due to fracture per unit length and unit width is constant and is equal to the fracture energy G_f of the material. The shear crack band model assumes a linear stress–strain relationship having a slope E_c up to the tensile strength f_t' and a strain-softening relationship having a slope E_t as seen in Fig. 8.10. The area under the diagram represents the fracture energy G_f in the following expression

$$G_f = w_c \int_0^\infty \sigma d\epsilon^f \qquad [8.21]$$

where ϵ^f = fracture strain causing softening.

An evaluation of Eq. 8.21 for an approximate linear stress–strain diagram gives

$$G_f = \frac{1}{2} w_c (f_t')^2 \left(\frac{1}{E_c} - \frac{1}{E_t} \right) \qquad [8.22]$$

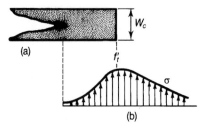

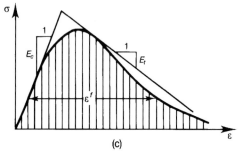

Fig. 8.10 Stress distribution at the fracture process zone: (a) fracture crack in a fixed band width w_c; (b) fracture stress f_t'; (c) stress–strain diagram

8.6.5   Fracture Mechanics Size Effect

The brief discussion on the size effect in Section 8.6.2 showed that the nominal stress σ_N at failure is a function of the geometry of similar structures:

Two-dimensional similarity

$$\sigma_N = \frac{P_u}{bd} \qquad\qquad [8.23a]$$

Three-dimensional similarity

$$\sigma_N = \frac{P_u}{d^2} \qquad\qquad [8.23b]$$

where P_u = maximum ultimate loads

    b = thickness of a two-dimensional structure

    d = characteristic dimension of a structure such as the depth of a beam or its span.

Figure 8.11 graphically illustrates the fracture zone in two concrete rectangular panels, *similar* in shape but different in size.[8.10] Each panel is assumed to have a weak spot from which fracture lines generate. As previously shown in Fig. 8.8(c) and also in this diagram, the area of the fracture zone in a brittle material such as concrete is quite large.

    h = width of the cracking band, assumed constant and independent of the structure size for similar structures having the same concrete properties

    a = fracture length at maximum load and a function of d (a/d = constant)

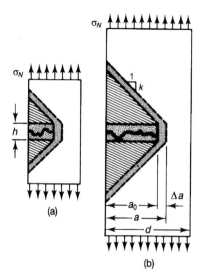

Fig. 8.11 Size effect on stored energy release in fracture[8.5, 8.10]: (a) small plate; (b) large plate

A fracture having a band thickness h and length a could release an elastic strain energy density $= \sigma_N^2/2E_c$ from the cross-hatched area in Fig. 8.11. As the fracture extends by Δa, additional strain energy is released from the densely cross-hatched boundary Δa fracture strip in the diagram. As the Δa dimension is proportional to the size of the structure, the area of the energy release (stress relief) zone increases[8.10] is as follows:

$$\Delta A = h\Delta a + 2ka\Delta a \qquad [8.24]$$

where $k =$ slope of the boundary fracture band in Fig. 8.11, being an empirical constant depending on the structure shape ($\simeq \pi/2$) for a panel).

The incremental strain energy in terms of Δa becomes

$$\Delta W = b(h\Delta a + 2ka\Delta a)\frac{\sigma_N^2}{2E} \qquad [8.25]$$

where, from before, $\sigma_N^2/2E =$ strain energy density.

Equating the incremental strain energy release to the dissipated energy, $\Delta W = G_f b\Delta a$ gives

$$\sigma_N^2[h + 2k(a/d)d] = 2EG_f \qquad [8.26]$$

Solving for σ_N in Eq. 8.26 gives the *size effect law equation*

$$\sigma_N = Bf_t'(1 + \beta)^{-\frac{1}{2}} \qquad [8.27]$$

where $\beta = d/d_0$, $d = hd/2ka$ and

$$B = \sqrt{2EG_f/hf_t'^2}$$

β is termed the *brittleness number* as in Section 8.6.3 or as in Eq. 8.20, and

$$B = \frac{\sqrt{2EG_f}}{f_t'\sqrt{h}} \qquad [8.28]$$

gives the limit nominal strength in plasticity.

The size law Eq. 8.28 is valid for specimens of the same size and *same* material constituents. The coarse aggregate is one major material constituent. Hence, it is suggested by Bažant[8.10] to define d_0 in relation to the maximum aggregate size d_a and to decrease the value of f_t' in Eq. 8.27 as the aggregate size is increased such that

$$f_t' = f_t^0[1 + \sqrt{c_0/d_a}] \qquad [8.29]$$

where f_t^0 and c_0 are constant for the particular structure. Figure 8.12 gives plots[8.5, 8.10] of comparisons in Eq. 8.27 with a value of $c_0 = 0.64$ in. and $f_t^0 = 183.3$ psi for specimens of different geometry and loading conditions.[8.14]

8.6.6 Fracture Resistance Curves

Fracture resistance curves (*R*-curves) are quasi-elastic graphical plots relating the extension of a crack from a notch as a function of the energy required for crack growth as a variable rather than a constant. The fracture resistance plot value vs. the crack extension c is called the *R*-curve. The crack propagation condition is $G = R(c)$ rather than $G = G_f$ previously discussed. If the value of $R(c)$ is known, the response is calculated in accordance with LEFM procedures, replacing G_f with $R(c)$.[8.5]

In lieu of this procedure, it is possible to define the *R*-curve in terms of the critical stress intensity factor K_{IC} discussed in Section 8.6.3 such that

$$K_{IR}^c = \sqrt{E'R(c)} \qquad [8.30]$$

using the crack propagation condition $K_I = K_{IR}^c$ instead of $K_I = K_{IC}$. The *R*-curve for any given geometry may be determined on the basis of the size effect law of Eq. 8.27, as it is applicable to size ranges of 1–20 as sufficient for most practical applications. The *R*-curve giving the required fracture energy per unit crack extension can be obtained from

$$R(c) = G_f \frac{g'(\alpha)}{g(\alpha)} \cdot \frac{c}{c_f} \qquad [8.31]$$

where $\alpha = a/d$, $\alpha_0 = a_0/d$,

$c = (a - a_0)$ = crack extension from the notch or initial crack tip

$g'(\alpha)$ and $g(\alpha_0)$ = nondimensional energy release rate defined by the total energy release rate $G = g(\alpha)P^2/Eb^2d$

c_f = $d_0 g(\alpha_0)/g'(\alpha_0)$

$$\frac{c}{c_f} = \frac{g'(\alpha)}{g(\alpha)} \left[\frac{g(\alpha)}{g'(\alpha)} - \alpha + \alpha_o \right] \qquad [8.32]$$

By knowing G_f and d_0, a series of α-values can be chosen and for each of them one can calculate c from Eq. 8.32 and the $R(c)$ from Eq. 8.31. Figure 8.13 shows typical *R*-curves for different specimen geometries. In summary, it is possible to apply such *R*-curves for many practical applications, simplifying the need for

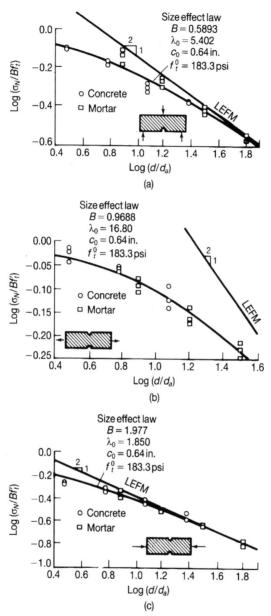

Fig. 8.12 Size effect law comparisons for specimens of different geometry and loading conditions[8.10]

more rigorous computations for crack length determination and the stresses at failure.

8.6.7 Application to Shear in Reinforced Concrete Beams

The conventional strength failure theories have not been able to provide an adequate explanation of the reasons for the decrease in shear strength of

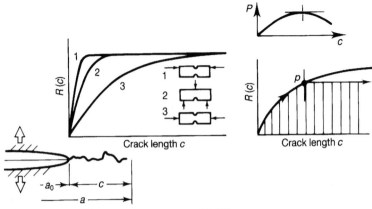

Fig. 8.13 *R*-curves for different specimen geometrics[8.5, 8.10]

reinforced concrete beams with the increase in their depth. The less slender beams are marked at failure by the transition in the failure mode from ductile flexural failure to the brittle mode of failure caused by shear. The ACI 318 code empirically takes into account the effect of the decrease in slenderness by the shear span/depth ratio embodied in the expression for the nominal shear strength (see Eqs 11.25a and b).

Karihaloo[8.15] discusses the change from linear behavior to nonlinear behavior and the application of fracture mechanics to the flexural and shear evaluation of longitudinally reinforced elements. As is well established in theory and laboratory tests, the first few cracks develop at the region of maximum moment at midspan of a simply supported beam where the shear force is insignificant if the load is uniformly distributed. These cracks are *normal* to the major principal tensile stress and are parallel to the direction of the applied gravity load. This behavior is consistent with fracture mode I of Fig. 8.8. As the cracks start to develop in regions closer to the support where the shear forces are no longer negligible, a mixed mode combination of modes I and II is created, with the cracks still essentially normal to the principal tensile stress, but no longer parallel to the applied load. While cracks always develop and grow normal to the major principal tensile stress, the direction of growth depends on the mode II component, causing the crack faces to "slide"[8.15] in an inclined direction. If longitudinal and transverse reinforcement are present, the inclined crack is prevented from opening further and ductile failure in flexure results as the beam reaches its ultimate capacity.

If the reinforcement ratio is increased without modifying the beam cross-sectional dimensions or if those dimensions are increased without increasing the reinforcement ratio for the same failure load or factored moment, diagonal tension failure precipitates (mode II). The sliding displacement of the inclined crack faces, calls into action aggregate interlock bond and dowel action of the reinforcement until failure occurs (see also the discussion in Section 8.7.1). The

Plate 42 Shear-friction interaction specimens (tests by Nawy et al.)

size effect law applied to the flexural shear behavior at failure resulted in the following expression by Bažant, et al.[8.14] for the nominal mean shear strength intensity v_c (psi) for beams without web reinforcement;

$$v_c = \frac{8\rho^{1/3}}{\sqrt{1 + d/(25g)}} [\sqrt{f_c'} + 3000\sqrt{\rho/(l_u/d)^5}] \qquad [8.33]$$

where ρ = steel reinforcement ratio
      d = effective beam depth to the centroid of the tensile reinforcement, in.
   g (namely, d_a) = maximum aggregate size in the mix, in.
      f_c' = cylinder compressive strength of the concrete, psi
      l = beam span, in.

The statistical expression in Eq. 3.33 is based on tests of relatively small-scale beam specimens. Its format has the advantage that it includes the aggregate size while maintaining the format of the ACI 318 code expression. The size effect does not seem to be significantly influenced by the presence of diagonal tension stirrups in the beams.

In summary, it should be remembered that while the discussions in Section 8.6 on fracture mechanics theory and the expressions presented give ample insight into the propagation of cracking in concrete structures and the importance of the size factor in determining the ultimate capacity of a structure, more progress needs to be made to simplify the analysis procedures and facilitate for the designer shortcut approximations in the application of the inelastic fracture theory and the size effect law.

8.7 SHEAR FRICTION TRANSFER IN TWO-LAYER HIGH STRENGTH CONCRETE SYSTEMS

8.7.1 Mechanics of Shear Friction Transfer

The problem of shear transfer in concrete structures arises when shear loads must be transmitted across a definite and often weak plane. Typical situations are encountered in corbels, nonmonolithic joints in concrete and composite elements where concrete is cast in place over a precast member. It is generally recognized that the shear transfer capacity in concrete elements[8.16, 8.17] can be attributed to any of the following factors: friction at the shear plane, interlocking action of the aggregates, dowel action of any reinforcement, and bond forces (apparent cohesion).

Consider the forces in Fig. 8.14 acting on a concrete element;

$\Delta V_b =$ intrinsic bond shear resistance
$\Delta V_f =$ shear friction resistance
$\Delta V_i =$ aggregate interlock resistance
$\Delta V_d =$ dowel resistance

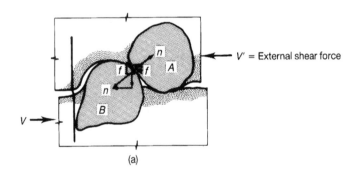

(a)

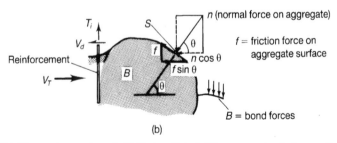

(b)

Fig. 8.14 Shear resistance through (1) friction, $F \sin \theta$, (2) aggregate interlock, $n \cos \theta$, and (3) dowel action, V_d[8.17]

Initially, all shear resistance is provided by intrinsic bonding. After cracking has started and slip has occurred, resistance is developed through friction, aggregate interlock, and dowel action. Shear friction is purely due to the surface shear resistance to slip. Aggregate interlock is due to the interlocking action of the aggregate at the failure plane. Dowel action shear resistance is a result of the steel reinforcement as shown in Fig. 8.14(b).

Summing up the resistances in the horizontal direction,

$$V_t = \Delta V_b + \Delta V_f + \Delta V_i + \Delta V_d \qquad [8.34]$$

The nominal shear stress intensity becomes

$$v_t = \frac{1}{A} \int_A \Delta V_t \qquad [8.35]$$

where $A =$ area of the shear plane. Idealizing the concrete mass as a brittle material containing microcracks, bond shear strength would be an *intrinsic* property of any given concrete. The resistance due to bond can be represented by $v_b = qdA$ where $q =$ strength per unit bond area.

If n' is the total number of bars and T_f is the load transferable by dowel action per bar, the expression for the total dowel force from Dulacska[8.18] modified such that the shear reinforcement is taken normal to the fracture plane yields a total dowel force,

$$n'T_f = \left[\frac{4A_s'n'}{\pi} \right] \left[\left(1 - \left(\frac{f_s}{f_y} \right)^2 \right) 1.51 \frac{f_c'}{f_y} \right]^{1/2} \qquad [8.36]$$

The shear stress over the cross-sectional area b_w of the failure plane is $v_d = n'T_f/w$. If $\tilde{p} = n'A_s'/b_w =$ reinforcement ratio for shear transfer reinforcement, the dowel action shear resistance intensity in Eq. 8.36 becomes

$$V_d = \left[\frac{4\tilde{p}f_y}{\pi} \right] \left[\left(1 - \left(\frac{f_s}{f_y} \right)^2 \right) 1.51 \frac{f_c'}{f_y} \right]^{1/2} \qquad [8.37]$$

This expression incorporates the condition that as the tension force in the shear-reinforcing steel approaches the yield point, v_d tends to become zero.

For friction and aggregate interlock, the contribution of the surface frictional force to the transfer strength (Fig. 8.14) would be

$$v_f = f \sin \theta \qquad [8.38a]$$

where $f =$ frictional zone in the surface.

The contribution due to aggregate interlock is

$$v_i = n \cos \theta \qquad [8.38b]$$

where $n =$ normal force per unit area.

If $T_i =$ tension force per unit area $= \tilde{\rho}A_s$, summing forces in the n direction, Fig. 8.14,

$$v_n = (\tilde{\rho}f_s + qdA)\sin\theta - v_d\cos\theta \qquad [8.38c]$$

The frictional force

$$f = \mu n \qquad [8.38d]$$

where $\mu =$ coefficient of friction between the aggregate and the cement mortar surrounding it. Recollecting terms and integrating these forces over the surface area of the aggregate and dividing by the cross-sectional area of the failure plane, the resistance v_f due to friction and v_i due to aggregate interlock can be defined as follows:

$$v_f = \mu\left[(\tilde{\rho}f_s + qk_1)\frac{\pi}{4} - \frac{1}{2}v_d\right]k_2 + [\mu(\tilde{\rho}f_s + qk_1)]k_3 \qquad [8.39]$$

$$v_i = [(\tilde{\rho}f_s + qk_1)/\pi - \tfrac{1}{2}v_d]k_2 \qquad [8.40]$$

where $k_1 =$ ratio of bond area to total shear area
$\quad k_2 =$ ratio of projected area of aggregate to total shear
$\quad k_3 = 1 - k_1 - k_2$
$\quad q \;=$ bond shear strength per unit area.

Adding the various components and rearranging terms gives

$$v_t = qk_1 + \left[\frac{4\tilde{\rho}f_y}{\pi}\right]\left[\left(1 - \frac{f_s}{f_y}\right)^2 1.51\frac{f'_c}{F_Y}\right]^{1/2}$$

$$\times \left[1 - \left(\frac{k_2}{2}\right)(1+\mu)\right] + [\tilde{\rho}f_s + qk_1]\left[\mu k_3 + k_2\pi\left(\frac{\mu}{4} + \frac{1}{\pi^2}\right)\right]$$

$$[8.41]$$

The constant terms $\frac{1}{2}$, $\pi/4$, π and others represent the shape of the aggregate in the matrix.

8.7.2   Members With No Shear Transfer Reinforcement ($\tilde{\rho} = 0$)

In members with no shear transfer reinforcement the general expression of Eq. 8.41 reduces to

$$v_t = qk_1 + qk_1\left[\mu k_3 + k_2\pi\left(\frac{\mu}{4} + \frac{1}{\pi^2}\right)\right] \qquad [8.42]$$

Because every term in this expression is a constant for a given surface, v_t is constant and is termed the *apparent cohesive strength* which is the bond strength of the material. In this case $v_t \simeq 150$ psi in this series of tests with no shear transfer reinforcement.

In normal strength concretes where the voids in the matrix are not substantially filled with fine particles, the magnitude of the shear resistance is relatively low as compared to high strength concrete. Taking silica fume high strength concrete as an example, the very fine silica fume particles (about one-hundredth the fineness of portland cement) fill most of the matrix voids and bridge all the microcracks. This induces compressive stress against the interaction planes between the aggregates, thereby contributing to development of *additional shear strength* through friction and aggregate interlock mechanisms, hence a higher total shear strength.

8.7.3   Members With Transverse Shear Reinforcement

When specimens with transverse reinforcement are subjected to shear along the shear plane, slipping takes place, leading to the introduction of stresses in the transverse reinforcement. The transverse steel develops its yield strength at the ultimate load capacity of a structural element[8.19].

If we take $\mu' = \mu k_3 + k_2 \pi (\mu/4 + 1/\pi^2)$ and $c' = q k_1 (1 + \mu')$ and substitute in Eq. 8.41, v_t becomes

$$v_t = \tilde{\rho} f_y \mu' + c' \qquad [8.43]$$

where c' = shear strength from bond action for cases with no shear reinforcement

μ' = apparent coefficient of friction, combining the effects of friction and aggregate interlock actions.

If I is termed as the shear reinforcing index $\tilde{\rho} f_y$, then

$$v_t = I \mu' + c' \qquad [8.44]$$

Eq. 8.44 is similar to the format developed by Hermansen and Cowan.[8.20]

At ultimate load, the compressive force across the crack after the separation of the shear plane faces is considered equivalent to the yield force in the reinforcement. The frictional resistance to shear along the crack is then equal to this force multiplied by the coefficient of friction of concrete μ'. This coefficient in Eq. 8.44 includes, therefore, this frictional shear resistance in addition to the dowel action and aggregate interlock shear resistances.[8.21]

Members Having Moderate Shear Reinforcement
In this case, when $\tilde{\rho} f_y$ is low, shear failure will proceed by yielding of the shear reinforcement so that $f_s = f_y$ in Eq. 8.41 leading to the expression in Eq. 8.42. Extensive tests of L-specimens described subsequently and tested at 28 days yielded a value of $\mu' = 0.609$ and $c' = 711$ so that

$$v_t = 0.609 I + 711 \qquad [8.45a]$$

Members Having High Shear Reinforcement
When $\tilde{\rho} f_y$ is very high, the aggregates on the shear plane may be dislocated or sheared off and as load is applied, k_1 and k_2 in Eq. 8.41 will equal zero. Shear transfer capacity will then be only due to friction and dowel action of the reinforcement. For a given cracking strength, as $\tilde{\rho}$ increases f_s decreases. Thus, for

high value of index I, $[1 - (f_s/f_y)^2]$ in Eq. 8.41 is almost equal to 1.0 and $\tilde{\rho} f_y$ becomes a constant. Test results in this case resulted in the values $\mu' = 0.20$ and $c' = 1140$, so that

$$v_t = 0.20I + 1140 \qquad [8.45b]$$

The values of these constants were obtained from extensive laboratory testing[8.16, 8.17] using among other tests, L-shaped specimens shown in Fig. 8.15. Polymer high strength concrete was used for casting the mating L-shaped prism against the precast 5000 psi normal strength concrete basic element to simulate two-layer systems in actual structures. The polymer system consisted of DER resin and CA-640 low viscosity hardener. The resin had an epoxy equivalent weight of 180–195 and a viscosity of 11 000 to 16 000 poise. Figure 8.16[8.16] shows that the slip value (in.) vs. the applied shear stress reaches 1500 psi (10.3 MPa). Figure 8.17[8.16] summarizes the relationships between the shear-friction strength index $I = \tilde{\rho} f_y$ and the shear transfer capacity.

8.7.4 Early Age High Strength Concrete Test Values for μ' and c' for Concrete Cast at Subfreezing Temperatures

Another series of tests was conducted[8.19,8.21] to evaluate the friction interaction strength in cold weather at early ages of 1–3 days. The L-shaped push off specimens had one L made of high strength methyl methacrylate polymer concrete (MMA) and magnesium phosphate concrete. The control specimens and

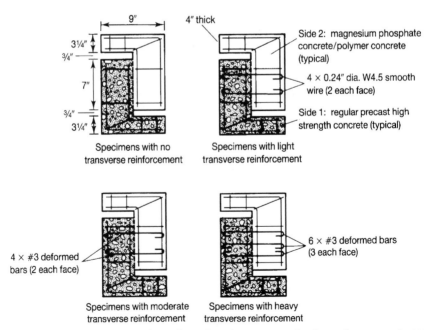

Fig. 8.15 Push-off shear test specimens (control specimens were made of nonpolymer concrete on both sides, cast monolithically)

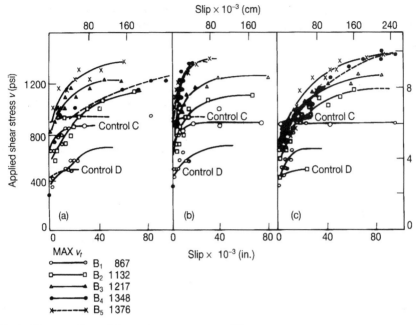

Fig. 8.16 L tests slip vs. failure transfer shear stress ϑ_t [8.16]

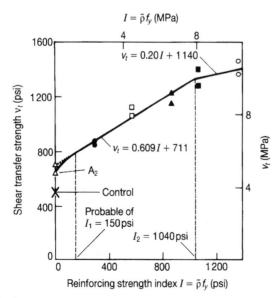

Fig. 8.17 Reinforcing strength index I vs. shear transfer strength α_t for two-layer system tested at 28 days[8.16]

the precast half of the test specimens had a high strength concrete mix comprising type III high early portland cement, 3/8in. (9.5 mm) maximum size coarse aggregate and natural riverbed sand with fineness modulus of 2.61.

Microsilica, superplasticizer, and a low water/cement ratio were used. All test specimens were air-cured for 24 hours in the mold, thereafter stored in the moisture curing room for 30 days prior to casting the mating half. The second half of each specimen (MMA or MP high strength polymer concrete) after being cast, was placed in a temperature-controlled room at a temperature of 15–20°F (-7 to -10°C). Specimens were allowed to thaw for 1–2 hours prior to testing in order to maintain uniform conditions during the test. Figure 8.18[8.21] shows the early age relationship between the shear-friction reinforcing index $I = \tilde{\rho} f_y$ and the shear transfer stress intensity v_t. Table 8.1 gives the values of the constants μ' and c' at 1, 3, and 7 days. Even at 1 day, the methyl methacrylate high strength polymer concrete gives

$$v_t = 0.54I + 890 \qquad\qquad [8.46a]$$

and at 3 days

$$v_t = 0.74I + 869 \qquad\qquad [8.46b]$$

giving relatively very high values of v_t at early age in comparison with those of the other mix experiments described in Section 8.7.3. In comparing the v_t values obtained in both series, it is clear that the ACI 318 code, which limits the maximum shear-friction strength for two-layer systems to 800 psi (5.5 MPa), is very conservative indeed, regardless of whether or not there is long-term or even early age (e.g. 1 day) exposure to subfreezing temperatures of 15–20°F.

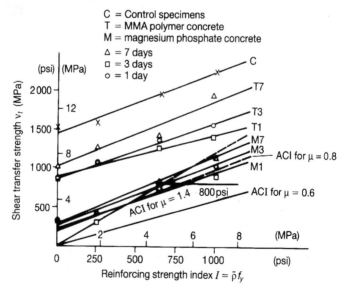

Fig. 8.18 Reinforcing strength index I vs. shear transfer strength θ_t for two-layer system tested at early age for polymer concrete placed at subfreezing temperature[8.21]

Table 8.1 Values of c' and μ' at early ages in 15–20°F temperatures[8.21]

Age	Magnesium phosphate concrete		MMA polymer concrete	
	c'	μ'	c'	μ'
1 day	248	0.68	890	0.54
3 days	279	0.78	869	0.74
7 days	278	0.88	1015	0.89

For control specimens, the above constants are $c' = 1458$ and $\mu' = 0.817$.

Plate 43 City Spire: tallest building in New York City, slenderness ratio 10 : 1 (Courtesy Portland Cement Association)

8.7.5 Freeze-thaw Performance of High Strength Two-layer Systems

Durability test results[8.23] are presented in Fig. 8.19, the relative dynamic modulus during the freeze–thaw cycles is given in Fig. 8.20, and the durability factor in Fig. 8.21. The relative dynamic modulus P_c is defined by the following expression:

$$P_c = \left(\frac{n_1^2}{n^2}\right) \times 100 \qquad [8.47]$$

where $n =$ fundamental transverse frequency at no freeze–thaw cycle
$\quad\quad\; n_1 =$ fundamental transverse frequency after N freeze cycles

The durability factor (DF) was computed using the expression

$$DF = \frac{PN}{M} \qquad [8.48]$$

where $P =$ relative dynamic modulus of N cycles, expressed as percentage
$\quad\quad\; N =$ number of cycles at which P reaches the specified minimum value for discontinuing the test, or the specified number of cycles at which the exposure is to be terminated, whichever is less
$\quad\quad\; M =$ specified number of cycles at which the exposure is to be terminated; it was taken as 300 cycles as ASTM specifies.

From Figs. 8.19, 8.20, and 8.21, it can be inferred that all the polymer concrete specimens increased in weight during the early periods of freeze–thaw cycles, whereas the control specimens made of plain concrete showed a decrease in weight. The increase in polymer content (Figs. 8.20, 8.21) leads to improved

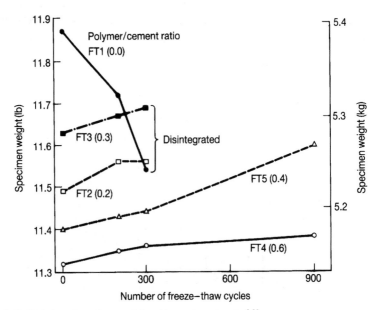

Fig. 8.19 Variation of specimen weight with number of cycles[8.23]

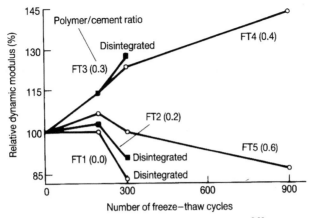

Fig. 8.20 Variation of relative dynamic modulus with number of cycles[8.23]

freeze–thaw durability. Specimens which had a polymer/cement ratio of 0.20–0.30 disintegrated before reaching 900 cycles while those with a P/C ratio of 0.4–0.6 withstood the 900 cycles of freezing and thawing; only 300 cycles are needed for the freezing and thawing test. The durability factor (DF) for the polymer concrete specimens was considerably higher than that of the control specimens.

8.8   CONFINEMENT IN HIGH STRENGTH CONCRETE

It is distinctly advantageous to use high strength concrete in columns of tall structures, resulting in significantly smaller column sizes, and additional floor space and reduced cost. Spiral transverse reinforcement leads to increased strength and ductility of the confined concrete. Concrete confined by rectangular ties also develops higher strength and ductility, but to a lesser degree. Although

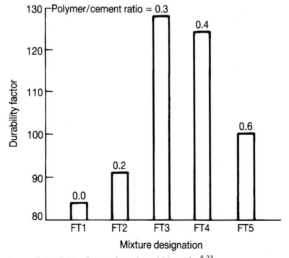

Fig. 8.21 Comparison of durability factors based on 300 cycles[8.23]

rectilinear confinement in rectangular sections is less effective than spiral confinement, rectangular sections often exhibit higher moment capacity than circular sections of the same lateral dimensions, particularly at large deformations.

There is no universal agreement on a model to define the stress–strain diagram of confined concrete which is basically subjected to a triaxial state of inelastic stress at yield.[8.24–8.31] Biaxial investigations for rectangular plate specimens[8.31] showed a maximum strength increase under biaxial loading from 29 to 47 percent at biaxial loading ratios σ_1/σ_2 between 0.2 and 0.5. Figure 8.22 gives ultimate biaxial envelopes for various σ_1/σ_2 ratios. Table 8.2 gives experimental test results[8.29] of very high strength triaxially loaded confined concretes having uniaxial compressive strengths of 13 000–17 100 psi (90–118 MPa). The confining pressure as listed in the table was 5, 10, or 15MPa. The corresponding experimental confining stress f_0 values exceeded f'_c by 50–65 percent.

Work by Traina and Mansour[8.24] on the biaxial strength and deformational behavior of plain and steel fiber concrete changes the mode of failure from the common tensile splitting to a shear type failure. They used volume fractions of steel fibers 0.5, 1.0, and 1.0 percent and an l/d ratio of 33–60. The biaxial principal stress ratios applied were $\sigma_2/\sigma_1 = 0.0$ (uniaxial), 0.5, and 1.0. Figure 8.23(a) gives the biaxial stress–strain relationship for plain concrete and Fig. 8.23(b) gives the fiber reinforced concrete relationship. The tests were conducted on cubes 3 in. × 3 in. × 3 in. (76 mm × 76 mm × 76 mm). The increase in the compressive strength due to biaxially or triaxially loaded specimens is qualitatively comparable to the axial capacity of compression members with the increase in the volume of the transverse confining reinforcement. A vast array of data exists in the literature on confining ties in columns and beam-column connections in seismic resisting structures.

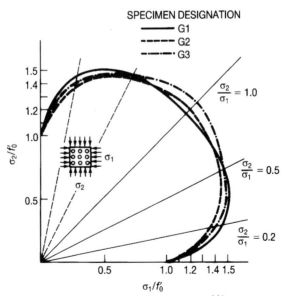

Fig. 8.22 Biaxial ultimate strength envelope under compression[8.31]

Table 8.2 Experimental results of very high strength concretes subjected to triaxial confining loading[8.29]

Mix no.	Age (days)	f_c (MPa)	f_r (MPa)	f_0 (MPa)
AH	28	108	5	144
			10	172
			15	194
BH	28	102	5	145
			10	158
			15	175
CH	28	96	5	125
			10	147
			15	163
DH	28	96	5	117
			10	144
			15	151
AH	90	118	5	154
			10	176
			15	199
BH	90	110	5	153
			10	164
			15	185
CH	90	100	5	128
			10	153
			15	170
DH	90	98	5	119
			10	146
			15	156
EH	90	58	1	68
			5	98
			10	122
			15	144

1 MPa = 145.038 lbf/in.^{2}

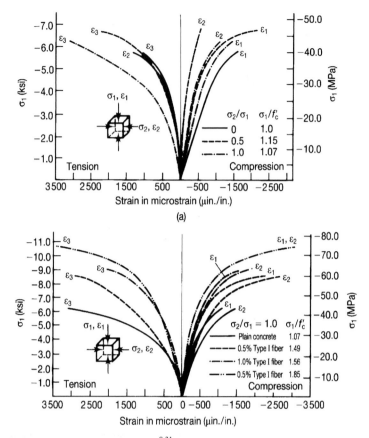

Fig. 8.23 Biaxial stress–strain relationships[8.31]: (a) plain concrete; (b) fibrous concrete

8.8.1 Confining Reinforcement Design

Studies of confinement effects resulted in a model[8.25] for peak stress f_0, of the confined concrete stress–strain diagram shown in Fig. 8.24 such that

$$f_0 = Kf_c' \qquad [8.49]$$

where

$$K = 1 + 0.0091\left(1 - \frac{0.245s}{d''}\right)\left(\rho'' + \frac{nd_b''}{8sd_b}\rho\right)\frac{f_{yv}}{\sqrt{f_c'}} \qquad [8.50]$$

where K = effective confinement factor = f_0/f_c'
  f_c' = concrete cylinder compressive strength
  s = center-to-center distance of transverse ties, in.
  d'' = length of one side of rectangular tie, in.
  n = number of longitudinal bars
  d_b'' = nominal diameter of tie, in.
  d_b = nominal diameter of longitudinal bar, in.
  f_{yv} = yield strength of the tie reinforcement, psi

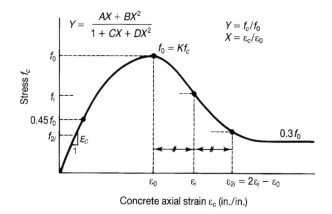

Fig. 8.24 Theoretical stress-strain plot of Eq. 8.58 for high strength confined concrete[8.25]

ρ'' = volumetric ratio of the transverse tie reinforcement
ρ = volumetric ratio of longitudinal reinforcement.

The peak strain ϵ_0 can be predicted from the following expression[8.22]

$$\epsilon_0 = 0.00265 + \frac{0.0035\left(1 - \frac{0.734s}{d_b''}\right)(\rho''f_{yv})^{2/3}}{\sqrt{f_c'}} \qquad [8.51]$$

By choosing ϵ_0, one can get the required confining reinforcement ratio ρ''. Alternatively, the design ratio ρ'' and spacing s give in Eq. 8.51 the peak strain ϵ_0 that the concrete can sustain at failure, thereby determining the degree of ductility that a concrete member has in high strength concretes.

Table 8.3[8.25] gives the properties of the specimens used to develop the confinement model and Table 8.4 shows the close correlation with models of other investigators. Figure 8.25 gives the stress–strain plots of the various investigations,[8.25] the solid line representing the model defined by Eqs. 8.49 and 8.50.

Recent work on deformation and curvature under uniaxial bending of eccentrically loaded high strength reinforced concrete columns is reported in Ref. 8.38. A constant size and spacing of lateral ties having a diameter of 0.16 in. (4 mm) and spaced at 2.4 in. (60 mm) on centers were used. Concrete cylinder compressive strengths, f_c' ranged between 7800 and 14 900 psi (54–103 MPa). The work resulted in an expression for the peak stress f_0 as a function of f_c' and the ratio of the concrete compressive strain ϵ_c to the peak strain ϵ_0 using a K multiplier in a manner comparable to that in Ref. 8.25.

The Uniform Building Code (UBC)[8.32] requires that all vertical reinforcement be confined by hoops or cross-ties producing an area of steel not less than (UBC, Sec. 1921.6)

$$A_{sh} = 0.09sh_cf_c'/f_{yh} \qquad [8.52]$$

where A_{sh} = total cross-sectional area of transverse reinforcement (including cross-ties) within spacing s and perpendicular to dimension h_c

Table 8.3 Properties of confined high strength concrete compression members[8.25]

Specimen (1)	Lateral steel volume ratio (2)	Longitudinal steel rebars (3)	Concrete cover (in.) (4)	Compressive cylinder strength f'_c (psi) (5)	ε'_c strain at stress f'_c (in./in.) (6)	Measured $E_c \times 10^6$ (psi) (7)
ACI-AC3	0.0164	8 #3	3/8	12 850	0.0022	5.383
API	0	0	—	12 850	0.0022	5.583
BCI-BC3	0.0082	8 #3	3/8	13 560	0.0025	5.709
BPI-BP2	0	0	—	13 560	0.0025	5.709
CCI-CC3	0.0055	8 #3	3/8	12 830	0.00226	5.580
CPI	0	0	—	12 830	0.00226	5.580
DCI-DC3	0.0028	8 #3	3/8	12 250	0.00229	5.486
DPI	0	0	—	12 250	0.00229	5.486
NCI-NC3	0.0082	8 #3	0	12 130	0.00209	5.453
NPI	0	0	—	12 130	0.00209	5.453
LCI-LC3	0.0055	4 #3	3/8	13 020	0.0024	5.641
LPI	0	0	—	13 020	0.0024	5.641

1 psi = 0.006895 MPa; 1 in. = 25.4 mm.

Table 8.4 Compression of test results of Eq. 8.49 with models by others[8.25]

Results and models (1)	Peak stress f_0 (psi) (2)	Peak strain ϵ_0 (in./in.) (3)	Strain at $0.85f'_c$, $\epsilon_{0.85}$ (in./in.) (4)
		Specimen group A	
Test results	14 360	0.00512	0.00757
Proposed model	14 580	0.00559	0.0082
Park et al. (1982)	14 030	0.00218	0.0165
Vallenas et al. (1977)	14 580	0.00684	0.0015
Fafitis and Shah (1985)	13 480	0.00486	0.00819
		Specimen group B	
Test results	14 730	0.0049	0.007
Proposed model	14 400	0.00414	0.006
Park et al. (1982)	14 150	0.00209	0.0052
Vallenas et al. (1977)	14 680	0.00419	0.00722
Fafitis and Shah (1985)	14 030	0.0041	0.0056
		Specimen group C	
Test results	13 190	0.00344	0.00417
Proposed model	13 340	0.00353	0.00465
Park et al. (1982)	13 220	0.00206	0.0377
Vallenas et al. (1977)	13 690	0.00338	0.0051
Fafitis and Shah (1985)	13 150	0.00379	0.0048
		Specimen group D	
Test results	13 180	0.0042	0.00637
Proposed model	13 010	0.00423	0.006
Park et al. (1982)	12 720	0.00209	0.0519
Vallenas et al. (1977)	13 350	0.00429	0.00734
Fafitis and Shah (1985)	12 610	0.004	0.0056

1 psi = 0.006895 MPa; 1 in. = 25.4 mm.

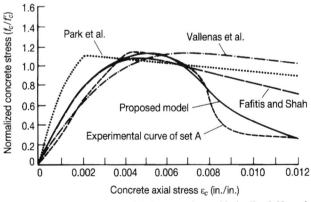

Fig. 8.25 Stress–strain plots of various models in comparison with the Eq. 8.58 model for high strength confined concrete[8.25]

s = spacing of transverse reinforcement along the longitudinal axis of a compressive member, in. (mm)

h_c = cross-sectional dimension of a column core or shear wall boundary zone measured center to center of confining reinforcement

f'_c = specified compressive strength of concrete, psi (MPa)

f_{yh} = specified yield strength of transverse reinforcement, psi (MPa)

8.8.2   Techniques for Confinement

Standard techniques for confining the main reinforcement in structural members involve the use of closed ties or spirals to enclose the reinforcing bars. Such use is equally applicable for confinement in seismic zones as well as in zones where earthquake effects are not a consideration. If the concrete section, such as a column or a shear wall, is relatively large, additional cross-ties are used to ensure adequate confinement of the concrete section. The ACI 318 code stipulates the requirements for size and spacing of the confining reinforcement in building structures.

In the case of large deep beams where strains are no longer linear, or in cases of stress concentration, such as under concentrated loading points or geometrical discontinuities, other types of confining reinforcement might be preferable. Headed reinforcing bars[8.36, 8.37] are advantageous when used in disturbed strain regions. They are also particularly suited in such structures where congestion of steel cannot be avoided such as in offshore oil platforms.

In summary, the discussion in this chapter presented a concise treatment of three major topics in the area of mechanics of concrete: microcracking, macrocracking, and fracture mechanics as applied to concrete; the shear friction interaction in multilayered high strength concrete systems; and the effect of confinement on increasing the uniaxial strength of high strength concrete. A theory and procedures are presented for determining the size effect influence on the behavior of structural systems. Expressions are given for determining the shear-friction value in two-layer elements such as bridge decks, using different dowel reinforcement levels, together with demonstrative test results that the present limitation in the ACI 318 code to a value of 800 psi (5.5 MPa) is very conservative even at early age (e.g. 1 day). Also presented are the results of extensive tests on high strength confined concretes and a verified expression is given in Eqs. 8.49 and 8.50 for evaluating the ultimate strain ϵ_0, hence the ductility of laterally confined high strength compression members. It should be noted that confinement can, with proper design, increase the ductility of a member severalfold, so it is essential in seismic areas.

REFERENCES

8.1   ACI Committee 224 Control of Cracking in Concrete Structures. *ACI 224 Report 224R-95* American Concrete Institute, Detroit. 1995

8.2   Griffith A A 1920 The Phenomena of Rupture and Flow in Solids. *Transactions, Royal Society of London* No. 221A, pp. 163–198

8.3   Kaplan M F 1961 Crack Propagation and the Fracture of Concrete. *Proceedings, ACI Journal* Vol. 58 No. 5, American Concrete Institute, Detroit, pp. 591–610

8.4   Naus D J 1971 Applicability of Linear Elastic Fracture Mechanics to Portland Cement Concretes, Ph. D. Thesis, University of Illinois, Urbana

8.5   ACI Committee 446 Fracture Mechanics of Concrete: Concepts, Models and Determination of Material Properties. *ACI Report 446.1R-91* Z P Bažant, chairman, American Concrete Institute, Detroit, 1991, pp. 1–146

8.6   Nawy E G, and Balaguru P N 1983 High Strength Concrete. *Handbook of Structural Concrete* McGraw Hill-Pitman, New York, 1983, Ch. 5, pp. 1–33

8.7   Hobbs D W 1983 Failure Criteria of Concrete. *Handbook of Structural Concrete* McGraw Hill-Pitman, New York, 1983, Ch. 10, pp. 1–40

8.8   Whittman F H 1979 Micromechanics of Achieving High Strength and Other Superior Properties. *Proceedings High Strength Concrete Conference* University of Illinois, Chicago, Nov. 1979, pp. 8–30

8.9   Jenq Y S, and Shah S P 1985 A Two Parameter Fracture Model for Concrete. *Proceedings, Journal of Engineering Mechanics* Vol. III No. 4, pp. 1227–1241

8.10 Bažant Z P 1992 Should Design Codes Consider Fracture Mechanics Size Effects. *Concrete Design Based on Fracture Mechanics. ACI SP 134-1* ed. Z P Bazant and W Gerstle, American Concrete Institute, Detroit, pp. 1–23

8.11 Bažant Z P, Ozbolt J, and Eligehausen R 1994 Fracture Size Effect: Review of Evidence for Concrete Structures. *Proceedings, ASCE J. Structural Division* 120(8), pp. 2377–2398

8.12 Bažant Z P, and Cedolin L 1991 *Stability of Structures: Elastic, Inelastic, Fracture and Damage Theories* Oxford University Press, New York, Ch. 12

8.13 Bažant Z P 1976 Instability, Ductility and Size Effect in Strain Softening Concrete. *Proceedings, ASCE J. Engineering Mechanics Division* Vol. 102 No. EM2, pp. 331–344

8.14 Bažant Z P, and Pfeiffer P A 1987 Determination of Fracture Energy Properties from Size Effect and Brittleness Number. *Proceedings, ACI Materials Journal* Vol. 84 No. 6, American Concrete Institute, Detroit, pp. 463–480

8.15 Karihaloo B L 1995 *Fracture Mechanics and Structural Concrete* Longman Group, London, and John Wiley, New York

8.16 Nawy E G 1985 Shear Transfer Behavior in Concrete and Polymer Concrete Two Layered Systems with Application to Infrastructure Rehabilitation and New Design. *ACI SP 89-4* American Concrete Institute, Detroit, pp. 51–90

8.17 Nawy E G, and Ukadike M M 1983 Shear Transfer in Concrete and Polymer Modified Concrete Members Subjected to Shearing Loads. *Proceedings, J. of Testing and Evaluation* Vol. 11 No. 2, pp. 89–99

8.18 Dulacska H 1972 Dowel Action of Reinforcement Crossing Cracks in Concrete. *Proceedings, ACI Journal* Vol. 69 No. 12, American Concrete Institute, Detroit, pp. 754–757

8.19 Nawy E G, and Kudlapur S T 1991 Shear Interaction of High Strength Two Layered Concretes at Early Ages Placed in Subfreezing Temperatures. *Transactions No. 1984* Transportation Research Board, National Research Council, Washington, D.C., pp. 37–52

8.20 Hermansen B R, and Cowan J 1974 Modified Shear Friction Theory for Bracket Design. *Proceedings, ACI Journal* Vol. 71 No. 2, American Concrete Institute, Detroit, pp. 55–57

8.21 Kudlapur S T, and Nawy E G 1992 Early Age Shear Friction Behavior of High Strength Concrete Layered Systems at Subfreezing Temperatures. *Proceedings Symposium on Designing Concrete Structures For Serviceability and Safety ACI SP 133-9* ed. E G Nawy and A Scanlon, American Concrete Institute, Detroit, Ch. 133, pp. 159–185

8.22   ASTM 1994 Concrete and Mineral Aggregates. *Annual Book of ASTM Standards* Section 4, Vol. 4.02, American Society for Testing and Materials, Philadelphia, pp. 1–527

8.23   Balaguru P N, Ukadike M, and Nawy E G 1987 Freeze Thaw Resistance of Polymer Modified Concrete. *ACI SP 100-48* American Concrete Institute, Detroit, pp. 863–876

8.24   Traina L A, and Mansour S A 1991 Biaxial Strength and Deformational Behavior of Plain and Steel Fiber Concrete. *ACI Materials Journal* Vol. 88 No. 4, American Concrete Institute, Detroit, pp. 354–362

8.25   Yong, Y K, Nour M G, and Nawy E G 1988 Behavior of Laterally Confined High Strength Concrete Under Axial Load. *Proceedings, ASCE J. Structural Division* Vol. 114 No. 2, pp. 332–351

8.26   Nawy E G, Danesi R F, and Grosco J J 1968 Rectangular Spiral Binder Effect on the Plastic Hinge Rotation Capacity in Reinforced Concrete Beams. *Proceedings, ACI Journal* Vol. 65 No. 12, American Concrete Institute, Detroit, pp. 1001–1010

8.27   Mander J M, Priestly M N, and Park R 1988 Theoretical Stress-Strain For Confined Concrete. *Proceedings, ASCE J. Structural Division* Vol. 114 No. 8, pp. 1804–1826.

8.28   Fafitis A, and Shah S P 1985 Lateral Reinforcement for High Strength Concrete Columns. *ACI SP-87* American Concrete Institute, Detroit, pp. 213–232

8.29   Setunge S, Attard M M, and Darvall P Le P 1993 Ultimate Strength of Confined Very High Strength Concrete. *Proceedings, ACI Structural Journal* Vol. 90 No. 563, American Concrete Institute, Detroit, pp. 632–641

8.30   Maguruma H, and Watanabe F 1990 Ductility Improvement of High Strength Concrete Columns with Lateral Confinement. *ACI SP 121-4* American Concrete Institute, Detroit, pp. 47–60

8.31   Chen R C, Carrasquillo R L, and Fowler D W 1985 Behavior of High Strength Concrete Under Uniaxial and Biaxial Compression. *ACI SP 87-14* American Concrete Institute, Detroit, pp. 251–273

8.32   ICBO-UBC Code 1994 Uniform Building Code Vol.II, International Conference of Building Officials (ICBO), Whittier, CA, pp. 1339

8.33   Mehta P K, and Aitcin P C 1990 Microstructural Basis of Selection of Materials and Mix Proportions for High Strength Concrete. *Proceedings 2nd International Symposium on High Strength Concrete, Berkeley. ACI SP 121-14* ed. W T Henter, pp. 265–286

8.34   Ronneberg H, and Sandvik M 1993 High Strength Concrete For North Sea Platforms. *ACI Compilation 17* American Concrete Institute, Detroit, pp. 61–66

8.35   Aitcin P C, Sarkar S L, and Laplante P 1993 Long-Term Characteristics of a Very High Strength Concrete. *ACI Compilation 17* American Concrete Institute, Detroit, pp. 42–46

8.36   Berner D E, Gerwick B C Jr, and Hoff G C 1991 T-Headed Stirrup Bars. *Concrete International* American Concrete Institute, Detroit

8.37   Berner D E, and Hoff G C 1994 Headed Reinforcement in Disturbed Strain Regions of Concrete Members. *Concrete International*, American Concrete Institute, Detroit, pp. 5

8.38   Lloyd N A, and Rangan B V 1995 High Strength Concrete Columns Under Eccentric Compression. *Research Report 1/95* Curtin University of Technology, Perth, Australia 199 p

9 High Strength Concrete Fiber Composites

9.1 HISTORICAL DEVELOPMENT

Fibers have been used to reinforce brittle materials from time immemorial, dating back to the Egyptian and Babylonian eras if not earlier. Straws were used to reinforce sunbaked bricks and mud-hut walls, horsehair was used to reinforce plaster, and asbestos fibers have been used to reinforce portland cement mortars. Research by Romualdi and Batson[9.1] and Romualdi and Mandel[9.2] on closely spaced random fibers in the late 1950s and early 1960s primarily on steel fibers heralded the era of using fiber composite concretes as we know them today. In addition, Shah,[9.3] Swamy,[9.4] and several other researchers in the United States, United Kingdom, and Russia embarked on extensive investigations in this area, exploring other fibers in addition to steel fibers. By the 1960s, steel fiber concrete started to be used in pavements in particular.

In the mid 1960s, Nawy and his team[9.5,9.6] conducted extensive work on the use of bundled and resin-impregnated glass fibers, forming deformed bars as main reinforcement in structural elements. Since that time considerable progress has been made in using fiber filaments as a supplement to concrete matrices to improve the mechanical properties of concrete, but not as a replacement for the main bar reinforcement in supported structural components. The science of fibrous concrete and composites has advanced to an extent that justifies extensive use in the years to come.

9.2 GENERAL CHARACTERISTICS

Concrete is weak in tension. Microcracks start to generate in the matrix of a structural element at about 10–15 percent of the ultimate load, propagating into macrocracks at 25–30 percent of the ultimate load. Consequently, plain concrete members cannot be expected to sustain large transverse loading without the addition of continuous bar reinforcing elements in the tensile zone of supported members such as beams or slabs. But the developing microcracking and macrocracking still cannot be arrested or slowed down by the sole use of main continuous reinforcement. The function of such reinforcement is to replace the

Plate 44 Under construction in Newfoundland, Hibernia is the first platform designed for iceberg impacts; 80 m water depth and 165 000 m³ of 70 MPa concrete (Courtesy Dr. George C. Hoff)

function of the tensile zone of a section and to assume the tension equilibrium force in the section.

Consequently, the addition of randomly spaced discontinuous fiber elements should aid in arresting the development or propagation of the microcracks which are known to generate at such an early stage of the loading history. While fibers have been used to reinforce brittle materials such as concrete since time immemorial, newly developed fibers have been extensively used in the past three decades worldwide. Different types are commercially available such as those made from steel, glass, polypropylene, or graphite. They have proven their ability to improve the mechanical properties of the concrete, both as a structure and a material, *not* as a replacement for the continuous bar reinforcements when they are needed, but in addition to them.

Concrete fiber composites are concrete elements made from a mix comprising hydraulic cements, fine and coarse aggregates, sometimes including pozzolanic cementitious materials, admixtures commonly used with conventional concrete, and a dispersion of discontinuous, small fibers made from steel, glass, organic polymers, or graphites. The fibers could also be vegetable fibers such as sisal or jute.

Generally, if the fibers are made from steel, the fiber length varies from 0.5 to 2.5 in. (12.7 to 63.5 mm). They are either round, produced by cutting or chopping wire, or flat, having typical cross sections of 0.006–0.016 in. (0.15–0.41 mm) in thickness and 0.01–0.035 in. (0.25–0.90 mm) in width, and produced by shearing sheets or flattening wire. The most common diameters of the round wires are 0.017–0.040 in. (0.45–1.0 mm).[9.7–9.9] The wires are usually crimped or deformed or have small heads on them for better bond within the matrix, and some are crescent-shaped in cross section.

The fiber content in a mixture, where steel fibers are used, usually varies from 0.25 to 2 percent by volume, namely, from 33 to 265 lb/yd^3 (20 to 165 kg/m^3). A fiber content of 50–60 lb/yd^3 is common in lightly loaded slabs on grade, precast elements, and composite steel deck topping. The upper end of the range, more difficult to apply, is used for security applications such as vaults, safes, and impact-resisting structures.

Glass fibers that are alkali resistant are also gaining wide use. These would normally contain zirconium (ZrO_2) to minimize or eliminate the alkaline corrosive attack on glass present in the cement paste. Synthetic fibers made from nylon or polypropylene have recently gained application, both loose and woven into geotextile form, as more information on their mechanical performance in the matrix is obtained and more understanding of their structural contribution to resisting cracking is determined.

The introduction of the fiber additions to concrete as of the early 1900s has aimed principally at enhancing the tensile strength of concrete. As is well known, the tensile strength is 8–14 percent of the compressive strength of normal concretes with the resulting cracking at low stress levels. Such a weakness is overcome partially by the addition of reinforcing bars that could be either steel or fiberglass bars as *main continuous reinforcement* in beams and one-way and two-way structural slabs or slabs on grade.[9.5, 9.6] The continuous reinforcing elements cannot stop the development of the microcracks as indicated earlier. Fibers, on the other hand, are discontinuous and randomly distributed in the matrix both in the tensile and compressive zones of a structural element. They are able to add to the stiffness and crack control performance through preventing the microcracks from propagating and widening and also increase ductility due to their energy absorption capacity. Common applications of fiber reinforced concrete include overlays in bridge decks, industrial floors, shotcrete applications, highway and airport pavements, thin shell structures, seismic and explosion-resisting structures, and superflat surface slabs on grade in warehouses for reduction of expansion joints.

Table 9.1, compiled from several sources including ACI reports,[9.7] describes the geometry and mechanical properties of various types of fibers that can be used as randomly dispersed filaments in a concrete matrix. As there is a wide range in each type of fiber, the designer would have to be guided by the manufacturer's data on each particular product and the experience with it before a decision is made on the selected type.

Table 9.1 Typical properties of fibers

Type of fiber	Diameter, in. × 10³ (mm)	Specific gravity (s.g.)	Tensile strength, psi × 10³ (GPa)[a]	Young's Modulus psi × 10⁶ (GPa)[a]	Ultimate elongation (%)
(1)	(2)	(3)[b]	(4)	(5)	(6)
Acrylic	0.6–0.13 (0.02–0.35)	1.1	30–60 (0.2–0.4)	0.3 (2)	1.1
Asbestos	0.05–0.80 (0.0015–0.02)	3.2	80–140 (0.6–1.0)	12–20 (83–138)	1–2
Cotton	6–24 (0.2–0.6)	1.5	60–100 (0.4–0.7)	0.7 (4.8)	3–10
Glass	0.2–0.6 (0.005–0.15)	2.5	150–380 (1.0–2.6)	10–11.5 (70–80)	1.5–3.5
Graphite	0.3–0.36 (0.008–0.009)	1.9	190–380 (1.0–2.6)	34–60 (230–415)	0.5–1.0
Kevlar	0.4 (0.010)	1.45	505–520 (3.5–3.6)	9.4 (65–133)	2.1–4.0
Nylon (high tenacity)	0.6–16 (0.02–0.40)	1.1	110–120 (0.76–0.82)	0.6 (4.1)	16–20
Polyester (high tenacity)	0.6–16 (0.02–0.40)	1.4	105–125 (0.72–0.86)	1.2 (8.3)	11–13
Polypropylene	0.6–16 (0.02–0.40)	0.95	80–110 (0.55–0.76)	0.5 (3.5)	15–25
Rayon (high tenacity)	0.8–15 (0.02–0.38)	1.5	60–90 (0.4–0.6)	1.0 (6.9)	10–25
Rock wool (Scandinavian)	0.5–30 (0.01–0.8)	2.7	70–110 (0.5–0.76)	~0.6	0.5–0.7
Sisal	0.4–4 (0.01–0.10)	1.5	115 (0.8)	—	3.0
Steel	4–40 (0.1–1.0)	7.84	50–300 (0.3–2.0)	29.0 (200)	0.5–3.5
Cement matrix	—	1.5–2.5	0.4–1.0 (0.003–0.007)	1.5–6.5 (10–45)	0.02

[a] GPa × 0.145 = 10⁶ lb/in.²
[b] Density = Col. 3 × 62.4 lb/ft³ = Col. 3 × 10³ kg/m³.

9.3   MIXTURE PROPORTIONING

Mixing of the fibers with the other mix constituents can be done by several methods. The method selected depends on the facilities available and the job requirements, namely, plant batching, ready-mixed concrete, or hand mixing in the laboratory. The most important factor is to ensure *uniform dispersion* of the fibers and the prevention of segregation or balling of the fibers during mixing. Segregation or balling during mixing is affected by many factors that can be summarized as follows:

1. aspect ratio l/d_f—most important
2. volume percentage of the fiber
3. coarse aggregate size, gradation, and quantity
4. water/cementitious ratio and method of mixing

A maximum aspect ratio of l/d_f and a steel fiber content in excess of 2 percent by volume make it difficult to have a uniform mix. While conventional mixing procedures can be used, it is advisable to use a 3/8 in. (9.7 mm) maximum aggregate size. The water requirement will vary from concrete without fibers, depending also on the type of cement replacement cementitious pozzolans used and their percentage by volume of the matrix. Tables 9.2 and 9.3 give typical mix proportions for normal weight fibrous reinforced concrete and fly ash fibrous concrete mixes.[9.7]

A workable method for mixing in a step-by-step chronological procedure can be summarized as follows:

1. Blend part of the fiber and aggregate before charging into the mixer.
2. Blend fine and coarse aggregate in the mixer, then add more fibers at the mixing speed. Lastly, add cement and water simultaneously or cement followed *immediately* by water and additives.
3. Add the balance of the fiber to the previously charged constituents. Add the remaining cementitious materials and water.
4. Continue mixing as required by normal practice.

Table 9.2 Typical proportions for normal weight fiber reinforced concrete[9.7]

Cement	550–950 lb/yd³
W/C ratio	0.4–0.6
Percentage of sand to aggregate	50–100%
Maximum aggregate	3/8 in.
Air content	6–9%
Fiber content	0.5–2.5 vol% of mix steel: 1% = 132 lb/yd³ glass: 1% = 42 lb/yd³ nylon: 1% = 19 lb/yd³

1 lb/yd³ = 0.5933 kg/m³.

Table 9.3 Typical fly ash fibrous concrete mix[9.7]

Cement	490 lb/yd^3
Fly ash	225 lb/yd^3
W/C ratio	0.54
Percentage of sand to aggregate	50%
Maximum size coarse aggregate	3/8 in.
Steel fiber content (0.010 × 0.022 × 1.0 in.)	1.5 vol%
Air-entraining agent	Manufacturer's recom.
Water-reducing agent	Manufacturer's recom.
Slump	5–6 in.

1 lb/yd^3 = 0.5933 kg/m^3.
1 in. = 2.54 cm.

5. Place the fibrous concrete in the forms. Fibrous concrete requires more vibrating than nonfibrous concrete. While internal vibration if carefully applied is acceptable, external vibration of the formwork and the surface is preferable in order to prevent segregation of the fibers.

9.4   MECHANICS OF FIBER REINFORCEMENT

9.4.1   First Cracking Load

Fiber reinforced concrete in flexure essentially undergoes a trilinear deformation behavior as shown in Fig. 9.1. Point *A* on the load–deflection diagram represents the first cracking load that can be termed the first-crack strength.[9.12] Normally, this is the same load level at which a nonreinforced element cracks. Hence, segment *OA* in the diagram would be the same and essentially have the same slope for both plain and fiber reinforced concrete.

Once the matrix is cracked, the applied load is transferred to the fibers which bridge and tie the crack from opening further. As the fibers deform, additional narrow cracks develop and continued cracking of the matrix takes place until the maximum load reaches point *B* of the load–deflection diagram. During this stage,

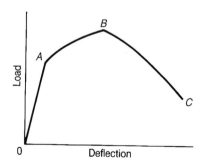

Fig. 9.1 Schematic load–deflection relationship of fiber reinforced concrete

Plate 45 Glass fibers (Courtesy American Concrete Institute)

debonding and pullout of some of the fibers occur. But the yield strength in most of the fibers is not reached.

In the falling branch *BC* of the load–deflection diagram, matrix cracking and fiber pullout continue. If the fibers are long enough to be able to maintain their bond with the surrounding gel, they may fail by yielding or by fracture of the fiber element depending on their size and spacing.

9.4.2   Critical Fiber Length: Length Factor

If l_c is the critical length of a fiber above which the fiber undergoes fracture rather than pullout when the crack intersects the fiber at its midpoint, it can be approximated by[9.12]

$$l_c = \frac{d_f}{2v_b}\sigma_f \qquad\qquad [9.1]$$

where d_f = fiber diameter
v_b = interfacial bond strength
σ_f = fiber strength

Bentur and Mindess[9.13] developed an expression to relate the average pullout work and the fiber matrix interfacial bond strength in terms of the critical fiber length, demonstrating that the strength of a composite increases continuously with the fiber length. This is of significance as it indicates that pullout work may go through a maximum and decrease as bond strength increases over a critical value. This loss of pullout work would be reduced to a typical range of $l = 10$ mm in cement-based composites to be discussed in Section 9.6. If a critical v_b value of 1.0 MPa is used and a small fiber diameter $d_f = 20$ μm—the increase in bond may result in reduced toughness.

9.4.3 Critical Fiber Spacing: Space Factor

The spacing of the fibers considerably affects cracking development in the matrix. The closer the spacing, the higher is the first cracking load of the matrix. This is due to the fact that the fibers reduce the stress intensity factor which controls fracture. The approach taken by Romualdi and Batson[9.1] to increase the tensile strength of the mortar was by increasing the stress intensity factor through decreasing the spacing of the fibers as crack arresters. Figure 9.2 due to Romualdi and Batson relates the tensile cracking stress to the spacing of the fibers for various volumetric percentages. Figure 9.3 compares the theoretical and experimental values to the ratio of the first cracking load to the cracking strength of plain concrete (strength ratio). Both diagrams demonstrate that the closer the spacing of the fibers, the higher is the strength ratio, namely, the higher is the tensile strength of the concrete up to the practical workability and cost-effectiveness limits.

Several expressions to define the spacing of the fibers have been developed. If s is the spacing of the fibers, one expression[9.1] gives

$$s = 13.8 d_f \sqrt{\frac{1.0}{\rho}} \qquad [9.2]$$

where d_f = diameter of the fiber
ρ = fiber percentage by volume of the matrix

Another expression due to McKee gives

$$s = 3 \sqrt{\frac{V}{\rho}} \qquad [9.3]$$

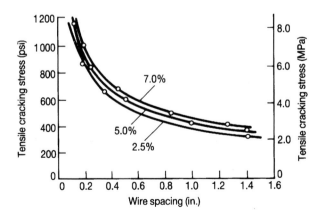

Fig. 9.2 Effect of steel fiber spacing on the tensile cracking stress in fibrous concrete for $\rho = 2.5$, 5.9, and 7.5 percent[9.1]

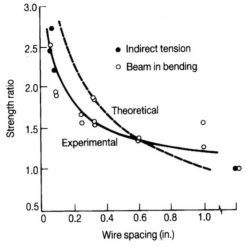

Fig. 9.3 Effect of fiber spacing on the strength ratio[9.2] (ratio = first cracking load of fibrous concrete divided by strength of plain concrete)

where V is the volume of one fiber element. Another expression due to Mindess and Young[9.12] taking also into account the length of the fiber, gives

$$s = 13.8 d_f \frac{\sqrt{l}}{\rho} \qquad\qquad [9.4]$$

9.4.4 Fiber Orientation: Fiber Efficiency Factor

The orientation of the fibers with respect to load determines the efficiency with which the randomly oriented fibers can resist the tensile forces in their direction. This is synonymous with the contribution of the bent bars and vertical shear stirrups in beams provided for resisting the inclined diagonal tension stress. If one assumes perfect randomness, the efficiency factor $= 0.41l$, but can vary between $0.33l$ and $0.65l$ close to the surface of the specimen as troweling or leveling can modify the orientation of the fibers.[9.12]

9.4.5 Static Flexural Strength Prediction: Beams With Fibers Only

For predicting the flexural strength, several methods could be applied depending on the type of fiber, the type of matrix, using empirical data from laboratory experiments, basing the design on the bonded area of the fiber, or using the law of mixtures. An empirical expression for the composite flexural strength based on a composite material approach can be[9.13]:

$$\sigma_c = A\sigma_m(1 - V_f) + BV_f \frac{l}{d} \qquad [9.5]$$

where σ_c = composite flexural strength
   σ_m = ultimate strength of the matrix
   V_f = volume fraction of the fibers adjusted for the effect of randomness
   A, B = constants
   l/d = aspect ratio of the fiber where l is the length and d is the diameter of the fiber

The constants A and B obtained from 4 in.× 4 in. × 12 in. (100 mm × 100 mm × 305 mm) model beam tests by Swamy et al. and adopted by ACI Committee 544[9.8] produced the following.

First crack composite flexural strength (psi)

$$\sigma_f = 0.843 f_r V_m + 425 V_f \frac{l}{d_f} \qquad [9.6]$$

where f_r = stress in the matrix (modulus of rupture of the plane mortar or concrete), psi
   V_m = volume fraction of the matrix = $1 - V_f$
   V_f = volume fraction of the fibers = $1 - V_m$
   l/d_f = ratio of the length to diameter of the fibers, namely, the aspect ratio

Ultimate composite flexural strength, psi

$$\sigma_{cu} = 0.97 f_r V_m + 494 V_f \frac{l}{d_f} \qquad [9.7]$$

9.5   MECHANICAL PROPERTIES OF FIBROUS CONCRETE STRUCTURAL ELEMENTS

9.5.1   Controlling Factors

From Section 9.4, it can be seen that the mechanical properties of fiber reinforced concretes are influenced by several factors. The major ones are

1. Type of fiber, namely, the fiber material and its shape
2. Aspect ratio l/d_f, namely, the ratio of the fiber length to its nominal diameter
3. Amount of fiber in percentage by volume ρ
4. Spacing of the fiber s
5. Strength of the concrete or mortar matrix
6. Size, shape, and preparation of the specimen

Hence, it is important to conduct laboratory tests to failure on the mixtures using specimen models similar in form to the elements being designed. As the fibers affect the performance of the end product in all material resistance capacities, such as flexure, shear, direct tension, and impact it is important to evaluate the test specimen performance with regard to those parameters.

The contribution of the fiber to tensile strength as discussed in Section 9.3 is due to its ability as reinforcement to assume the stress from the matrix when it cracks through interface shear friction interlock between the fiber and the matrix. This phenomenon is analogous to the shear-friction interlock hypothesis presented in Section 8.7 on the mechanism of shear-friction interlock. Hence, deformed or crimped fibers would have a greater influence than smooth and straight ones. The pullout resistance in zone *AB* of Fig. 9.1 is proportional to the interfacial surface area.[9.8] The nonround fiber cross sections and the smaller diameter round fibers induce a larger resistance per unit volume than the larger diameter fibers.

This is also analogous to the crack control behavior in traditionally reinforced structural members. There, a larger number of smaller diameter bars, more closely spaced, are more effective than a smaller number of large diameter for the same reinforcement volume percentage.[9.15] One reason is the larger surface interaction area between the fibers and the surrounding matrix resulting in a higher bond and shear-friction resistance.

9.5.2   Strength in Compression

The effect of the contribution of the fibers to the compressive strength of the concrete seems to be minor as seen in Fig. 9.4[9.16] for tests using steel fibers. However, the ductility and toughness are considerably enhanced as a function of

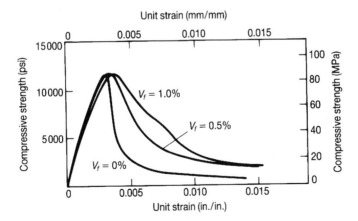

Fig. 9.4 Influence of volume fraction of steel fibers on stress–strain behavior for 13 000 psi concrete[9.16]

the increase in the volume fractions and aspect ratios of the fibers used. Hsu[9.16] shows in Fig. 9.4 the effect of the increase in volume fraction on the stress–strain relationship of the fibrous concrete through increasing the fiber volume from 0 to 1.5 per cent for concretes having a compressive strength of 13 100 psi (90.3 MPa). Figures 9.5 and 9.6 from Fanella and Naaman[9.17] depict a similar trend with respect to both a volume fraction ratio up to 3 per cent and an aspect ratio 47–100. Figure 9.7, from Shah, also demonstrates the influence of the increase in fiber content on the relative toughness of reinforced concrete members.

Toughness is a measure of the ability to absorb energy during deformation. It can be estimated from the area under the stress–strain or load–deformation diagrams. A toughness index (TI) expression proposed in Hsu and Hsu[9.16] gives

$$TI = 1.421RI + 1.035 \qquad [9.8]$$

where
RI = reinforcing index = $V_f(l/d_f)$
V_f = volume fraction
l/d_f = aspect ratio

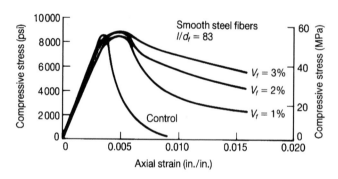

Fig. 9.5 Influence of volume fraction of steel fibers on stress–strain behavior for 9000 psi concrete[9.17]

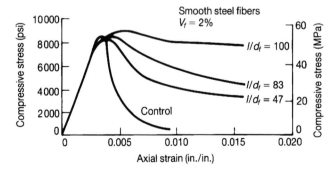

Fig. 9.6 Influence of aspect ratio of steel fibers on stress–strain behavior[9.17]

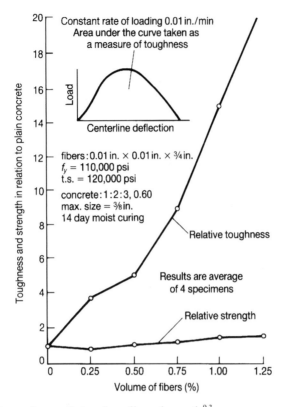

Fig. 9.7 Relative toughness and strength vs. fiber volume ratio[9.3]

Figure 9.8 gives the relationship of the toughness index to the reinforcing index of fibrous high strength concretes within the limitation of the type, aspect ratio, and volume fractions of the steel fibers used in those tests. In short, by increasing the volume fraction, both ductility and toughness have been shown to increase significantly within the practical limits of workable volume content of fiber in a concrete mix.

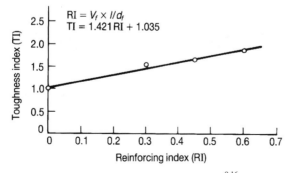

Fig. 9.8 Toughness index vs. reinforcing index of fibrous concrete[9.16]

9.5.3   Strength in Direct Tension

The effect of different shapes of the fiber filaments on the tensile stress behavior of steel fiber reinforced mortars in direct tension is demonstrated in Fig. 9.9. The descending portions of the plots show that the fibers with better anchorage quality increase the tensile resistance of the fiber concrete beyond the first cracking load.

9.5.4   Flexural Strength

Fibers seem to affect the magnitude of flexural strength in concrete and mortar elements to a much greater extent than they affect the strength of comparable elements subjected to direct tension or compression.[9.8] Two stages of loading portray the behavior. The first controlling stage is the *first cracking load stage* in the load–deflection diagram and the second controlling stage is the ultimate load stage. Both the first cracking load and the ultimate flexural capacity are affected as a function of the product of the fiber volume concentration ρ and the aspect ratio l/d_f. Fiber concentrations less than 0.5 percent of volume of the matrix and aspect ratios less than 50 seem to have a small effect on the flexural strength although they can still have a pronounced effect on the toughness of the concrete element as seen in Fig. 9.7.

The flexural strength of plain concrete beams containing steel fibers was defined in Section 9.4.4, Eqs. 9.6 and 9.7. For structural beams reinforced with both normal reinforcing bars and added fibers to the matrix, a modification of the standard expression for the nominal moment strength $M_n = A_s f_y (d - a/2)$, has to

Plate 46 Some shapes and sizes of steel fibers (Courtesy American Concrete Institute)

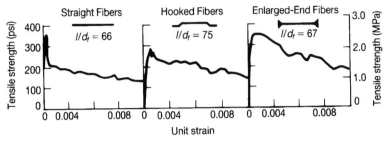

Fig. 9.9 Effect of shape of steel fiber on tensile stress in mortar specimens loaded in direct tension[9.3]

Plate 47 Fracture surface of steel fiber reinforced concrete (Courtesy American Concrete Institute)

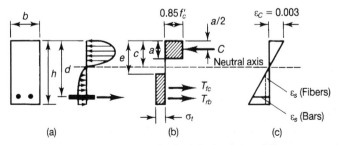

Fig. 9.10 Stress and strain distribution across depth of singly reinforced fibrous concrete beams: (a) assumed stress distribution; (b) equivalent stress block distribution; (c) strain distribution

be made in order to account for the shear-friction interaction of the fibers in preventing the flexural macrocracks from opening and propagating in the tensile zone of the concrete section, as seen in Fig. 9.10.[9.18] In this diagram, the standard hypothesis of neglecting the area of concrete in the tensile zone is, therefore, modified so that an additional equilibrium tensile force T_{fc}, is added to the section. This moves the neutral axis down, leading to a higher nominal moment strength M_n. The resulting expression[9.8, 9.18] for M_n becomes

$$M_n = A_s f_y \left(d - \frac{a}{2} \right) + \sigma_t b(h - e) \left(\frac{h}{2} + \frac{e}{2} - \frac{a}{2} \right) \qquad [9.9]$$

$$e = [\epsilon(\text{fibers}) + 0.003] \frac{c}{0.003} \qquad [9.10]$$

$$\sigma_t(\text{psi}) = \frac{1.12l}{d_f \rho_f F_{bc}} \qquad [9.11a]$$

$$\sigma_t(\text{MPa}) = \frac{0.00772l}{d_f \rho_f F_{bc}} \qquad [9.11b]$$

where
l = fiber length
d_f = fiber diameter
ρ_f = percentage by volume of the fibers
F_{be} = bond efficiency of the steel fiber depending on its characteristics and varies from 1.0 to 1.2
a = depth of the equivalent rectangular block
b = width of beam
c = depth to the neutral axis
d = effective depth of the beam to the center of the main tensile bar reinforcement
e = distance from the extreme compression fibers to the top of the tensile stress block of the fibrous concrete
ϵ_s = f_y/E_s of the bar reinforcement
ϵ_f = σ_f/E_c of the fibers developed at pullout at a dynamic bond stress of 333 psi
σ_t = tensile yield stress in the fiber
T_{fc} = tensile yield of the fibrous concrete = $\sigma_t b(h - e)$
T_{rb} = tensile yield force of the bar reinforcement = $A_s f_y$

9.5.5 Shear Strength

A combination of vertical stirrups and randomly distributed fibers in the matrix enhances the diagonal tension capacity of concrete beams. The degree of increase in the diagonal tension capacity is a function of the shear span/depth ratio of a beam. This ratio determines the mode of failure in normal beams that do not fall in the category of deep beams and brackets as detailed by Nawy.[9.19]

Williamson[9.20] found that when 1.66 percent by volume of straight steel fibers were used instead of stirrups, the shear capacity increased by 45 percent over beams without stirrups. When steel fibers with deformed ends were used at a volume ratio of 1.1 percent, the shear capacity increased by 45–67 percent and the beams failed by flexure. Using crimped-end fibers increased the shear capacity by almost 100 percent.

In general, as the shear span/depth ratio a/d decreased and the fiber volume increased, the shear strength increased proportionally. Tests by Sharma[9.21] resulted in the following expression in the ACI 544 Report[9.8] for the average shear stress v_c for beams in which steel fibers were added:

$$v_{cf} = \frac{2}{3}f'_t \left(\frac{d}{a}\right)^{\frac{1}{4}}$$

[9.12]

where
f'_t = tensile splitting strength
d = effective depth of a beam
a = shear span = distance from the point of application of the load to the face of the support when concentrated loads are acting or the clear beam span when distributed loads are acting

9.5.6   Environmental Effects

Freezing and Thawing
The addition of fibers to a matrix does not seem to have an appreciable improvement on the freezing and thawing performance of concrete since its resistance to such an environmental effect is controlled by permeability, void ratio, and freeze–thaw cycles. They tend, however, to hold the scaling concrete pieces together, thereby reducing the extent of apparent scaling.

Shrinkage and Creep
No appreciable improvement in the shrinkage and creep performance of concrete occurs by the addition of fibers but perhaps a slight decrease due to the need for more paste mortar in the mixture when fibers are also used. Cracking due to drying shrinkage in restrained elements can be slightly improved as the cracks are restrained from generating because of the bridging effect of the randomly distributed fibers.

9.5.7   Dynamic Loading Performance

The behavior of fibrous concrete elements under dynamic loading seems to be 3–10 times that of plain concrete. It was also found that the total energy absorbed by the steel fibrous concrete beams can be 40–100 times that for plain concrete beams depending on the type, deformed shape, and percentage by volume of the fibers.[9.8]

9.6   FIBER REINFORCED CEMENT COMPOSITES

9.6.1   General Characteristics

Fiber reinforced concretes are designed to contain a *maximum* of 2 percent by volume of fibers, using the same mix design procedures and placement as nonfibrous concretes. Fiber reinforced cement composites, on the other hand could contain a volume fraction, namely, a fiber content by volume, as high as 8–25 percent. Consequently, neither the design of the mixture, nor the constituent materials in the matrix can be similar to those of conventional fibrous or nonfibrous concretes. Either cement only or cement with sand is used in the mix and without a coarse aggregate, in order to achieve the high strength, ductility, and performance expected from this product.

In addition, the 1980s saw the development of cement compositions termed *macrodefect free cements (MDF)* having a high Young's modulus and flexural strength up to almost 30 000 psi (~200 MPa); and *densified cements (DSP)* having a particle size of 0.5 μm, less than one-twentieth that of portland cement. The void content in any matrix can be reduced with the addition of pozzolans such as silica fume to a negligible percentage.

With these developments as a background, the following are the types of cement-based composites that are being studied today:

1. Slurry infiltrated fiber concretes (SIFCON) and refractory use composite (SIFCA)
2. Densified small particles systems (DSP)
3. Compact reinforced composites (CRC)
4. Carbon fiber cement-based composites
5. Superstrength reactive powder concrete (RPC)

These cement-based composites can achieve a compressive strength in excess of 44 000 psi (300 MPa) and an energy absorption capacity, namely, ductility, that could be up to 1000 times that of plain concrete.[9.22]

9.6.2   Slurry Infiltrated Fiber Concretes (SIFCON)

Because of high volume fraction of the steel fibers (8–25 percent), the mix for a structural member is formulated by sprinkling the fiber into the formwork or over a substratum. Either the substratum is stacked with fibers to a prescribed height or the form is completely or partially filled with the fibers, depending on the requirement of the design. After the fibers are placed, a low viscosity cement slurry is poured or pumped into the fiber bed or into the formwork, infiltrating into the spaces between the fibers. Typical cement/fly ash/sand proportions can vary from 90/10/0 to 30/20/50 by weight.[9.23] The water/cementitious ratio (W/C + F) can range between 0.45 to 0.20 by weight, with a plasticizer content of 10–40 oz per 100 lb of the total cementitious weight (C + F). Batch trials of the slurry mix have to be particularly made with regard to the W/(C + F) ratio in order to arrive at the workable slurry mix that can fully penetrate the fibers' depth.

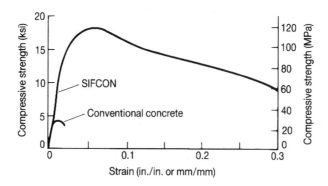

Fig. 9.11 Stress–strain relationship of SIFCON with rupture strain of around 0.45 in./in.[9.22]

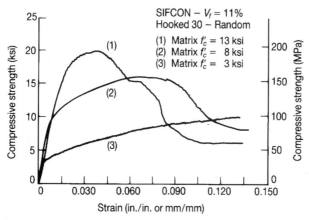

Fig. 9.12 Influence of matrix compressive strength on the stress–strain response of SIFCON in compression[9.23]

Figure 9.11 gives a stress–strain diagram for a slurry infiltrated fiber concrete (SIFCON) mix[9.24] with a compressive strength close to 18 000 psi but with a very large strain capability in the falling branch of the diagram.

Figure 9.12 gives the influence of the matrix compressive strength on the stress–strain response of SIFCON in compression.[9.23] The fiber content $V_f = 11$ percent resulted in total uniaxial strain in excess of 10 percent.

9.6.3   MDF and DSP Cement Composites

The densified small particle systems (DSP) and the compact reinforced composites (CRC) depend on gaining superhigh strength largely on the type of compact density cements used for the cement-based composites and the proper proportioning to considerably reduce or practically eliminate most of the voids in the paste.

9.6.4   Carbon Fiber Reinforced Cement Based Composites

Petroleum pitch-based carbon fibers have recently been developed for use as reinforcement for cement-based composites. Their diameter varies from 10 to 18 μm (0.0004 to 0.0007 in.) and their lengths vary from 1/8 to 1/2 in. (3 to 12 mm). They have a typical tensile strength of 60–110 ksi (400–750 MPa). They are incorporated in the cement-based composites in essentially the same manner as steel fibers in concrete and are uniformly distributed and randomly oriented.

Because of the very small length and the small diameter of the carbon fibers, a high fiber count is attained in the cementitious matrix at a typical volume fraction of 0.5–3 percent.[9.25] The spacing between the fibers is approximately 0.004 in. (0.1 mm) at a 3 percent fiber volume fraction. Their function is similar to that of the steel fibers in intercepting the microcracks from propagating and opening.

9.6.5   Superstrength Reactive Powder Concretes

Superstrength reactive powder concretes have compressive strengths of 30 000– 120 000 psi (200–800 MPa). The lower range in compressive strength is used today for construction of structural elements. The higher ranges are used in nonstructural applications such as flooring, safes, and storage compartments for nuclear waste. They are called superhigh strength concretes and possess very high ductility necessary for applications in structural systems.

The principal characteristic in such concretes is the use of a powder concrete in which aggregates and traditional sand are replaced by ground quartz less than 300 μm in size.[9.26] In this manner homogeneity of the mix is greatly improved and the distribution in the size of the particles is consequently reduced by almost two orders of magnitude. Another major improvement in the property of the hardened concrete is the increase in the Young's modulus value of the paste by almost a factor of three so that its value can reach 6×10^6 to 11×10^6 psi (55– 75 GPa) thereby reducing the effects of incompatibility of the moduli of the paste and the quartz powder. Richard and Cheyrezy[9.26] have developed the following mechanical characteristics of the RPC concrete:

1. Improvement in homogeneity resulting in a Young's modulus up to 11×10^6 psi (75 GPa).
2. Increase of dry compact density of the dry solids. While silica fume with its small particle size of 0.1–0.5 μm and an optimum mix content of 25 percent of cement by weight gives excellent dry compact density, additional amounts of precipitated silica further improve the dry compact density.
3. Increase of the density of concrete by maintaining the fresh concrete under pressure at the placement stage and during setting. This results in the removal of air bubbles, expulsion of excess water, and partial reduction of the plastic shrinkage during final set.
4. Improvement in microstructure through hot curing for 2 days at 194°F (90°C) to speed the activation of the pozzolanic reaction of the silica fume, resulting in a 30 percent gain in compressive strength.

Table 9.4 Mixture composition and concrete mechanical properties of superhigh strength reactive powder concrete (RPC)[9.26]

(1)	RPC 200 concrete (2)	RPC 800 concrete (3)
Portland cement, type V, lb/yd^3 (kg/m^3)	1 614 (955)	1 690 (1 000)
Fine sand (150–400 μm), lb/yd^3 (kg/m^3)	1 775 (1 051)	845 (500)
Ground quartz (4 μm), lb/yd^3 (kg/m^3)	—	659 (390)
Silica fume (18 m^2/g), lb/yd^3 (kg/m^3)	387 (229)	389 (230)
Precipitated silica (35 m^2/g), lb/yd^3 (kg/m^3)	16.9 (10)	—
Superplasticizer (polyacrylate), lb/yd^3 (kg/m^3)	22.0 (13)	30.4 (18)
Steel fibers, lb/yd^3 (kg/m^3)	323 (191)	1 065 (630)
Total water, gal/yd^3 (l/m^3)	31.2 (153)	36.7 (180)
Cylinder compressive strength, psi × 10^3 (MPa)	24–33 (170–230)	71–99 (490–680)
Flexural strength, psi × 10^3 (MPa)	3.6–8.7 (25–60)	6.5–14.8 (45–102)
Fracture energy (J/m^2)	15 000–40 000	1 200–2 000
Young's modulus, psi × 10^6 (GPa)	7.8–8.7×10^3 (54–60)	(9.8–10.9)10^3 (65–75)

1 l/m^3 = 0.2 gal/yd^3 = 1.69 lb/yd^3.   1 kg/m^3 = 1.69 lb/yd^3.
1 000 psi = 6.895 MPa.   1 l (water) = 2.204 lb = 0.264 gal.

5. Increase in ductile behavior through the addition of an adequate volume fraction of steel microfibers.

Table 9.4 adapted from Richard and Cheyrezy[9.26] gives the mix proportions for RPC concretes type 200 and type 800. It also lists the major mechanical properties of these concretes. Sulfate-resistant type V cement was used in all the mixtures.

9.6.6 Summary

The concretes described in the previous sections have demonstrated that strength, ductility, and performance of concretes and cement-based composites have achieved and will continue to achieve higher plateaus. A new era in construction materials technology has commenced. It promises a revolutionary impact on the manner in which constructed systems will emerge in the twenty-first century.

Considerable work needs to be done to enhance the practicability of the use of these materials and make them cost-effective. It is only with simplicity and practicability in application and the achievement of cost-effective competitive end product that these developments in the science of materials technology can gain universal acceptance.

REFERENCES

9.1 Romualdi J P, and Batson G B 1963 Mechanics of Crack Arrest in Concrete. *Proceedings, ASCE J. Engineering Mechanics Division* Vol. 89 EM3, pp. 147–168.
9.2 Romualdi J P, and Mandel J A 1964 Tensile Strength of Concrete Affected by

Uniformly Distributed Closely Spaced Short Lengths of Wire Reinforcement. *Proceedings, ACI Journal* Vol. 61 No. 6, American Concrete Institute, Detroit, pp. 657–671.

9.3   Shah S P, and Rangan B V 1971 Fiber Reinforced Concrete Properties. *Proceedings, ACI Journal* Vol. 68 No. 2, American Concrete Institute, Detroit, pp. 126–135.

9.4   Swamy R N 1975 Fiber Reinforcement of Cement and Concrete. *J. Materials and Structures* Vol. 8 No. 45, pp. 235–254.

9.5   Nawy E G, Neuwerth G E, and Phillips C J 1971 Behavior of Fiber Glass Reinforced Concrete Beams. *Proceedings, ASCE J. Structural Division* Vol. 97 No. ST9, Paper 8353, pp. 2203–2215.

9.6   Nawy E G, and Neuwerth G E 1977 Fiber Glass Reinforced Concrete Slabs and Beams. *Proceedings, ASCE J. Structural Division* Vol. 103 No. ST2, pp. 421–440.

9.7   ACI Committee 544 State-of-the-Art on Fiber Reinforced Concrete. *ACI Report 544.1R-82. Manual of Concrete Practice* Vol. 5, American Concrete Institute, Detroit, 1991.

9.8   ACI Committee 544 Guide for Specifying, Proportioning, Mixing, Placing and Finishing Steel Fiber Reinforced Concrete. *ACI Report 544.3R-93.* American Concrete Institute, Detroit, 1993, pp. 1–10.

9.9   ACI Committee 544 Design Considerations for Steel Fiber Reinforced Concrete. *ACI Report 544.R4-88* American Concrete Institute, Detroit, 1988, pp. 1–16.

9.10 ACI Committee 544 Measurement of Properties of Fiber Reinforced Concrete. *ACI Report 544.2R-89* American Concrete Institute, Detroit, 1989, pp. 1–12.

9.11 Shah S P 1983 Fiber Reinforced Concrete. *Handbook of Structural Concrete* McGraw-Hill, New York, Ch. 6, pp. 1–14.

9.12 Mindess S, and Young J F 1981 *Concrete* Prentice Hall, Englewood Cliffs, N.J.

9.13 Bentur A, and Mindess S 1990 *Fiber Reinforced Cementitious Deposits* Elsevier Applied Science, London.

9.14 Swamy R N, Mangat P S, and Rao C V 1974 The Mechanics of Fiber Reinforcement of Cement Matrices. *Fiber Reinforced Concrete. ACI SP-44* American Concrete Institute, Detroit, pp. 1–28.

9.15 Nawy E G, and Blair K 1971 Further Studies on Flexural Crack Control in Structural Slab Systems. *Proceedings International Symposium on Cracking, Deflection and Ultimate Load of Concrete Slab Systems. ACI SP-30,* ed. E G Nawy, American Concrete Institute, Detroit, Ch. 1, pp. 30–42.

9.16 Hsu L S, and Hsu T C T 1994 Stress-Strain Behavior of Steel-Fiber High-Strength Concrete Under Compression *Proceedings, ACI Structural Journal* Vol. 91 No. 4, American Concrete Institute, Detroit, pp. 448–457.

9.17 Fanella D A, and Naaman A E 1985 Stress–Strain Properties of Fiber Reinforced Concrete in Compression. *Proceedings, ACI Journal* Vol. 82 No. 4, American Concrete Institute, Detroit, pp. 475–483.

9.18 Henager C H, and Doherty T J 1976 Analysis of Fibrous Reinforced Concrete Beams. *Proceedings, ASCE J. Structural Division* Vol. 12 SF1, pp. 177–188.

9.19 Nawy E G 1996 *Reinforced Concrete—A Fundamental Approach* 3rd ed. (1st ed. 1985), Prentice Hall, Englewood Cliffs, N.J.

9.20 Williamson G R 1978 Steel Fibers as Web Reinforcement in Reinforced Concrete *Proceedings U.S. Army Service Conference, West Point,* Vol. 3, pp. 363–377.

9.21 Sharama A K 1986 Shear Strength of Steel Fiber Reinforced Concrete Beams. *Proceedings, ACI Journal* Vol. 83, No. 4, American Concrete Institute, Detroit, pp. 624–628.

9.22 Reinhardt H W, and Naaman A E (eds) 1992 High Performance Fiber Reinforced Cement Composites. *Proceedings International RILEM/ACI Workshop, Stuttgart* Chapman and Hall, New York.

9.23 Schneider B 1992 Development of SIFCON Through Applications. *Proceedings International RILEM/ACI Workshop, Stuttgart* Chapman and Hall, New York, pp. 177–194.

9.24 Naaman A E 1992 SIFCON: Tailored Properties for Structural Performance. *Proceedings International RILEM/ACI Workshop, Stuttgart* Chapman and Hall, New York, pp. 18–38.

9.25 Bayashi M Z 1992 Application of Carbon Fiber Reinforced Mortar in Composite Slab Construction. *Proceedings International RILEM/ACI Workshop, Stuttgart* Chapman and Hall, New York, pp. 507–517.

9.26 Richard P, and Cheyrezy M H 1994 Reactive Powder Concretes with High Ductility and 200–800 MPa Compressive Strength. *Proceedings V M Malhotra Symposium on Concrete Technology: Past, Present and Future ACI SP-144.* ed. P K Mehta, American Concrete Institute, Detroit, pp. 507–518.

10 Economics of High Strength Concrete

10.1 INTRODUCTION

Since the 1850s, concrete as a construction material has undergone a continuous evolutionary process. In 1801, F. Coignet published his statement on the principles of construction in concrete and Koenen in 1886 published the first manuscript on the theory and design of concrete structures. A strength of 2000 psi (13 MPa) was considered adequate at the turn of the twentieth century. Today, concretes having strengths of around 20 000 psi (138 MPa) are being used in columns of high-rise buildings and in a few European bridges. Concretes having strengths up to 100 000 psi (700–800 MPa) have been produced in France for special applications.

The accelerated developments in concrete research over the past 20 years have opened new and more proficient utilization of components available in nature, including industrial waste. The thrust in this accelerated activity has been made or justified because of the economical gains in producing stronger structures that are smaller in component dimensions while larger in the resulting space availability. Cost analysis of the use of high strength concrete as compared to normal strength concrete justifies its viability and utility.

Its use in high-rise structures, offshore platforms, and other special applications more than compensate for the increased cost of material and more rigorous quality control and assurance that are normally needed when high strength concrete is used.[10.1] It was demonstrated[10.2] that the cost of supporting 100 000 lb (445 kN) of service load is about $5 per storey in 1975 dollars for 6000 psi (41 MPa) concrete in the overall structural system. It drops to $3.65 for 9000 psi (62 MPa) concrete. This rate of drop should not be affected by today's costs since labor and material costs continue to be proportional. The reduction in cost is due to drastic reduction in member size, particularly in columns.

10.2 PRINCIPAL FACTORS AFFECTING COST

Cost of any product is affected by a variety of factors not the least of which is supply and demand. But demand is generated by knowledge and familiarity. A good knowledge by the design engineer and the constructor of the material behavior and performance of various concretes is always a contributor to a better

Plate 48 Bennett Bay Bridge, Idaho: 1730 ft segmental girder with two center spans of 520 ft and end spans of 320 ft (Courtesy Portland Cement Association)

design. With familiarity, trust is generated leading to increased application. The principal factors which affect the production, utilization, and costing of high strength concrete can be summarized as follows:

1. Research and development
2. Areas of application and performance requirements
3. Codes, standards, and engineering specifications
4. Selection of material components and the design mix
5. Quality control and assurance in production.

10.2.1 Research and Development

The previous chapters have presented a compact discourse of the vast research and development activities in the area of concrete materials that have been in progress, particularly over the past 10 years. It is evident that high strength concretes possess certain characteristics that differ from those of normal strength concretes, as influenced by internal changes caused by short-term and long-term loads and environmental conditions. Since the end product is a constructed system, the impact of material characteristics of high strength concrete on the code design expressions has to be established.[10.3]

The usual assumption for normal strength concrete has been to consider that concrete and steel reinforcement strains are identical until the reinforcement starts to yield. This assumption seems to be equally true for high strength concretes, both in beams and columns, as discussed in Chapter 11. The compressive stress distribution is directly related to the shape of the stress–strain curve in uniaxial compression. However, the stress–strain diagram for high strength concrete is almost *linear* up to failure as compared to normal strength concrete, which is essentially parabolic. This difference suggests that the equivalent rectangular block might not be accurate enough for design purposes if, in the case of beams, the members are overreinforced if they are prestressed.

No conclusive evidence exists at this time on the need for major changes in the provisions of the ACI 318 code parameters for design of very high strength concrete structures, namely, concretes with compressive strengths exceeding 12 000 psi (83 MPa). But more research and development are needed on the effect of the reduced ductility in higher strength concrete on the design parameters, particularly those that are more affected by the concrete strength than by reinforcement contribution, such as shear, torsion, development length, and repeated loadings, as discussed in Chapter 11. Costs would thus be affected by the design requirements if they differ in the case of high strength concrete. Evidence thus far indicates that the factor of high strength does not seem to have a major impact on the current approach to design, with modifications made as more research results are available.

10.2.2   Areas of Application and Performance Requirements

The performance of a concrete constructed system is greatly affected by the environment in which the system is to be placed. More intense requirements are needed in zones of high temperature fluctuations and seasonal changes. These factors include freeze–thaw, shrinkage cracking, effects of deleterious chemicals, and acid rain. Other requirements are needed for concrete placed under water or concrete in arctic zones and in special structures such as offshore oil platforms.

The listed placement conditions and other factors require a judicious selection of the type of concrete and its constituents, as well as the particular mix proportions that fit the needs of the particular environment. Different placement procedures, location, availability of materials, and levels of quality control and assurance are affected by each of these conditions. Thus, cost of production, placement, and finishings would be determined by the impact of all these factors on the production of the finished product.

10.2.3   Codes, Standards, and Engineering Specifications

It is essential to have a thorough understanding of the standards and codes of the particular zone in which a structural system is to be constructed, be it a building, a bridge, a highway, a tunnel, an offshore platform, or another superstructure or substructure. Together with this necessary understanding by the designer, the need to be well informed with the state of the art in high strength concrete is particularly paramount in proportioning in nonstandard cases. The resulting specifications that are generated by the engineer will determine the cost index of high strength concrete in comparison with normal strength concrete.

10.2.4 Selection of Material Components and the Design Mix

Superior quality has to be sought in the selection of all components of the high strength concrete mix. This can be achieved by more stringent control on quantity batching, laboratory and field testing, and elimination of deleterious materials. Material selection can be affected by availability and location. Transportation costs can be a factor in the cost of the finished product as the level of strength often determines the types of component materials that have to be used.

10.2.5 Quality Control and Assurance in Production and Workmanship

In order to achieve a high quality high strength concrete, a larger number of control tests has to be performed than in the case of normal strength concrete. Certified professional teams with experience in high strength materials should conduct or supervise these tests. Systematic sampling and periodic testing have to be done throughout the construction period. Testing procedures used for normal strength concrete might have to be updated for higher strength concretes. End specimen preparation is a typical example where end grinding produces better and more consistent results than end capping. Numerous standards exist by the American Society for Testing and Materials (ASTM) and the American Concrete Institute (ACI):

1. ASTM C9.03.01: Testing High Strength Concrete
2. ASTM C39: Compressive Strength of Cylinder Concrete Specimens
3. ACI 363: High Strength Concrete
4. Other standards such as from the CEB (Comité Euro International du Beton) and other codifying agencies.

Stringent controls, use of qualified personnel (ACI certified or equivalent) and strict adherence to testing requirements have an impact on the cost. The practice of choosing the lowest bidder has to be discouraged in favor of superior short-term and long-term quality, prequalified concrete suppliers, testing laboratories, and contractors.

10.3 ADVANTAGES OF USING HIGH STRENGTH CONCRETE

The advantages of using high strength concrete often balance the increase in material cost. The following are the major advantages that can be accomplished.

1. Reduction in member size, resulting in (a) increase in rentable space and (b) reduction in the volume of produced concrete with the accompanying saving in construction time.
2. Reduction in the self-weight and superimposed dead load with the accompanying saving in smaller foundations.
3. Reduction in formwork area and cost with the accompanying reduction in shoring and stripping time due to high early age gain in strength.

4. Construction of higher high-rise buildings with the accompanying saving in real estate costs in congested areas.
5. Longer spans and fewer beams for the same magnitude of loading.
6. Reduced axial shortening of compression supporting members.
7. Reduction in the number of supports and the supporting foundations due to the increase in spans.
8. Reduction in the thickness of floor slabs and supporting beam sections. This is a major component of the weight and cost of the majority of structures.
9. Superior long-term service performance under static, dynamic, and fatigue loading.
10. Low creep and shrinkage.
11. Greater stiffness as a result of a higher modulus E_c.
12. Higher resistance to freezing and thawing, chemical attack, and significantly improved long-term durability and crack propagation.
13. Reduced maintenance and repair costs.
14. Smaller depreciation as a fixed asset.

10.4   COST STUDIES AND COMPARISONS

The effect of the parameters presented in Section 10.3 influence cost nonuniformly. Conditions pertaining to each project, location, zone, season, execution duration, and the technical expertise of the field teams have variable effects on the costs of the different components and the totality of a project. This section will attempt to present cost comparisons in the use of high strength concrete in several large-scale projects. Particular savings are attained in using as high a concrete strength in columns as possible. This is due to the fact that compressive strength is the principal parameter resisting compressive loads. But savings in floor systems and in beams as well as principal bridge components are equally documented.

Table 10.1 In-place cost (1992) for concretes having 7 000–14 000 psi (48–96 MPa) strengths[10.4]

Type of material	Cost in place ($)
(1)	(2)
Reinforcement	760/ton
Concrete	
$f_c' = 7\,000$ (48)	80/yd^3
$f_c' = 9\,000$ (62)	85
$f_c' = 11\,000$ (76)	104
$f_c' = 14\,000$ (96)	123
Formwork	280

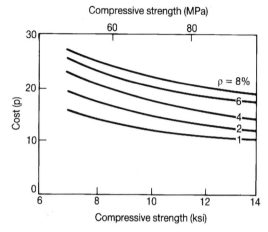

Fig. 10.1 Cost vs. concrete compressive strength for reinforcement ratios $\rho = 1$–8 percent[10.4] (cost of 40 in. × 40 in. column per foot of length per 1000 kip of design load, $1.4D + 1.7L$)

10.4.1   High Rise Buildings

Extensive cost analyses by Moreno of using high strength concrete[10.4] in buildings give cost comparisons for different compressive strength levels as shown in Table 10.1. The study examined several factors affecting the optimal design of high-rise building frames. These factors included lateral forces, building drift, foundation type, and the itemized costs of the construction materials. Estimates of the construction material costs were based on material costs per kip—454 lb of axial gravity load for square columns of sizes 20, 30, and 40 in. (51, 76, and 102 cm). The study did not include construction costs in columns of unbraced frames subjected to lateral loads. The increase in cost of concrete from $80/yd³ for $f'_c = 7000$ psi (48 MPa) to $129/yd³ for $f'c = 14\,000$ psi (96 MPa) seems to be more than *offset* by the drastic reduction in the size of the columns in the structure and a considerable reduction in the reinforcement percentage.

Table 10.1 was constructed on the basis of using columns 40 in. × 40 in. (102 cm × 102 cm) tied to nonslender columns carrying 1000 kips (4450 kN). Figure 10.1 gives a cost comparison for the range of steel percentages allowed in the ACI 318 code[10.3] varying between 1 and 8 percent. It should also be noted that the use of minimum reinforcement in the case of high strength concrete allows easier flow and compaction of the concrete in the member because of lack of congestion of the reinforcement leading to further reduction in labor costs.

10.4.2   Cost Comparisons as Affected by Loads and Height

A case study is presented from Nathan and Leatham[10.5] for two high-rise buildings comprising five and fifteen stories. Spans used were 15, 25, and 35 ft. (4.6, 7.6, and 10.7 m). The pricing had factored in the cost of slender columns in unbraced frames subjected to lateral seismic loading.

Table 10.2 Frame load and concrete strength data[10.5]

	f_c' (ksi)	
Configuration	5 Stories	15 Stories
15 ft span, 70 psf dead load		
50 psf live load		
4% lateral load	4, 8, 12	4, 8, 12
8% lateral load	4, 8, 12	4, 8, 12
100 psf live load		
4% lateral load	4, 8, 12	4, 8, 12
8% lateral load	4, 8, 12	4, 8, 12
150 psf live load		
4% lateral load	4, 8, 12	4, 8, 12
8% lateral load	4, 8, 12	4, 8, 12
25 ft span, 115 psf dead load		
50 psf live load		
4% lateral load	4, 8, 12	4, 8, 12
8% lateral load	4, 8, 12	4, 8, 12
100 psf live load		
4% lateral load	4, 8, 12	4, 8, 12
8% lateral load	4, 8, 12	4, 8, 12
150 psf live load		
4% lateral load	4, 8, 12	4, 8, 12
8% lateral load	4, 8, 12	4, 8, 12
35 ft span, 160 psf dead load		
50 psf live load		
4% lateral load	4, 8, 12	4, 8, 12
8% lateral load	4, 8, 12	4, 8, 12
100 psf live load		
4% lateral load	4, 8, 12	4, 8, 12
8% lateral load	4, 8, 12	4, 8, 12
150 psf live load		
4% lateral load	4, 8, 12	4, 8, 12
8% lateral load	4, 8, 12	4, 8, 12

Design Parameters

The building is box type without shear walls and subjected to uniform loading. The range of uniform load was at three levels as seen in Table 10.2, namely, 50 psf (2394 Pa) representing residential occupancy, 100 psf (4788 Pa) representing store or manufacturing occupancy and 150 psf (6732 Pa) representing storage or heavy manufacturing facilities. All columns had a slenderness ratio exceeding 22 for unbraced frames. Table 10.2 gives the frame geometry and load combinations. Figure 10.2 shows a cross section of the high-rise unbraced frame while Table 10.3 gives the column details that formed the basis of this study.

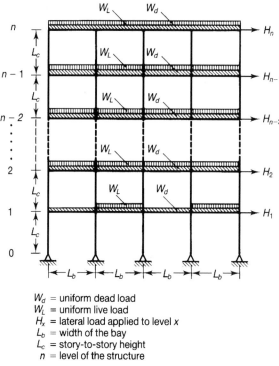

W_d = uniform dead load
W_L = uniform live load
H_x = lateral load applied to level x
L_b = width of the bay
L_c = story-to-story height
n = level of the structure

Fig. 10.2 Unbraced concrete frame in cost analysis[10.5]

Table 10.3 Column details[10.5]

	Column size			
Description	12 in. × 12 in.	18 in. × 18 in.	24 in. × 24 in.	36 in. × 36 in.
Form area (ft² of column area)	48	72	96	144
Column volume (yd³/12 ft length)	0.44	1.00	1.78	4.00
Span lengths (ft.)				
5 stories	15	25	35	—
15 stories	—	15	25	35
Reinforcing steel (%)				
5 stories				
4 000 psi	8.00	8.00	8.00	—
8 000 psi	5.92	5.43	4.65	—
12 000 psi	4.37	3.38	1.97	—
15 stories				
4 000 psi	—	8.00	8.00	8.00
8 000 psi	—	5.00	4.46	3.35
12 000 psi	—	3.31	1.76	1.07

Table 10.4 Cost analysis comparisons[10.5]

Breakdown of costs ($/yd³)	Column size			
	12 in.×12 in.	18 in.×18 in.	24 in.×24 in.	36 in.×36in.
	Five stories			
4 000 psi				
Formwork	359.68	233.28	170.64	—
Reinforcement	504.19	503.98	504.02	—
Column concrete	83.05	74.25	64.60	—
Floor slab concrete	0.00	0.00	0.00	—
Shoring equipment	0.00	0.00	0.00	—
Total	946.92	811.51	739.26	—
8 000 psi				
Formwork	359.68	233.28	170.64	—
Reinforcement	355.36	325.83	278.41	—
Column concrete	96.15	87.35	77.70	—
Floor slab concrete	56.52	32.23	23.47	—
Shoring equipment	−56.71	−25.20	−14.17	—
Total	811.00	653.50	536.05	—
12 000 psi				
Formwork	359.68	233.28	170.64	—
Reinforcement	262.42	196.18	114.25	—
Column concrete	114.85	106.05	96.40	—
Floor slab concrete	70.54	44.36	34.69	—
Shoring equipment	−113.41	−50.40	−28.35	—
Total	694.08	529.47	387.63	—
	Fifteen stories			
4 000 psi				
Formwork	—	233.28	170.64	108.72
Reinforcement	—	503.98	504.02	504.02
Column concrete	—	74.25	64.60	58.39
Floor slab concrete	—	0.00	0.00	0.00
Shoring equipment	—	0.00	0.00	0.00
Total	—	811.51	739.26	671.13
8 000 psi				
Formwork	—	233.28	170.64	108.72
Reinforcement	—	300.14	258.78	194.36
Column concrete	—	87.35	77.70	71.49
Floor slab concrete	—	28.85	21.07	11.43
Shoring equipment	—	−25.20	−14.17	−6.30
Total	—	624.42	514.02	379.70
12 000 psi				
Formwork	—	233.28	170.64	108.72
Reinforcement	—	192.05	102.07	62.11
Column concrete	—	106.05	96.40	90.19
Floor slab concrete	—	36.12	28.86	17.49
Shoring equipment	—	−50.40	−282.35	−12.60
Total	—	517.10	369.62	265.91

1000 psi = 6.895 MPa $\quad$ 1 ft² = 0.0929 m².
1 yd³ = 0.765 m³. $\quad$ 1 ft = 0.3048 m.
1 lb = 0.4536 kg.

Table 10.5 Engineeering New Record (ENR) unit cost pricing index

Item	Unit	Cost in 1992 ($)
(1)	(2)	(3)
Labor	ft^2	2.53–2.94
Bars, sizes #3–#7 (9.5–22.2 mm)	lb	0.23–0.34
Bars, sizes #8–#18 (25.4–57.3 mm)	lb	0.15–0.22
Concrete material		
$f_c' = 4\,000$–$12\,000$ psi	yd^3	46–86
Concrete placement, labor + equipment		
36 in. × 36 in. columns (91 × 91 mm)	yd^3	12–14
12 in. × 12 in. columns (30 mm × 30 mm)	yd^3	37–40
Formwork and shoring rental		
Based on 10 000 ft^2 (929 m^2) of contact area; rental per month for 6 months.	ft^2	1.05–1.20

Column Cost Comparison

As previously discussed in Section 10.3, cost is affected by numerous factors, not the least of which are the conditions and practices in the various geographical boundaries. Formwork, reinforcement percentage, strength and shape of the reinforcement (spiral or rectangular ties), size and shape of the concrete column, concrete strength, shoring of supported floors, and architectural finish control the cost of columns in particular. Consideration of all the identified variables resulted in the cost analysis shown in Table 10.4. Prices are broken into labor and material costs per square foot (0.1 m^2) of contact area with the formwork.

Labor costs were shown to vary between \$2.93 and \$2.53 per square foot (0.0929 m^2), for 12–36 in. (30–91 cm) square columns. Formwork costs in Table 10.4 were based on the cost of forming 1 yd^3 of concrete for a particular size column.[10.5] Table 10.5 gives a breakdown of item by item costs based on the

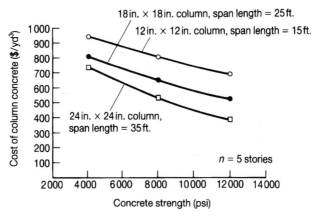

Fig. 10.3 Cost relationship to compressive strength of high strength concrete in a fifteen-story structure[10.5]

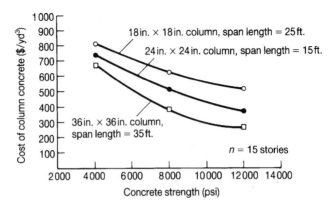

Fig. 10.4 Cost relationship to compressive strength of high strength concrete in a five-storey structure[10.5]

Engineering News Record Price Index for November 13, 1992. A graphical representation of the data presented in Table 10.4 is shown in Fig. 10.3 for the five-storey structure and Fig. 10.4 for the fifteen storey structure.[10.5]

It can be inferred from the presented data that an increase in column strength produces a significant reduction in the required reinforcement percentage with a relative reduction of almost 67 percent for 12 000 psi concrete (83 MPa) from the base 4000 psi concrete requirement. The reduction in cost of almost 42 percent is achieved by using a 12 000 psi (82.7 MPa) high strength concrete in lieu of normal strength concrete.

10.4.3   Relative Costs of Different Column Types

The arrangement of the confining ties in columns and whether they are rectangular or spiral affect the column behavior and capacity. Increased confinement increases the ductility and the axial strength as the value of the transverse stress introduced by the confining ties is increased. The discussion in Sections 8.8 and 11.2 on confinement clarify and demonstrate how the lateral confining stress f_2' impacts on the axial stress f_c. Additional confinement can also be achieved by use of composite sections comprising a steel tube filled with concrete. In this latter type, better fire protection, ideal curing conditions, and minimum loss in moisture can be achieved resulting in minimum creep and shrinkage.[10.5] Table 10.6 gives the relative costs of different column types to resist the same axial load. In the case of steel encased concrete columns, the change in tube thickness affects the column cost. Figure 10.5 gives relative cost ratio vs. column size for different steel tube thicknesses filled with 8700 psi (60 MPa) concrete.

Figure 10.6 for square columns 25 in. × 25 in. (60 cm × 60 cm) to 32 in. × 32 in. (80 cm × 80 cm) gives a relationship between cost ratio and column size for reinforcement percentages of 1–6 percent. It should be emphasized that a total

Plate 49 Skybridge, Vancouver, Canada: the world's longest transit bridge, 2020 ft long with cable stays (Courtesy Portland Cement Association)

percentage exceeding 2–3 percent results in congestion of reinforcement, causing increase in cost of material and labor. It is seen from Fig. 10.6 that it is difficult to justify the increase in cost for a steel percentage exceeding 1 percent in very high strength concrete columns.

10.5   HIGH STRENGTH CONCRETE IN PRESTRESSED BRIDGE GIRDERS

The same trend in cost saving in high-rise buildings is also established for bridge construction. The basic cost per cubic yard obviously increases with the increase in compressive strength. But, as in buildings, the cost increase is offset by the reduction in the volume of concrete required to construct the bridge. The cost of the prestressing strands, however, will not significantly change. This is because as the number of girders is reduced, the number of strands per girder has to be increased.

The most substantial saving in the use of high strength concrete comes from the reduction in nonmaterial costs associated with the girders as seen in Fig. 10.7.[10.7] These include a reduction in labor costs in the production of the girders, transportation costs, erection costs, and overhead expenses. In effect, therefore, it is the reduction in the number of girders in a particular project which substantially reduces the costs. Table 10.7[10.7] gives cost comparisons per foot between 6000 psi (42 MPa) and 10 000 psi (69 MPa). A saving of $196.50/ft

Table 10.6 Relative costs of different column types[10.6]

No.		Column	Relative Cost
1.		60 MPa reinforced concrete [8600 psi] 840 × 840 6Y24 [33"sq 6-1" bars] AS3600 ties (R10-360)	1.0
2.		120 MPa reinforced concrete [17 300 psi] 600 × 600 8Y24 [24"sq 8-1" bars] crawley (1989) ties (Y32-200)	0.79
3.		120 MPa reinforced concrete [17 300 psi] 660 × 660 8Y24 [26"sq 8-1" bars] AS3600 ties (R10-360)	0.77
4.		60 MPa [8600 psi] concrete in grade 250 steel tube 740 × 8 CHS [23" dia × $\frac{3}{8}$" thick]	0.98
5.		120 MPa [17,300 psi] concrete in grade 250 steel tube 570 × 8 CHS [23" dia × $\frac{5}{16}$" thick]	0.71
6.		steel column grade 350 600 × 40 flanges [24" × $1\frac{1}{2}$"] 520 × 40 web [21" × $1\frac{1}{2}$"]	2.21

($645/m) was achieved by using the 10 000 psi (69 MPa) concrete in the bridge girder. Comparison of costs of various mixes giving also the applicable mix proportions is given in Table 10.8. From both tables it is clear that the use of high strength concrete in the production of prestressed concrete girders enables the design and erection of more efficient, more cost-effective, and higher performance bridges.

10.6 SUMMARY

The cost data presented in this chapter are intended to serve as a guideline illustrating that higher strength concretes, though seemingly more expensive per se, result in a reduced cost of the structure. This reduction in cost is accomplished because of the reduction in the geometry of the structural components and the reduced labor costs by the decrease in reinforcement percentage,

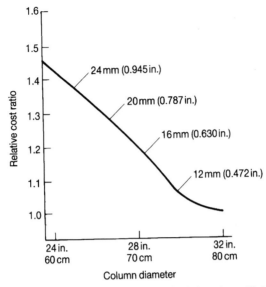

Fig. 10.5 Relative cost ratio vs. column diameter in a steel tubular column filled with high strength concrete[10.6]

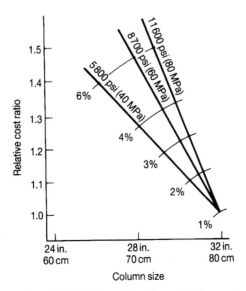

Fig. 10.6 Cost ratio vs. column size for different strengths and reinforcement ratios[10.6]

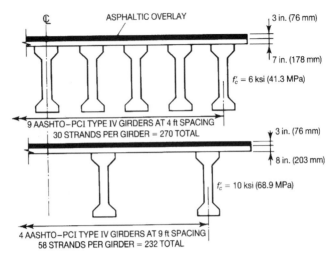

Fig. 10.7 Reduction in number of girders through use of high strength concrete in bridges[10.7]

Table 10.7 Cost comparisons (1992) for prestressed girders in Fig. 10.7[10.7]

Bridge item	Cost ($/ft)	
	6 000 psi fly ash	10 000 psi microsilica
Bridge deck[a]	$5.90 per ft^2 × 36 ft width = 212.40	$7.46 per ft^2 × 36 ft width = 268.56
Strands[b]	270 × $0.40 per strand = 108.00	232 × $0.40 per strand = 92.80
Girder concrete	9 girders × 0.203 yd^3 × $40 = 73.08	4 girders × 0.203 yd^3 × $85 = 69.02
Girder nonmaterial[c]	9 girders × $46.68 = 420.12	4 girders × $46.68 = 186.72
	Total = 813.60	Total = 617.10

[a]Cost of bridge deck is from the *Louisiana Bridge Design Manual* based on a 7 in. thick slab with a design span of 4 ft for the 6 000 psi girders, and 8 in. thick slab with a design span of 9 ft for the 10 000 psi girder design.
[b]The prestressing strand cost of $0.40 per ft includes provisions for material, labor for placement, waste, and overhead.
[c]The girder nonmaterial costs represent the labor and overhead of the prestressing plant as well as transportation and erection costs. 1 ft = 0.3048 m; 1 in. = 25.4 mm; 1 psi = 0.006895 MPa; 1 yd^3 = 0.7646 m^3.

Table 10.8 Relative costs (1992) of various mixes of different compressive strengths[10.7]

Mix proportions	6 000 psi[a]	6 000 psi fly ash	High f_c'	High f_c' fly ash	High f_c' microsilica
Cement, type III (lb/yd^3)	658	480	846	559	559
Fly ash (lb/yd^3)	0	178	0	205	209
Microsilica (lb/yd^3)	0	0	0	0	80
Coarse aggregate (lb/yd^3)	1 800	1 800	1 835	1 835	1 792
Fine aggregate (lb/yd^3)	1 200	1 200	1 174	1 213	1 051
Retarder (oz/yd^3)	20	20	25	15	26
HRWR (oz/yd^3)	72	72	270	220	112
Water (lb/yd^3)	263	363	291	200	234
W/C ratio	0.40	0.40	0.34	0.26	0.30
Total cost ($)	45.36	40.13	60.46	49.13	84.97

[a]6 000 psi mixes are representative of typical proportions.

Plate 50 Mercantile Exchange, Chicago: 9000 psi concrete (Courtesy Portland Cement Association)

smaller foundation, and the reduction in formwork and shoring. But a *team effort is required* to produce the most cost-effective structural system. This team effort in quality production and control can best be achieved by ensuring that the activities influencing the final quality, hence the final cost, of a concrete structure are

1. Based on clearly defined requirement of the concrete components, the placement procedure, and the curing techniques.
2. Well-dimensioned working drawings and precise specifications with regard to all phases of a project.
3. Correct and efficient execution of the drawings and specifications.
4. Systematic field supervision and use of a technically competent labor force well versed in the technology of high strength concrete proportioning and production.

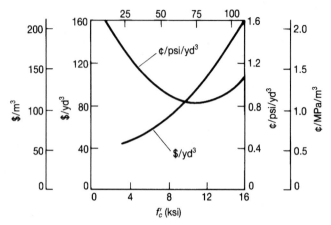

Fig. 10.8 Cost optimization of high strength concrete[10.8]

Since cost is the major factor in the choice of the material and the level of high strength to be used for the facility to be constructed, charts on cost/benefit data should be obtained from the ready-mix suppliers in order to make a studied judgement. A typical such chart is shown in Fig. 10.8 based on 1992 cost data due to Material Service Corporation, Chicago.[10.8] As stressed earlier, the cost/benefit ratio is highly dependent on the planning and teamwork at all phases of the project from inception to the turnkey stage. The polygon in Fig. 10.9[10.9] schematically demonstrates the various team activities involved in the production of a cost-effective constructed system.

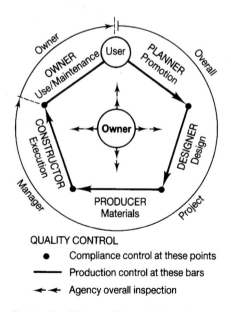

Fig. 10.9 Teamwork coordination for efficient quality control to produce cost-effective high strength concrete[10.9]

REFERENCES

10.1 ACI Committee 363 State-of-the-Art Report on High Strength Concrete. *ACI Report 363R-92* American Concrete Institute, Detroit, 1992, pp. 1–55

10.2 Schmidt W, and Hoffman E S 1975 Nine Thousand-psi Concrete—Why? Why Not. *ASCE Civil Engineering Journal* Vol. 45 No. 5, American Society of Civil Engineers, New York, pp. 52–55

10.3 ACI Committee 318 Building Code Requirements for Reinforced Concrete. *ACI 318-95* and Commentary *ACI 318R-95*. SI Versions *ACI 318M-95, ACI 318RM-95*. *ACI Standard 318-95* American Concrete Institute, Detroit, 1995

10.4 Moreno J, and Zils J 1985 Optimization of High Rise Concrete Buildings. *ACI SP-97* American Concrete Institute, Detroit, pp. 25–92

10.5 Smith G J, and Rad F N 1989 Economic Advantages of High Strength Concretes in Columns. *Concrete International, Design and Construction* Vol. 11 No. 4, American Concrete Institute, Detroit, pp. 37–43

10.6 Webb J 1993 High Strength Concrete: Economics, Design and Ductility. *Concrete International, Design and Construction* Vol. 15 No. 1, American Concrete Institute, Detroit, pp. 27–32

10.7 During T A, and Rear K B 1993 Braker Lane Bridge—High Strength Concrete in Prestressed Bridge Girders. *Proceedings, PCI Journal* Vol. 38 No. 3, pp. 46–51

10.8 Farny J A, and Panarese W C 1994 High Strength Concrete. *PCA Engineering Bulletin* TA 440.F35, Portland Cement Association, Skokie, Ill., pp. 1–48

10.9 Nawy E G 1996 *Reinforced Concrete—A Fundamental Approach* 3rd ed. (1st ed., 1985), Prentice Hall, Englewood Cliffs, N.J

11 Proportioning Concrete Structural Elements by ACI 318-95 Code: An Overview

11.1 STRUCTURAL CONCRETE

Structural concrete, whether normal weight or lightweight, is designed to have a compressive strength in excess of 3000 psi (20 MPa) in concrete structures. As the strength exceeds 6000 psi (42 MPa) such structures are defined today as high strength concrete structures. Concrete mixes designed to produce 6000–12 000 psi in compressive strength are easily obtainable today with silica fume replacing a portion of the cement content, having lower water/cement (W/C) and water/cementitious materials (W/C+P) ratios. Concretes having cylinder compressive strengths of around 20 000 psi (140 MPa) have been used in several buildings in the United States. Such strengths currently qualify such concrete as superhigh strength concrete.

11.1.1 Modulus of Concrete

The ACI 318 code[11.1, 11.2] stipulates that the concrete modulus E_c be evaluated from

$$E_c(\text{psi}) = 33w^{1.5}\sqrt{f_c'} \qquad [11.1a]$$

$$E_c(\text{MPa}) = 0.043w^{1.5}\sqrt{f_c'} \qquad [11.1b]$$

The expressions in Eq. 11.1a and 11.1b are applicable to strengths up to 6000 psi (42 MPa). Available research to date for concrete compressive strengths up to 12 000 psi (83 MPa) gives[11.2, 11.3] the following expressions:

$$E_c(\text{psi}) = (40\,000\sqrt{f_c'} + 10^6)\left(\frac{w_c}{145}\right)^{1.5} \qquad [11.2a]$$

$$E_c(\text{MPa}) = (3.32\sqrt{f_c'} + 6895)\left(\frac{w_c}{2320}\right)^{1.5} \qquad [11.2b]$$

where f_c' in Eqs. 11.1a and 11.2a is in psi and w_c ranges between 145 lb/ft³ for normal density concrete and 100 lb/ft³ for structural lightweight concrete; and f_c', in Eqs. 11.1b and 11.2b is in MPa and w_c ranges between 2400 kg/m³ for normal density concrete and 1765 kg/m³ for lightweight concrete. The modulus of

Plate 51 Toronto City Hall (Courtesy Portland Cement Association)

rupture of concrete can be taken as

$$f_r(\text{psi}) = 7.5\lambda\sqrt{f'_c} \qquad\qquad\qquad [11.3a]$$

$$f_r(\text{MPa}) = 0.623\sqrt{f'_c} \qquad\qquad\qquad [11.3b]$$

where $\lambda = 1.0$ for normal density stone aggregate concrete

$\qquad = 0.85$ for sand lightweight concrete

$\qquad = 0.75$ for all-lightweight concrete.

11.1.2 Creep of Concrete

Concrete creeps under sustained loading due to transverse flow of the material. The creep coefficient as a function of time can be calculated from[11.1, 11.3] the following expression

$$C_t = \left(\frac{t^{0.6}}{10 + t^{0.6}} \right) C_u \qquad [11.4]$$

where the time t is in days and C_u is the ultimate creep factor $= 2.35$. The short-term deflection is multiplied by C_t to get the long-term deflection to be added to the short-term (instantaneous) deflection value in order to get the total deflection.

11.1.3 Shrinkage of Concrete

Concrete also shrinks as the absorbed water evaporates and the chemical reaction of cement gel proceeds. For moist-cured concrete, the force shrinkage strain which occurs at any time t in days 7 days after placing the concrete can be evaluated from[11.3]

$$(\epsilon_{SH})_t = \left(\frac{t}{35 + t} \right) (\epsilon_{SH})_u \qquad [11.5a]$$

For steam-cured concrete, the shrinkage strain at any time t in days, 1–3 days after placement of the concrete is

$$(\epsilon_{SH})_t = \left(\frac{t}{55 + t} \right) (\epsilon_{SH})_u \qquad [11.5b]$$

where maximum $(\epsilon_{SH})_u$ can be taken as 780×10^{-6} in./in. (mm/mm).

Shrinkage and creep due to sustained load can also be evaluated from the ACI expression[11.1]

$$\lambda = \frac{\xi}{1 + 50\rho'} \qquad [11.5c]$$

and Fig. 11.3 for the factor ξ that ranges from a value of 2.0 for 5 years or more to 1.0 for 3 months of sustained loading.

$\rho' = $ compression steel percentage
$\quad = A_s'/bd$

Detailed discussion of Sections 11.1.1 to 11.1.3 are given in Chapter 6.

11.1.4 Control of Deflection

Serviceability is a major factor in designing structures to sustain an acceptable long-term behavior. It is controlled by limiting deflection and cracking in the members.[11.3]

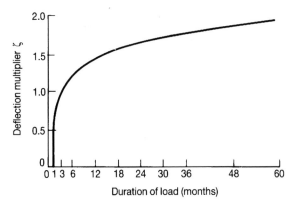

Fig. 11.1 Long-term deflection multipliers[11.1]

For deflection computation and control, the effective moment of inertia of a cracked section can be evaluated from the Branson equation:

$$I_e = \left(\frac{M_{cr}}{M_a}\right)I_g + \left[1 - \left(\frac{M_{cr}}{M_a}\right)^3\right]I_{cr} \leq I_g \qquad [11.6]$$

For *reinforced concrete beams*

$$M_{cr} = \text{cracking moment due to } \textit{total} \text{ load} = \frac{f_r I_g}{y_t}$$

y_t = distance from the neutral axis to the extreme tension fibers

M_a = maximum service load moment at the section under consideration

I_g = gross moment of inertia

In the case of *prestressed concrete*,

$$\left(\frac{M_{cr}}{M_a}\right) = \frac{f_{tl} - f_r}{f_L} \qquad [11.7]$$

where M_{cr} = moment due to that portion of the *live* load moment M_a that causes cracking

M_a = maximum service load (unfactored) *live* load moment

f_{tl} = total calculated stress in the member

f_L = calculated stress due to live load

For long-term deflection, Fig. 11.1 gives the required multipliers as a function of time.

11.1.5   Control of Cracking in Beams

Control of cracking in beams and one-way slabs can be made using the expression[11.4]

$$w_{max}(\text{in.}) = 0.076\beta f_s \sqrt[3]{d_c A} \qquad [11.8]$$

where w_{max} = crack width in units of 0.001 in. (0.0254 mm)

β $= (h - c)/(d - c)$

d_c = thickness of cover to the first layer of bars, in.

f_s = maximum stress in reinforcement at service load = $0.60f_y$, ksi

A = area of concrete in tension divided by number of bars, in.^{2}

     $= bt/\gamma_{bc}$ where γ_{bc} = number of bars at the tension side

11.2 STRUCTURAL DESIGN CONSIDERATIONS

11.2.1 General

As discussed in Chapter 10, high strength concretes have certain characteristics and engineering properties that differ from those of lower strength concretes.[11.5] These differences seem to have a larger effect as the strength increases beyond the present 6000 psi (42 MPa) plateau for normal strength concrete. High strength concretes are shown to be essentially linearly elastic up to failure with a steeper declining portion of the stress–strain diagram. In comparison, the stress–strain diagram of lower strength concretes is more parabolic in nature as seen in Fig. 11.2.[11.5] The stress–strain relationship of the steel reinforcement in this diagram is not to scale in its ordinate value but is intended to show the relative strain following the usual assumption of strain compatibility between the concrete and the steel reinforcement up to yield.

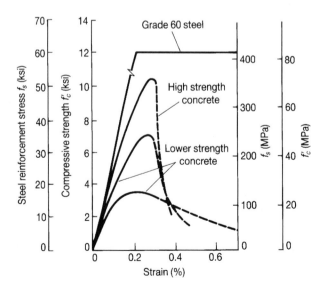

Fig. 11.2 Concrete and steel stress–strain relationships[11.5]

11.2.2   Axially Loaded Columns

The present design practice is to assume direct addition of the contribution of the steel and the concrete in calculating the ultimate state of failure in compression members. For lower strength concretes, when the concrete reaches the nonlinearity load level at a strain of 0.001 in./in. as seen in Fig. 11.2, the steel is still in the elastic range, assuming a larger share of the applied load. But, as the strain level approaches 0.002 in./in., the slope of the concrete stress–strain diagram approaches zero while the steel reaches its yield strain that would thereafter be idealized into a constant (horizontal) plateau. The strength of the column using the addition law would then be

$$P_n = 0.85 f'_c A_c + f_y A_s \tag{11.9}$$

where f'_c = concrete cylinder compressive strength
$\quad\quad f_y$ = yield strength of the reinforcement
$\quad\quad A_c$ = gross area of the concrete section
$\quad\quad A_s$ = area of the reinforcement

The factor 0.85 representing the adjustment in concrete strength between the cylinder test result and the actual concrete strength in the structural element has been shown by extensive tests to be sufficiently accurate for higher strength concretes.[11.5]

Confinement of the concrete in compression members through the use of spirals or closely spaced ties increases its compressive capacity. The increase in concrete strength due to the confining effect of the spirals can be represented by the following expression:

$$f'_2 = \frac{1}{4}[\bar{f}_c - f''_c] \tag{11.10a}$$

where f'_2 = concrete confining stress due to the spiral
$\quad\quad \bar{f}_c$ = compressive strength of the confined concrete
$\quad\quad f''_c$ = compressive strength of the unconfined column concrete.

The hoop tension force in the circular spiral is

$$2A_{sp}f_y = f'_2 D' s$$

or

$$f'_2 = \frac{2A_{sp}f_y}{D's} \tag{11.10b}$$

where A_{sp} = cross-sectional area of the spiral
$\quad\quad D'$ = diameter of concrete core
$\quad\quad s$ = spiral pitch

Equations 11.10a and 11.10b can be improved[11.5] leading to the following form for normal weight concrete

$$(\bar{f}_c - f''_c) = 4.0f'_2(1 - s/D') \tag{11.11a}$$

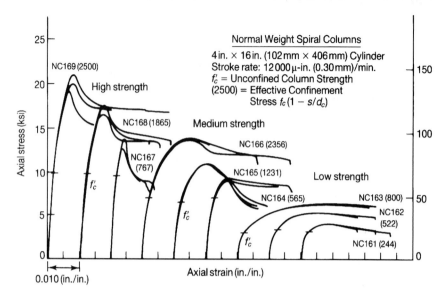

Fig. 11.3 Stress–strain diagrams of 4 in. × 6 in. normal weight spirally confined compression prisms[11.7]

For lightweight concrete

$$(\bar{f}_c - f_c'') = 1.8f_2'(1 - s/D') \qquad [11.11b]$$

Yong et al.[11.6], presented in more detail in Section 8.8, outlines the confining effect of rectangular ties on high strength concrete compression members. It gives the value of the peak stress $\bar{f}_c$ (Eqs. 8.58 and 8.59) and the peak strain ϵ_0 (Eq. 8.60). Figure 11.3[11.7] gives the results of peak stress comparisons versus axial strain for spirally reinforced members for low, medium, and high strength concretes. It shows for higher strength a lower strain at peak load and a steeper decline past the peak value. The strength gain in concrete due to confinement seems, however, to be well predicted for high strength concretes in the presently available expression.

11.2.3 Beams and Slabs

The Compressive Block
Design of concrete structural elements is based on the compressive stress distribution across the depth of the member as determined by the stress–strain diagram of the material. For high strength concretes, the difference in the shape of the stress–strain relationship previously discussed in connection with Fig. 11.2 results in differences in the shape of the compressive stress block. Figure 11.4 shows possible compressive blocks for use in design. Figure 11.4(c) could more accurately represent the stress distribution for higher strength concrete.

However, the computed strength of beams and eccentrically loaded columns depends on the reinforcement ratio. In the ACI 318 code provisions using the

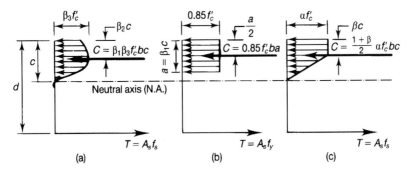

Fig. 11.4 Concrete compressive stress block: (a) standard stress block; (b) equivalent rectangular block; (c) modified trapezoidal block

equivalent rectangular block, the nominal moment strength of a singly reinforced beam is calculated using the following expression:

$$M_n = A_s f_y d \left[1 - 0.59 \rho \frac{f_y}{f_c'} \right] \qquad [11.12]$$

where the coefficient $0.59 = \beta_2 / \beta_1 \beta_3$, while a detailed evaluation of the factors β_1, β_2, and β_3 separately indicates a significant difference in their individual values, depending on the concrete strength.[11.5] Figure 11.5 shows that these differences collectively balance each other and that the combined coefficient $\beta_2 / \beta_1 \beta_3$ is well represented by the 0.59 value. Consequently, for strengths up to 12 000 psi (42 MPa), the present ACI 318 code expressions, requiring that beams be underreinforced, are equally applicable. For considerably higher strengths or

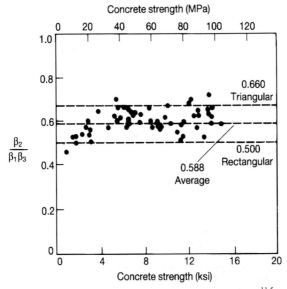

Fig. 11.5 Stress block parameter $\beta_2 / \beta_1 \beta_3$ vs. concrete compressive strength[11.5]

for members combining compression and bending or overreinforced members allowed in the codes, some differences in the value of $\beta_2/\beta_1\beta_3$ can be expected.

Compressive Limiting Strain
Although high strength concrete achieves its peak value at a unit strain slightly higher than that of normal strength concrete (Fig. 11.2), the ultimate strain is lower for high strength concrete unless confinement is provided. A limiting strain value allowed by the ACI 318 code equals 0.003 in./in. (mm/mm). Other codes allow a limiting strain of unconfined concrete of 0.0035 or 0.0038. The conservative ACI 0.003 value seems to be adequate for high strength concretes as well, although it is somewhat less conservative than for lower strength concretes.

Confinement and Ductility
As higher strength concrete is more brittle, confinement becomes more important in order to increase its ductility. If μ is the deflection ductility index,

$$\mu = \frac{\Delta_u}{\Delta_y} \tag{11.13}$$

where Δ_u = beam deflection at failure load
Δ_y = beam deflection at the load producing yield of the tensile reinforcement.

Table 11.1[11.8] shows the ductility index values of concretes in singly reinforced beams ranging in strength from 3700 psi (25 MPa) to 9265 psi (64 MPa). The corresponding reduction in the ductility index ranges from 3.54 to 1.07. Addition of compressive reinforcement and confinement to geometrically similar beams seems to increase the ductility index for $f_c' = 8500$ to a value of 5.61. Hence, the higher the concrete compressive strength, the more it becomes necessary to provide for confinement and/or the addition of compression steel A_s' while using the same expression for nominal moment strength applicable to normal strength concretes. It should be stated that cost would not be affected to any meaningful extent since diagonal tension and torsion stirrups have to be used anyway and in seismic regions closely spaced confining ties are a requirement.

Table 11.1 Deflection ductility index for singly reinforced beams[11.8]

Beam	f_c', psi (MPa)	ρ/ρ_b ratio[a]	Ductility index $\mu = \Delta_u/\Delta_y$
A1	3 700 (26)	0.51	3.54
A2	6 500 (45)	0.52	2.84
A3	8 535 (59)	0.29	2.53
A4	8 535 (59)	0.64	1.75
A5	9 264 (64)	0.87	1.14
A6(a)	8 755 (60)	1.11	1.07

[a]Ratio of tension reinforcement percentage to the balanced percentage.

Shear and Diagonal Tension

Design for shear in accordance with the ACI 318-95 code is based on permitting the plain concrete in the web to assume part of the nominal shear V_n. If V_c is the shear strength resistance of the concrete, the web stirrups resist a shear force $V_s = V_n - V_c$. High strength develops a relatively brittle failure, as previously discussed, with the aggregate interlock decreasing with the increase in the compressive strength. Hence the shear friction and diagonal tension failure capacity in beams might be unconservatively represented by the ACI 318 equations.[11.9] However, the strength of the diagonal struts in the beam shear truss model is increased through the mobilization of more stirrups and the increased load capacity of the struts themselves. No research data is currently available for definitive guidelines on the minimum web steel that can prevent brittle failure. All presently available work shows no unsafe use of the present ACI 318 code provisions in shear in the design of high strength concrete members.

11.3   REINFORCED CONCRETE MEMBERS

11.3.1   Flexural Strength

Singly Reinforced Beams

Flexural strength is determined from the strain and stress distribution across the depth of the concrete section. Figure 11.6[11.2] shows the stress distribution and forces. Taking moments of all the forces about tensile steel A_s gives for singly

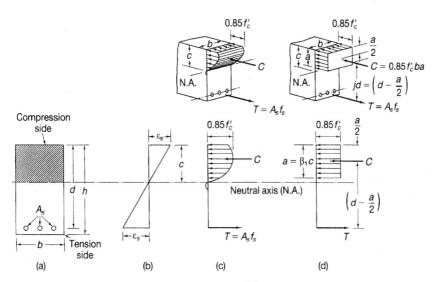

Fig. 11.6 Stress and strain distribution across beam depth[11.2]: (a) beam cross-section; (b) strain across depth; (c) actual stress block; (d) assumed equivalent stress block

reinforced beams ($A'_s = 0$) a nominal moment strength

$$M_n = A_s f_y \left(d - \frac{a}{2} \right)$$ [11.14a]

or

$$M_n = bd^2 \omega (1 - 0.59\omega)$$ [11.14b]

where ω = reinforcement index = $A_s/bd \times f_y/f'_c$.
    The reinforcement index

$$\rho = \frac{A_s}{bd} \leq 0.75\bar{\rho}_b$$ [11.15]

$$\bar{\rho}_b = \frac{0.85\beta_1 f'_c}{f_y} \times \frac{0.003E_s}{0.003E_s + f_y}$$ [11.16]

where $\beta_1 = 0.85$ and reduces at the rate of 0.05 per 1000 psi in excess of 4000 psi, namely,

$$\beta_1 = 0.85 - 0.05 \left(\frac{f'_c - 1000}{1000} \right)$$ [11.17]

β_1 not to be less than 0.65.

Doubly Reinforced Beams
For doubly reinforced sections (having compression steel),

$$M_n = (A_s - A'_s) f_y \left(d - \frac{a}{2} \right) + A'_s f_y (d - d')$$ [11.18]

    See Fig. 11.1, if compressive reinforcement is used in a doubly reinforced section[11.1] (see also Fig. 11.9). The reinforcement percentage ρ is

$$\rho \leq 0.75\bar{\rho}_b + \rho' \frac{f'_s}{f_y}$$ [11.19]

where f'_s = stress in compression.
    The depth of the compressive block is

$$a = \frac{A_s f_y - A'_s f'_s}{0.85 f'_c b}$$ [11.20]

where b = width of section at the compression side.

Flanged Sections
For flanged sections where the neutral axis falls outside the flange,

$$M_n = (A_s - A_{sf}) f_y \left(d - \frac{a}{2} \right) + A_{sf} f_y \left(d - \frac{h_f}{2} \right)$$ [11.21]

where $A_{sf} = \dfrac{0.85 f'_c (b - b_w) h_f}{f_y}$

b_w = web width
h_f = flange thickness.

The depth is given by

$$a = \frac{A_s f_y}{0.85 f_c' b} > h_f$$

and

$$\rho < \frac{b_w}{b} (\bar{\rho}_b + \rho_f) \tag{11.22a}$$

where $\bar{\rho}_b$ = reinforcement percentage for a singly reinforced beam,

$$\rho_f = 0.85 f_c' (b - b_w) \frac{h_f}{f_y b_w d} \tag{11.22b}$$

Minimum Reinforcement

In Eqs. 11.14c and 11.19a, the flexural reinforcement percentage ρ has to have a minimum value of $\rho_{min} = 3\sqrt{f_c'}/f_y$ for positive moment reinforcement, $\rho_{min} = 6\sqrt{f_c'}/f_y$ for negative moment reinforcement but always not less than $200/f_y$ where f_y is in psi units. The factored moment

$$M_u = \phi M_n \tag{11.23}$$

where $\phi = 0.90$ for flexure.

11.3.2   Shear Strength

External transverse load is resisted by internal shear in order to maintain section equilibrium. As concrete is weak in tension, the principal tensile stress in a beam cannot exceed the tensile strength of the concrete. The principal stress is composed of two components: shear stress and flexural stress. It is important that the beam web be reinforced in order to prevent shear diagonal cracks from opening. The resistance of the plain concrete in the web sustains part of the shear stress and the balance has to be borne by the diagonal tension reinforcement. The shear resistance of the plain concrete is called the nominal shear strength V_c. The nominal V_c is

$$V_c = 2.0\lambda \sqrt{f_c'} b_w d \text{ lbs} < 3.5\lambda \sqrt{f_c'} \tag{11.24a}$$

$$V_c = \left(\frac{\sqrt{f_c'}}{6}\right) b_w \, d \text{ Newtons} \tag{11.24b}$$

or

$$V_c = \left[1.9\lambda \sqrt{f_c'} + 2500 \rho_w \frac{V_u d}{M_u}\right] b_w d \text{ lbs} \leq 3.5\lambda \sqrt{f_c'} \tag{11.25a}$$

$$V_c = \frac{1}{7}\left(\sqrt{f_c'} + 120 \rho_w \frac{V_u d}{M_u}\right) b_w d \text{ Newtons} \tag{11.25b}$$

The λ values are given in Section 11.1.

$$\rho_w = \frac{A_s}{b_w d} \quad \text{and} \quad \frac{V_u d}{M_u} \le 1.0$$

No web steel is needed if $V_u < V_c/2$. The critical section for calculating V_n is at a distance d from the support face. Spacing of the web stirrups:

$$s = \frac{A_v f_y d}{(V_u/\phi - V_c)} \qquad [11.26]$$

where A_v = cross-sectional area of web steel and $\phi = 0.85$ for shear and torsion. The transverse web steel is designed to carry the shear load $V_s = V_n - V_c$. The spacing of the stirrups is governed by the following:

$$V_s \ge 4\sqrt{f_c'} : s = \frac{d}{4}$$

$$V_s \le 2\sqrt{f_c'} : s = \frac{d}{2}$$

$$V_s \ge 8\sqrt{f_c'} : \text{enlarge section}$$

The minimum sectional area of the stirrups is $A_{v,\min} = \dfrac{50 b_w s}{f_y}$ and

$\qquad s_{\max} = d/2$ where shear is to be considered

$\qquad d$ = effective depth to the center of the tensile reinforcement

$\qquad f_y$ = yield strength of steel in psi.

11.3.3 Torsional Strength

The space truss analogy theory is used for the analysis and design of concrete members subjected to torsion. It is based on the shear flow concept in a hollow tube and the summation of the forces in the space truss elements[11.1, 11.2, 11.10, 11.11]. The ACI 318-95 code stipulates disregarding the concrete nominal strength T_c in torsion and assigning all the torque to the longitudinal reinforcement A_l and the transverse reinforcement A_t, assuming that essentially the volume of the longitudinal bars is equivalent to the volume of the *closed* transverse hoops or stirrups. The critical section is taken at a distance d from the face of the support for the purpose of calculating the torque T_u. Sections that are subjected to combined torsion and shear should be designed for torsion if the factored torsional moment T_u exceeds the following value for nonprestressed members:

$$T_u > \phi \sqrt{f_c'} \left(\frac{A_{cp}^2}{p_{cp}} \right) \qquad [11.27]$$

where A_{cp} = area enclosed by the outside perimeter of concrete cross-section
$\qquad p_{cp}$ = outside perimeter of the cross section A_{cp}, in.

Two types of torsion are considered:

1. Equilibrium torsion where no redistribution of torsional moment is possible. In this case, *all* the factored torsional moment is designed for.
2. Compatibility torsion where redistribution of the torsional moment occurs in a continuous floor system. In this case, the *maximum* torsional moment to be provided for is

$$T_u = 4\phi\sqrt{f_c'}\left(\frac{A_{cp}^2}{P_{cp}}\right) \qquad\qquad [11.28]$$

The concrete section has to be enlarged if

$$\sqrt{\left(\frac{V_u}{b_wd}\right)^2 + \left(\frac{T_up_h}{1.7\,A_{oh}^2}\right)^2} > \phi\left(\frac{V_c}{b_wd} + 8\sqrt{f_c'}\right) \qquad\qquad [11.29]$$

where p_h = perimeter of centerline of outermost closed transverse torsional reinforcement, in.

A_{oh} = area enclosed by centerline of the outermost closed transverse torsional reinforcement, in.^{2}

The transverse torsional reinforcement should be chosen with such size and spacing s that

$$\frac{A_t}{2} = \frac{T_n}{2A_{oh}f_y\cot\theta} \qquad\qquad [11.30]$$

where A_{oh} = gross area enclosed by the shear path $= 0.85A_{oh}$

θ = angle of compression diagonals

   $= 45°$ in reinforced concrete

   $= 37\frac{1}{2}°$ in prestressed concrete

The longitudinal torsional reinforcement A_1 to be equally divided along the four faces of the beam is

$$A_1 = \frac{A_t}{s}p_h\left(\frac{f_{yv}}{f_{yl}}\right)\cot^2\theta \qquad\qquad [11.31]$$

$$A_{1,\,min} = \frac{5\sqrt{f_c'}A_{cp}}{f_{yl}} - \left(\frac{A_t}{s}\right)p_h\frac{f_{yv}}{f_{yl}} \qquad\qquad [11.32]$$

where f_{yv} = yield strength of the transverse reinforcement

f_{yl} = yield strength of the longitudinal reinforcement.

The minimum area of transverse reinforcement is

$$A_v + 2A_t \geq \frac{50b_ws}{f_y} \qquad\qquad [11.33]$$

Maximum $s = 12$ in.

In SI units, the following are equivalent expressions:

Eq. 11.27: $\dfrac{\phi\sqrt{f_c'}}{12}\left(\dfrac{A_{cp}^2}{P_{cp}}\right)$

Eq. 11.28: $\dfrac{\phi\sqrt{f_c'}}{3}\left(\dfrac{A_{cp}^2}{P_{cp}}\right)$

Eq. 11.29: the right hand expression is $\phi\left(\dfrac{V_c}{b_wd} + \dfrac{8\sqrt{f_c'}}{12}\right)$ MPa

Eq. 11.32: $A_{1,\min} = \dfrac{5\sqrt{f_c'}A_{cp}}{12f_{yl}} - \left(\dfrac{A_t}{s}\right)p_h\left(\dfrac{f_{yv}}{f_{yl}}\right)$

Eq. 11.33: $A_v + 2A_t \geq \dfrac{0.35b_ws}{f_y}$ where f_y is in MPa. Maximum $s = 300$ mm.

11.3.4 Compression Members: Columns

Nonslender Columns

Flexural members such as beams are designed in such a manner that the reinforcement ratio ρ cannot exceed 75 percent of the balanced ratio ρ_b and for practical reasons not to exceed 50 percent. Compression members, on the other hand, are proportioned on the basis of the magnitude of eccentricity. If P_{nb} is the balanced axial load where failure occurs simultaneously by crushing of the concrete on the compression side and yielding of the reinforcement of the tension side, then

$$P_n < P_{nb} \text{ is tension failure } (e > e_b)$$
$$P_n = P_{nb} \text{ balanced failure } (e = e_b)$$
$$P_n > P_{nb} \text{ compression failure } (e < e_b)$$

$$P_{nb} = 0.85f_c'ba_b + A_s'f_s' - A_sf_y \qquad [11.34]$$
$$M_{nb} = 0.85\,f_c'ba_b\left(\bar{y} - \dfrac{a_b}{2}\right) + A_s'f_s'(\bar{y} - d') + A_s \qquad [11.35]$$

where

$$f_s' = E_s\left[\dfrac{0.003(c - d')}{c}\right] \leq f_y \qquad [11.36]$$

The force P_n and the moment M_n at ultimate for any other eccentricity level is

$$P_n = 0.85f_c'ba + A_s'f_s' - A_sf_y \qquad [11.37]$$

$$M_n = P_ne = 0.85f_c'\,ba\left(\bar{y} - \dfrac{a}{2}\right) + A_s'\,f_s'(\bar{y} - d') \qquad [11.38]$$

where

$$f_s = E_s\left[\dfrac{0.003(d - c)}{c}\right] \leq f_y \qquad [11.39]$$

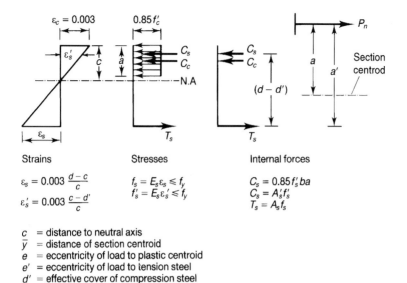

$$\varepsilon_c = 0.003 \qquad 0.85 f_c'$$

Strains   Stresses   Internal forces

$$\varepsilon_s = 0.003 \frac{d-c}{c}$$

$$\varepsilon_s' = 0.003 \frac{c-d'}{c}$$

$$f_s = E_s \varepsilon_s \leq f_y$$
$$f_s' = E_s \varepsilon_s' \leq f_y$$

$$C_s = 0.85 f_c' \, ba$$
$$C_s = A_s' f_s'$$
$$T_s = A_s f_s$$

c = distance to neutral axis
$\bar{y}$ = distance of section centroid
e = eccentricity of load to plastic centroid
e' = eccentricity of load to tension steel
d' = effective cover of compression steel

Fig. 11.7 Stresses and forces in columns[11.11]

c = depth to the neutral axis
$\bar{y}$ = distance from the compression extreme fibers to the center of gravity of the section
a = depth of the equivalent rectangular block = $\beta_1 c$ where β_1 is defined in Eq. 11.20(b).

The geometry of the compression member section and the forces acting on the section are shown in Fig. 11.7. Equations 11.37 and 11.38 are obtained from equilibrium of forces and moments.

Slender Columns
If the compression member is slender, namely, the slenderness ratio kl_u/r exceeds 22 for unbraced members and $(34 - 12M_1/M_2)$ for braced members, failure will occur by buckling and not by material failure. In such a case, if kl_u/r is less than 100, a first-order analysis can be performed such as the moment magnification method. If $kl_u/r > 100$, the $P - \Delta$ effects have to be considered and a second-order analysis has to be performed. The latter is a lengthy process and more reasonably executed using canned computer programs.

Moment Magnification Solution ($kl_u/r < 100$)
The larger moment M_2 is magnified such that

$$M_c = \delta_{ns} M_2 \qquad\qquad [11.40]$$

where δ_{ns} = magnification factor. The column is then designed for a moment M_c as a nonslender column. The subscript ns = nonside sway, s = side sway.

$$\delta_{ns} = \frac{C_m}{1 - (P_u/0.75P_c)} \geq 1.0 \qquad [11.41]$$

$$P_c = \frac{\pi^2 EI}{(kl_u)^2} \qquad [11.42]$$

EI should be taken as

$$EI = \frac{0.2E_cI_g + E_sI_{se}}{1 + \beta_d} \qquad [11.43a]$$

or

$$EI = \frac{0.4E_cI_g}{1 + \beta_d} \qquad [11.43b]$$

$$C_m = 0.6 + 0.4\frac{M_1}{M_2} \geq 0.4 \qquad [11.44]$$

If there is side sway

$$M_1 = M_{1ns} + \delta_s M_{1s} \qquad [11.45a]$$
$$M_2 = M_{2ns} + \delta_s M_{2s} \qquad [11.45b]$$

where

$$\delta_s M_s = \frac{M_s}{1 - (\sum P_u/0.75P_c)} \geq M_s \qquad [11.46]$$

The nonsway moment M_{2ns} is unmagnified provided that the maximum moment is along the column height and not at its ends. Otherwise, its value has to be multiplied by the nonsway magnifier δ_{ns}. The effective length factor k when there is single curvature can be obtained from the Jackson and Morland chart of Fig. 11.8(a). For double curvature, the length factor k can be obtained from Fig. 11.8(b). Discussion of the $P - \Delta$ effect and the second-order analysis is given in Nawy.[11.2]

11.3.5 Two-Way Slabs and Plates

There are several methods of designing two-way concrete slabs and plates :

1. The ACI direct design method
2. The ACI equivalent frame method, where effects of lateral loads can be considered
3. The yield line theory
4. The strip method
5. Elastic solutions

Plate 52 Automation through robotics technology for placing high volumes of well-controlled concrete (Courtesy American Concrete Institute)

The subject is too extensive to cover in this overview on concrete structures. However, serviceability as controlled by deflection and cracking limitation, being of major importance, can be briefly presented.

Deflection Control

The thickness of two-way slabs for deflection control should be determined as follows:

Flat Plate

Use Table 11.2.

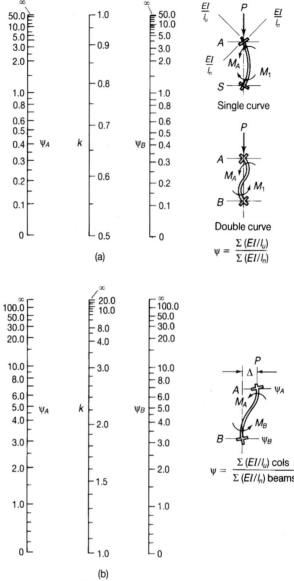

Fig. 11.8 Slender columns end effect factor k: (a) single curvature; (b) double curvature

Slab on Beams

Use Table 11.2 for $\alpha_m \leq 0.2$,

$$0.2 < \alpha_m < 2.0, \ h \geq \frac{l_n(0.8 + f_y/200\,000)}{36 + 5\beta(\alpha_m - 0.2)} \qquad [11.47]$$

but not less than 5.0 in.

$$\alpha_m > 2.0, \ h \geq \frac{l_n(0.8 + f_y/200\,000)}{36 + 9\beta} \qquad [11.48]$$

Table 11.2 Minimum thickness of slabs without interior beams $(\alpha_m = 0)^a$

	Without drop panels			With drop panels		
Yield strength f_y (psi)	Exterior panels without edge beams	Exterior panels with edge beams	Interior panels	Exterior panels without edge beams	Exterior panels with edge beams	Interior panels
40 000	$\dfrac{l_n}{33}$	$\dfrac{l_n}{36}$	$\dfrac{l_n}{36}$	$\dfrac{l_n}{36}$	$\dfrac{l_n}{40}$	$\dfrac{l_n}{40}$
60 000	$\dfrac{l_n}{30}$	$\dfrac{l_n}{33}$	$\dfrac{l_n}{33}$	$\dfrac{l_n}{33}$	$\dfrac{l_n}{36}$	$\dfrac{l_n}{36}$
75 000	$\dfrac{l_n}{28}$	$\dfrac{l_n}{31}$	$\dfrac{l_n}{31}$	$\dfrac{l_n}{31}$	$\dfrac{l_n}{34}$	$\dfrac{l_n}{34}$

$^a l_n$ = effective span.

where α_m = average value of α for all beams on edges of a panel

$$\alpha = \frac{\text{flexural stiffness of beam section}}{\text{flexural thickness of slab width bounded laterally by centerline of the adjacent panels on each side of beam}}$$

β = aspect ratio, long span/short span

Crack Control

For crack control in two-way slabs and plates, the maximum computed weighted crack width due to flexural load[11.2, 11.4] is

$$w_{max}(\text{in.}) = k\beta f_s \sqrt{\frac{s_1 s_2 d_c}{d_b}} \cdot \frac{8}{\pi} \qquad [11.49]$$

For w_{max} (mm), multiply Eq. 11.40 by 0.145 and use MPa for f_s (see Section 6.5.2)

where k = fracture coefficient
$\quad\quad\quad$ = 2.8×10^{-5} for square uniformly loaded slab
$\quad\quad\quad$ = 2.1×10^{-5} when $0.5 < \beta < 0.75$ or for concentrated load
$\quad\quad\quad$ = 1.6×10^{-5} for $\beta < 0.5$
$\quad\quad$ β = $1.25 = (h - c)/(d - c)$, where c = depth to neutral axis
$\quad\quad$ f_s = $0.40 f_y$, kip/in.^{2}
$\quad\quad$ h = total slab or plate thickness
$\quad\quad$ s_1 = spacing in direction 1, closest to the tensile extreme fibers, in.
$\quad\quad$ s_2 = spacing in the perpendicular direction, in.
$\quad\quad$ d_c = concrete cover to centroid of reinforcement, in.
$\quad\quad$ d_{b1} = diameter of the reinforcement in direction 1, closest to the concrete outer fibers, in.

Table 11.3 Tolerable crack widths

Exposure condition	Tolerable crack width, in.	(mm)
Dry air or protective membrane	0.016	0.41
Humidity, moist air, soil	0.012	0.30
Deicing chemicals	0.007	0.18
Seawater and seawater spray: wetting and drying	0.006	0.15
Water-retaining structures (excluding nonpressure pipes)	0.004	0.10

The tolerable crack widths in concrete elements are given in Table 11.3. In SI Units, Eq. 11.49 becomes

$$w_{max}(mm) = 0.145k\beta f_s \sqrt{G_I}$$

where f_s is in MPa; s_1, s_2, d_c, and d_{b1} are in millimeters.

11.4 PRESTRESSED CONCRETE

11.4.1 General Principles

Reinforced concrete is weak in tension but strong in compression. To maximize utilization of its material properties, an internal compressive force is induced on the structural element through the use of highly stressed prestressing tendons to precompress the member prior to application of the external gravity live load and superimposed dead load. A typical effect of the prestressing action is shown in Fig. 11.9 using a straight tendon as is usually the case in precast elements.[11.11] For elements cast in situ, the tendon can be either harped or usually draped in a parabolic form. Figure 11.10 gives the stress and strain distributions across the beam depth and the forces acting on the section in a prestressed concrete beam.

Stresses due to Prestressing plus Self-Weight

$$f^t = -\frac{P_i}{A_c}\left(1 - \frac{ec_t}{r^2}\right) - \frac{M_D}{S^t} \qquad [11.50a]$$

$$f_b = -\frac{P_i}{A_c}\left(1 + \frac{ec_b}{r^2}\right) + \frac{M_D}{S_b} \qquad [11.50b]$$

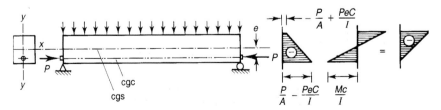

Fig. 11.9 Stress distribution at service load in prestressed beam with constant tendon eccentricity[11.11]

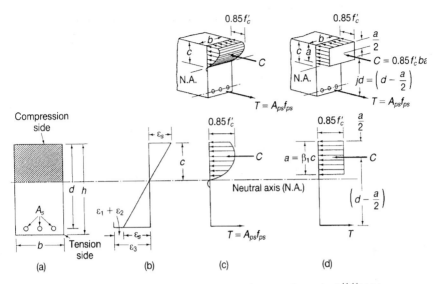

Fig. 11.10 Stress and strain distribution across prestressed concrete beam depth[11.11:] (a) beam cross-section; (b) strain across depth; (c) actual stress block; (d) assumed equivalent block

Stresses at Service Load

$$f^t = -\frac{P_e}{A_c}\left(1 - \frac{ec_t}{r^2}\right) - \frac{M_T}{S^t} \qquad [11.51a]$$

$$f_b = \frac{P_e}{A_c}\left(1 + \frac{ec_b}{r^2}\right) + \frac{M_T}{S_b} \qquad [11.51b]$$

11.4.2   Minimum Section Modulus for Variable Eccentricity Tendon

$$S^t \geq \frac{(1 - \gamma)M_D + M_{SD} + M_L}{\gamma f_{ti} - f_c} \qquad [11.52a]$$

$$S_b \geq \frac{(1 - \gamma)M_D + M_{SD} + M_L}{f_t - \gamma f_{ci}} \qquad [11.52b]$$

where γ = percentage loss in prestress
  M_D = self-weight moment
  M_{SD} = superimposed dead load moment
  M_L = live load moment
  f_{ti} = initial tensile stress in concrete
  f_c = service load concrete compressive strength
  f_t = service load concrete tensile strength
  f_{ci} = initial compressive stress in concrete
  S^t = section modulus at top fibers (simple span)
  S_b = section modulus at bottom fibers (simple span)

11.4.3 Minimum Section Modulus for Constant Tendon Eccentricity

$$S^t \geq \frac{M_D + M_{SD} + M_L}{\gamma f_{ti} - f_c} \qquad [11.53a]$$

$$S_b \geq \frac{M_D + M_{SD} + M_L}{f_t - \gamma f_{ci}} \qquad [11.53b]$$

11.4.4 Maximum Allowable Stresses

Concrete Stresses (ACI 318)

$$f'_{ci} \cong 0.75 f'_c \text{ psi}$$
$$f_{ci} \cong 0.60 f'_{ci} \text{ psi}$$

Plate 53 225 West Wacker Drive, Chicago: 14 000 psi concrete (Courtesy Portland Cement Association)

$$f_{ti} = 3\sqrt{f'_{ci}} \text{ psi on span } (\sqrt{f'_{ci}}/4 \text{ MPa})$$
$$= 6\sqrt{f'_{ci}} \text{ psi at support } (\sqrt{f'_{ci}}/2 \text{ MPa})$$
$$f_c = 0.45 f'_c$$
$$f_t = 6\sqrt{f'_c} \ (\sqrt{f'_c}/2 \text{ MPa})$$
$$= 12\sqrt{f'_c} \text{ psi if deflection verified } (\sqrt{f'_c} \text{ MPa})$$

Reinforcing Tendon Stresses

Tendon jacking : $f_{ps} = 0.94 f_{py} \leq 0.80 f_{pu}$

Immediately after prestress transfer : $f_{ps} = 0.82 f_{py} \leq 0.74 f_{pu}$

Posttensioned members at anchorage immediately after tendon
anchorage : $f_{ps} = 0.70 f_{pu}$

where f_{pu} = ultimate strength of tendon

f_{py} = yield strength of tendon

f_{ps} = stress allowed in tendon

A prestressed concrete section is designed for both the service load and the ultimate load. A typical distribution of stress at service load at midspan is shown in Fig. 11.9. Expressions for the ultimate load evaluation are essentially similar to those of reinforced concrete elements, taking into consideration that both prestressing tendons and mild steel bars are used. Figure 11.10 gives the compressive stress block and the equilibrium forces. Note its similarity to Fig. 11.6. For details, refer to a prestressed concrete textbook such as ACI Committee 435 Report.[11.3]

11.5   SHEAR AND TORSION IN PRESTRESSED ELEMENTS

11.5.1   Shear Strength

ACI Short Method if $f_{pe} > 0.40 f_{pu} <$?tf = "P7B6C" >

The nominal shear stress of the concrete in the web is

$$V_c(\text{lb}) = \left(0.60\lambda\sqrt{f'_c} + \frac{700 V_u d}{M_u} \right) b_w d \qquad\qquad [11.54a]$$

$$V_c \geq 2\lambda\sqrt{f_c'}b_wd \leq 5\lambda\sqrt{f_c'}b_wd$$

$$\frac{V_ud}{M_u} \leq 1.0$$

$$V_c(\text{newton}) = \left(\frac{\sqrt{f_c'}}{20} + \frac{5V_ud}{M_u}\right)b_wd \qquad [11.54b]$$

$$V_c \geq \frac{\sqrt{f_c'}}{6}b_wd \leq 0.40\sqrt{f_c'}b_wd$$

$$\frac{V_ud}{M_u} \leq 1.0$$

Detailed Method

The smaller of the values obtained from flexural shear V_{ce} or web shear V_{cw} has to be used in the design.

Flexural Shear

$$V_{ci}(\text{lb}) = 0.6\sqrt{f_c'}b_wd + V_d + \frac{V_iM_{cr}}{M_{max}} \qquad [11.55a]$$

$$\geq 1.7\sqrt{f_c'}b_wd$$

where $M_{cr} = S_b(6\sqrt{f_c'} + f_{ce} - f_d)$

S_b = section modulus at the extreme tensile fibers
V_d = shear force at section due to unfactored dead load
V_i = factored shear force due to externally applied load
f_{ce} = compressive stress in concrete due to effective prestress only at the tension face of section
f_d = stress due to unfactored dead load at extreme fibers in tension.

$$V_{ci}(\text{newton}) = \left(\frac{\sqrt{f_c'}}{20}\right)b_wd + V_d + \frac{V_iM_{cr}}{M_{max}} \qquad [11.55b]$$

Web Shear

$$V_{cw}(\text{lb}) = (3.5\sqrt{f_c'} + 0.3\bar{f}_{ce})b_wd + V_p$$
$$V_{cw}(\text{newton}) = (0.3\sqrt{f_c'} + \bar{f}_c)b_wd + V_p \qquad [11.56]$$

where $\bar{f}_c$ = compressive stress at center of gravity of section due to externally applied load
V_p = vertical component of prestressing force.

The critical section for calculating V_u and T_u is taken at distance ($h/2$) from the face of the support.

Minimum Shear Reinforcement

For prestressed members subjected to shear, the minimum transverse web stirrups are the smaller of

$$A_v(\text{in.}^2) = \frac{50b_w s}{f_y} \qquad [11.57\text{a}]$$

or

$$A_v = \frac{A_{ps} f_{pu} s}{80 f_y d}\sqrt{\frac{d_p}{b_w}} \qquad [11.57\text{b}]$$

where f_y is in psi.

11.5.2 Torsional Strength

As discussed in Section 11.2.3 the nominal torsional strength T_c is disregarded and all the torque is assumed by longitudinal bars and the transverse closed hoops. The expressions used in the case of prestressed concrete elements are essentially the same as those for reinforced concrete elements with the following adjustments to Eqs. 11.27 and 11.29:

Multiply the right side by

$$\sqrt{1 + \frac{3f_{ce}}{\sqrt{f_c'}}}$$

For hollow sections, the left side of Eq. 11.29 becomes ,

$$\left(\frac{V_u}{B_w d}\right) + \left(\frac{T_u p_h}{1.7 A_{oh}^2}\right)$$

The maximum spacing of the closed hoops $= 1/8 p_h \le 12$ in. and the longitudinal bar diameter not less than $1/16s$ where $s =$ spacing of the hoop steel.

11.6   WALLS AND FOOTINGS

The design of walls and footings should be viewed in the context of designing a one-way or two-way cantilever slab in the case of footings and one-way vertical cantilevers in the case of reinforced concrete walls. The criteria and expressions for proportioning their geometry are the same as those presented in the previous sections of this chapter. Shear V_u in one-way footings is taken at a distance d from the face of the vertical concrete wall or columns and at $d/2$ in the case of two-way footings. The nominal shear strength (capacity) V_c of the *one-way slab footing* is

$$V_c = 2\sqrt{f_c'} b_w d \qquad [11.58]$$

For two-way slab footings, the nominal shear strength V_c should be the smaller of

$$V_c = 4\sqrt{f'_c}b_0 d \qquad \qquad [11.59a]$$

$$V_c = \left(2 + \frac{4}{\beta_c}\right)\sqrt{f'_c}b_0 d \qquad \qquad [11.59b]$$

$$V_c = \left(\frac{\alpha_s d}{b_0} + 2\right)\sqrt{f'_c}b_0 d \qquad \qquad [11.59c]$$

where b_0 = perimeter shear failure length at distance $d/2$ from all faces of columns; if column size is $c_1 \times c_2$, then

$b_0 = 2(c_1 + d/2) + 2(c_2 + d/2)$ for an interior column
β_c = ratio of long side/short side of reaction area
α_s = 40 for interior columns, 30 for end columns, and 20 for corner columns.

The same requirement for shear in Eq. 11.59 applies to the shear design of two-way-action structural slabs and plates.

REFERENCES

11.1   ACI Committee 318 Building Code Requirements For Reinforced Concrete. *ACI 318-95* and Commentary *ACI 318R-95. ACI 318-95 Standard* American Concrete Institute, Detroit, 1996.

11.2   Nawy E G 1996 *Reinforced Concrete—A Fundamental Approach* 3rd ed. (1st ed. 1985), Prentice Hall, Englewood Cliffs, N.J.

11.3   ACI Committee 435 Control of Deflection in Concrete Structures. *ACI Report 435* chairman, E G Nawy, American Concrete Institute, Detroit, 1995, pp. 77.

11.4   ACI Committee 224 1990 Control of Cracking in Concrete Structures. *ACI Report 244* American Concrete Institute, Detroit, pp. 43.

11.5   ACI Committee 363 State-of-the-Art on High Strength Concrete. *ACI Report 363R-92* American Concrete Institute, Detroit, 1992, pp. 1–55.

11.6   Yong Y K, Nour M G, and Nawy E G 1988 Behavior of Laterally Confined High Strength Concrete Under Axial Loads. *Proceedings, ASCE J. Structural Engineering Division* Vol. 114 No. 2, pp. 332–351.

11.7   Martinez S, Nilsen A H, and Slate F O 1984 Spirally-Reinforced High Strength Concrete Columns. *Proceedings, ACI Journal* Vol. 81 No. 5, American Concrete Institute, Detroit, pp. 431–442.

11.8   Pastor J A, Nilsen A H, and Slate F O 1984 Behavior of High Strength Concrete Beams. *Cornell University Report No. 84-3* Dept. of Structural Engineering, Cornell University, Ithaca.

11.9   Ahmed S H, and Liu D M 1987 Flexure-Shear Interaction of Reinforced High Strength Concrete Beams. *Proceedings, ACI Structural Journal* Vol. 84 No. 4, American Concrete Institute, Detroit, pp. 330–341.

11.10 Hsu, and Thomas T C 1993 *Unified Theory of Reinforced Concrete* CRS Press, Boca Raton, Fla.

11.11 Nawy E G 1996 *Prestressed Concrete—A Fundamental Approach* 2nd ed. (1st ed. 1989), Prentice Hall, Englewood Cliffs, N.J.

12 High Strength Concrete in the Twenty-First Century

12.1 THE NEXT MILLENNIUM

Revolutionary evolutions of new materials of construction and new modifications and improvements in the behavior of traditional materials have been taking place in the past two decades. These evolutions have been considerably facilitated by increased knowledge of the molecular structure of materials, studies of long-term failures, development of more powerful instrumentation, monitoring techniques, and instruments, decrease in cost-effectiveness of traditional materials, and the need for stronger and better performing materials suitable for larger structures, longer spans, and more ductility. The last two decades of the twentieth century can be described as the decades of concrete admixtures. The twenty-first century will be the millennium of high strength, high performance concrete.

Concrete structural systems constructed from 15 000–20 000 psi (103–138 MPa) concretes are being built today. But, in spite of these tremendous advances in concrete technology and development of high performance concretes, there is still ample scope for new development, new components or admixtures, microstructural studies, blended cement compositions, better material selection proportioning, placement techniques, long-term performance, and all the other factors discussed in Chapter 10, including new structural design formulations compatible with the behavior of these new materials. It will be a century of challenge to the materials scientist, the technologist, and the design engineer.

The present state of the art in concrete materials research has demonstrated that the use of pozzolans and slags as cementitious replacements for part of the cement in concretes not only contributes to higher strength but also to energy conservation and a major solution to the disposal of industrial by-products. The recent advances in material proportioning and use of fly ash, blast furnace slag, silica fume, and natural pozzolans is noteworthy. The development of new cements, such as macrodefect free cements (MDF) and densified cements (DSP), and the advances in composites such as the slurry infiltrated fiber concrete (SIFCON), have all permitted attainment of compressive strength levels of 45 000 psi (300 MPa) with buildings and bridges being built using concretes in excess of 25 000 psi (175 MPa). Massive construction projects utilizing these advances are being undertaken throughout the world, such as the recently

Plate 54 Water Tower Place, Chicago: 9000 psi concrete (Courtesy Portland Cement Association)

completed undersea tunnel connecting the British Isles to France, using special techniques but not necessarily very high concrete strength.

Deterioration of the infrastructure mandates replacement or rehabilitation. Rehabilitation often requires new materials and techniques compatible with the parent system. In all these, concrete in various forms and compositions is the only suitable material. Adding the factor of rapid population growth, particularly in the underdeveloped parts of the world, and the continually increasing urbanization and industrialization, it is clear that the twenty-first century will become the golden age of high performance concrete.

12.2   HIGH STRENGTH CONCRETE CONSTRUCTION AND NEEDS

As indicated in Chapter 7, the construction industry in the United States is responsible for in excess of $425 billion in new construction (1992), which amounts to approximately 7.3 percent of the gross domestic product (GDP) and in excess of 6 million relatively skilled and highly paid jobs.[12.1] More than 500 million tons of concrete are annually produced in the United States and several times this volume worldwide. This demand will accelerate because of a rapid escalation of population in many parts of the world, particularly in developing countries. Only seven urban areas held more than 5 million people in 1950[12.2]: New York, London, Paris, the Rhine–Ruhr zone, Tokyo–Yokohama, Shanghai,

Table 12.1 Largest world metropolitan areas[12.2]

1980 Population (millions)		2000 Population (millions)	
1. Tokyo–Yokohama	17.0	Mexico City	26.3
2. New York	15.6	Sao Paulo	24.0
3. Mexico City	15.0	Tokyo-Yokohama	17.1
4. Sao Paulo	12.8	Calcutta	16.6
5. Shanghai	11.8	Bombay	16.0
6. Buenos Aires	10.1	New York	15.5
7. London	10.0	Seoul	13.5
8. Calcutta	9.5	Shanghai	13.5
9. Los Angeles	9.5	Rio de Janeiro	13.3
10. Rhine–Ruhr	9.3	New Delhi	13.3
11. Rio de Janeiro	9.2	Buenos Aires	13.2
12. Beijing	9.1	Cairo	13.2
13. Paris	8.8	Jakarta	12.8
14. Bombay	8.5	Baghdad	12.8
15. Seoul	8.5	Tehran	12.7
16. Moscow	8.2	Karachi	12.2
17. Osaka–Kobe	8.0	Istanbul	11.9
18. Tianjin	7.7	Los Angeles	11.3
19. Cairo	7.3	Dhaka	11.2
20. Chicago	6.8	Manila	11.1

and Buenos Aires. By 1980, 34 centers held 5 million people and by the year 2000, this number will reach 60 or more.

Table 12.1 lists the largest 20 metropolitan areas in the world and the change or explosion in population growth by the turn of the century. This growth is particularly significant in countries less developed than the United States and Europe. Many of the less developed world centers lack adequate housing, running water, sewage facilities and adequate transportation. From these statistics, it is evident that the twenty-first century would have to encompass doubling or tripling the utilization of concrete so as to solve the infrastructure needs of these sprawling urban areas. It might not be unreasonable to expect that where land becomes scarce, construction of floating residential concrete satellites becomes necessary using high strength, high performance concrete. On our planet, no other materials are as abundant as the aggregates, sand, and pozzolans, and no other materials are as economical as concrete in meeting the exploding demands of population growth.

More growth requires more industrialization. The need for increased production of steel and other metals results in industrial by-products that can be detrimental to the environment. Some of these by-products include fly ash, bottom ash, blast furnace slag, and silica fume. Extremely large quantities of these by-products have to be disposed of for ecological considerations.

Table 12.2 details the world production of fly ash which in 1989 was in excess of 500 billion tons, and in the United States alone was in excess of 65 million tons. If 25–35 percent of this tonnage can be gainfully used to replace cement in

Table 12.2 Coal ash production and utilization in the world[12.3] (1989)

Country	Production (thousands of tons)		Utilization (thousands of tons)															
	Fly ash	Bottom ash and boiler slag	Cement raw material	Blended cement	Cement replacement	Grout	Nonaerated blocks	Aerated blocks	Lightweight aggregates	Bricks or ceramics	Asphalt filler	Structural, land, or embankment fill	Pavement base course or subgrade	Filler for mines, quarries, or pits	Other	Total	Percent of production
Australia	5 539	1 024			710						10		30	20		770	11.4
Austria	341	43		78								18				96	25
Belgium	872	150	65	174	309		96			3	55	100	21		3	826	80.8
Bulgaria	5 300	1 060			20		50		30			10			5	65	1
Canada	3 463	1 096	132		445	3		5			1	610	55	40	20	1 288	27.2
Chile	200	18														0	
China	55 000	7 500		369	1 907				62	4 059		1 200	2 500	4 600	1 500	16 197	25.9
Colombia	450	300		104			12	1	1			8			15	141	18.8
Czechoslovakia	13 783	4 334	8		23		9	312	91	29		934		39		1 445	8
Denmark	840	86	215	63	118			11			17	319	40			783	84.6
Finland	434	49	10	55	192							75	55	25		412	85.3
France	2 288	421	236	209	438			128				105			433	1 549	57.2
Germany (East)	12 479	6 578		550	155							4 258	1 045	700	448	7 156	37.6
Germany (West)	7 980	4 330		150	1 250	200	530		320		50		1 530	6 420	260	10 710	87
Greece	5 730	516		757												757	13.2
Hong Kong	1 012	112		58	105					74		271		616		1 124	100

Table 12.2 (*Continued*)

Hungary	3 880	937		145		3		239				168	12	29	597		12.3
India	36 000	4 000	210												800		2
Israel	370	40	40		20									35	250		61
Italy	1 249	775	161	250	27		28		3	61	126	2	35		1 266		91.7
Japan	3 341	919	459	170		61	61			2	84	30	131	139	1 758		46.2
Korea (South)	1 929	214	100	100											100		4.6
Mexico	1 360	240	21	3			18						3		45		2.8
Netherlands	765	90	250	65	3	120		30	125		120	50		3	760		82.6
Norway	0	0	95 (imported from Denmark)												95		100
Poland	26 300	3 200	78	260	920		345		12			270	1 570	1 000	4 455		15.1
Romania	7 000	20 000	10	10	120		5				600				745		2.8
South Africa	28 000	32 000	250	72	89	20	21					40			492		0.8
Spain	7 391	1 304	1 100	300							100				1 500		17.3
Sweden	225	25		10	10										10		4
Taiwan	1 089	272		393			49							4	446		32.8
Thailand	1 000	90													0		
Turkey	15 250	1 865													0		
U.K.	13 300	2 200	50	820	250	890	522				850		40	1 195	5 467		35.3
U.S.A.	48 458	16 776	821	5 239	220				204		2 529	1 300	20	5 641	15 974		24.4
USSR (Former)	90 000	35 000	1 293	4 240	10	78	842		980		4 007	200	48		11 500		9.2
Yugoslavia (Former)	12 147	1 190	50	470	15	27	65						5	123	985		7.4
Total	90 564	414 675	147 650	2 778	7 365	17 521	721	1 627	2 757	1 212	5 599	1 457	16 393	7 241	14 358	10 809	16.1

Plate 55 Under construction, Ronald McDonald House, New York City: flat plate high-rise high strength reinforced concrete building (Courtesy *New York Construction News*)

the production of concrete, considerable savings in material and energy costs are achieved. Added to this the improvement of concrete quality and achievement of considerably higher strengths accentuates the importance of utilizing this by-product. The same is applicable to blast furnace slag and silica fume.

It is conceivable that the statistics of Table 12.2 could increase by 20–30 percent over the next 25 years, and other applications would be developed to consume this ecologically harmful by-product. In summary, the twenty-first century will be marked by considerably more extensive use of such admixtures as fly ash and silica fume and possibly other newly discovered fillers for the production of the high strength concretes described in the previous chapters.

12.3 DESIGN AND REHABILITATION CONSIDERATIONS

Deterioration of the infrastructure and rapid population growth in the past two decades have created a sizable backlog, particularly in the United States, of badly

Plate 56 Superstructure for Gulfaks C, a Norwegian-owned offshore oil platform in the North Sea (Courtesy American Concrete Institute)

needed repair and replacement. Cohen[12.4] outlines how the concrete industry in New York has to be ready to do its part in the additional $30–50 billion federal infrastructure investment program for this area. Repair and replacement activities in airports, bridges, roads, mass transit, water supply, sanitary facilities, affordable housing, and other civilian structures have to be undertaken even in an emergency manner at the turn of the century.

High performance concrete combined with good architecture and efficient structural design can result in cost-effective and, at the same time, durable long-life structural systems. As indicated in Chapter 11, some of the design parameters in codes such as the ACI 318 building code might not be affected in a major way. But, this view can only be substantiated by massive research particularly in the areas of shear, torsion, stability, stiffness, cracking, and deflection. The increase in high strength results in slenderer members, different behavior, and less ductility. All these parameters can only be clarified by additional extensive research on the micro- and macrostructural response of the material to external loading and its impact on the design provisions and expressions that are in use today.

The use of 30 000–40 000 psi (206–275 MPa) concrete expected in the twenty-first century and reinforcement with yield strength in excess of 85 000 psi (590 MPa) will require the generation of new or modified rational expressions for design of high strength concrete buildings, bridges, and marine structures. While noncorroding materials other than steel reinforcement can and are being used such as fiberglass, resin-impregnated bundled fiber glass rods,[12.2] or carbon fibers, reinforcing steel rods will continue to be dominant because of the limitations of the other media at present. It is expected that extensive research will continue to be undertaken to produce reinforcement with more ductility than available today.

More knowledge will be developed to design, build, and rehabilitate concrete structural frames that are almost immune to the seismic effects of earthquakes, thereby resisting the massive destruction caused by such earthquakes as the Northridge, California, earthquake of 1994. Advances in the design of connections for precast elements for use in both seismic and nonseismic regions will result in massive use of precast high strength concrete structures, creating universal standardization of factory-produced major structural concrete elements. Here also, considerable additional research on the strength and ductility of connections would have to be undertaken. In summary, structural research on the efficient utilization of the newly developed materials and compositions through research, development, and design will be the hallmark of the twenty-first century.

12.4   CONSTRUCTIBILITY CONSIDERATIONS

Technology transfer for *correct use* by the design engineer and the field constructor requires adequate detailed knowledge of the basics. The extensive advances in concrete technology have not permeated the design engineer's reservoir of knowledge. Unfortunately, weakness exists in the curricula of most if not all universities by not providing formal adequate theoretical and experimental instruction in concrete materials technology. As a consequence, the design engineer lacks in many cases an appreciation of what techniques and selection decisions are best for proportioning a structural system.

This book is intended to fill, in some measure, this serious gap in the training of engineers to cope with the developing concrete technology of the twenty-first century. It is no longer enough to be a good designer. The computer can perform many of the analysis tasks that the engineer used to perform. Engineering curricula at the turn of the century have to rectify the existing deficiency in concrete materials instruction, particularly in the United States, if the profession is to succeed in facing the challenges of a society that will require faster, more durable, and more economical structures and habitats.

Equally important is the knowledge and training of the field constructor. The new concretes require skills and knowledge of the behavior of ingredients far more than did low strength concretes in the past. As detailed in other chapters of the book, mix proportioning that results in high performance, high strength concretes is a complicated process. It requires the know-how on the interaction of the natural pozzolans, the slag, the fly ash, and the silica fume with the portland or blended cements. It requires experience in the contribution of other admixtures such as the air-entraining agents, the superplasticizers (high range water-reducing agents), and the loss of air entrainment. It requires good knowledge of interpreting laboratory test data, the effect of loading rate on the test results, and the errors induced by the testing machine loading pattern. It requires knowledge of the production process, the effects of aggregate moisture content, the techniques for placement of concrete in the forms, and the curing and preparation of test specimens.

In order to have personnel able, conversant, and proficient as concrete technologists, prescribed training and certification of field personnel is mandatory if the emerging technology in high strength concretes is to be successfully transferred to full and cost-effective application. The turn of the century will be marked by new testing procedures and by expected mandatory certification requirements for all concrete technologists, based on laboratory and field training, required by all federal, state, and local agencies. Only with such stringent requirements can the exploding information in the production of high strength durable concretes be transferred to real applications in the massive construction activities needed in the next century.

12.5   EXPECTATIONS AND CONCLUSIONS

High strength durable concrete will dominate the new and rehabilitated infrastructure in the next millennium. It will have to contain pozzolanic admixtures, particularly fly ash and silica fume, to minimize or eliminate voids in the concrete matrix. In developing countries, where the availability of silica fume is limited, rice husk ash will be used as the substitute supplement to reduce the voids in order to enhance strength and long-term performance. Fiber reinforced concretes and fiber composites will be extensively used. Mixing procedures and equipment will have to be considerably modified using high speed mixers instead of truck mixing, and robotic technology to place concrete in the forms.

Instrumentation of the infrastructure, both newly constructed and existing, will be a standard procedure to monitor performance. The information superhighway will be put to full use as fiber-optic sensing becomes more refined. Use of both embedded and surface fiber-optic sensors will be routinely used for remote real-time sensing of deterioration of materials and components at centers miles away from the source.[12.6–12.9] Hence safety would be enhanced and impending failures prevented.

Engineering education will have to adapt to this highly sophisticated materials technology by the inclusion of adequate instruction to equip the graduating engineers with the know-how to proportion concrete constituents. Certification of materials personnel will become standard through mandatory requirement by owners and governmental agencies. If this is the way the industry and the

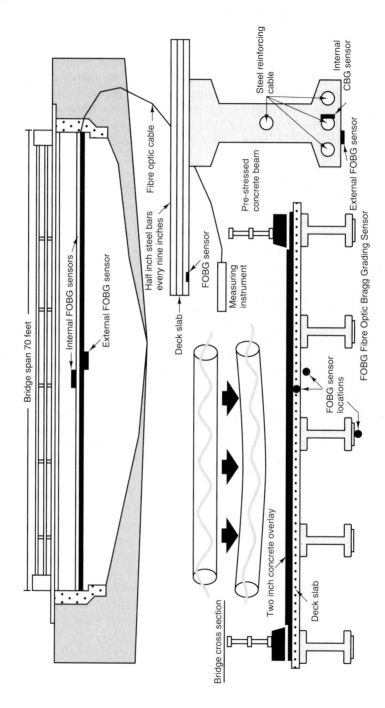

Plate 57 Schematic of Fiber Optic Bragg Sensor Instrumentation of a Bridge Deck[12.8,12.9] (Courtesy Thomas Kerr, Home News, New Brunswick, N.J.)

profession are heading as we approach the year 2000, the next century will be the golden age of high performance concrete.

REFERENCES

12.1   U.S. Department of Commerce 1992 *U.S. Industrial Output* U.S. Department of Commerce, Washington D.C., 1992.

12.2   Mehta P K, and Montiero P J M 1993 *Concrete-Structure Properties and Materials* 2nd ed., Prentice Hall, Englewood Cliffs, N.J.

12.3   Manz O E, Faber J H, and Takagi H 1987–1989 Worldwide Production of Fly Ash and Utilization in Concrete. *Proceedings CANMET/ACI Conference on Fly Ash, Silica Fume, Slag and Natural Pozzolan in Concrete, Norway. ACI SP-114* ed. V M Malhotra, American Concrete Institute, Detroit, 1989.

12.4   Cohen E 1992 Industry Must be Ready To Meet 21st Century Challenges. *New York Construction News* Nov. 1992, pp. 5–6.

12.5   Neville A 1992 Concrete in the Year 2000. *Proceedings International Conference on Advances in Concrete Technology, Athens* 2nd ed., ed. V M Malhotra, CANMET, Natural Resources Canada, Ottawa, pp. 1–17.

12.6   Nawy E G 1996 *Reinforced Concrete—A Fundamental Approach* 3rd ed.(1st ed., 1985), Prentice Hall, Englewood Cliffs, N.J.

12.7   Chen B, Latimer K, Mahar M H, and Nawy E G 1994 Use of Fiber Optic Sensors for Remote Deformation Evaluation of Existing and New Structures. *Structural Materials Technology Conference, Atlantic City* ed. R J Scancella and M E Callahan, Technomic Publishing, Basel, Switzerland, pp. 159–168.

12.8   Chen B, and Nawy E G 1994 Structural Behavior Evaluation of High Strength Concrete Beams Reinforced with Prestressed Prisms Using Fiber Optic Sensors. *Proceedings, ACI Journal* Vol. 91 S69, American Concrete Institute, Detroit, pp. 708–718.

12.9   Chen B, Prohaska J D, Maher M H, Snitzer E, and Nawy E G 1994 Fiber Optic Sensors For Strength Evaluation and Early Warning of Impending Failure in Structural Components. *Rutgers University Technical Report* Rutgers University Dept. of Civil Engineering, Piscataway, 210 pp.

A Appendix

Plate 58 Empire State Performing Arts Center, Albany, New York, (Courtesy of New York Office of General Services)

Table A.1 PI unit conversion to SI units: general

Quantity	To convert from PI	To SI	Divide by
Area	ft^2	m^2	10.76
Density	lb/ft^3	kg/m^3	0.0624
	lb/yd^3	kg/m^3	1.685
	g/cm^3	kg/m^3	0.0010
Energy	Btu	MJ	957.8
	cal	J	0.2390
Fracture toughness	$lb/in.^2 \sqrt{in.}$	$MN{\cdot}m^{-3/2}$	9.100×10^{-4}
Length	in.	mm	0.039
	in.	m	39.37
	ft	m	3.281
Mass	lb	kg	2.204
	ton	metric ton	1.102
Permeability	ft/s	m/s	3.281
	ft/yr	m/s	1.035×10^8
Power	Btu/h	W	3.412
Pressure	mm Hg	Pa	0.0075
Specific energy	Btu/lb	MJ/kg	429.9
	Btu/ton	J/kg	0.8598
	cal/g	J/g	0.2390
Specific surface area	cm^2/g	m^2/kg	10.00
Specific volume (yield)	ft^3/lb	m^3/kg	16.02
	yd^3/lb	m^3/kg	0.5933
	cm^3/g	m^3/kg	1000.0
Stress	$lb/in.^2$	MPa	145.0
	$10^4\ lb/in.^2$	GPa	0.145
Surface energy	$in.\ lb/in.^2$	J/m^2	0.0057
	erg/cm^2	J/m^2	0.0010
Surface tension	$dyne/cm^3$	N/m	0.0010
Temperature	°F	°C	9/5°C+32
Temperature difference	°F	°C or K	1.800
Thermal coefficient of expansion	$°F^{-1}$	$°C^{-1}$	1.800
Thermal conductivity	Btu/f·h·°F	W/m·K	0.5778
Thermal diffusivity	ft^2/h	m^2/h	10.76
Volume	ft^3	m^3	35.31
	yd^3	m^3	1.308
	fl. oz	ml	0.0338

1 gram water $= 0.035$ oz $= 2.205 \times 10^{-3}$ lb

Table A.2 PI unit conversion to SI units: load and stress intensity

N/m^2	$= Pa$
MPa	$= N/mm^2 = 10^6 \ N/m^2$
lb × 4.448	$= N$
lb/in^2 × 0.006895	$= MPa$
lb/ft^2 × 0.4788	$= kPa$
lb/ft × 14.593	$= N/m$
lb/ft^3 × 16.02	$= kg/m^3$
in.-lb × 0.113	$= Nm$
1 kg_{force}	$= 9.806 \ N$

Table A.3 PI unit conversion to MKS metric units

lb × 0.45	$= kgf$
9000 lb	$= 4082 \ kgf$
psi × 0.07	$= kgf/cm^2$
1000 psi	$= 70.3 \ kgf/cm^2$
$\sqrt{f_c'}$ psi × 0.27	$= \sqrt{f_c'} \ kgf/cm^2$

Table A.4 Chemical analysis by XRF of cement, fly ash, and silica fume[7.7]

Oxide (Mix no.)	Cement[a] (1,2,3,4,5)	Cement[b] (6)	Fly ash (2,5)	Fly ash (6)	Silica fume (2,3)	Silica fume (4,5)	Silica fume (6)
SiO_2	20.39	20.17	35.51	31.91	93.52	93.83	93.19
Al_2O_3	4.80	4.85	18.87	16.69	0.85	0.21	0.67
Fe_2O_3	2.19	2.33	5.49	5.16	0.11	0.00	0.16
CaO	62.27	62.47	25.85	33.85	0.78	0.56	0.68
MgO	4.22	3.76	4.42	4.57	0.55	0.07	0.48
SO_3	2.71	3.79	2.58	3.01	0.12	0.03	0.19
Na_2O	0.09	0.18	1.42	1.24	0.28	0.15	0.30
K_2O	0.65	1.18	0.38	0.53	0.54	0.46	0.44
TiO_2	0.26	0.24	1.96	1.39	0.06	0.01	0.06
P_2O_5	0.18	0.05	1.16	0.87	0.12	0.06	0.11
Mn_2O_3	0.08	0.06	0.05	0.04	0.05	0.04	0.05
SrO	0.03	0.04	0.35	0.31	0.01	0.01	0.01
L.O.I	1.27	1.02	0.79	0.53	2.78	3.95	3.20
Total	99.14	100.14	98.83	100.10	99.77	99.38	99.54

[a]Calculated compounds per ASTM C-150-89: C_3S 53%, C_2S 19%, C_3A 10%, C_4AF 7%.
[b]Calculated compounds per ASTM C-150-89: C_3S 53%, C_2S 18%, C_3A 10%, C_4AF 7%.

Table A.5 Physical properties[a] of some heavyweight aggregates[5.8]

Material	Chemical composition	Classification[b]	Bulk specific gravity	Unit weight $(kg/m^3)^c$
Goethite	$Fe_2O_3 \cdot H_2O$	N	3.5–3.7	2 100–2 250
Limonite	Impure Fe_2O_3	N	3.4–4.0	2 100–2 400
Barite	$BaSO_4$	N	4.0–4.6	2 300–2 550
Ilmenite	$FeTiO_3$	N	4.3–4.8	2 550–2 700
Magnetite	Fe_3O_4	N	4.2–5.2	2 400–3 050
Hematite	Fe_2O_3	N	4.9–5.3	2 900–3 200
Ferrophosphorus	$Fe_2O_3–P_2O_3$	S	5.8–6.8	3 200–4 150
Steel	Fe (scrap iron steel punchings)	S	6.2–7.8	3 700–4 650

[a]See ASTM C638.
[b]N, naturally occurring; S, synthetic products.
[c]$kg/m^3 \times 0.062 = lb/ft^3$.

Table A.6 Density classification of concrete aggregates[5.8]

Category	Unit weight of dry-rodded aggregate $(kg/m^3)^a$	Unit weight of concrete $(kg/m^3)^a$	Typical concrete strengths $(MPa)^a$	Typical applications
Ultralightweight	< 500	300–1 100	< 7	Nonstructural insulating material
Lightweight	500–800	1 100–1 600	7–14	Masonry units
Structural lightweight	650–1 100	1 450–1 900	17–35	Structural
Normal weight	1 100–1 750	2 100–2 550	20–40	Structural
Heavyweight	>2 100	2 900–6 100	20–40	Radiation shielding

[a]$kg/m^3 \times 0.062 = lb/ft^3$; $MPa \times 145 = lb/in.^3$

Table A.7 Typical solid wastes that have been considered as aggregate for concrete[5.8]

Material	Composition	Industry	Annual amount (10^6 tons)
Mineral waste	Natural rocks	Mining and mineral processing	2000
Blast furnace slags	Silicates or aluminosilicates of calcuim and magnesium silicate glasses	Iron and steel	30
Metallurgical slags	Silicates, aluminosilicates, and glasses	Metal refining	30
Fly ash	Silica glasses	Electric power	50
Municipal wastes	Paper, glass, plastics, and metals	Commercial and household wastes	200
Rubber	Synthetic rubbers	Scrapped tires	5
Incinerator	Container glass, metals, and silica glasses	Municipal and industrial	5
Building rubble	Brick, concrete, and reinforcing steel	Demolition	25

Table A.8 High strength high-rise buildings

Building	Location	Year[a]	Total stories	Maximum design concrete strength, psi (MPa)	
S.F. Financial Center	Miami	1982	53	7 000	(48.2)
Petrocanada Building	Calgary	1982	34	7 250	(50.0)
Lake Point Tower	Chicago	1965	70	7 500	(51.7)
1130 S. Michigan Ave.	Chicago	—	—	7 500	(51.7)
Texas Commerce Tower	Houston	1981	75	7 500	(51.7)
Helmsley Palace Hotel	New York	1978	53	8 000	(55.2)
Trump Tower	New York	—	68	8 000	(55.2)
City Center Project	Minneapolis	1981	52	8 000	(55.2)
Collins Place	Melbourne	—	44	8 000	(55.2)
Larimer Place Condominium	Denver	1980	31	8 000	(55.2)
499 Park Avenue	New York	—	27	8 500	(58.6)
Royal Bank Plaza	Toronto	1975	43	8 800	(60.7)
Richmond-Adelaide Center	Toronto	1978	33	8 800	(60.7)
Melbourne Central	Melbourne	1991	55	8 700–9 425	(60.0–65.0)
Bourke Place	Melbourne	1990	55	8 700–9 425	(60.0–65.0)
530 Collins Strove	Melbourne	1990	39	8 700–9 425	(60.0–65.0)
Midcontinental Plaza	Chicago	1972	50	9 000	(62.1)
Water Tower Place	Chicago	1975	79	9 000[f]	(62.1)
River Plaza	Chicago	1976	56	9 000[b]	(62.1)
Columbia Center	Seattle	1983	76	9 500	(65.5)
Interfirst Plaza	Dallas	1983	72	10 000	(68.9)
Scotia Plaza	Toronto	1988	68	10 000	(68.9)
Century Square	Seattle	1988	42	11 000[g]	(75.4)
Eugene Terrace	Chicago	1987	44	11 000	(75.4)
La Laurentienne Building	Montreal	1984	—	11 600	(80.0)
One Peachtree Center	Georgia	—	60	12 000	(82.7)
311 S. Wacker Drive	Chicago	1988	70	12 000[d]	(82.7)
Chicago Mercantile Exchange East	Chicago	1982	40	14 000[c]	(96.5)
900 N. Michigan Annex	Chicago	1986	15	14 000	(96.5)
Two Union Square	Seattle	1987	62	20 000[e]	(137.9)
225 W. Wacker Drive	Chicago	1988	30	14 000	(96.5)
Pacific First Center	Seattle	1992	36	18 000	(124.1)

[a] Year in which high strength concrete was cast.
[b] Two experimental columns of 11 000 psi strength were also included.
[c] Two experimental columns of 14 000 psi strength were also included.
[d] 9 000 psi also used in floor slabs of lower levels.
[e] 19 000 psi indirectly specified to achieve a high modulus of elasticity.
[f] First 28 lower stories. [g] The upper 30 floors.

Table A.9 Mix proportions of recent high-rise buildings[8.30]

Mix	Description of concrete	Avg. 28 day compressive strength (MPa)	Component materials in 1 m³ concrete batch (kg/m³)								Water to cementitious ratio by weight
			PC	FA	BFS	SF	Total water	Fine aggregate	Coarse aggregate	Superplasticizer L (m³)	
1	Water Tower Place, Chicago	65	500	60	—	—	178	608	1068	—[a]	0.32
2	Commerce Tower, Houston	65	390	100	—	—	161	575	1141	—[a]	0.33
3	Inter First Plaza, Dallas	80	360	150	—	—	148	603	1157	3[a]	0.29
4	Nova Scotia Plaza, Toronto	82	315	—	135	36	145	745	1130	6	0.30
5	Experimental Column, Montreal	90	500	—	—	30	135	700	1100	15	0.25
6	Laboratory Mixture	70	485	—	—	—	130	762	1143	3.4	0.27
7	Laboratory Mixture	72	317	—	167	—	133	749	1145	7.0	0.28
8	Laboratory Mixture	80	315	—	155	35	143	744	1142	7.5	0.29
9	Laboratory Mixture	82	449	—	—	39	130	758	1149	11.0	0.27
10	Laboratory Mixture	91	427	—	—	59	132	754	1139	14.9	0.27
11	Laboratory Mixture	93	450	—	—	50	140	687	1108	17	0.28
12	Laboratory Mixture	97	500	—	—	42	138	675	1130	10	0.25
13	Laboratory Mixture	100	486	—	—	54	135	661	1112	20	0.25
14	Laboratory Mixture	103	580	—	—	70	140	620	1025	12	0.22
15	Laboratory Mixture	107	517	—	—	58	126	641	1126	25	0.22
16	Two Union Square, Seattle	120	564	—	—	44	124	682	1100	21	0.20

[a]Mixes 1 and 2 contained only a normal water-reducing admixture; mix 3 also contained a normal water-reducing admixture in addition to a superplasticizer.

Table A.10 Concrete platforms in the North Sea.[8.31]

Platform	Designer/contractor	Construction site	Delivered	Concrete volume (m^3)	Water depth (m)
Ekofisk 1	Doris/Selmer-Heyer	Stavanger	1973	80 000	70
Beryl A	Norwegian Contractors	Stavanger	1975	52 000	118
Beryl B	Norwegian Contractors	Stavanger	1975	64 000	140
Frigg CDP-1	Howard Doris/ Norwegian Contractors	Åndalanes	1975	60 000	104
Brent D	Norwegian Contractors	Stavanger	1976	68 000	140
Frigg MP-2	Howard Doris/ Skanska Doris	Stromstad	1976	60 000	94
Frigg TP-1	Sea Tank/McAlpine	Ardyne Point	1976	49 000	104
Statfjord A	Norwegian Contractors	Stavanger	1977	87 000	145
Frigg TCP-2	Norwegian Contractors	Åndalanes	1977	50 000	104
Dunlin A	Andoc	Rotterdam	1977	90 000	153
Brent C	Sea Tank/McAlpine	Ardyne Point	1978	105 500	141
Cormorant A	Sea Tank/McAlpine	Ardyne Point	1978	120 000	149
Ninian Central	Howard Doris	Loch Kishorn	1978	140 000	136
Statfjord B	Norwegian Contractors	Stavanger	1981	140 000	145
Statfjord C	Norwegian Contractors	Stavanger	1984	130 000	145
Gulfaks A	Norwegian Contractors	Stavanger	1986	125 000	135
Gulfaks B	Norwegian Contractors	Stavanger	1987	100 000	141
Oseberg A	Norwegian Contractors	Stavanger	1988	120 000	109
Gulfaks C	Norwegian Contractors	Stavanger/Vats	1989	240 000	216
[a]Ekofisk PB	Doris/Peconor Ekofisk J/V	Rotterdam/ Ålfjorden	1989	106 000	75
[b]Sleipner A	Norwegian Contractors	Stavanger	1992	77 000	82
		Total volume		2 063 000	

[a]Under construction

Author Index

Subject Index